POLITICAL RETURNS

Irony in Politics and Theory
from Plato
to the Antinuclear Movement

POLITICAL RETURNS

Irony in Politics and Theory
from Plato
to the Antinuclear Movement

John Evan Seery

Westview Press
BOULDER, SAN FRANCISCO, & OXFORD

Published in 1990 in the United States of America by Westview Press, Inc., 5500 Central Avenue, Boulder, Colorado 80301, and in the United Kingdom by Westview Press, Inc., 36 Lonsdale Road, Summertown, Oxford OX2 7EW

Library of Congress Cataloging in Publication Data
Seery, John Evan.
  Political returns : irony in politics and theory from Plato
to the antinuclear movement / by John Evan Seery.
    p. cm.
  ISBN 0-8133-7936-9.
  ISBN 0-8133-7964-4 (if published as pbk.)
  1. Political science—History. 2. Antinuclear movement.
3. Irony—Political aspects. I. Title.
JA81.S39 1990
320.5'09—dc20   90-11989
                                                               CIP

Printed and bound in the United States of America

The paper used in this publication meets the requirements
of the American National Standard for Permanence of Paper
for Printed Library Materials Z39.48-1984.

10   9   8   7   6   5   4   3   2   1

At a time like this, scorching irony,
not convincing argument, is needed.

--Frederick Douglass,
"What to the Slave Is the Fourth of July?"

Contents

Acknowledgments

Authors routinely want to use this semipublic space to express feelings of deep gratitude toward their friends, supporters, colleagues; and so do I. But last-minute doubts creep in: Maybe my coconspirators won't want to be named; a book hardly repays their generosity nor discharges my lifelong debts; maybe this whole exercise is presumptuously self-indulgent; maybe, for balance, I should say a few words about the people who weren't very helpful at all; and so on. If I proceed with this curious convention, I know that I will need to find the right combination of words warmly thanking these people for their wonderful contributions on the one hand, while relieving them of any lingering responsibilities on the other. Compounding all of these typical troubles is that I am attempting to thank my associates at the outset of a book on *irony*. Who will believe me? Is it too late for sincerity? How can I attach an acknowledgments page that isn't flip, glib, and self-protective? The enemies of irony shall cry, "Aha--he's turning earnest! We knew it couldn't last!" But I've been deadly serious throughout the writing of this entire book (more or less), and irony was consistent with that effort, providing far more than comic relief.

This book began as a dissertation at the University of California, Berkeley, which was about the only place in the world in the early 1980s that would have permitted a dissertation coupling irony and nuclear affairs. At the time, I felt myself fortunate to be there, and that sense has been only heightened in retrospect. Hanna Pitkin, my adviser, was never wildly enthusiastic about irony, but she stuck with me nonetheless, showing her care through hours upon hours of detailed, clearheaded (if perhaps secretly ambivalent) commentary and criticism. Her labors were painstaking, and my respect grew into fondness into gratitude. Paul Thomas was present at every important juncture in my graduate career; it was he who first prompted me to write about nuclear politics, and then about Plato, and then about Marx. His inspiration and friendship sustain me to this day. Reinhard Bendix knew what I was doing before I did, and I always left his office *begeistert* and with a clearer sense of my ironic mission. I treasured my time spent with Reinhard and Jane Bendix and wouldn't trade those conversations for anything in the world. Also at Berkeley, John Traugott's quiet counsel gave me needed shots of confidence or kept me from going crazy, and Lowell Dittmer showed me a living example of how scholarship, decency, and understatement can all be combined. I also want to thank the Danforth Foundation and the Mabelle McLeod Lewis Foundation for their support during these graduate years.

An earlier version of the above committee, my professors at Amherst College--William Kennick, Tracy B. Strong, and George Kateb--set high standards, never patronized, and yet looked past students' youthful indiscretions, believing in possibilities. Such teachers change lives (albeit short of redemption), and these three taught me and still show me, through their words and in their persons, the integrity of the study of political theory and philosophy.

At Stanford University I met a true colleague and kindred spirit, Daniel Conway, whose ideas have energized and transformed my thinking, such that I'm no longer certain how to disentangle his thinking from mine, nor do I think it necessary. This book owes much to him. Also at Stanford, David Riggs proved to me that senior faculty members can actually talk to, take an interest in, and try to learn from junior faculty. I thank him for his encouragement.

Thanks as well to Spencer Carr, Marykay Scott, Marian Safran, Libby Barstow, Lynn Arts, and all others at Westview Press, whose professionalism made the task of publishing a first book an enjoyable experience.

Of course I want also to thank my overly proud parents, who never discouraged my waywardly cosmopolitan pretensions, though such tendencies took me away from the Midwest. Last, though I'm tempted to cite, in order to thank, numerous friends, relatives, former coworkers, classmates, colleagues, students, and ex-teammates on my softball team, I shall mention but three such persons, who must stand for the rest: Shey Tata, Bill Blagborne, and Kim Peasley. Without their companionship, all theory would be gray, indeed.

John Evan Seery

Introduction
to
The Morality of Hell

I recognize the tokens of the ancient flames.
–Vergil, *The Aeneid*
--Dante, *Purgatorio*

Think how Christianity ruined hell for all of us. The early Christians--Peter and Paul were the primary culprits[1]--stripped away its fictionality; they presented hell as *literal*.[2] No longer would a journey into hell be regarded as a pleasant experience after all, an act of remembrance and renewal, a goad to the imagination, a benign displacement, a joyful awakening. Now hell would be turned into a site of supposedly real punishment and eternal suffering, a scary pit of fire,[3] a concept the purpose of which could only be to bedevil, threaten, frighten, discipline, and deter us, but a concept whose conceptuality Peter and Paul would never dare confess. Eternal *judgment* became possible as never before, goodness and good rewards now separated geographically from evil, and clear-cut consequences to follow from an admittedly mysterious theology.

Why does it matter that hell has been perverted? Why not just thank the Christians for introducing an extreme, if compelling, form of utilitarian logic into the world and forgive them for their ghastly excesses? What has been lost or altered?

Much depends upon what hell, that entire experience of descending imaginatively into a nether region, once was. For unless we tour pre-Christian, Hellenic hell, we may miss a crucial and still abiding feature of Western morality and Western politics.[4] Christianity has induced us to look not only downward too literally, but upward as well. Western moral topographers tend to relegate our "highest" ideals, our best principles, to transcendental spheres; and only recently (say, the last 150 years) have our most progressive philosophers and antiphilosophers begun to debase, decenter, and deconstruct these ideals, to bring them back down to earth, as it were (Hegel, Nietzsche, Heidegger, Foucault, Derrida, and Richard Rorty come to mind). But a long alternative tradition exists and persists, of looking wittingly below ground, and not literally beyond, for a critical moral vantage, for a self-created perspective upon this world, for a foil close to home. Indeed, whatever moral continuity is to be found in the West is to be found in hell, in Hades and Tartarus, in inferno traveling, in *katabasis* and *anastasis*, in descent and return: from Homer and the Greek tragedians, to Plato, to Vergil and Cicero, to Christ, to Plutarch and Lucian, to Dante, to Cervantes, Shakespeare, Milton, and Goethe, to Nietzsche. Let us be as precise as possible about the origins[5] of this epic underbelly to Western morality: It begins with Orpheus.[6]

Who was Orpheus?[7] Why is his story so suggestive, why did it leave such a legacy?[8] He has been called the founder of many things: Orpheus, the founder of civilization, the harmonizer, the great initiate; Orpheus, the first poet, musician, and artist; Orpheus, the great lover, the first homosexual as well; Orpheus, the first go-between, the first reconciler, between life and death, between body and soul, and between Apollo and Dionysus. Who was this Odysseus before Odysseus, an Aeneas before Aeneas, a Christ before Christ, Dante before Dante, Faust before Faust, and Zarathustra before Zarathustra? Why has this tale endured and continued to entice?

Orphic[9] scholars recognize three clear parts to the Orpheus narrative: Orpheus' civic and lyrical activities, Orpheus' underworldly affairs, and Orpheus' final dismemberment and swansong singing.[10] To be sure, the tale has many sides to it, is richly ambiguous, has undergone numerous transformations, and altogether can accommodate several nicely plausible readings. But let us avoid becoming too distracted with nuances and distinctions, for Orpheus' story is essentially a story about love[11] and therefore, more generally, about human relationships. What exactly makes this love story so poignant, eerie, and tragic (if finally uplifting)?

Orpheus descends into the underworld to look for Eurydice, his snakebitten lover.[12] Thus begins a narrative strategy of indirection, of juxtaposing the worldliness and vitality of love with the other-worldliness of death. What is the significance of looking for one's lover in hell? Or, to frame that question more philosophically, what does it mean to regard, in anticipatory fashion, one's present lover as dead, to imagine one's lover already dead, to look at the whole notion of love, in other words, from the perspective of death? Orpheus' descent teaches us about love by testing and playing upon its limits: Does love endure, even after the separation that is death? Orpheus' descent begins by reversing our initial expectations: Death is not the forbidding obstacle one might normally assume but can be overcome, at least for now, by an artistic spell. Herein lies the power and pathos of Orpheus' dedication to Eurydice: To look for love in hell, after death, after the cessation of life, is to suggest that love may indeed be more powerful than death, that a love may defy death--though all the while our countervailing selves know better, for this after all is but a figurative triumph.[13] Let us assign a preliminary name to this strategy of indirection, to this reversal of expectations, to this suggestion that an exercise in fictionality may produce very real sentiments indeed: It is *irony*.[14] The essential irony contained in Orpheus' descent is to be found in the bare suggestion, the unspoken premise of the tale, that one may care about someone, or care about anything alive and worldly, in the face of death.[15] Orpheus' love, a love that skirts--even as it acknowledges--the limitations imposed by death, represents not blind devotion or superabundant desire but rather, to use that word again, irony.[16]

Orpheus' tragedy, farther on, is that he succumbs to a need for literalism.[17] The source of tragedy in the tale, we might say, begins with the defeat of irony. Orpheus' shortcoming is that he desires to see Eurydice directly, to have direct ocular proof of her existence;[18] he can no longer play along with the extraordinary fictionality of his circumstances, he can no longer sustain an ironic love. At the moment he turns around to see her, he ceases to be playful, cunning, Dionysian, theoretical, ironic. Love cannot conquer all, that is starkly true. Only the irony that inspired the original descent into hell is capable of withstanding such knowledge.

Our glance cast downward, we can begin to discern the now murky connections among pre-Christian hell, Western morality, and irony. Hell in the Orpheus tale is a laboratory prop, a heuristic device, a visual construct, a figurative ploy, a mathematical extrapolation to infinity--all designed to help us put our relationships to others into a longer-term perspective, in short, to prompt us to examine the value of our lives and loves from within the inevitable context of human mortality. That we shall all die is, of course, literally a cliché.[19] The Orpheus tale exploits this literalism, reiterates it, doubles it, in a way exaggerates it, and thereby confronts and partially undermines it.[20] The descent into hell requires a suspension of literalness, a fictionalization of death; but that newly won playfulness about death permits a new detachment toward the attachments of life.[21] Love is cast into sharp relief; in the liminal zone of hell it can be examined as if from afar, as if we infernal travelers had gone on vacation.   To affirm love, in turn, by subjecting it to the scrutiny of everlasting torment, by viewing it as already lost, dead, or mutilated, requires a strange, a self-knowingly strange, cast of mind.   Here, down deep (speaking very expansively) we begin to see the first beginnings of Western morality, in the insight that the affirmation of others is to be attained only *via negativa*, by indirection, by imaginary detachment, that is to say, through an acceptance of a pretense or a kind of proviso, namely that caring about another human being matters at all (rather than not) in view of human finitude.[22]

But if we really want to see the original ironic connections between hell and Western morality, we must look to Homer, as one who wittingly invokes the Orpheus myth.[23] With Homer begins a series of subsequent Orphic excursions, led by Western[24] poets, writers, musicians, philosophers, and artists who in their infernal activities pay mock-homage to Orpheus, all the while aware that the "epic" tradition they invoke and further is at once mock-epic, conscious that their fiction is built upon another fiction, a long line of fictions, all of which nonetheless constitute a very real tradition of discourse.[25] Why did Homer first draw upon Orpheus, an act that has inspired so many others?[26]

We should not be distracted by the easy observation that Homer uses the Orpheus descent to produce, after all, a tale of heroic regeneration.[27] No, Odysseus' confrontation with death in the underworld reproduces, and underscores, the original strain of irony from the initial descent. Odysseus' descent serves the same moral mission. To descend to see your vanquished enemies, dead warriors, and neglected parents; to view human life, in anticipatory fashion, as divested of all life's blood; to imagine humans as mere shades of themselves; to consider human life itself *in extremis*--what does this mean? Homer has been misunderstood.   The Hegels and Nietzsches see only the externals of the poetry; they think Homer is glorifying the "premoral" hero, one who understands and celebrates only the visible, even if tragic, consequences of his actions. But that customary "heroic" reading doesn't take hell fully into account.

The Homeric hero may indeed be "premoral," but this cannot be *Homer's* point.   Rather, Homer seems already to have anticipated the modern deconstructionist view of Western morality. He already realizes that a fully rounded, self-internalized, truly anticonsequentialist moral code is an impossibility. He seems to know that he cannot *discursively* change his heroes' angry characters, cannot alter their bloodthirsty behaviors through syllogistic suasion. Instead, he *shows us* the extended consequences of their actions, highlighting these consequences through artful exaggeration. Lest one take these images too literally, Homer includes a tip-off as to their mock-mythic origins: Orpheus. Homer's invoking Orpheus (by way of Odysseus' descent) serves as a tacit admission of the fictionality, the citationality, of his entire enterprise, which amounts to a virtual admission that moral horizons can never, alas, be built upon externalities and visible consequences. To this end we are repeatedly reminded that Homer has complete control over his poetic amplifications. He has the gods laugh at us, quarrel over us, intervene in our affairs, threaten divine retribution; and sometimes a Homeric warrior has the audacity to do battle with a god!

We latter-day readers must not presume that Homer is some manipulator of the masses or some naïve wit who takes himself and his tale completely seriously. His use of the gods, the very notion of their immortality in conspicuous contrast to our affairs, and the sheer idea of an afterlife or an underworld are meant to lend in his works an odd validity to human matters, an obliquely heightened sense of place and importance: Worldly action has something like divine, or eternal, significance, it is suggested. But meanwhile Homer undercuts his images, he lets us in on his secrets, he pokes fun at his own devices, he puts everything into perspective: "Such was the fate of Hektor, breaker of horses" (now dead and of course no longer breaking horses). Finally we realize: His works are not some glorification of honorific warfare in the face of death, not after all a testimony to the supreme greatness of humans-as-heroes, and certainly not a bible primarily about the gods and their otherworlds. Instead Homer reminds us of the limitations and dangers occasioned by the fact of human mortality; and he indirectly teaches us that human self-affirmation, or human moral restraint, is not something to be merely discovered in nature or above it, but rather is something achieved, by looking up and down, back and forth, between here and an imaginative elsewhere.

"Tragedy provokes irony"--that is Homer's theme, a perspective not "grounded" in some Greek aesthetic phenomenology but one proffered instead as a working hypothesis, as a claim with numerous conditions attached.[28] To repeat, Homer has been misunderstood. How unfortunate that misreception, for it may well mean that an entire Greek attitude, perhaps an entire epic tradition that such an attitude engendered, subsequently has been misreceived as well. It is beyond our purview here to attempt to explain adequately how an entire poetic tradition could be misread. Still, a quick conjecture suggests itself. If Homer's hell represents the beginning of "anticonsequentialist" moral discourse, Homer went about his task by ironically begging the point, through a poetic exploitation of visible externalities. Certainly he must have been aware of the risks he was taking; perhaps he gave his auditors too much credit for their abilities of *hineinlesen*, of reading into the work and between the lines, of listening critically. What we can easily note is that an ironic method is extremely vulnerable to being misunderstood, so that Homer's auditors, then and now, might easily take him either all too literally and "mythically" or else dismiss him as a manipulative purveyor of myths.

Skipping over the descents of some of the other ancient Greek dramatic ironists--Sophocles, Euripedes, Aeschylus[29]--we might quickly consider the next major high point in our underworldly epic tradition: Socrates and Plato.[30] In the context of the above discussion of Homer's Orphic enterprise, we must stress the essential *continuity* between Homer's moral mission and that of Socrates and Plato--despite those moderns who insist that Socratic and Platonic "rationalism" was at war with Greek tragedy. To placate such persons, by respecting some less-than-obvious differences between Homeric poetry and Platonic philosophy, we might suggest that what Socrates and Plato were trying to do was to bring the hell of the tragic poets aboveground, thus making their moral irony more explicit, more accessible, and seemingly more discursive for an audience of demanding sophists. But such an effort, we must note, would not constitute an essential *break* with Homer. Rather, their attempt to make irony more dialogical would suggest that Socrates and Plato were hoping to correct a prevalent *misreading* of Homer.   Socrates and Plato, as the proper heirs to Homer's irony, seemed to know that Homer, in almost every word he issued, was attempting to *disabuse* humans of their apparent need to rely upon the gods--and all such cognitive equivalents--for moral instruction.[31] While Homer, to make this point, took the gods as his ironic allies, so did Socrates and Plato take Homer as their apparent foil, as a new god to the Greeks, from whom they would indirectly preach moral independence to *their* auditors.[32]

This affinity between Plato and Homer becomes most apparent (to the extent that it ever becomes apparent) precisely in Plato's references to Orpheus: for instance in the Myth of Er, when the tale-teller chastises Orpheus for being a lukewarm lover, because he refused to die heroically in order to be reunited with his lover. Or in the *Apology*, when Socrates states that he is willing to die ten times over, because it would be a pleasure to see Orpheus (and Homer) in the underworld.[33] If Socrates' irony represented an attempt at shaking his interlocutors' reliance upon formulaic ways of thinking, so too was Plato engaging in an essentially ironic effort, in an attempt at disabusing his readers of relying upon Plato's own text as a moral self-help manual (more on this in Chapter 2).

What generally can be said about subsequent "Orpheus" efforts--
and the surprisingly extensive list of those paying homage to Orpheus
includes the names of Isocrates, Aristophanes, Vergil, Cicero, Horace,
Ovid, Seneca, Plutarch, Lucian, Boethius, Augustine, Dante, Chaucer,
Rabelais, Cervantes, Shakespeare, Monteverdi, Descartes, Calderón de
la Barca, Milton, Gluck, Haydn, Goethe, Novalis, Balzac, Baudelaire,
Browning, Dostoyevski, Rodin, Rimbaud, Valéry, Rilke, Thomas Mann,
Wallace Stevens, Joyce, Eliot, Robert Lowell, Stravinsky, Henry
Miller, Tennessee Williams, George Bernard Shaw, H.D., Ralph
Ellison, Sartre, Jean Anouilh, Muriel Rukeyser, Jean Cocteau, Varuhan
Boghosian, Thomas Pynchon[34]--is that latter-day Orphic poets are
conscious that their descents have an ancestry and that they are paying
tribute to the original Orpheus myth,[35] whatever their particular
twists, turns, reversals, and mediations upon it. This implicit admission deepens the artificiality of the entire enterprise, even though
invoking such a past lends immediate credence to the descent at hand.
Such technique, of tacitly or explicitly invoking previous authors in the
context of the world of the dead, is not simply *technique*, deployed for
dramatic effect. Indeed, invoking dead Orphic poets is perfectly
compatible with the original Orphic moral mission: One becomes able
to confront the dead, think about the dead, engage with the dead,
through an act of fiction. Latter-day Orphism puts the past into a
dialogue with the present in order to attest[36] to an unexpected
connection between the two. No work exemplifies this protracted moral
affirmation, in defiance of all space and time, better than Dante's
Commedia.

That Dante, at least in part, draws upon the Orphic myth--in a
line from Homer, to Vergil, to Augustine[37]--would seem obvious
enough.[38] In fact, it could be argued that Dante's *Descensus ad Inferos*
owes more to Orphic sentiment than to Christology if only because
Dante takes love of a girl, Beatrice, as his model of unconditional
moral affirmation, whereas Christ knew no such lovers (Mary, Mary
Magdaline, Martha, and Joanna hardly count).[39] Furthermore, the
idea of a poet-artist qua Christian pilgrim would certainly seem more
inspired by Orphic creativity than by anything Christ ever did.[40] But
if Dante's descent ultimately owes so much to Orpheus, then how can
the implicit irony of that journey be at all compatible with Christian
orthodoxy, which by most counts is completely devoid of irony?[41] We
know that the Christian *anastasis*, Christ's particular version of
descent and ascension, was never a part of the original Christological
cycles and most likely was an early contrivance.[42] But even so, the
mere fact that the early Christians were capable of imaginative

embellishment does little to explain Dante's odd merging of Orphic and Christian imagery.[43]

John Freccero has explicated beautifully an overall "irony" that informs Dante's descent.[44] Dante-the-pilgrim, confused and over-whelmed, confronts the inscription over the gates of hell at the "same" time, in much the same way as Dante's readers (following both Dante-the-pilgrim and Dante-the-poet) confront these words at the beginning of the third canto (*"Lasciate ogne speranza, voi ch'intrate"*). This effect typifies what Freccero, following Paul de Man, defines as "irony," namely the unexpected disclaiming of a work of fiction *as* fictional; an artistry, in other words, the central fiction of which is to deny its own fictionality. For Freccero, such irony establishes for Dante's reader the vivid sensuality and "temporality" of the pilgrim's journey, for now it is suggested that the poetic scheme in hell is no *mere* scheme at all, that the pilgrim's experience should count as a moving reality applicable to the reader's life as well.

But we want to add to this account the suggestion that the irony of Dante's descent bespeaks much more than an authorial strategy of poetic intrigue or disingenuous overstatement. The irony does more than merely to disclaim and thus to beguile in order to instruct; it also implies a moral outlook, more affirmative after all than judgmental. To be sure, Dante's pretense establishes a poetic verisimilitude that seems all too real; his poetry creates an uncannily perceptible world of visible consequences in the afterlife. Surely the strategy produces the effect of promising eternally punishing consequences for one's temporal acts. That is a frightening thought. But the correlation between sin and punishment is too direct, too immediate (often too humorous), to be finally credible to the careful reader that Dante assumes. Surely that reader must eventually surmise: For the punishments to be so remi-niscent of the original act, the temporal must already admit of the eternal. An extrapolation to infinity is unnecessary. Our wayward acts must be, in some sense, eternal punishments in and of themselves. That thought may be even more frightening than the first (for the punishment doesn't even abide temporary deferment). Lest we succumb to a second-order literalism (seeing souls, for instance, where Dante speaks of bodies), we need to remind ourselves of the possibility that Dante may be attempting to disabuse us of the idea that there need be literal punishments for one to pursue righteousness; he may ultimately be trying to subvert a Christianity that subscribes to a utilitarian "improvement-morality." He may be attempting to disabuse us of the practice of pursuing goodness or godliness on the promise of rewards and the threat of punishments--even though his *Inferno, Purgatorio,* and *Paradiso* seem upon first blush to be exploiting and advocating such a variety of calculating Christian logic. Here we can begin to see how the irony of Orphism may be at all compatible with an original strain of what to some would appear to be a sacrilegious Christianity: For what was Christ's role as mediator if not to suggest that the sacred is already present in the secular, and that the human already partakes of the divine--all of which would tend to spiritually undermine Christ's indispensability?

Likewise, Dante's retroactive merging of the pagan and Christian worlds (e.g., the creation of a limbo for virtuous pagans) was not, one suspects, an act of desperate, revisionist theology but rather a mission informed by a sustained ironic Orphism:[45] All redemption is a homecoming.[46] We are who we are and need not view ourselves as intrinsically perverse nor all of human history as radically discontinuous. But to realize this unexpected point, we might need to take creative leave of our senses. At the height of the *Paradiso*, at the point where we have learned finally how no longer to rely upon guides, Dante indirectly allows us to catch a glimpse of an expansive vision suggesting that all things, past, present, and future, are somehow interconnected, bound through something like creative faith or an all-embracing poise.[47] If only for that brief moment, our fleeting insight confirms the ecstatic vision. Our own poetic powers, shown the way by Dante, strain to make this appreciative leap. But the attempt alone is enough. We now at least possess a *notion* of redemptive affirmation, which was perhaps Christ's original message in humblest form, before any extravagance. Our act of reading in that moment *becomes* that which has been symbolized and sought; the fiction ceases then to be merely fictional.[48] Such is the shamanism of Dante's poetry.

Dante presents an expansive moral outlook that affirms through poetic irony. What could such poetry have to do with Western politics?[49]

Cleanth Brooks once claimed that all poetry is "ironic" because poetry must admit its own form and the "pressures" of context in order to project beyond itself.[50] That definition of poetry may seem a little formulaic, but what Brooks appears to have meant is that in order for a poet to engage a reader so that the poet's words convey sense rather than gibberish, the poet must first admit (somehow) the fictionality of the entire enterprise. Poetic intention may be conveyed, and often is assumed, in a variety of ways; but the point is that once the reader is alerted to the presence of a *context* for poetry, then and only then can he or she begin to make sense of sentence fragments, elliptical phrases, rhyme schemes, and so on.

We might take a cue from Brooks's definition of poetry and apply it analogously to politics. Politics does not make sense unless its

participants tacitly admit the "pressures" of context and attempt to
project beyond them by way of irony. We need to elaborate. Politics, of
course, is the art, or the rough-and-tumble, of diverse persons trying to
live together. Certainly the imperatives of brute survival provide
some of the mundane pressures of "context" for politics; but the fullest
sense of political context, the "parameters" of such activity, is
provided by the fact that all human life ends in death--which by
definition constitutes the termination of political activity per se.
Those who hold that the imperatives of survival provide *all* of the
pressures of context for politics elide its fundamental strangeness. How
can such activity be at all meaningful in view of its ultimate futility?
How can one affirm the idea of trying to live with others when one
knows that all of one's efforts eventually will be for naught? We can
eliminate one answer: In view of the fact of death, we must conclude
that we do not pursue politics, we do not affirm a life in common, for the
sake of ultimate *consequences*. Politics *literally* does not make sense in
the face of death. And by parity of reason, an anxious attachment to
survival does not make sufficient sense in view of death and thus cannot
fully define the meaning of politics. We want to suggest instead that
politics acquires its meaning and form and direction only by recognizing
its essential if underlying irony: that all is part pretense, play, fiction,
temporality, construct, indirection. Politics is *ironic*, because it requires
an acceptance of the pretense, the possible fiction, that living together
matters in the face of death; it requires a fundamental reversal of
sensibilities, an outlook that can somehow affirm worldliness
notwithstanding the ultimate of consequences.

My claim: that an ironic outlook informed the moral mission of the
Greek tragedians, as evidenced in their Orphic descents, and that that
same sense of ironic connection, concocted first in hell, originally
informed the general Greek concept of politics.[51] Irony helped to unify
the ancient polis, but that unity was self-consciously imaginative,
detached from all consequentialist concerns, both earthbound and
heavenward. To the extent, then, that we have misunderstood the
Orphic-epic tradition, we have also misunderstood the ancient Greeks'
ironic attitude toward politics. Furthermore, to the extent that the
Greeks provided us with *our* concept of politics, our misreading means
that we may well have lost touch with the underlying irony of our own
enterprise. Some of this is not altogether new: Many contemporary
political theorists have claimed that the ancient Greeks provide us
with our concept of politics.[52] Some have subsequently endorsed what
they thought to be the Greeks' original intention, others have viewed
it as an anachronism and a potentially dangerous one at that. But the
prevalent understanding has been that the Greeks sought to unify the

body politic through various transcendentalist or organic schema (the standard readings of Plato and Aristotle, respectively, come to mind). According to such a view of the Greeks' position, political communities supposedly have something *literally* in common that holds them therefore definitively together.

The above alternative account, emphasizing images of underworldly descent rather than claims to transcendence or to organicism, would suggest that the Greeks understood political unity as *essentially* ironic; that one's moral and political connections to other human beings are to be drawn by way of a roundabout process of negative ratiocination; and that life with others might be thought meaningful after all, not because of an ultimate, essentialist purpose but thanks rather to certain temporary postures of pretense.

How far have we wandered from hell? What has been lost along the way? Our contemporary tendency to avoid hell at all costs would seem to suggest that we may no longer be able to view life ironically, no longer able to provide for ourselves an ironic "justification" of life. And of course that inability would extend to an inability to regard others, other human lives, ironically, all of which would impose certain constraints upon our political possibilities. What does this mean? Can we even still think about an "ironic" justification for life? For politics?

After Nietzsche's devastating critique of Kant's "deontological" ethics, the idea of pursuing something "for its own sake" has been pushed much out of favor today. Surely "life" must be pursued for its benefits, both the postmodernist and the neorationalist will contend, and surely these benefits will accord (for the post-Nietzschean) with the somehow naturally human, perhaps with biological imperatives, or deep structures of mind and personality, symbolic functions of culture and language, tradition and historicity, the tendencies of ethnicity and gender, and of course, with French "desire." The idea of pursuing life "for its own sake," it is claimed, is a self-deception. Isn't life, mustn't life, oughtn't life be lived for a *reason*, an interest, a natural inclination? Doesn't life (call it Heideggerian thrownness) provide internally its own momentum and logic and purpose (even once one has smashed all previous idols and abandoned all aporias)? And shouldn't postmodern "morality" tend toward, and take advantage of, that which is intrinsically life-promotional?

The modern preoccupation with "life" as the sole source of vitality can be related to an evident longing to reduce "morality" to a matter of basic mechanics, to simple ends-means calculations, to "rational" problem-solving: pursue the necessary, avoid the contingent. What this stance actually does is to eliminate any *real* choice in moral deliberation, for it forecloses entirely the radical option that life may not admit of an inherent reason for itself.

What is "ironic" (here used in the simple sense of "unexpected") about the act of looking to hell, a fictive death, for moral guidance is that we are normally accustomed to looking at "life" for our principles of living. Looking at death in order to learn about life (as opposed to indulging in death to learn about death per se) betrays a partial detachment toward life, a way of admitting the option that life may not admit of any inherent "reason" for itself and that, therefore, one must look elsewhere for guidance, by default.

The problem-solver, the "consequentialist" ethicist, even the postmodern pragmatist, seem to have a hard time grasping a truly "anticonsequentialist" morality. He or she will insist that moral affirmation must be based upon *something*, must be "grounded," and that the anticonsequentialist simply isn't admitting what this something is. He or she will portray the anticonsequentialist's position as a principled dedication to the purity of "good intentions," or as an aversion to "dirty hands," or else as an unflagging loyalty to an inarticulate absolutism or an ill-defined mysticism or an unreconstructed humanism. Furthermore, he or she might dismiss "anticonsequentialism" precisely because of its potential for producing dangerous or imprudent consequences (as in, "The path to hell is paved with good intentions," or "Damn the torpedoes, full steam ahead").

But what the critics of anticonsequentialism seem never to consider is the possibility that an "anticonsequentialist" moral outlook could under certain circumstances turn out to be the most beneficial stance "for life" after all. Such would be the case if indeed "life" happens to fail at some point to provide any good reasons for itself. Or to put it more positively: In potentially tragic times, the ironic anticonsequentialist does not ask for and would not require a *reason* or reasons to affirm the value of living. In politics, the ironist would have an advantage of being able to affirm the value of diverse persons living together even though one might not be able to say that such activity leads anywhere, represents anything, or that the various constituencies involved have anything literally, naturally, or practically in common with one another.

Why attempt, then, to recapture a lost sense of moral and political irony? The question is tricky, for irony, a pose that tends to be obsessively self-deprecating, would seem to preclude outright advocacy. My preliminary response to this question is simply that the times again invite, nay provoke, irony, and I hope to bring that ironic sensibility to the surface of current political debate. Specifically, I am struck by the overwhelming failure of modern democratic liberalism to issue a coherent moral and political denunciation of the use, or the *threat* of the use, of thermonuclear weapons. By now a pluralistic theory of preferences has proven itself utterly incapable of providing a general critique of the possibility of nuclear destruction.[53] And moral absolutists are of little help either, insofar as they are, as a matter of principle, indifferent to the realities of the modern age, and but a scant few listen to them anyway. Utilitarians are able and often all too eager to provide a rationale for nuclear arms buildup, but not for clearly condemning the *prospect* of annihilating great numbers of human beings.[54] Concerned liberal theorists such as John Rawls strive to find the right configuration of words that might eventually inform a more unified political stance, but Rawls's approach has captured the imagination mainly of other like-minded analytic philosophers and has failed to translate into a widely accepted politics.[55] All claims to "rationalism" fade in the face of death, and no veil of ignorance can hide that fact.

Has Rawls--by some counts the leading political theorist of the postwar period--ever thought about hell? To his credit, Rawls has attempted to bring Kant's transcendentalism down to earth, but his critics usually produce equally down-to-earth complications that confound the general theory. Rawls's failure finally to produce theoretical unity in the nuclear age is telling for the state of contemporary theory. Where has he gone wrong? Where has contemporary theory run aground? Just *listen* to the major concepts, the grandest of issues and debates circulating in contemporary political theory, and note how singly preoccupied these are with concerns drawn exclusively from "life,"[56] and by the same token how lacking they are in any implied acknowledgment of the ultimate fact of human mortality,[57] and thus how unwittingly self-trivializing most accounts become when all is said and done: the "good" life, "power," "rights," "justice," "property," "interests," "preferences," "desires," "liberty," "obligation," "authority," "representation," "negative versus positive freedom," "individualism versus community," "public versus private," "separateness versus attachment," "difference versus identity." "Equality" is about the only concept that retains its grammatical integrity when viewed from the perspective of death.[58]

There is one major school of thought in contemporary political theory that takes death as its point of departure for thinking about politics. I am thinking of that cluster of thinkers concerned with distinguishing between "just" and "unjust" wars, a tradition running from Augustine to Hobbes. But even this school doesn't descend headlong into hell. Michael Walzer, arguably the best modern commentator in the "just war" tradition, is one of the few who sets his

sights directly and explicitly toward hell.[59] But even Walzer's notion
of hell is gravely limited, mainly because it is devoid of all irony.

Walzer discusses hell extensively in order to challenge the
Clausewitzian sentiment that all "war is hell" allegedly because war
is limitless in its potential for ruthlessness and escalating cruelties.
Some wars are *not* hell, Walzer reminds us; and most fighting *can* be
stopped short of oblivion. Walzer thinks war *is* hell "whenever men
are forced to fight, whenever the limit of consent is breached." Hence
war is hell "most of the time"; but Walzer wants to insist upon the idea
of individual consent as the deciding test of morality in wartime,
which establishes "the boundaries of hell." It is an admirable project.
Walzer wants to impose some sense of order, decency, and restraint upon
modern wartime madness, and he wants to lend his support to wartime
conventions and rules of fair play. The ends do not always justify the
means, even in times of war, and not all forms of aggression are
excusable due to the supposedly inevitable hellishness of war. To distinguish between hell and not-hell in times of war, Walzer implicitly
challenges even Dante's famous description: "When we say, war is
hell, it is the victims of the fighting that we have in mind. In fact,
then, war is the very opposite of hell in the theological sense, and is
hellish only when the opposition is strict. For in hell, presumably,
only those people suffer who deserve to suffer, who have chosen
activities for which punishment is the appropriate divine response,
knowing that this is so."[60]

Whatever the shortcomings of his interpretation of Dante and the
Christian tradition, Walzer's own notion of hell, by contrast, is
earthbound, aboveground, decidedly literal. In fact he recommends
that "poetic images" of death be avoided, for when such images enter
into moral and political thought, they "obscure our critical judgment."[61]
Though an "aboveground" moral theorist, Walzer doesn't want to be
understood as a "consequentialist." The hellishness or not-hellishness
of war should not be staked upon outcomes; moral reasoning should not
be held hostage to consequences (Walzer thinks the policy of nuclear
deterrence is immoral). But in response to Walzer, we want to say that
a *thoroughly* "anticonsequentialist" morality would need to project
even beyond the current psychological dispositions of the actors
involved. What Dante's hell can do that Walzer's hell cannot is to
assess the validity of consent from a detached, anticipatory perspective, allowing the possibility that one could repudiate one's current
position after the fact, that is, somehow after death. Then perhaps,
only after one is dead and gone, might one be able to see clearly one's
mortal connections to other humans; only from the perspective of hell
can one perhaps see that death defeats *all* justifications for war (as

Achilles lamented, Death visits the noblest hero just as surely as the commonest rogue). Though the main force of Walzer's analysis is directed against those who wish to justify war at virtually any cost, his reasoning also commits him to justify, under certain conditions, the deliberate killing of members of other polities. Political attachments somehow sanction death, and Walzer's moral and political theory stops at the national border. Given Walzer's limited conception of hell, his otherwise impeccable analysis that modern war need not escalate into a veritable hell on earth, is hardly reassuring, especially in an age of nuclear weaponry.

I propose that Rawls, Walzer, and other political theorists who seem to be looking for a general affirmation, an expansive ground of justification, for the very idea of politics and political community in the nuclear age should look not upward nor even earnestly downward to earth but rather to (pre-Christian) hell.[62] There one can discover the idea of political community as *ironic*, an idea that I find--oddly--to hold out more promise for redirecting the politics of modernity than most other political theories now in vogue. Indeed, one of the claims of the present work is that this ironic perspective is not completely buried in the modern world. I shall contend that the antinuclear movement or at least certain voices in that sometimes overly apocalyptic movement are now the modern heirs to the moral irony of the Orphic-epic tradition. Resurrecting that irony, establishing its long legacy, and revealing its political importance are all part of the task that follows.

*   *   *

As suggested above, the eventual aim of this work is to present a political theory of the antinuclear movement. But who really *needs* a political theory of the antinuclear movement? you, my reader, might ask at this outset. The activists are already committed to their causes, the skeptics are already skeptical, and the apathetic won't bother to wade through such a laborious work in the first place! And further-more, what *good*, what real effect, can such a work possibly accomplish? Books are books; theories are theories; and the world, especially this nuclear world of ours, will go about its business, with little regard for the paltry efforts of academic writers.

Sadly, I must admit that my worthy reader's initial charges are indeed formidable, and I doubt whether I can meet those objections in the few pages of an introduction. Allow me to respond modestly by noting that if we grant that the enterprises of book-writing and even political theorizing hold some potential value in and of themselves, then a young, aspiring book writer and political theorist in the late twentieth century (such as I) could choose to write on any of a number of topics that recommend themselves as important, topical, and theoretically interesting, to wit: the politics of gender relations, of cultural confrontation, of international relations, of human rights, of technology, of genetics and disease, of economics, of ecology, and so forth.   Yet all of these latter topics--I am speaking now very broadly-- seem to be framed or conditioned by the presumption that the world will continue to exist in the near, the "foreseeable" future; whereas an investigation of the "nuclear issue" does not depend upon that particular operational conceit.   My very preliminary justification for addressing the nuclear issue, then, is that such an enterprise may well entail the fewest of presumptions, the lowest of expectations, the barest of prerequisites, for one to commit one's words to paper.

By "the antinuclear movement," I mean that diffuse, sometimes motley collection of groups and individuals involved in an array of activities generally designed to issue a protest against either the sheer existence of or else the unreasonable accumulation of thermonuclear weaponry in the arsenals of various national governments.   (I am less concerned in this book with the various activities of those who oppose nuclear-power plants, though often these movements overlap.)   To refer to the antinuclear movement as a "movement" is only a recent possi- bility, despite the fact that numerous individuals have voiced opposition to the "Bomb" ever since its development in the 1940s. Several well-publicized events come to mind as having helped define the movement qua *movement*: the "Freeze" campaign in the United States in the late 1970s and early 1980s; the emergence of the Green party in West Germany as a significant political force; the staged protests such as the Greenham Common women's peace camp in England, and demonstrations, rallies, peace marches, and acts of civil disobedience elsewhere; the declaration of nuclear-free zones, for example by New Zealand and numerous municipalities; and the awarding of the Nobel Peace Prize to the Physicians for Social Responsibility in 1985.   (France's sinking of the Greenpeace ship and the Chernobyl incident could also be given honorable mentions.)

Nevertheless, the vitality of the antinuclear movement as a unified movement remains open to question.   True, a myriad of localized peace groups have now been institutionalized and are unlikely to recede into oblivion; but the antinuclear movement as a movement often seems adrift.   It is uncoordinated, unable to bring together its diverse components.   It is extremely susceptible to the charge that it has not really produced tangible, long-term results.   It often appears to have lost momentum as a whole.   It is in danger of being upstaged by minor "arms control" treaties (often a ruse for arms modernization) and any new national commitment to a "strategic defense" approach to deterrence. Its sense of mission is perversely threatened by the prospect that superpower relations might improve. I want to suggest that these shortcomings are indicative of the movement's failure to comprehend itself theoretically, to articulate its purposes and directions in more coherent fashion than simply to state a shared opposition to the nuclear bomb.

I should hope that the theory expressed herein might give some focus to the antinuclear movement, both for insiders and for those on the sidelines. Yet that theory is not simply a construction, a design imposed from without by an act of the imagination. Instead, I base this theory of antinuclearism on evidence taken from the movement itself. But note: I have been very selective. I'm not sympathetic with large portions of the movement and consider much of the movement to be theoretically uninteresting and even embarrassing. Much of the movement I find to be overly sentimental, politically naïve, wistfully wishful, occasionally excessive. I have little patience with peace movements that virtually require hand-holding, song-singing, or flower-picking. I don't care much for European antinuclearism, with its tiresome blend of insipid nationalism and obligatory anti-Americanism. Instead, I've seized upon a particular *moment* I observed in a California antinuclear demonstration, taken this moment out of context, and generalized it as exemplary, as indicating the *spirit* of antinuclearism at its best.

Thumbing through the pages of this book, the curious reader will notice that the bulk of the work is apparently *not* devoted to the antinuclear movement. Instead, he or she will find chapters on the ancient Greeks, Plato's *Republic*, irony and literary theory, and nineteenth-century aesthetics. Only the next-to-last chapter has as its explicit topic the twentieth-century antinuclear movement. These earlier chapters, and the sequence of chapters, are not gratuitous; they do pertain to the final topic. The book has a difficult, and somewhat protracted, thesis to present. Hence I think it well to provide my cautious reader with a map so that the terrain upon which he or she is about to embark shall not seem so hazardous and forbidding. (If chapters seem to digress, I ask for my reader's forbearance; for the book has a final aim but it is also sometimes at odds with itself, and part of my digressive long-windedness is meant to reaffirm the value of scholarship for its own sake, even though we theorists and academics, too, live under the threat of nuclear destruction.)

Chapter 1 is about the enterprise of political theory in the nuclear age. I examine some of the claims leveled against political theory in the 1950s, charges alleging that political theory was no longer "viable." That such a view of theory emerged during the development of nuclear weaponry was hardly coincidental, I propose. The bomb, in other words, posed a challenge, both logically and historically, to the enterprise of political theorizing. But during this period certain other theorists attempted to revitalize political theory. These theorists turned to the ancient Greeks for inspiration. I take my departure from one of these revisionist theorists, Sheldon Wolin. Examining Wolin's attempt to restore an element of communitarianism to political theorizing by sketching a continuity between the Greeks and moderns, I retain Wolin's basic project while altering his conclusion. In brief, I argue that Wolin's view of communitarianism, from the Greeks to the modern world, was insufficiently *ironic*. Therewith, this book becomes a book also about the relationship between irony and political theory. Essentially, I argue that Wolin overlooked the significance of irony in ancient Greek political thought; and that oversight is extremely suggestive for rethinking the modern concept of politics as well as the modern practice of political theorizing. An ironic view of politics suggests a way of generalizing Greek communitarianism beyond the spatial confines of the polis.

Next I try to bear out this claim about the presence of irony in ancient Greek theorizing through an intensive rereading of Plato's *Republic*. Chapter 2 is really the centerpiece of the entire book. The *Republic*, I contend, is a profoundly ironic work. It lays the basis for the idea of an "ironic" political community. Plato attempts to extend, now in written form, Socrates' project of ironic examination and interpersonal engagement; but Plato also tries to surpass Socrates' personal project by sketching the political implications of irony. En route to this reading I try to defend Platonic irony against its Hegelian detractors, and I also try to steal away the notion of Platonic irony from two major schools of ironic criticism, those headed by Leo Strauss and by Jacques Derrida, respectively. Both Strauss and Derrida wrote seminal interpretations of Plato's *Republic* and both staked their understanding of irony upon their readings of the *Republic*. My reading contests both of their notions of irony and in the process offers a rival understanding of the politics of irony.

In Chapter 3 I trace the etymological history of the term *irony* from the Greeks up to the present. In brief, after the Greeks, irony became viewed as an isolated rhetorical figure, largely divested of its philosophical significance. But I argue that these later tropological renderings of irony were really unfortunate departures from the Greek understanding of irony, and that a philosophical or conceptual view of irony needs to underwrite any rhetorical or strictly literary interpretation of irony. (This chapter is placed after the reading of the *Republic*, mainly in order to resist formulaic applications of irony, especially with respect to the *Republic*.)

Chapter 4 examines closely the ironic theorists of the nineteenth century, those who returned to the Greeks for an account of irony. These theorists--Goethe, Hegel, the Schlegel brothers, Kierkegaard, and others--attempted to translate an aesthetic notion of irony into a concept of "political irony" (to use Thomas Mann's phrase). Their nineteenth-century efforts, I suggest, can be viewed as instructive for the twentieth century; for although these theorists perceived a need for bringing irony and politics closer together in the modern period, they also, I contend, failed to sustain their own efforts. One who dabbles in an ironic politics ought to know beforehand some of the dangers and risks--not merely the attractions and potential benefits--involved in that effort. Finally, however, we must remember the very attempt at reconciling politics and irony--more so than the failures--for the attempt alone reveals an ethics of affirmation from which we can extract some measure of hope. In the same ironic spirit that these Germans embraced the Greeks, so shall we try to understand these Germans' latter-day efforts.

Chapter 5 presents a close rereading of Thomas Mann's *Reflections of a Nonpolitical Man* in order to examine a successful transition from ironic art to ironic politics, and therewith a transition from the nineteenth to the twentieth centuries. Almost without exception, commentators view Mann's book as an appalling, reactionary defense of his own defense of Germany during World War I--and it is. While not excusing Mann's general excesses, this chapter contends that the book also in effect announces Mann's oblique endorsement of democracy, which would mark Mann's turn to democracy at an earlier date than is commonly realized. The key to that announcement is found in Mann's discussion of "political irony," a phrase that has drawn scant attention in secondary sources. In explicating that term, I review Mann's expressed view of an antagonism that he sees between art and politics, and of an unexpected relationship between them, by way of irony. All of this turns on a discussion of Nietzsche (which involves a dispute with Mann's brother, Heinrich) regarding the proper way to apply Nietzschean aesthetics to modern politics. The chapter argues, then, that though Mann's book is indeed a partial attempt to rationalize his prowar, antidemocratic tendencies, even more important are his countervailing sentiments conveyed therein. In an attempt to show the larger political implications of Mann's hidden change of heart, the chapter compares Mann's particular act of "self-reversal" with two other twentieth-century, Nietzschean-inspired acts of aesthetic self-renewal, namely those suggested by French theorist Jacques Derrida and American theorist George Kateb.

Finally, these chapters lead up to and culminate in Chapter 6, in a claim regarding the presence of irony in certain forms of nonviolent resistance and, specifically, in some of the activities of the modern antinuclear movement. There I contend that the antinuclear activists are more than Socratic gadflies, *that they are making a very "Platonic," that is, philosophically ironic, claim about the nature of politics and political community in the twentieth century.* Specifically, their implicit contention that all of the world's peoples have something "in common" by virtue of the shared possibility of collective destruction is very reminiscent of Plato's attempt to sketch a vision of politics on the basis of a shared pretense, a noble lie. Thus the antinuclear activists follow in and extend a tradition of anticonsequentialist communitarianism, now on a grandly cosmopolitan scale. I shall argue that the antinuclear movement employs a notion of politics that has well-established precedents in the history of political theory, namely an ironic tradition of going below ground, into a theoretical underworld, to view the activity of this world from the perspective of death and destruction. The notion of a tradition of *ironic political communitarianism* separates me from most "postmodernist" accounts of the nuclear age, which generally see the current tendencies toward apocalypse as unprecedented. Contrariwise, I am saying that the appropriate genealogical investigation of our nuclear woes begins with Socrates and Plato (sometimes referred to as the "Homer to Holocaust" axis of Western thought), and that earlier discussions of politics can indeed help us think through our contemporary problems.

A final word to you, my reader: I have struggled to refrain myself from lapsing into irony in this work about irony, but the temptation to try my own hand is a strong one. I realize, however, that many readers find it hard to enjoy a work with shifting perspectives and multiple textual strategies. So to avoid confusion, and to add to my reader's enjoyment, I've decided to outline the several senses of the title of this book, "Political Returns." Of course, the inspiration for the central theme of "returning" comes from Homer's *Odyssey*, a theme that harks back to Orpheus and is echoed again in Plato's *Republic*, in the Allegory of the Cave, and that is manifest throughout the *Republic* in Plato's relation to Homer as ironic educator. *My* act, then, of returning to Orpheus, Homer, Plato, and the Greeks, is undertaken in the same spirit of self-conscious mimicry. By "returning" I also mean to allude to the ancient theorist's act of returning to his home polis, after observing the religious festivals of neighboring poleis; and this sense recalls the

Hebraic theme of exile and return. I also mean to allude to the scholastic vision of affirmative unification, as in the Thomistic notion of a cosmic "emanation and return"; and if Nietzsche's "eternal return" surfaces hauntingly as well, that's fine with me. Elsewhere I argue that rhetorical irony is best defined as an activity of "returning" to the page, to the written text. All of these acts of returning are in turn suggestive for the activity and theoretical posture of the antinuclear movement: returning to the precious politics of the Greeks in the nuclear age; returning to an age of no nuclear weapons; returning in the military sense of retiring a weapon; achieving "political returns" in the sense of election results; attaining returns in the sense of tangible consequences. In brief, I understand the act of theoretic returning as a kind of ironic affirmation of worldly activity, that is, as an affirmation that overcomes one's countervailing tendencies toward cynicism and tragedy. To repeat, Odysseus is the best exemplar of an ironic return to the human world, with Orpheus, his poetic forebear, as the great mediator and spiritual unifier.

Recalling the earlier inquiry, I can perhaps now offer my reader a stronger justification for this book: The project at hand is proffered in a spirit of irony. That is to say, *I am well aware that the world probably cannot be spared from great nuclear devastation by attending carefully to a trope.* But I am sufficiently intrigued by the possibility, however remote, that a trope just might save the world from nuclear annihilation; and I thought it worth my reader's while to alert him or her to this possibility, even though I realize that this book might be subjecting my reader to an effort that may prove to have been in vain (and can never be proven to have been successful). In a world that seems ever resistant to the lessons of theory, to the extent that such efforts are increasingly held in contempt, beneath contempt, and sometimes in self-contempt, a spirit of irony, of acknowledging the very real discrepancies between theory and practice and cautiously proceeding in spite of them, may need to inform as well those works in political theory whose designs are far more grand or self-assured than this one.

Notes

1. For the claim that Christianity borrowed directly from Orphic sources, see A. Dieterich, *Nekyia: Beiträge zur Erklärung der neuentdeckten Petrusapokalypse*, 2d ed., annotated by R. Wünsch (Leipzig and Berlin: Teubner, 1913). Also see Vittorio D. Macchioro, *From Orpheus to Paul: A History of Orphism* (New York: Henry Holt and Company, 1930). Macchioro's point is that Orphism was not representative of the rest of ancient Greek

religion, but that it gradually won the day and eventually culminated in Christian doctrines.

2. See D.P. Walker, *The Decline of Hell: Seventeenth-Century Discussions of Eternal Torment* (Chicago: University of Chicago Press, 1964). Walker's main thesis is that the doctrine of hell went unchallenged until the mid-seventeenth century, mainly because it was based upon strong scriptural authority and proved valuable as a deterrent device as well.

3. For the general transition from depicting hell as mud to depicting it as fiery, see Martha Himmelfarb, *Tours of Hell: An Apocalyptic Form in Jewish and Christian Literature* (Philadelphia: University of Pennsylvania Press, 1983), pp. 107ff.

4. Quickly I must mention Himmelfarb's main contention. She takes issue with Dieterich's tracing of a direct lineage from Greek Orphism to Christianity; i.e., Peter's apocalypse, she suggests, is not simply a reworked version of Greek myths. Himmelfarb complicates the Orphic-Christianity connection by resurrecting a number of Jewish and other cultural tours of hell. Her broader point is that there is no necessary thread of connection among all the various Western tours of hell and that, moreover, the notion of hell is not confined to the West. She mentions, for instance, the presence of hell in Ethiopian, Muslim, Zoroastrian, and Buddhist texts. Himmelfarb, *Tours of Hell*. See also John Block Friedman's wonderful book, *Orpheus in the Middle Ages* (Cambridge: Harvard University Press, 1970), for Orphic influences upon Hellenistic Jews.

5. Precision here is impossible. As Raymond J. Clark points out in his excellent book on the "catabatic" tradition, the Greek underworldly motif probably had origins dating back to Babylonian and Sumerian tales. And there were other catabatic excursions in Greek mythology, those namely of Heracles, Theseus, Dionysus, and Pollux. But like Clark, in his thesis about Virgil, I am focusing on the Orpheus tale as the most influential for later descent writers. *Catabasis: Virgil and the Wisdom Tradition* (Amsterdam: Gruner, 1979).

6. I realize that any quest for the origins of anything "Orphic" is problematic (cf. Himmelfarb, West, Clark, Linforth, Dodds). By most counts the Orpheus story probably derived from northern shamanism, then descended into the Hellenic world, through Thrace; and there it became a generic name for a wide assortment of poems, tales, songs, cults, and so forth. But thereafter it is difficult to trace the connection between the Orpheus narrative and the various cults and movements that have been alleged to have been "Orphic." Many commentators throw up their hands at all of this confusion, and thus one must issue the disclaimer that the term Orphism does not necessarily denote a univocal meaning. On the study of this protean phenomenon, West warns: "The magic of Orpheus' song drew animals and trees; the magic of his name has attracted a more unruly following, a motley crowd of romantics and mystics, of impostors and poetasters, of dizzy philosophers and disoriented scholars. The disorientation of the scholars is understandable after so many centuries in which Orpheus was all things to all men." M.L. West, *The Orphic Poems* (Oxford: Clarendon Press, 1983), p. 1;

Himmelfarb, *Tours of Hell*; Ivan M. Linforth, *The Arts of Orpheus* (Berkeley: University of California Press, 1941); E.R. Dodds, *The Greeks and the Irrational* (Berkeley: University of California Press, 1963).

7. The first mention of the name Orpheus is to be found in a mid-sixth-century fragment by the poet Ibycus. The phrase refers to "famous Orpheus," which is of note because Ibycus wrote some 150 years before Aristophanes and Plato. See Emmet Robbins, "Famous Orpheus," *Orpheus: The Metamorphoses of a Myth*, ed. John Warden (Toronto: University of Toronto Press, 1982), pp. 3-23. See also: C.M. Bowra, "Orpheus and Eurydice," *Classical Quarterly* (1952), pp. 113-24; Walter A. Strauss, *Descent and Return: The Orphic Theme in Modern Literature* (Cambridge: Harvard University Press, 1971); W.K.C. Guthrie, *Orpheus and Greek Religion* (New York: W.W. Norton & Co., 1966); Karl Kérenyi, *Pythagoras und Orpheus* (Zurich: Rhein-Verlag, 1950); Erich Heller, *The Disinherited Mind: Essays in Modern German Literature and Thought* (Cambridge: Bowes & Bowes, 1952); and Charles Segal, *Orpheus: The Myth of the Poet* (Baltimore: Johns Hopkins University Press, 1989).

8. Again, I am well aware that the movement called Orphism takes a different route or routes from the stories associated with Orpheus the man. On this point, see John Warden, "Introduction," *Orpheus: The Metamorphoses of a Myth*, ed. Warden, p. xi.

9. My use of the term Orphic in the paper refers to the "Orpheus" tale, not specifically to the religious movement called Orphism.

10. See Strauss, *Descent and Return*, p. 6.

11. Robbins contends that the idea of romantic love was of little interest to the early Greeks and that the emphasis on the tragedy and passion of the lost love owes more to the Alexandrian age and to Vergil and Ovid than to the original Orphic tales. In fact, he contends, Orpheus represented to the Greeks more of a shaman figure than a lover. But in the *Symposium* Plato *does* include the tale as part of his discussion about the power of love. Robbins's point is still well taken, namely that one must distinguish between the meaning of love for the Greeks and the later heightening of romantic passions through the anguish of separation. Robbins, "Famous Orpheus." I am also aware of Denis de Rougemont's famous thesis about the late origins of romantic love, but I do not think his thesis undermines my reading of Orphism. Denis de Rougemont, *Love in the Western World*, trans. Montgomery Belgion (Princeton: Princeton University Press, 1983). For an account of the development of a "love-interest" in the catabatic tradition, including Dionysus' concern for Semele, see Clark, *Catabasis*, p.99ff.

12. For a general account of the tale (most probably based upon those of Apollonius of Rhodes and Ovid), see Robert Graves, *The Greek Myths* (Baltimore: Penguin Books, 1948), pp. 111-113; Bertrand Mathieu has a nice synopsis also, in *Orpheus in Brooklyn: Orphism, Rimbaud, and Henry Miller* (The Hague-Paris: Mouton, 1976), pp. 6-18

13. Peter Dronke describes well the pathos of the Orpheus: "The story of Orpheus and Eurydice is no mere sentimental Hellenistic tale of love and

death. Nor is the happy ending a mere literary eccentricity. Rather it brings out a profundity which the better-known version tends to disguise--it gives a fuller clarity to the myth's most essential, most universal trait: the intimation that the here and the beyond are not irrevocably opposed to each other, that they form one world, that one who is endowed with a more-than-human power of vision . . . or endowed with a more-than-human power of love, can know this greater whole, can pass from here to beyond and back again, and can 'redeem' others, giving them this same power, giving them 'a new life.' " Dronke, "The Return of Eurydice," *Classica et Mediaevalia* (1962), pp. 205-206.

14. Heller's lament, repeated in Strauss, indicates, I think, the tendency of modern scholars to overread the literalism of the ancient Greeks: "The attempt of scholars to unravel the complex of historical reminiscences, the images, insights, feelings that make up the story of Dionysus, Apollo and Orpheus in modern German literature and thought, and then to relate it to what may be the Greek reality of these divine creatures, is as heroic as it is doomed to failure. For a scholar's guarded steps cannot possibly keep pace with the rush and dance of the passions of the mind swirling around those names and arrested only for brief moments in innumerable figurations. Nietzsche, from *The Birth of Tragedy* onwards, is seeking spiritual employment in the service of a god who is a synthesis of Dionysus and Apollo. In this composite Nietzschean deity, Apollo, it is true, more and more loses his name to the other god, but by no means the power of his artistic creativeness, forever articulating but the Dionysian chaos in distinct shapes, sounds and images, which are Dionysian only because they still aglow with the heat of the primeval fire." Strauss, *Descent and Return*, p. 19; Heller, *The Disinherited Mind*, p. 109.

15. Though he doesn't connect Orphism with irony, Segal notices a "double aspect" of Orphic power that in turn, he contends, corresponds to a "double aspect of the power of language itself." *Orpheus: The Myth of the Poet*, p. 8.

16. To those who might say at this point that my reading ignores Eurydice's perspective on the whole affair, I would respond by noting that the tale itself tends to marginalize (to say the least) dead Eurydice and her sentiments. Segal notes that modern poetry, Rilke's in particular, shifts emphasis to Eurydice; and H.D.'s "Eurydice" sharply rebukes Orpheus for his presumptuous airs (maybe Eurydice would prefer to remain dead). *Ibid.*, pp. 29, 176.

17. As Robbins points out, the idea of an unsuccessful return is emphasized only in later Latinate versions. For instance, Euripedes' play *Alcestis* (438 B.C.) refers to Orpheus as successful in bringing back his wife from Hades. Plato speaks in the *Symposium* of the failure of Orpheus, but as Robbins points out, Plato's stress on Orpheus' failure seems to have been intended as a deliberate *reversal* of the common Orpheus story, informing us that Orpheus' wife was a phantom, and thus alluding (as in the *Republic* 586c) that the war at Troy was fought over a phantom, for Helen was never at present at Ilium. In short, Plato's reversal counts as some complicated play upon Homer's works. See also *ibid*, pp. 8ff; Clark, *Catabasis*, pp. 108ff; and Dronke, "The Return of Eurydice."

18. Cf. Stanley Cavell, *The Claim of Reason: Wittgenstein, Skepticism, Morality and Tragedy* (Oxford: Clarendon Press, 1979), p. 496.

19. Here I can point out the differences between Maurice Blanchot's interpretation of the Orpheus story and mine. In general, Blanchot takes death, art, and love far too "seriously" and melodramatically for my money. He reads the Orpheus story as a call to die more profoundly, which I think elides the underlying irony of Orpheus' art. Blanchot wants to discover a new brand of authenticity, and a new freedom from death, in the space of literature; but I think this undermines art's own fictionality. Strauss has a nice discussion of Blanchot, in *Descent and Return*, pp. 251ff. With respect to Rilke's treatment of the Orpheus tale, I prefer Lowell over Blanchot. See Maurice Blanchot, *The Space of Literature*, trans. Ann Smock (Lincoln: University of Nebraska Press, 1982); Robert Lowell, "Orpheus, Eurydice and Hermes," *Imitations* (New York: Farrar, Straus and Giroux, 1978).

20. Clark and Segal point out that the tale of Orpheus' descent and ascent probably repeats the ancient pattern of fertility myths, in which a vegetative maiden is restored to life after a period of barrenness. Hence a strong resemblance can be drawn between Orpheus' descent and that of Dionysus. Also Orpheus' tale resonates with Gilgamesh's journey to the land of Utnapishtim to recover his lost companion, Enkidu. Clark, *Catabasis*, p. 15ff; Segal, *Orpheus: The Myth of the Poet*, pp. 9, 157.

21. Here I must insist upon a fundamental difference between an "ironic" reading of Orphic descents and Bakhtin's "carnivalesque" treatment of Rabelais. Bakhtin is interested, as I am, in exploring the nether regions for an alternativen and affirmative moral outlook; but I cannot finally reconcile the morality of irony with his "materialism." His point is well taken--that laughter, food, sex, death, and popular culture in general can all be joyful--but I cannot extend his association of the lower body and lower culture and the underworld with the general tradition of what I understand to be Orphic morality. Mikhail Bakhtin, *Rabelais and His World*, trans. Helene Iswolsky (Cambridge, Mass: MIT Press, 1968).

22. Clark distinguishes between descents in a "fertility tradition" and those in a "wisdom tradition." The former restore life and vitality, and the latter provide the infernal traveler with insight and knowledge, but not necessarily any triumph over death. *Catabasis*, p. 15ff; and Segal, *Orpheus: The Myth of the Poet*, p. 157.

23. As Robbins points out, clearly the Argonautic myth was well known to the author of the *Odyssey* and the *Iliad*. Page contends that the *Odyssey* as a whole represents an uprooting and replanting of the tale of Jason (and "not at all deeply"). To see the connections to Orpheus in Homer, see K. Meuli, *Odyssee und Argonautika* (Basel, 1921), and Denys Page, *Folktales in Homer's Odyssey* (Cambridge: Harvard University Press, 1973). Robbins points out that the idea of a "threshold" to Tartarus appears in both the *Iliad* and the *Odyssey*, which would seem to be a reference to the songs of Orpheus. It might also be noted that Orpheus was believed to have founded the Orphic mysteries, one of whose sacred books was the *Katabasis*. As Voegelin has argued, *katabasis* is a

key word in the *Odyssey*, which is then echoed by Plato in the *Republic*. Eric Voegelin, *Plato and Aristotle*, Vol. 3 of *Order and History*, (Baton Rouge: Louisiana State University Press, 1966), p. 53. Finally, of interest is a passage in the *Cratylus* (402b), where Socrates traces a line in the *Iliad* back to Orpheus.

24. Though it should again be added that the descent motif is not confined to the West. Himmelfarb, *Tours of Hell*. Fritz Graf mentions the Near Eastern parallels with Orphism, as well as Pacific Asian and North American Indian resemblances. "Orpheus: A Poet among Men," *Interpretations of Greek Mythology*, ed. Jan Bremmer (London and Sydney: Croom Helm, 1987). Clark, challenging Ganshini'etz's "mistrust" of Near Eastern influences, mentions the descents of Ianna and Ishtar, though he also says these tales are to be contrasted with those of Orpheus and Dionysus. *Catabasis*, pp. 23, 107.

25. Roger B. Salomon, *Desperate Storytelling: Post-Romantic Elaborations of the Mock-Heroic Mode* (Athens and London: University of Georgia Press, 1987).

26. Dodds scoffs at the idea (once put forward by Wilamowitz) that the great sinners in the *Odyssey* are an "Orphic interpolation." He wants to contend that in the classical age the fear of punishment after death was not confined to "Orphic" or Pythagorean circles, but "might haunt any guilty conscience." The evidence he cites, however, is sketchy. Dodds, *The Greeks and the Irrational*, pp. 148ff, 168-9.

27. Orpheus appears generally as a cultural hero, a benefactor of mankind, the "educator of heroes"; and though the Greeks regarded him as a civilizing hero, later writers depict him as embodying an antirational, anti-Promethean strain in our Western culture. See Segal, *Orpheus: The Myth of the Poet*, p. 10.

28. See Ian Johnston's fine book on the tragic ironies of Homer's *Iliad*. Johnston's treatment of Homer's irony becomes a little too fatalistic for my designs, and ultimately his thesis serves to depoliticize both irony and war in general (in fact Johnston explicitly recommends that we moderns take more seriously the idea that warfare and human conflict might be cosmically inevitable). Ian C. Johnston, *The Ironies of War: An Introduction to Homer's Iliad* (Lanham, Maryland: University Press of America, 1988).

29. One could also mention Aristophanes, Pythagoras, Posidenios, Aenocrites, Heraclides, Hermesianax.

30. The corpus of Plato's works contains numerous references to Orphism. West especially notes that Plato mentions that a "hubbub of books by Orpheus and Musaeus" exists (*Republic* 364e-5a, 364b-c-366a-b). See West on Orphism, *The Orphic Poems*, pp. 21-24; and Linforth, *The Arts of Orpheus*, pp. 75ff.

31. Supporting this view of Plato's "anticonsequentialism," we might note the Gyges' ring and cap of Hades stories are both *katabasis* scenes (*Republic*, 359c, 612b). The Hades story is a reference to the *Iliad* (5.844f).

32. A passage in which Plato seems to be playing with these contrasts is *Republic* 364e, where Orpheus is said to have been the first to reveal to men the meaning of rites of initiation (*teletai*). Guthrie notes that this passage

suggests that literary authority was made to take responsibility for such rites. Guthrie, *Orpheus and Greek Religion*, p. 17.

33. As I argue in Chapter 3, we cannot take Plato's disparagement of Orpheus as indicating his privileging of philosophy over poetry (the standard interpretation), since Plato himself employs the Orphic *katabasis* motif throughout the *Republic*.

34. This list can actually go on. See M. Owen Lee, "Orpheus and Eurydice: Some Modern Versions," *Classical Quarterly* (1952), pp. 113-126. Also of note is Bruce Mazlish's connecting Freud's psychoanalytic activity with the epic descent, by way of W.H. Auden's "In Memory of Sigmund Freud." Mazlish, *James and John Stuart Mill: Father and Son in the Nineteenth Century* (New York: Basic Books, 1975), pp. 13-14.

35. Strauss makes this point with respect to the "modern" Orphic. *Descent and Return*, p. 10.

36. Cf. Ronald R. MacDonald, *The Burial-Places of Memory: Epic Underworlds in Vergil, Dante, and Milton* (Amherst: University of Massachusetts Press, 1987), pp. 13ff. MacDonald makes this point nicely, though his main contention is that one returns to a past Orphic in order to learn from history so as not to repeat it.

37. One could trace the influence of Orpheus to Augustine by way of the Neoplatonists, including Boethius. Augustine himself mentions that Orpheus "spoke the truth in spite of himself but made no attempt to live up to it." Orpheus thus represented a pagan embodiment of the word (*Contra Faustum* 13:15). See Patricia Vicari, "Sparagmos: Orpheus Among the Christians," *Orpheus: The Metamorphoses of a Myth*, ed. Warden, p. 66.

38. See Himmelfarb's summary of the literature outlining the theories of Dante's debt to Muslim sources. Though Himmelfarb makes the case that Dante's inferno has certain features in common with non-Western sources, this affinity alone cannot account for Dante's deliberate invoking of Orpheus and of the Western tradition from Homer to Vergil. Dante places Orpheus, for instance, in the "philosophical family" of virtuous pagans. Himmelfarb, *Tours of Hell*, p. 39.

39. See Vicari's excellent essay "Sparagmos: Orpheus Among the Christians," which expounds on the assimilation of the Orpheus motif into Christianity. For instance, the idea of Christ as a shepherd was probably derived from a pagan icon showing Orpheus among the animals, often sheep. The leap to transform Christ into a lover was first attempted in an anonymous piece *Ovid Moralises*, appearing at the end of thirteen century. Therein we find the first explicit connection between Eve and Eurydice, which Vicari posits was an attempt to wed the myth of Orpheus with the more familiar one of Adam-Christus; in any event, some association can be drawn between the serpent who bit Eurydice, and the one that bit Eve, etc. Strauss notes that the attempt to reconcile Orpheus and Christ, removing Gnostic baggage, had shifted emphasis by the romantic period: "The question is no longer one of reconciling Orpheus and Christ, but one of a world vision that makes the sacred possible at all." Strauss, *Descent and Return*, p. 12.

40. Eleanor Irwin's essay "The Songs of Orpheus and the New Song of Christ" is a fascinating account of how Clement of Alexandria, a second-century Christian apologist, tried to demonstrate Christ's musical aptitude, comparing it with that of Orpheus, and arguing that Christ's song of the Word was more harmonious than Orpheus'. Orpheus' songs, for one thing, charmed only beasts instead of men. Clement tried to trace Christian musicology back to the Hebrew Bible, with the young David as a lyre-player. Irwin, "The Songs of Orpheus and the New Song of Christ," *Orpheus: The Metamorphoses of a Myth,* ed. Warden, pp. 51-62.

41. Cf. David L. Hall, *Eros and Irony: A Prelude to Philosophical Anarchism* (Albany: State University of New York Press, 1982), pp. 221ff. To say that Christian orthodoxy is devoid of irony is not, however, to say that all literature inspired by Christianity is lacking in irony. See especially Edmund Reiss, "Medieval Irony," *Journal of the History of Ideas* 42, No. 2 (April-June, 1981), pp. 209-226.

42. See Anna D. Kartsonis, *Anastasis: The Making of an Image* (Princeton: Princeton University Press, 1986). Kartsonis notes that early Christian artists confronted a fundamental logistical problem in trying to depict a triumphant, but dead, Christ.

43. Those who discern a direct lineage from the Orphic cults to Christianity usually make note of the close association of Orphism with Pythagoreanism and of Pythagoreanism with Gnosticism. Hence one can see many similar traits between Orphism and Gnosticism (texts as a special way of obtaining knowledge of the cosmos and of salvation; the notion of the body as a prison or tomb). Dodds, for one, wants to avoid drawing any intermediary connection between Pythagoreanism and Orphism. Strauss sees a clear link between certain ethical ideals of Orphism and those of Judaism and Christianity. Dodds, *The Greeks and the Irrational,* pp. 149ff; Strauss, *Descent and Return,* pp. 7-9. On the use of the Orpheus myth in Christianity, see also Dronke, "The Return of Eurydice," p. 209.

44. John Freccero, "Infernal Irony: The Gates of Hell," *Dante: The Poetics of Conversion* (Cambridge: Harvard University Press, 1986), pp. 93-109.

45. Vicari makes a similar point, namely that Orpheus provides the general inspiration for viewing Christ as shaman or go-between between Hebraic and Greek cultures. "Sparagmos: Orpheus Among the Christians."

46. Strauss repeats this formulation from Novalis's *Heinrich von Ofterdingen.* Strauss calls it "traditional apocalyptic thinking," a variant of "romantic Christianity." To my mind, however, this summary of Novalis doesn't explain the influence of the Schlegels upon him. Strauss, *Descent and Return,* pp. 36ff.

47. John Warden defines "Orphic unity" as an insistence on the unity and singleness of the Cosmos. He mentions that the Orphic poet Musaeus wrote that "everything comes to be out of one and is resolved into one" (*Diogenes Laertius* 1.3). Warden, "Orpheus and Ficino," *Orpheus: The Metamorphoses of a Myth,* ed. Warden, pp. 85-110.

48. See Freccero's last two chapters, "The Final Image: *Paradiso* XXXIII, 144," and "The Significance of *Terza Rima*," *Dante: The Poetics of Conversion*, pp. 245-271.

49. It should be remembered that Dante himself claimed that his *Commedia* could be interpreted on four different allegorical levels--literal, political, moral, and mystical--and only the literal layer of signification was concerned with the state of souls after death.

50. Cleanth Brooks, "Irony as Principle of Structure," *Literary Opinion in America*, ed. Morton Zabel (New York: Harper and Brothers, 1937), and *The Well Wrought Urn* (London: Dennis Dobson, 1947).

51. Walter Burkert notes that Orphic theogony traditionally portrayed generations of kings among the gods. "Oriental and Greek Mythology: The Meeting of Parallels," *Interpretations of Greek Mythology*, ed. Bremmer; cf. Herbert Marcuse's treatment of Orpheus. Marcuse opposes the "Orphic" and the "Promethean" as modes of liberation: The Orphic charms and transforms being; the Promethean rebels and reforms being. Marcuse, *Eros and Civilization: A Philosophical Inquiry into Freud* (Boston: Beacon Press, 1955), pp. 162, 171.

52. Here we need at least to mention the works of Butler and Bernal, both of which confound the Hellenocentric view of the West. See E.M. Butler, *The Tyranny of Greece over Germany* (Boston: Beacon Press, 1958); and Martin Bernal, *Black Athena: The Afroasiatic Roots of Classical Civilization* (New Brunswick, N.J.: Rutgers University Press, 1987).

53. Note that Robert Dahl's mode of analysis in his book on nuclear policy shifts from the descriptive to the prescriptive. *Controlling Nuclear Weapons: Democracy Versus Guardianship* (Syracuse: Syracuse University Press, 1985).

54. See Derek Parfit, *Reasons and Persons* (Oxford: Clarendon Press, 1984), pp. 453-454.

55. John Rawls, *A Theory of Justice* (Cambridge: Harvard University Press, 1971).

56. Wendy Brown insists otherwise, contending that Western political theory has systematically steered its (manly) attention away from "life." A return to a concern for "life," she explains, would entail "learning how to engage regeneratively . . . with ourselves as bodily creatures," for the body, not to be severed from the head of course, is "the locus of our freedom." For the most part her forceful book works its case "for life" by deconstructing an implicit opposition between "mortality" and "immortality" (the politics of manhood characteristically strives for the heroic glory of the latter), rather than an opposition between "life" and "death." Symptomatic of this tendency is that Brown's extended discussions of Aristotle, Machiavelli, and Weber barely mention that these three thinkers were students of classical tragedy--and a possible connection between tragedy and irony is far from Brown's concerns. Nonetheless, to the extent that her book envisions a way in which we humans and political animals might be able to become more accepting of death, in some non-trivializing sense, seeing death as an integral part of the rhythms of life I suppose, then I should welcome this extraordinary accomplishment--but

such feats ought not be confined to the realm of theory. Wendy Brown, *Manhood and Politics: A Feminist Reading in Political Theory* (Totowa, N.J.: Rowman & Littlefield, 1988).

57. Cf. Michael J. Sandel: "Following Aristotle [communitarian critics of liberalism] argue that we cannot justify political arrangements without reference to common purposes and ends, and that we cannot conceive our personhood without reference to our role as citizens, and as participants in a common life." "Introduction," *Liberalism and Its Critics*, ed. Sandel (Oxford: Basil Blackwell, 1984), p. 5.

58. Cf. George Kateb's call for a greater awareness of death while alive and theorizing, in "Thinking about Human Extinction (1): Nietzsche and Heidegger," *Raritan* 6, No. 2 (Fall, 1986), p. 25. Michel Foucault seems to call for a lesser connection between writing and death, in "What is an Author?" *The Foucault Reader*, ed. Paul Rabinow (New York: Pantheon Books, 1984), p. 102. George Armstrong Kelly's very instructive monograph, "Mortal Politics in Eighteenth-Century France," attempts to link a concern about death with issues of revolution, war, punishment, the state, and of politics and political philosophy generally; and the project shows "how politics bestows special tension on the meaning of death" and how "death may be said to inhere in politics." But one of the final lessons, the author asserts, is that Hobbes was basically right to think "that politics is a sovereign that keeps death at bay." And by "death," we learn, Kelly really means killing and being killed--thus he is interested in the use of war and cataclysmic coercion as means toward the "production and maintenance of the preservative state." This is not a theory about how death sets the moral parameters to politics; rather, the purposes of politics are presumed, and the lessons of the story are mainly historical. George Armstrong Kelly, "Mortal Politics," *Historical Reflections* 13, No. 1 (Spring, 1986).

59. Michael Walzer, *Just and Unjust Wars: A Moral Argument with Historical Illustrations* (New York: Basic Books, 1977), pp. 21-33.

60. *Ibid.*, p. 30.

61. *Ibid.*, p. 31.

62. Though I draw upon Dante, I've avoided the Christian tradition of political theorizing for several reasons. Mainly I stand in agreement with René Girard in his claim that Christianity after all heralds the violent end of the world, whatever apparently peaceful holding patterns it inspires in the meantime. See Girard, "Generative Violence and the Extinction of the Social Order," trans. Thomas Wieser, *Salgamundi*, No. 63-4 (Spring/Summer, 1984), pp. 204-237.

1

Politics and Ironic Vision

The mere observing of a thing is no use whatsoever. Observing turns
into beholding, beholding into thinking, thinking into establishing
connections, so that one may say that every attentive glance we cast
upon the world is an act of theorizing. However, this ought to be done
consciously, with self-criticism, with freedom, and, to use a daring
word, with irony.

--Goethe, *Schriften zur Farbenlehre*

The reconstruction of political thought proved to be a long and
arduous process extending over several centuries and manifesting
odd twists and turns. It was a process that began in paradox and
ended in irony.

--Sheldon Wolin, *Politics and Vision*

Political theory is about borders and boundaries. In making this
remark as an opening, a remark I intend to be more modest and provisional than bold and definitive, I am fully aware of the customary
claim that political theory is about "wholes" and "interconnections,"
that it is a characteristic way of thinking "broadly" about politics and
political matters. Indeed, the attempt consciously to enlarge, rather
than restrict, one's perspective upon political phenomena is what
draws together theorists even of diverging political persuasions. For
instance, Leo Strauss writes that political philosophy assumes a
"comprehensive character,"[1] whereas Sheldon Wolin, by no means an
advocate of Strauss's brand of conservatism, portrays the theorist as
attempting to grasp politics "in the round" and "to explain its workings

as a unified whole."[2] This perspective Wolin unabashedly labels as "radical"[3] precisely, it would seem, because Wolin's radicalism strives for Straussian-like comprehensiveness. Although by emphasizing theory's concern with borders and boundaries, that is to say, a concern fundamentally with parts and divisions rather than with wholes and connections,[4] I may appear to be challenging conventional wisdom, actually I am not taking issue with Strauss or Wolin[5] or any of my theoretical forebears who take a "holistic"[6] approach toward politics. Instead, I want to forward only the preliminary suggestion that while "wholes" should be given their due, they are but one side to political theory, a side that theorists ought to put into theoretical perspective.

The Greeks typically are credited with having assigned a special significance to the activity of theorizing.[7] Initially the word *theoria* stood for the activities of persons called *theoroi*, who were public emissaries sent by city officials to attend and to observe the religious festivals of neighboring Greek cities. A *theoros* was a "spectator" or an "onlooker." The verb *theorein* meant "to behold," or "to take in," a spectacle, in the sense of physically seeing it.[8] Gradually *theorein* acquired the connotation of a long journey undertaken "to see" different lands and to observe different institutions.[9] Upon his return to his home city, the *theoros* would present the results of his investigations to the highest political authority. From Aristotle we know that such information was valued for its own sake, not for the sake of some immediate or "practical" end, and that the *bios theoretikos*, a life of observation and philosophic contemplation, was considered highest and most virtuous.[10]

I want to emphasize that there were *two* legs to the theorist's journey, first his leaving the city and then his returning. This philological vignette is perhaps a commonplace among practicing political theorists, yet I think theorists frequently misread its significance. Hannah Arendt, for example, writes that the tradition of political philosophizing "began with the philosopher turning away from politics and then returning";[11] but Arendt immediately inserts the proviso that the reason the philosopher returns is "in order to impose his standards on human affairs."[12] Wolin finishes his account of the classical quest with a list of "some of the features which were to become the distinguishing marks of a theory."[13] He names these features as: the "observation of practice"; the "achievement of perspective upon one's own society by an act of liberation"; and, finally, the "process of appraising the importance of what had been observed in light of what was known."[14] Whereas Arendt writes of the imposition of standards, Wolin speaks of appraisal and comparison; yet he too notes that each theorist eventually (though not "automatically") makes a "decision" about "what the world is like,"[15] a decision that then informs and colors his theory. For Wolin, theory involves a paradox, for theory begins with a decision, thus a selection of a *particular* perspective, yet the theorist aims at the "whole." He quotes Tocqueville to explain this paradox:

> My present object is to embrace the whole from one point of view: the remarks I shall make will be less detailed, but they will be more sure. I shall perceive each object less distinctly, but I shall descry the principal facts with more certainty. A traveler who has just left a vast city climbs the neighboring hill; as he goes farther off, he loses sight of the men whom he has just quitted: their dwellings are confused in a dense mass; he can no longer distinguish the public squares and can scarcely trace out the great thoroughfares; but his eye has less difficulty in following the boundaries of the whole. . . . The details of the immense picture are lost in the shade, but I conceive a clear idea of the entire subject.[16]

Wolin explains further that the classical theorist understands that his vision of the whole involves distortion, yet he seeks an overall synthesis. Although I am greatly indebted to Wolin's masterful accounts of political theory as a discipline and a vocation, I often suspect that his conception of theory, beginning with his reading of Plato, leans too far in the direction of Arendt's view of "imposition." Moreover, his articulation of the theorist's activity as the making and subsequent enforcing of an initial decision exhibits a tendency toward advocacy that I find all too prevalent in many works of and about political theory. In response, I shall stress throughout this book, if only as a recurring leitmotif, that the theorist's task, like his journey, is twofold; and that his perspective is not simply visionary, unifying, and holistic, but is in a way double. It is within the larger purview of this book to draw out some of the implications of seeing doubly for politics and political theory.[17]

Death Reports

Perhaps we should pause, however, to consider whether all of this proposed intellectual toil is worth the effort. Perhaps the concern over the nature of theoretical inquiry as regards politics is in service of a lost cause, a dead issue. That, at least, was the opinion of many in an earlier generation of political thinkers, a generation that pronounced, for better or worse, the field of political theory "dead." In the early 1950s, David Easton (1953)[18] and Alfred Cobban (1953)[19] each observed that political theory was in "decline," while T.D. Weldon (1953) voiced his strong objections to the view that the enterprise of political theory was any longer viable.[20]   In 1956, Peter Laslett declared that "for the moment, anyway, political philosophy is dead,"[21] and Robert Dahl in 1958 issued another pronouncement that political theory was "permanently" dead in the "English-speaking world" and that outside the West it was either "imprisoned or moribund."[22] Small wonder, then, that looking back over a decade of such death sentences, Daniel Bell delivered the postmortem decree, stating that the 1950s had "exhausted" political theorizing, a development Bell hailed as the "end of ideology."[23]

This morbid mood was not confined to those who welcomed political theory's demise. Leo Strauss announced in 1954 that the field was in "a state of decay and perhaps of putrefaction, if it has not vanished altogether."[24] In the early 1950s, Hannah Arendt stated similarly that the Western tradition of political thought had ended "definitely in the theories of Karl Marx."[25] In 1957, Judith Shklar presented her claim that "utopianism is dead,"[26] the significance of which, Shklar argued, was that "without that grain of baseless optimism no genuine political theory can be constructed."[27] Hence, the "entire tradition of political theory," Shklar surmised, is "at a standstill."[28] Even Wolin, who agreed with Shklar that political theory requires an element of radicalism,[29] published an analysis similar to Shklar's, testifying to the protracted historical decline of political theory--though Wolin's outlook in his *Politics and Vision* was certainly more hopeful and less skeptical than Shklar's in her *After Utopia*.

Assuming that political theory did die sometime in the 1950s, who or what, according to the witnesses, killed it? From the various reports we can piece together *ex post facto* a forensic analysis of intertwining causes and culprits. For Judith Shklar, the death of political philosophy can be traced through an elaborate autopsy of the history of ideas since the Enlightenment. Shklar did not finger any one suspect or point to any culminating *coup de grâce*, but instead observed that it was a "slow and intricate process" that produced the present "spirit of the age" in which it is "impossible to believe strongly that the power of human reason expressing itself in political action is capable of achieving its end."[30] In short, nineteenth-century Romantic and religious thought, in their rebellions against the optimism of the Enlightenment, went too far. The Romantics killed God in order to celebrate man in his full immediacy; but what they did not foresee was that, in Shklar's words, "the death of God has left man with no way of rendering the world comprehensible."[31] Romantic theories of irrationalism could not sustain themselves once the thrill of aestheticism wore off. Religious doctrines of imperfection ended in fatalism. Both developments dealt death blows to philosophy: "All philosophy can pretend to be now is an open admission of the failure of all understanding."[32] Shklar's argument was cogent and neatly circular: Political theory depends upon the possibility and belief that the intellect is self-determining, yet in opposing the Enlightenment, the intellect rebelled against itself and thus denied its own power of determination. Hence political theory succumbs to skepticism.

If Shklar was unrelenting and undiscriminating in her acceptance, reflected in her own skepticism, of post-Enlightenment thought, others argued, some in blame and some in praise, that the ascendancy of science and the scientific method in modern thought is what dealt political philosophy its death blow. Dante Germino traced the beginning of the decline of political theory to the rise of "positivism" in postrevolutionary France. The first assault upon political theory, according to Germino, came from within the "social sciences," beginning with Antoine Destutt de Tracy, followed by Auguste Comte, and culminating in the twentieth century in the work of Arnold Brecht and David Easton in the United States.[33] Positivism launched an attack against "ideology," in other words, against the independent reality and validity of all "ideas." Ideas were then considered "epiphenomenal," mere reflections of direct sense experience and of more general biological and natural conditions. Eventually, positivism limited its attack to "metaphysics," those purely ethical or speculative judgments that were considered capable neither of cognition nor of verification through scientific experiment. In the 1920s and 1930s, Germino continued, American political scientists, influenced by the work of Tracy and Comte and others, adhered to the view that "facts" and "values" were to be strictly and methodologically distinguished, a distinction that resulted in the separation and classification of studies as either "metaphysical" or "empirical." Political theory or political philosophy, the political scientists argued, had been superseded by the scientific method, which promised distortion-free access to political reality.

Surely Germino was right to emphasize, in contrast to Shklar's sweeping intellectual overview, the particular tension between the social sciences and political theory; but I think it was somewhat misleading for Germino to portray the positivists' rejection of political theory as fundamentally a dispute over epistemology and methodology. David Easton, for counterexample, agreed with Shklar that Friedrich Nietzsche's philosophy represented and foreshadowed the fragmentation of ethics in modern times, a problem wider and more formidable than Germino might realize. But according to Easton's account of the decline of political theory, a Shklarian analysis, with its exclusive concern with the history of ideas, was symptomatic of the problem itself.[34] For Easton, the dispute was not confined to the realm of the intellect. The problem with political theory was that it failed to keep pace with a post-Nietzschean *world*, a world in which "men can act on the basis of widely divergent ethical standards."[35] He emphasized, however, that "ethical pluralism" is but a reflection of "empirical pluralism,"[36] which induces the recognition of the existence of a "multiplicity of social groups."[37] Social and political scientists *therefore* recognize a "multiplicity of causes, especially of a group nature, that influence social policy"; whereas political theorists stubbornly adhere to the viewing of "social causation in terms of single factors," or else political theorists are reduced to the study of political *history*, the study of causes and values relative to particular historical contexts.[38]

Robert Dahl echoed Easton when he touted the virtues of political science over political theory on the basis of a substantively superior methodology, proclaiming that political theory was dead because "so many of the interesting political problems have been solved."[39] Like that of Easton, Dahl's pronouncement issued first from a claim about political "reality"; only as a secondary matter was Dahl concerned with epistemological and methodological issues. That is, Dahl was convinced that not social science, but *political pluralism* as a factual phenomenon had rendered political theory anachronistic. The political world, he and other political scientists contended, consists of many distinct groups; social and political science "works," in turn, *because* it implicitly respects the distinctions and differences among these various groups. Political theory, however, in its generalizing and systematizing way, lumps these groups together and thus cannot possibly comprehend the complexity of a heterogeneous social and political world.

Such a view, of course, was an extension of and elaboration upon an older liberal tradition, articulated in earlier forms by J.S. Mill, Tocqueville, and Madison. As Madison wrote, and as America seemed to demonstrate to later enthusiastic political scientists such as Easton and Dahl, a political "system"[40] needs neither a sense of public-spiritedness nor some theoretical "bond" in order to "function" and to hold a people formally together. The political *process* made political theory, first factually, then intellectually, obsolete. On similar, albeit "sociological," grounds, Daniel Bell (citing Karl Popper among many others) argued that the complexities of social life in America had obviated the generalizing approach of political philosophy.

To summarize: The sharpest critics of political theory attributed its decline to the same "holistic" and generalizing nature of the enterprise that defenders of political theory proclaimed as its prime virtue and distinguishing feature. In the way I have formulated the development of the critics' case--that political theory is not so much intellectually or methodologically "dead" as it is factually obsolete-- it would seem that the challenge to political theory is indeed formidable, since the critics meet the theorists on their own terms. Hence the criticism warrants serious review.

To be sure, a group of dedicated theorists responded to the charges brought against them and their occupation in the 1950s. This group-- including Wolin, Arendt, Strauss, Germino, and Eric Voegelin--sought not only to defend theory but also to restore its vitality.[41] A thread connecting all of these writers was the idea that the task of repairing political theory necessitated a return to the Greeks, thus a recon-sideration of the premises of the entire Western tradition in light of the modern world. These writers seemed to suggest that the primary factor responsible for the flurry of pronouncements over theory's decline and death was the rise of fascist and totalitarian regimes in the twentieth century. Fascist and totalitarian regimes in many respects resembled the generalizing and idealizing approaches to politics that theory seemed to have been advocating all along, beginning with the Greeks. Hence the debate in the 1950s over the relevance of theory-- though it may have had long historical underpinnings, as Shklar and Germino claim--could be understood in large part as an aftermath to World War II. The post-World War II defender of theory posed the problem as one of needing to find some way of retaining the substance of the Western political tradition while preventing its horrible excesses: How do you adapt the Greeks to the twentieth century? Sheldon Wolin was one of the most outspoken on the issue of the decline of political theory; and because his response, I think, successfully reasserts some of theory's cardinal virtues and yet at the same time reveals some of its lingering defects, I shall turn first to an examination of Wolin's writings on the matter, paying particular attention to his understand-ing of the theoretical relation between Greek politics and modernity.

Wolin and Community

In his brilliant, impressive (and award-winning[42]) book, *Politics and Vision*, Wolin analyzes the rise and fall of Western political theory throughout the ages according to a scheme of a "metaphysics" of political theory (political space, time, and energy) that he outlines early in the book. I will not attempt to summarize the early and middle chapters of the book, on the Greek city-state, the Roman Empire, and the influence of Christianity up to Machiavelli and Hobbes. I will pass over this valuable material, for in an important respect the book leads up to and culminates in the last chapters, on liberalism, the decline of political philosophy, and the age of organization. If I am right to think that the book represents what is fundamentally a reply to the critics of political theory, then the key to Wolin's argument is his turning the claims of the liberals and the pluralists back upon themselves. Rather than having "solved" so many political problems, as Dahl contended, liberalism and its cousin, pluralism, have attenuated the significance of the political element in modern times, according to Wolin; and the decline of political theory is actually attributable to, and a reflection of, the prevailing trend toward the decline of *politics*. Wolin's critique of liberalism begins early in his historical scheme (and hence early in the book), in his analysis of early Christianity. Christianity promoted a confrontation between the "social" and "political" realms. The notion that there was something more divinely natural about social than political relationships carried over into later thought, and, according to Wolin, "the antinomy has [not] been laid to rest."[43] "The belief persisted that society represented a spontaneous and natural grouping, while the political stood for the coercive, the involuntary."[44]

Society was to be seen as the sum of a multiplicity of voluntary bodies and natural associations. Politics became "government" or "the state," an artificial and compulsory controller of the naturally human. Locke, the classical economists, the French liberals, and the English utilitarians added the "economic" group to the natural sphere of society and further enforced, according to Wolin, the separation between society and the political realm. Wolin then argues that the liberal view of the primacy of societal relations informs the liberal critique of philosophy, a critique that in turn lends itself to the adoption of a scientific method as an alternative outlook. Wolin makes the point in a section about Thomas Hobbes, who Wolin claims had no genuine theory of society: "The case usually advanced for the superiority of the social sciences over traditional political philosophy rests on much the same assumption as the case made against Hobbes: that political phenomena are best explained as the resultant of social factors, and hence political institutions and beliefs are best understood by a method which gets 'behind' them to the 'underlying' social processes which dictate the shape of things political."[45]

The issue, however, is not over methodology, argues Wolin, but is "substantive"; it concerns the status of politics and the political.[46]

Herein lies the crux of Wolin's argument, informing retroactively the historical approach of the entire book:

> When modern social science asserts that political phenomena are to be explained by resolving them into sociological, psychological, or economic components, it is saying that there are no distinctively political phenomena and hence no special set of problems. On its face, this assertion appears to be a purely descriptive statement, devoid of evaluative overtones and therefore innocent. Actually, it is nothing of the sort. It rests upon an evaluation which remains concealed because its historical origins are not well understood. It is possible to view politics in terms of more "fundamental" factors, if it is believed that the political possesses no distinctive significance, pertains to no unique function, and occupies no loftier plane than, say, that of any large-scale organization.[47]

Politics and Vision, in other words, is a study of the history of the status of the political, but it would be a gross distortion to say that Wolin is engaging in historical sociology or the sociology of knowledge. Rather, Wolin takes his departure from the Greeks, who, he contends, originally gave definition to the political realm; and thereafter, subsequent renderings of the political necessarily bear a relation (hence the word *continuity* in the book's subtitle) to the Greek meaning of the term, even if in particular periods the political realm undergoes transformations that alter this meaning (hence the word *innovation*). But by drawing a "tradition of discourse" starting from the Greeks and extending into the present, Wolin sets the terms for his analysis and critique of liberalism and the modern age. Whereas the liberals presume the primacy of the *social*, Wolin now can presume, against the liberals' argument, the primacy of the *communal*--which in Wolin's mind is synonymous with the "substantively" political. Thus liberalism renders neither politics nor a generalizing political theory obsolete but rather represents the "diffusion"[48] of the political, and the "chopping up"[49] of the political community. Hence Locke, in Wolin's terms, "substitutes" private interest for "collective conscience."[50] For Wolin, the loss of political community encourages or forces the individual to withdraw unto himself, even if liberal theorists hail his independence as a natural virtue.

Yet Wolin's argument is tricky, for he must walk a fine line. He still wishes to retain for the modern age the validity of the *res communitas*--and therewith the validity of political theory--so he formulates a kind of reverse Hegelian teleology, suggesting that notions of politics and community are implicitly present, even if they have become attenuated and diffuse, somewhere in the modern world. From his historical vantage point beginning with the Greeks, Wolin can argue that later liberal theory attempted to fashion a substitute for lost community.[51] Wolin goes on to claim that this shift in liberalism, from the individual to society, led, not to a harmonious relationship between "the individual" and "society," but to a kind of social conformism. The result, according to Wolin's gripping analysis, is that liberalism, which originally set the individual *against* the government and sought to liberate him from political authority, eventually subjected this individual to the greater (because insidi-ously concealed) controls and constraints of society. Moreover, the problem in shifting the locus of authority from the political to the social was that the shift from the integrally political to the diffusely social left the entire issue of authority, let alone the issue of freedom, inexplicitly posed and theoretically misunderstood.

Wolin extends his theme of the "implicitness" of politics under liberalism to his reading of the present age--which he calls the age of organization. Modern organizations, in collaboration with their intellectual analogue, modern social science, attempt to "dissect"[52] political man, to compartmentalize him, in order to confer some semblance of management upon the parts of society; but this approach is only a symptom of rather than an antidote to the larger problem. Wolin does not argue that bureaucratization and organization defeat politics altogether; rather, he contends that the triumph of large-scale administrative structures represents indeed the triumph of theory, a world "deliberately created" rather than "historically articulated." But--"in another sense, the embodiment of theory in the world has resulted in a world impervious to theory."[53] Theory has triumphed but has become "submerged," its original significance diluted and altered. In conjunction with the diffusion of political theory, political authority, properly understood, has been trivialized and depreciated. Political authority has been transferred to the "private" realm, to the bureau, the association, the group--a development that Wolin calls the "fragmentation of the political."[54] Throughout his analysis, Wolin's operational premise is that organizations, however much they may absorb elements of the political, are poor substitutes for a viable community. The questionable aspect of this analysis is the extent to which Wolin's premise over-determines his conclusion.

Wolin advances the bold argument that the rise of totalitarian regimes in the twentieth century demonstrated--"perhaps perverse-ly"--that "the political animal is not extinct."[55]

> One of the most striking [aspects of modern totalitarianism] is the
> radically political character of these systems. It is illustrated by the

attempt of totalitarian governments to render the political factor all-pervasive and the ultimate referent of existence. By deliberate policy, they have extended political control into every significant human relationship and organized every important group in terms of the goals of the regime. No effort has been spared to arouse among the citizens a strong sense of involvement and identification with the political order. Time and again they have puzzled critics by the ability to muster widespread popular support. This suggests that totalitarian systems have been able to tap successfully the potential for participation which nontotalitarian societies have only diverted.[56]

Wolin concedes that totalitarian systems should not serve as a model for political participation, and he takes note of the argument that "the fragmentation of the political and its assignment to other associations and organizations are the necessary price for achieving some measure of individual self-determination, freedom, and participation in the modern world." Nonetheless, Wolin holds to the view that the "political" has meaning only in terms of a general constituency, "and no multiplication of fragmentary constituencies will provide a substitute."[57] Further, he cites Aristotle to back the claim that a political association in service of comprehensive, community-wide goals has a stronger claim on men's loyalties and promotes individual participation better than any "lesser association," such as the family or the religious group. The task, then, for theorists of nontotalitarian societies is "to temper the excesses of pluralism," to strive for an "integrative form of direction" that is "broader than that supplied by any group or organization."[58] Political theory, therefore, *must* once again be viewed in holistic terms, "as that form of knowledge which deals with what is general and integrative to men, a life of common involvements."[59]

If it is not obvious, I will confess to being fascinated by Wolin's words and to indulging in an urge to rehearse his defense of political theory. Yet much as I value his arguments, or maybe the sentiments that underlie them, I do not think that the book puts to rest the liberal challenge to political theory. Wolin, it seems to me, has simply reasserted the value of community against the liberals' objections, and he has used a complex reading of history to shore up his claim. But I do not think he can he simply assume and assert the implicit superiority of *res communitas* and thereby claim that anything short of the Greek experience--notwithstanding the intervening historical circumstances and "innovations" in the meaning of politics--is a poor "substitute" for the real thing. Moreover, if his claim is tenuous that the genuinely political is seemingly ever present because it is implicitly and episodically articulated, there is a further problem in his case, for Wolin never proves, but only assumes, the *value* of the general and integrative political experience. Instead, his preference for community seems almost aesthetic. And I think the liberal can reply, in good utilitarian fashion: What does it *matter* if we moderns suffer from a diminished sense of what was once understood as politics or that our "system" eliminates the "need for greatness"?[60] (We do quite well, thank you, without greatness or epic theory.) Why *not* leave the "political element" sublimated, if it is for the most part obsolete?

Wolin seems to touch upon the *need* for a modern community when he portrays the individual in Western democracies as politically indifferent and apathetic (despite the "surface appearance of vitality"[61]). But Wolin immediately retracts this charge by contending that "the problem is not one of apathy, or of the decline of the political, but the absorption of the political into non-political institutions and activities."[62] Wolin has to perform a difficult balancing act: On the one hand, he wants to account for the decline of political theory, while on the other hand, he wants to assert its continued, if covert, validity. But the countercharge of absorption simply leads back to the issue of community and thus begs the question.

Moreover, Wolin simply does not address certain points expressed by those who endorse the view that a "Madisonian" approach to politics is the best way to deal with, as it were, a "post-Nietzschean" political world. Wolin's response to Madisonian pluralists seems, judging from what he says and especially from what he does not say, to be wholly inadequate. Wolin's reading of Madison is that Madison's solution to the problem of group conflict was to dissipate its intensity over a wide geographical area.[63] Space, not a process of checks and balances, provided Madison with his solution, and it is solely on the issue of political space that Wolin challenges Madison. Yet if a Madisonian "system" eliminates the *need* for "public-spiritedness," then it does little good to charge that the system is a poor substitute for community. Space is irrelevant. What is worse, Wolin does not seem fully to appreciate the benefits that accrue to the individual under such a system,[64] and he seems too quick to dismiss the general virtue of the system as a check against tyrannical majoritarianism, not to mention totalitarianism.

Macpherson and Human Nature

Where Wolin may falter in his critique of liberalism (and hence in his defense of political theory), C.B. Macpherson picks up the charge; a review of Macpherson's well-known challenge to liberalism provides a telling contrast to Wolin's overview, and it is additionally revealing for what Macpherson has to say about political theory.

Like Wolin, Macpherson explains that his interest in liberalism is connected to his observation of the paradox that political theory is so much in decline in an age in which so many fundamental political issues crowd upon us.[65] But Macpherson's thesis is not that the liberal-democratic theory that informs our politics today has "sublimated" classical philosophy or that it has "abandoned human nature," as Wolin claims. Instead, Macpherson argues that the political theory of the past 150 years represents an uneasy and contradictory attempt to reconcile two mutually incompatible models of human nature.

Macpherson unravels these two versions of human essence by locating them within a historical scheme that draws heavily upon analogous developments in economics. "Classical political theory"--by which Macpherson means the seventeenth- and eighteenth-century tradition ranging from Locke to Bentham--grew up with the market. The general form of such theorizing was that it sought to articulate a notion of political obligation as a simple postulate of some version of human nature. Explanation *meant* justification.[66] Macpherson contends that classical theory revealed a particular vision of human nature, which he calls "possessive individualism"; and he suggests further that such an understanding was related, whether as cause or effect, to the rise of markets. Such theories embrace the market as a model of natural equilibrium and utility maximization. To view a mechanical maximization of utility as the ultimate justification of a particular kind of society is, according to Macpherson, to view man as a consumer, as an appropriator of utilities: "It is only when man is seen as essentially a bundle of appetites demanding satisfaction that the good society is the one which maximizes satisfactions."[67] Even though theorists such as Hobbes and Bentham may seem to have depicted diverse conceptions of human nature, their theories did require, and rested upon, a fundamental proposition regarding human nature; for implicitly in the claims of market equilibrium and maximization are the propositions that such processes are *equitable* because they apply to all, and that they are indeed universally satisfying because all men are essentially alike.

Possessive individualism, then, can be roughly summarized as follows: (1) Man, the individual, is seen as natural proprietor of his own capacities, a being whose essence is freedom to use his capacities in search of satisfaction. Everyone is free, for everyone at least possesses himself. (2) Society is seen as a lot of free, equal individuals relating to each other through their possessions. *Exchange* is the fundamental relation of society. (3) Political society is seen as a rational device for the protection of property, including capacities; thus, life and liberty are viewed as possessions.[68]

Macpherson contends that in the mid-nineteenth century such theory became untenable, for the market had clearly created a dominant and a subservient class, one free and the other exploited; and a class-conscious proletariat emerged. The result, according to Macpherson, was not so much that these developments put the bourgeoisie on the defensive intellectually but that "the actual change in society made it impossible for bourgeois thinkers either to stay honestly and clearly within the old assumptions or to abandon them."[69] After 1848, then, one finds either "apologetics" or "syncretism" in the theory of liberalism, both representing attempts at abandoning possessive individualism while maintaining bourgeois values. In short, thinkers such as J.S. Mill and T.H. Green attempted, according to Macpherson, to reconcile bourgeois individualism with *social democracy*. But the emergence of a working class made it difficult to make meaningful statements about human nature as such,[70] and thus emerged an attempt "to moralize" the relation of the individual to society, as opposed to simply postulating the relationship between the individual and society as naturally harmonious, tending toward a point of equilibrium. Nonetheless, the nineteenth century idealism that formed in rebellion to the crass materialism of the eighteenth century (such as J.S. Mill's rebellion against the older utilitarians) revealed a distinct conception of human nature to rival that of the equilibrium model.

Nineteenth-century thinkers affirmed man's human powers, his uniquely *human* capacities, as an inspired doer, a creator, an enjoyer of his particularly human attributes. Instead of being a bundle of base appetites, man was seen as an expender--and not just a consumer--of energies. Upon this reading, Nietzsche is closer to J.S. Mill than one might otherwise suppose.

The problem was that the two views of human essence were intermixed in the confused theory of the time. J.S. Mill could not abandon his father's individualism, but the young Mill needed the second version of man's essence, as an enjoyer, to challenge crass materialism and yet to retain some justification for the market model. The difficulty was that the notions of equilibrium and unlimited activity were inherently hard to reconcile, for they led to the contradiction "between equal freedom to realize one's human powers and freedom of unlimited appropriation of others' powers, or between the maximization of powers in the ethical sense and the maximization of powers in the descriptive market sense."[71]

Macpherson notes that J.S. Mill exhausted himself looking for ways of patching up the contradictions between liberalism and social democracy. T.H. Green and other neoidealists tried to convert the notion of the state into a moral idea rather than a Benthamite mechanism--but that "attempt to return to the concept of the Greek city-state" diverted attention from the class basis of political problems and, according to Macpherson, ended only in the argument that "the frustration of humanity was due to faulty political concepts."[72] Pluralism was (and is) another attempt to resolve the inherent contradictions in liberal theory, and it attempts to do so by "turning social thought away from class by emphasizing the multiplicity and moral value of group life."[73] The essential problem, according to pluralists, "is to get the right relation between the authority of the state and spontaneous (moral) group life."[74] Macpherson criticizes this alleged solution because it "again neglects or leaves concealed or overshadowed the problem of getting men clear of the class relation of the market."[75]

What, then, are we to do, according to Macpherson? He states his case in the conditional. If the adequacy of political theory is to be assessed according to its ability to analyze human nature, then it must be said that there has been no political theory of classical quality since Bentham. The reason for this failure is that political theorists have not taken into account "a class difference" in human nature, or at least in concepts of human nature. Liberalism, he contends, refuses to do precisely this, for taking into account a class difference leads to the necessary conclusion that to have real democracy, a bifurcated human nature must be overcome. Hence "human nature" must be changed. And the proponents of liberalism "have become increasingly anti-liberal" in rejecting the possibility of mass transformation. But the cost of refusing to make some compromise, Macpherson ominously suggests, only "widens the gulf between liberal-democratic and mass-democratic concepts."[76]

In short, Macpherson offers no quick fix for political theory. His critique of liberalism leads in a direction that is suggestive rather than definitive. What he offers in fact for political theory is a negative proposition, suggesting that terribly and uncontrollably revolutionary consequences lie ahead unless the tradition of political theory is revived. In his passing comments, he seems to be saying that political theory should and must return to the "classical" tradition, that is, to the time when theory issued from general speculation concerning the integrative "nature" of humankind; yet Macpherson also seems to be advocating the position that political theory must at the same time recognize irreducible divisions, or "class divisions," in the nature of human beings.[77] In other words: Macpherson's "theory" is plagued by the same contradictory conditions that beset the liberals he analyzes, though he himself recognizes and admits this dilemma.[78] Nonetheless, though Macpherson's critique of liberalism may not extricate political theory from the quandaries posed by liberalism, at least Macpherson turns the dispute between political theory and liberalism away from Wolin's focus upon the fallacies of method due to the failure to recognize political community, and instead reveals the dispute to be a direct confrontation over the right to make claims regarding the general "nature" of human beings. Moreover, Macpherson's critique of liberalism and pluralism carries a special weight insofar as Macpherson's argument does not require that he downplay liberal fears of majoritarian tyrannies. Wolin, however, does not sufficiently speak to the fear that a generalizing approach, for all its grand implications tending toward the "community," may in fact hold unfortunate and deleterious *political* consequences when put into practice.

Wolin and Visual Commonness

The liberal challenge to political theory focuses on the question of how to achieve theoretical unity while respecting (actual?) diversity. Macpherson's reply is powerful because he argues that the liberals do *not* forsake generalizing claims about human nature; rather the liberals are either evasive or ambiguous about their claims. Yet Wolin's kind of defense of political theory--i.e., that a singular commitment to community endures despite appearances--typifies a trend among various writers who responded to the charges brought against theory in the 1950s. Indeed, the writings of Leo Strauss, Eric Voegelin, and Hannah Arendt bore a strong resemblance to Wolin's defense of theory insofar as all of these writers looked to the Greeks for some grounding of their conceptions of human nature, politics, and theory. Voegelin's transcendentally oriented psyche, Strauss's revealed philosophy, and Arendt's public world were all heavily indebted to the Greeks. Voegelin, Strauss, and Arendt looked to the Greeks not *just* as "authority figures" or as founders of a tradition but because these later theorists genuinely believed that the Greeks in some sense had "gotten it right" in their apprehension of the "whole"--as if the whole were a natural or noumenal category, some kind of worldly given. The critics of political theory had taken issue with theory's penchant for classical broadness, and they argued that contemporary theory had failed to account for diversity and plurality in human affairs. Such neglect, they had charged, invites the excesses of totalitarianism when grandiose theoretical designs are put into practice. Voegelin, Strauss, and Arendt felt, however, that they could distinguish *on principle* an acceptable theory of politics from intellectual fascism or totalitarianism (and thereby erect a theoretical *safeguard* against fascism and totalitarianism), because they felt themselves to be privy to some comprehensive proposition regarding some ineluctable aspect of human nature, some higher validity that necessarily attaches to the common realm, some view of the whole of the human enterprise that has endured in some latent fashion ever since the Greeks. Voegelin, Strauss, and Arendt--like Wolin--looked to the Greeks in order to reassert a substantive view of the "whole" against a liberal tradition that had cast aspersions upon political wholeness.[79]

Whether they succeeded in "proving" their propositions is debatable, but their sweeping claims should at least arouse our suspicion. The question must be asked: Need political theory really become a branch of natural philosophy, anthropology, or Greek philology in order to stave off the liberal sociologists, psychologists, and economists and prevent them from tearing at its skin?

In reply, I want to suggest the possibility that these post-World War II theorists seriously misread the Greeks, and that instead the modern defense of political theory can and should take a different turn. I think there is evidence that the Greeks themselves were more *ambivalent* about their views of the political "whole" than contemporary theorists have realized (one need think here only of Aeschylus' *Oresteia*). Theory was and is a way of thinking that *detaches* one from everyday discourse, and that detachment permits a glimpse of the whole from afar; but as suggested by the etymology of the word *theorein*, theory does not stop once it detaches: It is not simply the advocacy of what one has envisioned in the light of religious festivity. Rather, theory, at least in the classical sense, also entails a *return* to the city, thus the appraisal of the particular features of the polis in light of one's enlarged perspective. Theory, in short, involves a *double* perspective--not straight advocacy--and a double way of seeing means that theory is primarily a *questioning* enterprise, a way of comparing, checking, rethinking, and revising.

When I say that political theory is "about" boundaries and borders, I am not suggesting that theory mainly involves the observance and enforcement of boundaries and borders already in place. Rather, my reading of the theorist's journey is that he or she is always negotiating the placement of borders, in light of some vision of the whole. To be more precise: Political theory is principally concerned with the boundaries of the whole political unit, the definition of the political community. Who are we?--as members of a polity--is the first question of the enterprise, a question that precedes the practical question, What shall we do? But in saying that the theorist asks Who are we? I mean that that question itself is fundamentally *theoretical*, as opposed to being a "philosophical" question (if by philosophy we understand an activity that strives to ascertain universal, unchanging, apodictic truths). The theoretical definition of a political community is a matter involving conceptual boundaries, a question of inside and outside; philosophical or anthropological speculation concerning the essential nature of the human animal is at best of secondary importance. The concern with boundaries has a domestic dimension, of definition from *within*. The theorist may address himself or herself to domestic issues such as the relation of the individual to the larger polity, or of the distinctions and borders between the public and the private realms, between ruler and ruled, man and woman, the political and the social (or other) realms, and so on. He or she may attend to the unifying concepts that bind and define a people from within: justice, authority, contract, legitimacy, power. In addition, the theorist needs to pay attention to "foreign" affairs, to the matter of definition from *without*. This effort may focus on the importance of geography, language, ethnicity, religion, and so on, upon domestic definition and consolidation.[80] A focus upon external definition also examines, as an *issue*, the nature of the imputed difference between citizen and noncitizen. Many factors may bear upon the definition of a polity, but the formation of a political unit is not simply a straight extension of some "natural" principle, some ineluctable view of human nature, or even some ingrained tradition. All political definition, those ties and relationships between persons that are uniquely *political*, is, to a great degree, abstract, intangible, conceptual, negotiated--which is to say, theoretical.

To explain what I mean, let me return to my critique of Wolin, in order then to outline my own, contrasting view. At the outset of *Politics and Vision*, Wolin links "political philosophy" to "philosophy." He explains first that political philosophy is not "an essence with an external nature" but rather is a "complex activity." Nonetheless, political philosophy bears a fixed relationship to philosophy, he contends, in that the latter discipline seeks truths or knowledge of a "public" nature. One of the "essential qualities" of what is political is its relationship to what is "public," Wolin states, and he notes that this relationship between the political and the public has "powerfully shaped the view of political theorists about their subject matter."[81] Citing Cicero, Wolin then associates the notion of commonwealth with *res publica*, thus extracting from the notion of publicness the idea of commonness. In syllogistic fashion, Wolin concludes: "Of all the authoritative institutions in society, the political arrangement has been singled out as uniquely concerned with what is "common" to the whole community."[82] For Wolin, "the political" is tantamount to "the public," which is tantamount to "the common."

Wolin qualifies and amends his basic argument. He insists that the field of politics--in a "radical sense"--is a "created one."[83] But he retreats a bit from this assertion with the negative rejoinder that the political philosopher is not "at liberty to call 'political' whatever he chooses."[84] The meaningful realm of the political apparently has a solid, ontological base, separate from the theorist's constructions, though Wolin adds that "the task of defining what is political is a continual one."[85] If the origin of the concept of politics is somewhat confusing to the reader at this point, Wolin settles on the conclusion that "the words 'public,' 'common,' and 'general' have a long tradition of usage which has made them synonymous for what is political. For this reason, they serve as important clues to the subject matter of political philosophy."[86] From here, Wolin accepts as his working premise that "the Western political tradition has looked upon the political order as a common order"; and he ends the section ("Political Philosophy and the Political") with an extended commentary on the "commonness" of the political order.[87]

From the above discussion, it is clear that Wolin makes a conceptual shift in his argument and calls the result an equation or equivalence. He relates the political to the public and the public to commonness and ends up equating the political with the common, as if they were "synonymous." I want to suggest that that equation, or transitive logic, informs not only Wolin's views of the Greek city-state but also his conception of political theory that is expressed in the book overall.

To put it briefly, Wolin's account of the meaning of the polis, the Greek city-state, radiates outward from the concept of *commonness*. He claims that the political thought of Plato and Aristotle was strongly *political* because it "dealt with subjects of common concern, and because all of the members were implicated in a common life." Although his argument is scattered rather than compact, Wolin suggests that the *spatial dimensions* of the polis were largely responsible for promoting commonness in the Greek city-state. The relatively small size of the polis permitted the identification of politics with *paideia*, with a common moral and civilizing education. Such moral and civil relationships could occur effectively only within close confines, in a face-to-face, or directly "visual," relationship.[88]

Wolin makes these points, however, only through a contrastive account of the polis's decline. The polis was overlaid by giant state forms and gradually ceased to be *the* politically significant unit,[89]

Wolin explains. Beginning in the Hellenistic age and accelerating during the Roman Republic, "an attempt repeatedly was made to adjust the categories of political thought to the unprecedented situation where masses of men, scattered over great distances and differentiated by race and culture, had been gathered into a single society and governed by a single authority."[90] Wolin astutely argues that the new dimensions of space posed political problems "that had been obscured by the homogeneity of the Greek polis: problems of the admissible limits of political conflict, the role of institutions in containing and ordering these conflicts, and, above all, the implications of conducting politics on the basis of interests."[91] In short, the problem with the expansion of political space and the breakdown of homogeneity was that the concept of politics became increasingly *abstract* and distant. Wolin claims that the personification of authority figures and the use of symbolism were two ways of responding to heterogeneity and the abstract character of political life.[92] Wolin's explanation of this development is telling:

> With the development of impersonal organization, the locus of power and decision had grown far removed from the lives of the vast majority. There seemed to be little connection between the milieu surrounding political decisions and the tiny circle of the individual's experience. Politics, in other words, was conducted in a way incomprehensible to the categories of ordinary thought and experience. The "visual politics" of an earlier age, when men could see and feel the forms of public action and make meaningful comparisons with their own experience, was giving way to "abstract politics," politics from a distance, where men were informed about public actions which bore little or no resemblance to the economy of the household or the affairs of the marketplace.[93]

The shift from "visual" to "abstract" politics meant that the "decline of the *polis* as the nuclear center of human existence had apparently deprived political thought of its basic unit of analysis, one that it was unable to replace."[94] Wolin writes *Politics and Vision* with an unmistakable sense of this loss in mind. "Without the *polis*," he begins his story, "political philosophy had been reduced to the status of a subject-matter in search of a relevant context."[95]

In fairness to Wolin's book, I should note that the decline or irrelevance of later political philosophy is not all that *Politics and Vision* is about, for Wolin includes the thesis that Christianity unexpectedly rejuvenated the concept of the political. Yet, for all the talk of "continuity" in his book, I am not sure that Wolin himself ever recovers from the loss of the polis. The book on the whole is an admirable, though perhaps rearguard, attempt not to admit defeat. Wolin continues to scan the history of political thought in search of some substantive communal tie that would accommodate diversity and distance. Yet he never seems to be able to reconstruct a viable concept of politics, relevant to spatially enlarged and heterogeneous societies, once the polis is deemed obsolete.

I think Wolin's difficulties in reformulating the concept of the political and in revitalizing political theory begin with his reading of the Greek concept of politics. I submit that he attaches the concept of the political too closely to the concept of commonness, a concept of commonness that is based upon spatial metaphors and visual imagery. From other theorists knowledgeable about the Greeks, such as Arendt,[96] we have gained an appreciation for certain distinguishing features of Greek political life that Wolin does not emphasize. Wolin mentions, but does not emphasize, that the Greek realm of politics was in principle distinguishable from the realm of the *oikos*, the household, or the family. (Wolin even suggests that the relationship between the family and the political should be understood more as an extension, rather than a separation, of the former from the latter.[97]) Wolin mentions, but does not emphasize, that the concept of the political was enforced through a sharp distinction between citizen and noncitizen. (Wolin in fact suggests that the polis contributed to its own demise, promoting--apparently because of their conceptual compatibility with the polis--the relations of "isopolity" and "sympolity"[98] with neighboring poleis.) If the Greek conception of "the political" was synonymous with a "visual" concept of "commonness," then Wolin needs to explain how the political became conceptually delimited away from the visual, affective ties of the family. He also needs to explain how the political realm became consolidated in contradistinction to the Homeric conception of a common Greek culture. If we understand the polis and the political as representing an important *break* with Homeric culture, then we must clarify the nature of this development. The activity of politics, in other words, appears to have been defined *against* both family life and Greek culture (despite however much it might have represented an extension of them). That definition, I suggest, was inherently and primarily "abstract" (for what, after all, were the concrete, *visual* differences between citizen and family member, or citizen and barbarian?). I contend that what gave the Greek concept of the political its uniqueness and characteristic definition was indeed more "abstract" than "visual."[99] Wolin mentions that politics is a created sphere, but one does not gain the sense from his account that the Greek city-state represented a triumph of conceptual consolidation, instead of being above all a natural extension of associations given by spatial conditions.

Wolin's emphasis on visual commonness is related to his understanding of commonness as that which forms the basis for general agreement, which in turn is that which permits benign conflict and conflict mediation. For instance, in a section in which Wolin mentions Aristotle's criticism of Plato, Wolin explains that Greek commonness entailed "unity," but that "unity" was not the same as "uniformity":

> Plato was correct in emphasizing that a common set of values and purposes was necessary if a society was to express its solidarity and to act purposefully. It does not follow, however, that this aspect of unity must be extended to every aspect of life or even to every important aspect of life. Unity, in short, is not synonymous with uniformity, as Plato was inclined to think that it was. . . . To put it somewhat differently, an area of agreement provides the foundation for statecraft; it permits political authority to deal with areas of difference with the assurance that some problems have been temporarily solved. The metaphor might be slightly altered to point to one other contribution of unity; that is, it serves as a stepping stone from an area of agreement to one of disagreement.[100]

But within this scheme, Wolin does not adequately explain why "commonness" should have permitted "difference." Or rather, Wolin does not distinguish between the different kinds of difference. He needs to explain, for instance, why "commonness" permitted differences in debate and discussion, but *not* in cultural, ethnic, linguistic, or residential matters. The closest he comes to an explanation is his suggestion, bare at best, that the concept of "unity" was anchored in a "visual" metaphor and, as metaphor, permitted benign differences, thus forbidding all-out "uniformity"; but as *mere* metaphor, the concept of "unity" could not accommodate the starker differences of race, color, language, and so forth. Yet Wolin's distinctions between visual and abstract and between unity and uniformity do not provide an account for the distinguishing boundaries between the political and nonpolitical spheres, whether domestic (the family), or foreign (barbarians, noncitizens, citizens of other poleis). Without addressing the meaning of the limits and borders of the political, Wolin has not yet put his finger on the precise location of the Greek conceptual realm of politics.

If, however, my implied, alternative reading of Greek political life is correct, then the key to understanding the Greek concept of politics is in the recognition that "the political" was fundamentally of an "abstract" character, that it was foremost a "theoretical" tie and not simply a direct extension of some "natural" or "visual" relationship.[101] (In my reading of Plato's *Republic*, presented in the next chapter, I try to show how Plato himself resists an understanding of politics as moored fundamentally in *visual* metaphors.) Moreover, I have suggested in preliminary fashion that the abstract character of politics was in some way related to the formation of borders and boundaries.

One could reasonably interject the objection that there seems to be a contradiction in my exposition and critique of Wolin, for in the first part of this chapter I was implicitly repudiating a "holistic" approach to political theory and now I am implicitly encouraging a recognition of theoretical "abstractness" in the Greek concept of politics. One would think that abstractness would go hand in hand with generality. I concede that abstractness does, in part, connote generality. But I want to recover the sense in which abstractness is *not* synonymous with generality and does not exclusively entail a "holistic" understanding. By emphasizing the great "abstractness" of the Greek concept of the political, I am drawing attention to the extent to which the realm of politics is primarily a product of deliberate definition, of construction or convention, of human artifice and intervention. And here is the point I think is often overlooked: That the "activity" or "realm" of politics is the product of self-conscious definition, a triumph of conceptual consolidation, betrays, because it necessarily presupposes, *a process of questioning and negotiation and hence an incorporated acknowledgment of difference.*

In the case of the Greeks, the "abstractness" of the concept of the political means that the Greeks themselves acknowledged--and the degree of consciousness here is beside the point--that the tie between citizen and citizen was of an altogether different nature from that tie between family member and family member (which, incidentally, invites the question whether even the "blood" ties of the family can be considered "visual"). In other words, inhering in the concept of political association was an acknowledgment of nonpolitical differences. My complaint about Wolin's "holistic" concept of "commonness" is that it obscures the implicit acknowledgment of boundaries and borders that is contained within the Greek concept of politics. In short, the holistic approach to political theory tends to detach and then to impose a single vision upon the concept of politics, whereas I am suggesting a version of political theory, based as Wolin's is upon a cautious reading of the Greeks, that entertains a double perspective on the city--a view of theory as a truly two-legged journey. And I want to suggest further that a recovery of this doubleness, this self-conscious ambivalence, within the abstract nature of politics holds the potential for establishing greater theoretical continuity between the Greek concept of politics and the modern version than does Wolin's "visionary" scheme, for it frees the concept of politics from the common confines of the parochial polis.

I find partial support for this view of theory in a review article written by John Schaar, on Michael Walzer's book *Spheres of Justice: A Defense of Pluralism and Equality*.   Schaar praises Walzer for asserting a view of justice that serves as a corrective to prevailing ways of theorizing about justice. Too often, according to Schaar, theorists of justice (e.g., John Rawls[102]) seek a single, comprehensive principle that is supposed to apply to all persons and to all circumstances. Schaar calls these theories formalistic and universalistic. He says that such theories have power in achieving great generality, but their weakness is that they lose touch with concrete empirical conditions. Walzer, however, argues that justice is spherical and plural.   Different standards apply to different situations, a view that, according to Schaar, recognizes real flesh-and-blood people, "ordinary persons living together under diverse and changing conditions of history, culture, and economy."[103] If we pay attention to real history and real societies, then we see, Walzer contends, that no single distributive principle of justice is possible. Schaar welcomes this perspective, one he calls at various points sociological, historical, pluralist, and conventional.

Yet, although Schaar strongly encourages Walzer's approach as a corrective measure and fresh perspective, he faults the author and the book for their onesidedness. He explains that Walzer's view of justice entails not only the idea that the spheres of justice are many but also the more questionable assertion that the spheres are logically separate and must remain autonomous. Justice for Walzer, then, has two dimensions: (1) establishing principles within the respective spheres; and (2) policing the borders *between* spheres. Justice, therefore, is also "boundary keeping." But Schaar does not think the matter can be settled so easily. Walzer has set the boundaries too rigidly, as if by fiat. Schaar contends that there are overlapping problems *between* spheres and a need to set priorities *among* spheres. Walzer's pluralistic notion of justice affords no trans-spherical regulation. For instance, even granting Walzer the idea that capital should never dominate outside the sphere of the market, Schaar points out that for Marx, capitalism is unjust precisely because capital dominates labor *inside* the market. It is unjust because it gives too many things over to that sphere; indeed, perhaps the entire sphere of distribution is unjust. But "Walzer's theory does not enable him to say anything about which matters *should* be contained within a sphere, and which should not, where the boundaries should be drawn and when they should be revised."[104]

Schaar explains that Walzer's shortcoming is that he accepts what people *say* is just but cannot elaborate *standards* for judging (a common charge against liberals). Inherent in the enterprise of theorizing about such matters is a tension, according to Schaar, between practice and standard, between sociology and philosophy. The philosophers' views of justice have become much too detached and formalistic in their musings on the subject, but Walzer has gone too far in the other direction. He gives too much to pluralism and too little to principle. Schaar goes on to espouse the view that the entire dichotomy between universals and particulars, or wholes and boundaries, or philosophy and sociology, may be misconceived and that there is a way of judging and theorizing free from such dichotomization. He finds the starting point for theorizing about justice, not in sociology or philosophy, but in economics: "If we don't get the economic basis of society right, there is little hope of getting anything else right."[105]

I am uncertain of Schaar's proposal, reminiscent of Macpherson's class analysis, that we should ease the inherent tension between philosophy and sociology by looking to economics, but I point to his review article not to endorse this particular solution but to draw attention to the frame of mind, and the view of theory, that brought him to that point of compromise. Whereas Wolin considered himself as a political theorist to be *combatting* the sociologists, Schaar's initial animosity is directed against those who exclude the pluralistic perspective that sociology often promotes. Schaar is against detachment, against transcendental yearnings, against holistic and universalizing methods; and he is for an acknowledgment of boundaries and a recognition of diversity--though in the end he wishes that boundaries and borders be questioned and revised, not simply acknowledged and enforced.

My theoretical aim in this work is to accomplish something along the lines of Schaar's general perspective (though I'm far less optimistic that the tension between philosophy and sociology admits of a *literal* reconciliation). If I need admit my ulterior motives at the outset, I should say that one of my concerns is that I want to recover the value of ambivalence, of tentativeness, of inquiry, within the activity of political theorizing. I do this in face of what I perceive to be a prevailing imperative within political theory circles toward *advocacy*, toward the need to find, affirm, and defend particular renditions of the nature of human beings, of the self or psyche, and then to build in word sketches political societies on the basis of these all-encompassing definitions.[106] I am not against advocacy per se, nor do I stand on principle against definition; but I am sensitive to and look with disfavor upon the tendency of theorists to pass in the course of their intellectual narratives beyond engagement and toward rigidity, beyond spirited inquiry and toward argumentation. To lay my alternative sensibility out as a doctrine: The spirit of theory is to be found in the activity of questioning rather than in the activity of answering. By this spirit I do not mean some hollow skepticism or coy liberalism. I find this spirit expressed characteristically in the person of Socrates (which should come as no great surprise). Drawing from his personal example, and from Plato's writings, I take quite seriously the importance of *irony* in the twin and intertwining activities of questioning and theorizing, especially as regards politics. I hope to show that irony, which I will define as a particular way of thinking, bears a special inner relationship to politics, and therewith to the activity of theorizing about politics. And it is upon the tradition of Socrates that I draw when I propose, in this book, to assert the significance of an element of irony in the theoretical understanding of politics, of that activity of uniquely defining "who we are" as political fellows.

A complete response to Wolin, and hence a recovery of the intimate relationship between irony and political theorizing in the ancient Greek world, would require a study of the epic poets and, therewith, a study of the extent to which the polis emerged out of a robust sense of tragedy. Such a study, of course, would focus upon Homer. My own view is that Homer's generally ironic sensibility has been vastly underestimated. To indulge in the gory details of *war* in order to learn about human *life* and human association; to investigate the ways of the *immortals* in order to discover the abilities as well as the limitations of *mortals*; to descend finally into the underworld in order to find one's way in *this* world: All of these Homeric reversals attest to the poet's appreciation of the significance of death and destruction *for life*, to the poignancy of human existence because of tragedy, to the supreme irony that human life and community should go on at all.

Nonetheless, an exhaustive study of Homer's irony, or that of the tragic poets after him, would be too digressive for my present purposes. Instead, I shall limit my remarks about irony in the ancient world to a careful study of Plato's *Republic*. A close reading of the irony of that work should suffice to provide a response to Wolin's thesis about the nature of political community for the Greeks. To anticipate: Plato's *Republic* suggests a view of political community that is based upon a pretense or lie--a stance, I suggest, that necessarily presupposes a tragic outlook. Recovering the sense in which politics represents an ironic triumph over tragedy could, in turn, revitalize the modern enterprise of political theorizing. Briefly--by the politics of irony I understand a way of entering into and sustaining a uniquely political relationship such that that relationship does not depend upon mutual and unadulterated adherence by the parties concerned to some *particular* notion of self, man, god, nature, or community. That may be an overly negative definition and I may be overstating the negativity of irony, but what I want to propose in preliminary fashion, and with respect to the foregoing discussion, is that irony provides a way of defining, of negotiating the borders around, political communities *without* forsaking or obscuring the vital differences that human beings recognize among themselves.

If tenable, such a notion would potentially hold great implications for political theory. Of course one typically substantiates such bold claims by forwarding an argument of *implicitness*: It was there all along, buried in the tradition of political theory; it didn't arise from nowhere; and hence I am acting as mere facilitator, making political theorists more *aware* of what they already implicitly know. (The supreme irony of political theory, arguably the most self-aware of disciplines, may be that its Socratic-ironic foundations remain largely unexamined.) I do think irony can be so substantiated, and I do intend to examine certain nodal moments in the history of political theory in which irony has played a key role. But I should emphasize that the point I am attempting to make by writing this book is thematic and conceptual, not primarily historical or sociological. I do not intend to survey the history of political theory in order to identify which theorists were ironic and which were not, or how aware and how not, why and why not, and so on. Nor am I making an outright declaration that all political theorists are ironists, and I wish strongly to discourage at the outset such a reading of my project. Like many theorists, I am beginning with the beginning of Western political theory--with the Greeks--and I am following the customary procedure in claiming that even if political theory's ironic origins have been forgotten, they have not been lost altogether.[107] Yet, since I care not to delve into the historical sociology of irony in all epic points of the tradition, my thematic argument belongs, following Wolin's scheme, more on the side of preserving a thread of "continuity" in the tradition than on the side of advancing a case for the various "innovations" along the way.

*   *   *

Much of the foregoing discourse begs my initial question: What if none of this matters, because theory is dead in the modern age and will remain dead despite innovative attempts to revive it? My first reaction (disregarding the preceding discussion) is to circumvent the problem completely: The answer to the question as far as I am concerned is that this book is not even "about" theory, nor is it about the conditions that would render theory "viable" or "possible." This is not another work in metatheory, or meta-metatheory, or critical theory, or supercritical theory, or poststructural, postmodern, posthermeneutical, postlinguistic metacritical quasideconstructionist theory. I do not intend to investigate, in the words of Clifford Geertz, the turtles on top of turtles on top of other turtles "all the way down";[108] nor will I pursue, in the words of Arendt, the infinite series of new Archimedean points all the way out to the "absolute void behind the universe";[109] nor will I, in the words of Richard Rorty, "manipulate jargon" endlessly.[110]

There is a specific reason for my resisting the high-tech vocabulary currently filling the pages of many theory journals. As much as the next theorist, I enjoy ruminating upon *a priori* conditions, underlying causes, grand schemes, synthetic models, first foundations, and final justifications. The beauty of irony, however, is that one can use it effectively and discuss it coherently without having to rely upon a preconfirmed ontology, or a certified epistemology, or a prepackaged methodology. I shall explain in Chapter 3 the reason for this anomaly. But for now I will give but a preview of the political consequences of irony's extraordinary character: The politics of irony can operate successfully even in the absence of, in the words of the sociologist, universalistic behavior-orienting norms. Allow me to leap from this cryptic proposition to reveal, prematurely, my wildest fantasies and greatest expectations for irony: I foresee the theory of irony as a way of recommending peoples as diverse as Jew and Arab, white South African and black South African, or American and Russian to enter into genuinely political relationships, i.e., relationships that could mitigate ingrained differences and mediate longstanding disputes.

If I may be presumptuous beyond restraint, allow me to suggest that the decisive question for our time is not the *possibility* but the *necessity* of theory. By now it is a commonplace within theory circles to say that political theorizing arises out of times of political crisis. We have been living in crisis. With cruise and Pershing missiles in place in Europe, the Soviet Union's response time for countermanding a "launch on warning" (triggered even by computer error) has dwindled down to a mere seven minutes (at the time of writing). One need not cultivate a keen sense of the apocalyptic to let the realization sink in that nuclear annihilation is upon us, literally less than a half hour away. A person only casually acquainted with the business of political theory would suppose that the prospect of thermonuclear destruction would provide abundant grist for the theorist's mill. All the appropriate issues are involved in one way or another in the "nuclear issue": the boundaries of the political; the questions and concepts of justice, authority, community, legitimacy, law, power; the issues of war and peace. And since the theorist's method is particularly well suited to political problems of a large and unwieldy nature, one would think that theorists and the nuclear crisis would be a perfect match. Perhaps it is foolhardy to entertain distant and hypothetical scenarios, but on the surface of things it would seem that *if* the world of nations is to avert nuclear warfare through deliberate policy (as opposed to happenstance and to "muddling through"), then the effort requires theoretical intervention and coordination of some sort. Yes, not only is nuclear peril *the* big political issue of the day, but it is also ripe for theoretical plucking.

Yet the distinction between the possibility and the necessity of theory does not settle the score, for the distinction is far from absolute. What *does* matter is that even the slightest suspicion that theory is nowadays necessary does indeed provide a resounding reply to those persons who once denied its sheer possibility. The thermonuclear bomb has transformed the world since the 1950s. A protracted arms race, the horizontal proliferation of nuclear weapons, and an increase in the destructive potential of individual warheads and missiles now subjects those pluralists and those post-Nietzscheans to a cruel irony: The bomb has created the basis for a world community of sorts, for a new anthropology, simply because all persons and all peoples might well experience the same death. All have a stake in world politics; all are oriented toward the same potential future. This does not mean that the bomb is a new god to which some perverse religious valence can be attributed. It does mean that all human beings have a theoretical common denominator in the practical possibility of collective death, a common denominator that perhaps now holds greater world significance than does the lowest common denominator among human beings, namely the natural inevitability of individual death.

The thermonuclear bomb has also subjected those liberals and those positivists who defended a "process-oriented" political system on the grounds that it prevented totalitarianism and preserved individual freedom to a similar, perhaps crueler, irony: The international policies of deterrence, of mutual assured destruction (MAD), of launch on warning, of all-encompassing "defensive" shields, have created a new brand of totalitarianism, a world totalitarianism, a scheme of international relations that relies deliberately upon a "balance of terror," the terror of which and threat of force of which far surpass that proposed and employed by national totalitarian and fascist systems.[111] The bomb contains an intrinsic terror, but now a form of *political* terrorism, merely *based* upon the technology of the bomb, has become the deliberate policy of major governments. (One can view Henry Kissinger's sad efforts to reassert the viability of conventional war as an attempt at denying the idea that international nuclear affairs are in fact terrible and totalizing.) Indeed, to the extent to which military strategists seek to make deterrence scenarios more credible by eliminating "the human element" from their calculations, the *meaning* of the bomb is that it threatens to eliminate *politics* from the world altogether. One could state with considerable justification that the phrase "international politics" is an anachronism, a misnomer.

But the failures of "foreign policy" only reflect back upon the failures of "domestic policy." Liberalism, with its once ingenious plan to pit faction against faction, might prevent tyrannies of the majority and the internal rise of national totalitarianism but, due to nuclear terrors, it has been proved an utter disaster in preventing the rise of international totalitarianism. At the very end of his book, in the very last sentence, Sheldon Wolin issues a brand new charge against liberalism, thus shifting his argument at the last possible moment. Instead of arguing, as he has up to that end point, that the failure of liberalism is marked by a diminution in the quality of domestic political life (because the notion of community has subsided), Wolin now suggests that the failure of liberalism is to be found, not in the absence of a quality, but in direct negative consequences--dire consequences--and that these consequences are due to liberalism's inherent inability to address large-scale political problems: "Political theory must once again be viewed as that form of knowledge which deals with what is general and integrative to men, a life of common involvements. The urgency of these tasks is obvious, for human existence is not going to be decided at the lesser level of small associations: it is the political order that is making fateful decisions about man's survival in an age haunted by the possibility of unlimited destruction."[112]

The bomb, then, vindicates Sheldon Wolin's book, vindicates political theory. But whereas Wolin simply asserts or assumes the value of community and the literal connection between the concept of the political and the concept of community, I wish to encourage, by this book, a rethinking of the concept of politics by way of a discussion of irony. Perhaps this project is not so far from Wolin's as I have suggested, but the contrast to be made is that whereas his connection between the concepts of community and politics is *literal*, mine is *ironic*.

It should become increasingly clear to the reader in the course of this book that by irony I mean something more than simply a rhetorical technique, a trope, or figure of speech. In the next chapter I shall argue that one ought to read Plato's philosophy as a natural extension of Socrates' ironic manner, that in fact the political theory of justice under discussion in the *Republic* is necessarily connected to the irony in and of that book. Socrates' irony implies a philosophy--in the spirited rather than the lettered sense of the term *philosophy*--which in turn entails a certain orientation tending toward the political. Ultimately, I think the substance of irony involves a particular way of thinking about life and death; irony--as a "philosophy" or "mode of con-sciousness"--is an anticipation of death in a way that has implications for life, including implications for politics and nuclear affairs.

Other contemporary political theorists have observed a relation-ship between irony and political theory;[113] but they tend to define irony narrowly, as a verbal technique or manner of presentation; and thus they miss its philosophical, and therewith political, significance. To return to John Schaar's review article to illustrate my point: Schaar is, I think, onto something when he notes that Walzer's analysis of Marx misses Marx's irony and hence "appears even to miss the whole point of *Capital*":

> The passage Walzer quotes is embedded within one of Marx's characteristic mock dialogues between capitalist and worker. The worker cannot understand why he should get so little and the capitalist so much. The capitalist is explaining that he too contributes to production and creates value, for which, of course, he should be rewarded. As he explains this with the aid of the political economists, his hired overseers "hide their smiles." Later, the capitalist breaks into a "hearty laugh," and the "cause of his laughter" is that he knows he has taken from the worker twice what he has given, and that the laws of political economy explain that his "good fortune" is "no injustice at all" to the worker. To dispel all doubt as to his intent, Marx footnotes his mock dialogue with some thunder from Luther: "Extol thyself, put on finery and adorn thyself . . . but whoever takes more or better than he gives, that is usury, and not service, and wrong done to his neighbor, as when one steals and robs."[114]

In the next paragraph, Schaar explains that "Marx's whole point" is that capitalism is in its entirety unjust, not simply that it distributes goods poorly. Marx analyzes capitalism first according to a principle of justice, and this principle then informs his economic analysis proper: "*Capital* is more than an analysis of an economic system; it is equally a theory of justice, and one of the greatest ever written." My one quibble with Schaar's very sensible explanation is that he fails to draw an explicit connection between Marx's irony and Marx's theory of justice. Perhaps that needn't concern Schaar in a review article, for the effort would certainly require a longer work; and, as I shall suggest in Chapter 5, I am uncertain whether or how far the ironic passages in Marx's later writings indicate a more generally ironic outlook in his political thought. Nonetheless, Schaar's apparent assumption that these matters are divorced is typical of the few political theorists who have touched upon irony.

To cite a few other examples: Hayden White, in *Metahistory*,[115] puts irony to the fore of his analysis of nineteenth-century historical writing (in which he covers, *inter alios*, Hegel, Marx, Nietzsche, and Croce); and Thomas Spragens, Jr., in *The Irony of Liberal Reason*, deploys irony extensively in his discussion of liberalism.[116] But both writers define irony very strictly: For White, irony is one of Kenneth Burke's four tropes, and an analysis of its tropological significance reveals, according to Burke and White, an attitude of unending skepticism and eternal fatalism. For Spragens, too, irony is pretty much synonymous with skepticism, and he cites only Reinhold Niebuhr to support him in that assumption. Irony's rhetorical logic of reversal translates for Spragens into a skeptical and detached attitude toward the universe as a whole, in other words, a view of the world in which the ups and the downs pretty much balance each other. I shall argue that even if irony for the most part can be understood in rhetorical, literary, or tropological terms, and even if irony for the most part reveals an underlying and noncommittal skepticism, irony contains within itself more than a rhetorical mechanism that signifies skepticism.[117] I shall argue that, despite its negative character, irony leads in a positive direction, signifying an ethos, a mode of consciousness, a spirit, that tends toward politics and the political.

The extent to which irony figures in the writings, even the entire "philosophy" of Leo Strauss, has been ignored by his readers, especially his critics. Strauss bases many of his conclusions regarding Socratic thought and Platonic philosophy upon a particular understanding of irony; but I shall argue, in a close examination of Strauss's reading of the *Republic*, that the philosophic conclusions he extracts from irony are peculiar to him and are not contained within the logic and operation of irony properly understood. This misunderstanding of irony is also due, I contend, to Strauss's particularly narrow understanding of irony also as a strictly rhetorical technique and mode of written presentation.

Finally, Richard Rorty has added his name to the list, starting with Socrates, of those who have attempted to think about politics and political theory by way of irony.[118] For Rorty, irony is *the* trope of today's world, whether you call that world modern or postmodern. Irony, according to Rorty, represents a general way of thinking common to a cluster of modern thinkers, ranging from Proust to Heidegger. But while ironists such as Hegel, Nietzsche, and Derrida can teach us much, their teaching on irony is of limited import, applicable only to the "private realm." Irony is of little public use, says Rorty: It is "largely irrelevant to public life and to political questions."[119] And the "later Derrida" teaches us that we should not attempt to reconcile irony with theory (Heidegger's mistake), especially *political* theory. No public heroism, and none of that political-theory-as-a-vocation stuff.

And yet, Rorty's *Contingency, Irony, and Solidarity* is a book about politics and political theory and specifically a book about how to combine private irony and a liberal democratic politics. Following the tradition of epic political theorizing, he fancies a "utopia" in which liberalism and ironism might be conjoined at least in the paradigmatic person of that regime--the "liberal ironist." As ironist, such a person believes that there is no answer to the question, Why *not* be cruel? As liberal, such a person nonetheless avoids committing acts of cruelty, in the name of "human solidarity." This avoidance isn't well grounded and well theorized, but that's Rorty's point. Irony may be fundamentally nonpolitical and provides no sure "foundation" for a political order, but Rorty maintains that irony is, at least, *not incompatible with* the goals of cruelty-avoidance and human solidarity and thus liberal democracy. Those goals will have to be nurtured primarily by other means--Rorty suggests poetry and certain works of literature. But the real key to this public-private compromise is the ironist, who drops the demand for theoretical unity and just decides, leaplike, Kierkegaard-like, to hold her contradictions and all of her unfounded views somehow together. The concession to politics has been made, and Rorty's liberal decency shines through (and appreciative readers might actually follow his do-as-I-do, not as-I-say example).

Rorty's belief in the essential antagonism between irony and politics presupposes an acquaintance with his earlier retelling of the Hegel-Nietzsche-Heideggerian story about the Western tradition of philosophy. It is a grand story, an epic rise and fall. Beginning roughly with Plato, the Western mind sought a rational justification for its world, and to that end it concocted, and successfully promulgated, the notion of a transcendental ideal--an ideal that was universally applicable because (presumably) it hovered so high. Ever since Plato, the Western mind has been seeking one version or another of this ultimate ideal; but starting sometime during the late eighteenth or early nineteenth century, various philosophers discredited this act of upward gazing, and they started lugging the transcendental back down to earth. One demystifying effort built upon another, until by Heidegger's day, most of those in the philosophic community had disabused themselves entirely of searching for universal answers, whether transcendent or earthbound. The French refined such labors, the American pragmatists were helpful, a few others contributed as well, and then Rorty summarized the proceedings, throwing in a special emphasis for literature and literary criticism.

But one wants to contest and to retell this long story and not to let it pass as the final word. Rorty mentions at one point that the ironist distrusts the metaphysician's metaphor of a vertical view downward from above, for which the ironist wants to substitute the historicist metaphor of looking back on the past along a horizontal axis.[120] In this quick topographical mapping of the Western tradition, Rorty reveals that he has missed the long, alternative Western tradition of moral, philosophical, and political discourse outlined in the introductory chapter, namely the tradition of *katabasis*. Rorty's entire reading of the West is staked on the belief that Plato is a metaphysician, not an ironist. If we can show Rorty wrong about Plato, then we shall be in a position to restore a theoretical and historical connection between politics and irony.

Let me reiterate a point I made earlier: This book, despite appearances, is not fundamentally "about" theory. And even though throughout the book I will betray my unbounded fascination with irony as a subject matter unto itself, I must emphasize at the outset that my overriding concern in writing this book is with the nuclear issue. To be sure, I shall give theory and irony their due, but I have my priorities. One could say much about theory and irony as matters entirely separate from nuclear affairs, and I have been selective in deciding what to exclude as superfluous to my chosen end (though the path I take toward my final destination meanders). Nevertheless, theory and irony are, I think, the appropriate media for addressing, if not combatting intellectually, the nuclear problem, and I have enlisted them especially for that reason.

In this chapter, to sum, I have addressed the question of the decline of theory in the modern age, in particular because the earlier discussions and debates conducted in the 1950s still bear upon the current dilemma--and yet, I have suggested, there are countervailing reasons to think that the earlier debate no longer pertains to the present crisis. I suggested that the decline in the credibility of communal or utopian theorizing was necessarily tied, not only to the long-term traditions of positivism, liberalism, and pluralism, but more directly to the experiences associated with World War II, namely the rise of fascist and totalitarian regimes. I proposed that the debates over theory, both pro and con, had to be put into perspective with respect to these traumatic world events. Such a perspective, however, frees one to theorize anew. For the world has since entered a new era, and so must our theories. A prominent political theorist wrote some twenty years ago that the goal of political theorizing was no longer to envision grand utopias but simply to avert annihilation.[121] The solemnest irony of our times may well be, however, that a dose of utopianism is the only theoretical, if not practical, recourse against the bomb. This book, then, is an attempt to rethink politics and political theory, to go beyond the post-World War II era. For mine is not the generation of the last holocaust but must be forever poised toward the next.

Notes

1. Leo Strauss, "What Is Political Philosophy?" *Journal of Politics* 19 (August, 1957), p. 345.

2. Sheldon Wolin, "Political Theory: 2, Trends and Goals," *International Encyclopedia of the Social Sciences*, Vol. 12 (1968), p. 322.

3. *Ibid.*, p. 321, and *idem*, "Political Theory as a Vocation," *American Political Science Review* 63 (December, 1969), p. 1078.

4. I am presenting this scheme of distinctions somewhat factitiously, for of course "political wholes" are frequently conceived with their edges and borders intact. As I remark in the passage, the point I am making is one of emphasis, in an attempt to force the issue of the relation between "wholes" and "particulars."

5. Even Strauss and Wolin counsel against excessive generalizing. Strauss writes that "men are constantly tempted to force the issue by imposing unity on phenomena, by absolutizing either knowledge of homogeneity or knowledge of ends." Wolin also is well aware of the relation between "wholeness" and "distortion." Strauss, "What Is Political Philosophy?" p. 322; Wolin, "Trends and Goals," p. 322.

6. Larry D. Spence, "Political Theory as a Vacation," *Polity* 12 (Summer, 1980), p. 699.

7. For a reply to Strauss's insistence that Greek political philosophy was not associated with the notion of "theory" until the nineteenth century, see Dante Germino, "The Revival of Political Theory," *Journal of Politics* 25 (August, 1963), pp. 441-442. *What Is Political Philosophy? and Other Studies* (Glencoe, Illinois: The Free Press, 1959), p. 88. Also see Germino, *Beyond Ideology* (New York: Harper and Row Publishers, 1967), chapters 1, 2, and passim.

8. Germino, "The Revival of Political Theory," p. 441.

9. Wolin, "Trends and Goals," p. 319.

10. Germino, "The Revival of Political Theory," p. 441. The citations of Aristotle that Germino notes are from *Ethics* 1, 6, 10 and *Metaphysics* 1.2.

11. Hannah Arendt, *Between Past and Future* (New York: Viking Press, 1954), p. 17.

12. *Ibid.*, p. 18.

13. Wolin, "Trends and Goals," p. 319.

14. *Ibid.*

15. *Ibid.*, p. 322.

16. *Ibid.* (Alexis de Tocqueville, *Democracy in America*, 1835, Vol. 1, Chapter 18; trans. by Wolin).

17. On different notions of doubleness in political thought, see George Kateb, "Hannah Arendt: Alienation and America," *Raritan* 3 (Summer, 1983), pp. 27-28; and Arendt, *Between Past and Future*, p. 245.

18. David Easton, *The Political System* (New York: Alfred A. Knopf, 1953).

19. Alfred Cobban, "The Decline of Political Theory," *Political Science Quarterly* 68 (September, 1953), pp. 321-338.

20. T.D. Weldon, "Political Principles," *Philosophy, Politics, and Society* I, ed. Peter Laslett (Oxford: Basil Blackwell, 1956), pp. 22-34.

21. Peter Laslett, "Introduction," *Philosophy, Politics and Society* I, p. vii.

22. Robert A. Dahl, "Political Theory: Truth or Consequences," *World Politics* 11 (October, 1958), pp. 89-102.

23. Daniel Bell, *The End of Ideology: On the Exhaustion of Political Ideas in the Fifties* (New York: Free Press, 1960).

24. Strauss, "What Is Political Philosophy?" p. 345.

25. Arendt, *Between Past and Future*, p. 17.

26. Judith Shklar, *After Utopia: The Decline of Political Faith* (Princeton: Princeton University Press, 1957), p. 268.

27. *Ibid.*, p. 271.

28. *Ibid.*, p. 269.

29. *Ibid.*, p. 268.

30. *Ibid.*, p. ix.

31. *Ibid.*, p. 120.

32. *Ibid.*

33. Germino, "The Revival of Political Theory," pp. 452-454.

34. Strauss makes a similar argument, claiming that a historical study of the failures of political philosophy cannot invalidate political philosophy altogether. *What Is Political Philosophy? and Other Studies*, p. 62.

35. Easton, *The Political System*, p. 264.

36. *Ibid.*, p. 269.

37. *Ibid.*

38. Though Easton's proposed solution to the problems of political theory is to reassign political theory the task of value construction, thereby liberating it from the positivist requirements for verification.

39. Dahl, "Political Theory: Truth or Consequences," p. 87.

40. Note that systems-theorists distinguish the "system" from the "systematizing" approach of political theory, but it is dubious whether their approach avoids such generalizing.

41. Germino lists other revivalists as: C.J. Friedrich, John Hallowell, Karl Jaspers, Bertrand de Jouvenel, Jacques Maritain, Yves Simon, and perhaps Michael Oakeshott.

42. Wolin's book *Politics and Vision* received the 1985 Benjamin Evans Lippincott Award in Political Theory, awarded by the American Political Science Association. Sheldon S. Wolin, *Politics and Vision: Continuity and*

Innovation in Western Political Thought (Boston: Little, Brown & Company, 1960), p. 96.

43. Wolin, *Politics and Vision*, p. 130.
44. *Ibid.*
45. *Ibid.*, p. 287.
46. *Ibid.*, p. 288.
47. *Ibid.*
48. *Ibid.*, p. 353.
49. *Ibid.*, p. 430.
50. *Ibid.*, p. 331.
51. *Ibid.*, p. 350.
52. *Ibid.*, p. 430.
53. *Idem*, "Political Theory as a Vocation," p. 108.
54. *Idem*, *Politics and Vision*, p. 433.
55. *Ibid.*, p. 354.
56. *Ibid.*
57. *Ibid.*, p. 433.
58. *Ibid.*, p. 434.
59. *Ibid.*
60. *Ibid.*, p. 392.
61. *Ibid.*, p. 353.
62. *Ibid.*
63. *Ibid.*, p. 322.
64. Kateb criticizes Arendt on similar grounds. See "Hannah Arendt: Alienation and America."
65. C.B. Macpherson, *Democratic Theory: Essays in Retrieval* (Oxford: Clarendon Press, 1973), p. 195.
66. *Ibid.*, p. 197.
67. *Ibid.*, p. 4.
68. *Ibid.*, p. 199.
69. *Ibid.*, p. 196.
70. *Ibid.*, p. 202.
71. *Ibid.*, p. 23.
72. *Ibid.*, p. 201.
73. *Ibid.*
74. *Ibid.*
75. *Ibid.*
76. *Ibid.*, p. 202.
77. *Ibid.*, pp. 202-203.
78. *Ibid.*, p. 203.
79. This is not to say that Arendt's interest in the Greeks was simply to recover the Greek tradition as an end in itself; rather, I agree with those commentators who argue that Arendt used the Greeks to offer a subversive interpretation of modernity. See Stan Draenos, "The Totalitarian Theme in Horkheimer and Arendt," *Salgamundi* (Spring, 1982), p. 166; and George Kateb,

Hannah Arendt: Politics, Conscience, Evil (Totowa, N.J.: Rowman & Allanheld, 1984), p. 149.

80. I am not denying in this section that the "importance of geography, language, ethnicity, and religion, etc." is also *conceptual*, a matter of conceptualization; rather, I am suggesting something along the lines that political definition is essentially, or almost exclusively, "conceptual" or "theoretical" or "abstract" or "conventional," that political relationships are not essentially based upon "natural" categories (to whatever extent one might consider geography, language, etc. more "natural" than "conceptual"). Whether this emphasis represents a qualitative rather than quantitative difference in comparison with all other forms of conceptual self-definition (including family relations, ethnic relations, religious affiliation, etc.), I am unprepared to say. I could have written this section with a different set of adjectives testifying to the unique character of political relations--my point is imprecise, but what I am trying to convey is the sense in which political relationships are more strange, more unexpected, more contrived than all other forms of membership and exchange that human beings recognize for themselves. Hence I am interested in the extent to which the political realm *differs* from the family, the religious sect, the social unit, even though politics may also be regarded as intimately connected with these other areas of life. In this regard, my theoretical focus differs from psychoanalytic, sociological, or economic approaches to politics, although I am sympathetic with contemporary efforts to bring politics *closer* to these concerns, as part of an ongoing project of rethinking the "nature" of the political.

81. Wolin, *Politics and Vision*, p. 2.

82. *Ibid.*

83. *Ibid.*, p. 5.

84. *Ibid.*

85. *Ibid.*, p. 10.

86. *Ibid.*, p. 9.

87. *Ibid.*, p. 10.

88. *Ibid.*, p. 77. The term *visual* is Wolin's, not mine. But I believe Wolin uses *visual* rather than *visible* deliberately: He wishes to retain and convey the ambiguity inherent in the relationship between "direct" sensual engagement and "abstract" conceptualization. "Visual" means, according to the dictionary, "perceptible by sight" and is listed as being synonymous with "visible." But "visual" also connotes "perceptible by mind." In other words, Wolin is making a claim about the Greek *concept* of politics, arguing that the Greeks *based* the concept upon "visible" criteria--even though the concept was a concept, not some concrete given. I think he avoids the word *visible* because he does not wish to suggest that the Greek concept of politics was formed by some unmediated sensual experience (i.e., Wolin is not a positivist).

89. *Ibid.*, p. 70.

90. *Ibid.*, p. 71.

91. *Ibid.*

92. *Ibid.*, pp. 76-77.

93. *Ibid.*, p. 77.

94. *Ibid.*, p. 94.

95. *Ibid.*

96. Hannah Arendt, *The Human Condition* (Chicago: University of Chicago Press, 1958), chapter 2 especially.

97. Wolin, *Politics and Vision*, p. 77.

98. *Ibid.*, p. 73.

99. See above, note 88. Because Wolin's use of "visual" rather than "visible" is (I think) deliberate, his distinction between "abstract" and "visual" may not be as stark as it appears at first glance. Clearly, Wolin knows that the Greek concept of politics and the post-Greek concept of politics are both "abstract"--his point however is comparative. *My* point is that Wolin, *despite* his comparative conceptual insight, has not made the Greek concept "abstract" enough, has not respected the extent to which the Greeks themselves (or at least certain Greeks) consciously regarded the political sphere as "invisible" and *not* based upon mundane or face-to-face criteria.

100. Wolin, *Politics and Vision*, p. 64.

101. See above, notes 88 and 99. I continue to beg here the question of the separation between "natural" and "abstract" categories. Hanna Pitkin has rightly reminded me that *all* "concepts" are "abstract." Just as you can see a tree or a person, you can also see Athens, or Manhattan, or freedom, or justice, or cruelty. It just takes the right context. Yet I think the context of the concept of politics cannot so simply be presumed, for the strange thing about the concept of politics--unlike the concepts of forestness, personness, citydom, freedom, justice, or cruelty--is that the conceptualization of the political in large part *determines* the "context" of politics (i.e., there is a cart-and-horse relationship here); thus one cannot simply refer to "the" context in order to confirm instances and essences. On this score, I think Wolin is right: After the Greeks, one cannot "see" politics. I would add only that the same was true for the Greeks, too (and I based this claim upon my reading of the *Republic*).

102. Rawls in his more recent work has been attempting to formulate principles of political justification that are not "general and comprehensive" and yet can provide overlapping consensus for all persons within a liberal democratic polity.

103. John H. Schaar, "The Question of Justice," *Raritan* 3 (Fall, 1983), p. 108.

104. *Ibid.*, p. 114.

105. *Ibid.*, p. 122.

106. I also stand opposed, however, to those theorists who contend, in a confusing sweep of logic, that "everything" is but a fiction, a myth, a story, a narrative.

107. E.g., see Arendt, *Between Past and Future*, p. 25.

108. Clifford Geertz, *The Interpretation of Cultures* (New York: Basic Books, 1973), p. 29.

109. Arendt, *Between Past and Future*, p. 278.

110. Richard Rorty, *Contingency, Irony, and Solidarity* (Cambridge: Cambridge University Press, 1989).

111. Arendt equated the radical evil of concentration-camp totalitarianism with the terror of the hydrogen bomb; but she did so in order to make a point about the former rather than the latter. And in the very next paragraph after having made this equation, Arendt states that life in the concentration camp has no parallel. See Arendt, *The Origins of Totalitarianism* (New York and London: Harcourt Brace Jovanovich, 1951), pp. 443-444. By the way, Gunther Anders argued that "to threaten with atomic weapons is totalitarianism." See his essay in *A Matter of Life*, ed. Clara Urquhart (London: Jonathan Cape, 1963), pp. 16-17.

112. Wolin, *Politics and Vision*, p. 434.

113. It is noteworthy that Wolin mentions irony frequently with regard to Weber's personal politics: "Weber's leader is a political hero, rising to heights of moral passion and grandeur, harried by a deep sense of responsibility. But, at bottom, he is a figure as futile and pathetic as his classical counterpart. The fate of the classical hero was that he could never overcome contingency or *fortuna*; the special irony of the modern hero is that he struggles in a world where contingency has been routed by bureaucratized procedures and nothing remains for the hero to contend against" (p. 423); and "[The separation of facts and values] was equally the result of a desperate effort on Weber's part to secure some sphere where affirmation was possible and, most important, where bureaucratic and scientific rationality were impossible. Yet the matter did not rest there, for Weber left a final irony for personal action to contemplate: each individual bore the awful responsibility for choice at this ultimate level but each was denied anything like the scientist's sense of certainty." *Ibid.*, p. 424.

114. Schaar, "The Question of Justice," p. 118.

115. Hayden White, *Metahistory: The Historical Imagination in Nineteenth-Century Europe* (Baltimore: Johns Hopkins University Press, 1973).

116. Thomas Spragens, Jr., *The Irony of Liberal Reason* (Chicago: University of Chicago Press, 1981).

117. John S. Nelson follows Thomas Spragens's lead in viewing irony as rhetorical subversion, and he similarly understands irony as a way of avoiding commitments and thereby a way of comprehending intellectual pluralism. See "Political Theory as Political Rhetoric," in *What Should Political Theory Be Now?* ed. John S. Nelson (Albany: State University of New York Press, 1983), pp. 236-237. But as I will argue in Chapters 3 and 5, especially with respect to Thomas Mann, such a view of irony misses entirely the real heart of irony, which necessarily involves commitment.

118. Rorty, *Contingency, Irony, and Solidarity* .

119. *Ibid.*, p. 83.

120. *Ibid.*, p. 96.

121. George Kateb, *Utopia and Its Enemies* (New York: Schocken Books, 1972), p. vii.

2

Plato's Ironic Republic

He who would explain to us when men like Plato spoke in earnest, when in jest or half-jest, what they wrote from conviction and what merely for the sake of the argument, would certainly render us an extraordinary service and contribute greatly to our education.
--Goethe, "Plato, als Mitgenosse einer christlichen Offenbarung"

Why examine Plato's *Republic* yet again? Scholars have already pored over Plato's words countless times, exhibiting a devotion (or sustained rancor) second perhaps only to that of biblical exegetes. One would suppose that the arguments of the *Republic* have all been thoroughly explicated, analyzed, and digested; the issues raised by Plato have all been previously addressed, clarified, if not settled and laid to rest. The "tradition" of Platonic commentary is rich and time-honored and, one might suspect, complete. Thus to venture back to the well-traveled terrain of Plato's polis surely requires an explanation. And to propose further, as I shall eventually, that a reconsideration of Plato's *Republic* is not simply an academic exercise of little more than antiquarian interest but rather bears significantly upon contemporary political issues, such as the worldwide proliferation of thermonuclear weapons, is a claim that surely requires more elaborate justification.

My general purpose in proposing a reconsideration of the *Republic* is to focus renewed attention upon the concept of politics. To be sure, many modern political theorists have similarly turned to the Greeks for edification; but, as I suggested in Chapter 1, the results of these retrospective investigations still seem very much open to question. Using Sheldon Wolin's view of the Greeks as my test case, I argued that we have not yet grasped the uniqueness and complexity of the ancient polis. I offered critical evidence suggesting that the Greek notion of politics represented a triumph of theorizing, a construct of conceptualization, but that within the theoretical unity of the polis certain differences were necessarily acknowledged and inherently incorporated. I proposed, then, that perhaps we moderns have underestimated the extent to which the Greek concept of politics was itself a product of self-conscious ambivalence; that the Greeks themselves were aware of certain tensions involved in the very idea of politics; and that these ambivalences and tensions have not been sufficiently accommodated within, for example, Wolin's general notion of political community (based as it is upon the Greeks). The reinterpretation of the Greek concept of politics may in turn hold important implications for our understanding and practice of politics.

Quickly I must qualify these extravagant claims. I shall not try to prove my point for *all* Greeks, nor shall I be at all specific in identifying any details of time and place. Thus I am returning to the *Republic* not because it is necessarily representative but because it is indicative on its own terms--and I make no broader historical, sociological, or genealogical claims beyond that.[1] What I am doing instead is to illustrate an insight, to document an interpretive hunch, namely that, in certain circles at least, the Greeks understood politics as an art of constructing theoretical ties among human beings so that such beings might live together, despite differences.

I want to spell out the specific thesis of this chapter in advance, in order to avoid possible misreadings and to accommodate inevitable digressions. I am attempting to articulate a particular reading of the *Republic* that will contribute, directly I think, to a heightened understanding of Plato's concept of politics, which eventually should cast some light upon our own concept and practice of politics. This reading is an *ironic* one, or more precisely, it is one that is sensitive to Plato's ironies. Stated outright, I am contending that the *Republic* is a profoundly ironic work; but the full meaning of this claim requires further elaboration on the nature of irony in general and on the nature of Plato's irony in particular. That Plato's work contains ironies is, to be sure, no new insight[2]--other commentators, inspired by the ironies of Socrates' method, have discussed irony in connection with Plato's writings. But no one, save perhaps Goethe, has distinguished carefully between *Plato's* irony as a written philosophical stance and *Socrates'* irony as method and manner. That the two need to be distinguished, and only thereafter should be considered jointly, will be a major contention of mine. But for now I am claiming only that Plato's irony for the most part goes unappreciated and deserves consideration. Further, I wish to show that an ironic reading of the *Republic* is crucial for following Plato's thought on the relationship between philosophy and politics and that, finally, an understanding of this relationship as ironic holds significance for contemporary discussions pertaining to politics and philosophy.

Though the *Republic* has been subjected repeatedly to interpretive scrutiny, controversy over the book still abounds. At issue has been Socrates' logic (whether philosophically impeccable), Plato's political motives (whether aristocratic, conservative, reactionary, utopian, or radical), and the point and purpose of the book on the whole (whether philosophical, political, poetic, personal). Even a renewed interest in the subtleties of the ancient Greek language has settled few scores. Yet despite the great expenditure of scholarly labor on the matter, perhaps the discord generated by the book is not surprising after all. For the politics of the twentieth century--roughly characterized, *inter alia*, by the experiences of revolutionary movements, world ideologies, holocausts, and wars of mass destruction--has incited a reexamination of the relation between philosophy and politics, and the *Republic* has often been the starting point for these inquiries.[3]

Spearheading the campaign to reconsider the *Republic* in light of modern political developments was the now-legendary scholar Karl Popper. Popper not only reappropriated the *Republic* from the clutches of philosophical purists, declaring it to be at bottom a political document, but he also proclaimed that Plato's book was the source of most of the world's modern evils. In *The Open Society and Its Enemies*, Popper branded Plato as the forerunner of Marxism, totalitarianism, fascism, and antihumanism--all of which he claimed were versions of "historicist" thought in general. Although debates over the insights and anxieties of Popper have of late calmed a bit, the lines of opposition that he drew, between Platonism and liberalism, are still particularly telling. For not only did Popper take a hostile view toward what he understood to be Plato's political program, but he also declared an intellectual war between "philosophy" and "empiricism"; and he imputed to each thought system a respective political agenda. Thus, if we may take a cue from Popper, at stake in the rereading of Plato is not only the modern status of "the political" but also the status of the form of intellectual discourse appropriate to modern political practice. Thanks to Popper, then, the question of empiricism, or of the nature of science generally, as a legitimating doctrine for the modern nation-state becomes a pregnant topic in relation to Plato's thought and further warrants another return to the *Republic*.

In the following section, I will review and comment upon some of the previous attempts at reading the *Republic*. The survey is by no means exhaustive, first because such would be an impossible task, but principally because my purposes are not to classify systematically all possible lines of interpretation (a needless task). Rather, I present my selective review in order to place my ironic reading of the *Republic* in relation to other readings, especially those readings that advance claims about the status of the *Republic* as a political text. But my prodding commentary upon secondary commentary serves another purpose beyond simple scholarly comparison (which usually is a front for scholarly one-upmanship). If, as I shall argue, a central theme of the *Republic* is that of *returning*, and if irony plays heavily in that score, then a reasonable and related focus of attention is to catalogue other returns to the text. If, as I say, the *Republic* is a profoundly ironic work, how then has the irony affected other readers?[4]

Literalists

An older generation of learned Platonic scholars--including names such as Cornford, Adam, Grube, Nettleship, Shorey, and Taylor-- assumed the burden of mediating between Plato's text and the public.[5] Those scholars concerned themselves with providing translations and running narratives; and when they did venture from straight explication to engaged analysis, generally they restricted themselves to such endeavors as restating in their own terms Plato's "principle" of justice; rewording Plato's "one over the many" argument; scrutinizing several of Socrates' "definitions" for loopholes in the logic; elaborating upon central topics such as the education of the guardians, the banishment of the poets, or the tripartite division of the soul and its correspondence to the city. They tended to use categoric subtitles such as "Plato's Doctrine of X and X" and "Plato's Theory of So and So." Briefly--and my purpose here is not to disparage an older generation of scholars whose concerns no longer coincide with ours--members of this earlier group of scholars viewed their own relationship to the *Republic* as strictly formal and academic, i.e., that as informed readers of Plato they were to translate obscure passages, explicate arguments, and finally to provide *answers* to the questions posed by the book. Again, my intent is not to disparage, but I do wonder what strange blend of immodesty and deference motivated those commentators who presumed themselves to be able to restate Plato's position, only better (a classic example is Shorey's book *What Plato Said*). One finds, however, this tradition carried on admirably and forcefully in certain essays of Vlastos' *Plato I* and *Plato II*, e.g., whether the *Republic* is "utilitarian" or not, whether the "main line of argumentation" is "fallacious," and so on.[6]

In the same way that the above authors can be grouped together as having read the *Republic* mainly as a (more or less) formal philosophical text, so can Popper's criticisms be regarded as having issued from a similar perspective on the book, also taking it foremost as a logical piece. The difference was that Popper emphasized the political ramifications of the logic rather than focusing upon questions of, for instance, justice and art as matters of abstract argument. But, to repeat, the assumption that the book follows, and advocates, a singular logic brings Popper into close company with the older generation of Platonic scholars. Popper in *The Open Society* set out to enumerate, in order to attack, the various features of Plato's political program--the "formula" as he called them. Following the leads of Crossman and Fite, Popper charged that Plato embraces in his *Republic*: (1) a class society with a rigid class system, which separates the ruling class from the ruled; (2) a system of intellectual censorship and manipulative propaganda, described in sections such as (as he calls it) the "Myth of Blood and Soil"; (3) a collectivism that oppresses the individual and is "anti-equalitarian." His chapters build to a climax with the charge that Plato's books encompass a plan of "utopian engineering," the hallmark of which is "an uncompromising radicalism." He concluded his book as he began, with the proposition that Plato's *Republic* not only anticipates modern totalitarianism but, more, is "fundamentally identical with it"[7] (whatever that means).

For the record, I should note that Bertrand Russell followed Popper's teachings on Plato, emphasizing with equal vehemence the point that insidious consequences are unleashed upon politics whenever philosophic ideals take hold. Russell garnered evidence for his case by pointing to the deleterious effects of philosophy in the allegedly similar cases of the Nazis, the Soviets, and the Catholics. I should also note the curiosity that Sheldon Wolin's commentary upon Plato is a watered-down version of Popper's dated liberal criticism. Wolin likewise asserts that Plato, in eliminating the conflict that is the agon of an open, democratic society, essentially eliminates politics from his polis. Both Popper and Wolin (as well as Arendt) charge Plato with the erudite error of regarding politics as a matter of artistic design and philosophic engineering rather than active participation by individuals.[8]

Susan Okin offers still another interpretation[9] of the *Republic* that also extracts a distinct line of argumentation from the work, and in this respect her reading parallels Popper's, though the conclusions she draws, or her evaluations of them, are very different. She focuses on the status of women in the *Republic*, in particular the status of the female guardians. She notes that Plato apparently approves of women sharing equally in citizenship (a radical departure from the prevailing Greek sentiments of his day). And at least with regard to the guardian class, Plato prescribes what amounts to a radically feminist perspective (according to some accounts of feminism): abolition of the family (along with the abolition of private property), and the abolition of traditional sex roles. Whereas Popper feels threatened by Plato's proposals, regarding them as anti-individualist, Okin approves of Plato's *Republic* (unlike his *Laws*) insofar as Plato attempts to consider women as persons in their own right. For her, the *Republic* issues a trenchant statement redefining (and inverting) the distinction between nature and convention with respect to matters of gender.

I suggest that all of the above readings of and reactions to Plato's *Republic* can be categorized in similar fashion, namely that all take Plato pretty much *at his word*--through Socrates as his direct spokesman--though each may interpret the word of Plato differently. In other words, commentators such as Shorey, Popper, and Okin take the book *literally* (according to their own understandings of the literal meaning of the book), presuming that Plato's overall point in the *Republic*, or even the meaning of the book separate from the author's intentions, corresponds directly to a straight reading of Socrates' speeches. This reading strategy informs these authors' conclusions, prompting the suspicion that Plato is advocating some position through Socrates as his mouthpiece. For a literal reading of the text urges one to accept the expressed purpose of the dialogue as a quest for the "ideal" of justice, in the city and the soul; and this acceptance entails that one respect the implied division between the "ideal" and the "real" (or "actual"), in other words the division between the essential world and the apparent world. Such a reading of the book forces, in due course, the question of whether such a division is literally true. Or, in more ethical terms, the choice presented is between "what ought to be" and "what is," between enlightenment and shadowy illusion. The juxtaposition forces a choice: One must either entertain the *Republic* as a wonderful vision that Plato has graciously shared with us, or else one can view it as a dreadful imposition, one of frightful standards wished upon humanity without regard for the frailties of the individual. According to the latter view, the *Republic* holds the possibility for terrible consequences, which necessarily manifest themselves either in Plato's faulty logic or in his faulty politics. According to the former view, the *Republic* awakens us to certain absolute and profound truths about human nature and the ways of the world.

If I may interject at this point a personal aside, I must say that even in my first impressions of the book I never felt as singularly reverential as Plato's admirers seem to be nor as singularly threatened as his detractors seem to be. (If anything, my early encounters with the book left me confused, though the bewilderment itself piqued my interest.) I never felt that Socrates' musings were designed to proselytize, nor did I suspect Socrates to be an advocate of propagandism and a prophet of communism. In short, I never took the book as literally as these readings require. In addition, the tendentious interpretations that a literal reading encourages seem to be held only at the expense of ignoring or overlooking certain passages and rejoinders in which Socrates says-- equally literally, if one takes everything at face value--that he does not think his just state is at all feasible. Do these provisos, then, make Plato less of a totalitarian or less of a feminist? For now, I will leave my criticism of the above critics confined to this: If the *Republic* is ironic (and profoundly so!), they seem to have missed it.[10]

Dramatists

Another school of commentary--inspired by the inimitable Leo Strauss--does not take the *Republic* quite so literally as did its older counterparts. Instead, the Straussians emphasize the importance of the dramatic design and character development implicit in the text. By reading "between the lines"[11] of the text and by drawing upon all hidden clues, they purport to be able to decipher the concealed meaning of the book. That Glaucon protests against vegetarianism,[12] for instance, may count as evidence for interpreting Plato's grander intentions and ulterior motives in a particular passage, whereas the "argument itself," the "exoteric" text, is viewed as a kind of window dressing or theater prop.

Strauss employs his technique, however, tendentiously. The main lesson he draws from his dramatic insight is that philosophy and philosophical justice consist of a deliberate abstraction from "eros."[13] This means that the dictates of philosophy militate against the natural concerns of the body and, conversely, that the common run of human beings (who evidently let their bodily passions govern them) will naturally repudiate philosophy.[14] The philosopher, then, ever prone to public persecution, must use indirect methods to pursue philosophic knowledge and to transmit his truths, lest he come to bodily harm. Strauss contends that an example of such indirect transmission occurs in Socrates' exchanges with Thrasymachus, as viewed over the course of the book. When he first breaks onto the scene, Thrasymachus argues with Socrates in a violent, vicious manner, an unruly display that reveals that Thrasymachus is ruled by his temper (and accordingly he advances a definition of justice that reflects his tyrannical temper).[15] Yet one observes toward the end of his exchange with Socrates that Thrasymachus has calmed down somewhat. Even though Thrasymachus has not been convinced by Socrates' arguments, he has been "tamed" by them.[16] By *showing* us Thrasymachus' character development, Plato has meanwhile conveyed to us a hidden philosophical point: Philosophical logic alone cannot change people's natures--at best they can be tamed--but there is something to be said for the taming of such tyrants.[17] Hence the dramatic form reveals at least two levels of complexity, and as Strauss's students we learn to abstract from the literal text in order to discern Plato's hidden and higher points. As readers who can distinguish between exoteric texts and esoteric teachings, we ourselves learn how to engage in philosophy, in the art of thinking independently, of abstracting from the corporeal world.

Yet Strauss does not stop here, with the satisfaction of knowing that he is pursuing, and enabling a select few others to pursue, the private virtues of philosophy. He goes on to draw certain conclusions about politics from his hard-won philosophic insight. Strauss garners textual evidence in support of the claim that Plato reveals a vision of a perfect city *not* so that we might aspire to it as a real worldly possibility. Rather, Plato artfully relegates his "utopia" to the sphere of the impossible precisely so that we may understand the marked difference between the possible and the purely visionary when it matters in an actual political setting.[18] A just city is impossible, we learn, because it abstracts from human nature.[19] The fictional portrayal of a perfect city in the *Republic*, then, is but a limiting concept[20] for real politics. The philosopher's perfected version of justice embraces a vision of a common humanity, according to which all humans see themselves as brothers and sisters. Yet worldly circumstances behoove even the philosopher to reject the ideals of communism and brotherhood for the sake of freedom and self-preservation.[21] The philosopher then must accept two mutually exclusive yet mutually reinforcing versions of justice,[22] a "perfect" or "philosophical" justice and a "worldly" or "political" justice. Worldly justice, then, will entail that one be able to distinguish friend from foe,[23] and that one even be capable of hating one's enemies[24] (even despite one's higher brotherly sentiments).

Thus for Strauss, the text of the *Republic* conceals a complex logic of reversal and substitution. The book is only ostensibly about the "state," for the apparent "political argument . . . conceals the transpolitical argument" and the transpolitical argument in turn "sets limits" to what is really political.[25] In short, Plato is but floating a trial balloon in the *Republic*. He parrots Socrates in order to convey to us the message that what attracts the idealistic philosopher repels us (as common folk or as prudent philosophers). The ideal of a world in which the sexes enjoy equality[26] and in which property is shared communally,[27] for instance, belongs solely to the philosopher's perverse palate, whereas in real terms such ideals are, for the rest of us, "against human nature." In short, Strauss's entire argument about Plato's philosophic utopia affords backhanded support for a worldly politics that is exclusivistic,[28] patriotic,[29] militaristic,[30] inegalitarian,[31] anticommunist,[32] meritocratic,[33] and democratic[34] (albeit in Strauss's authoritarian and "second-best" sense of democracy). Whereas Popper decried Plato's "utopianism" as a threat to liberal democracy, Strauss now agrees with Popper's view of the basic opposition between utopia and democracy but accepts Plato as an indirect ally in the battle.

If Popper fell victim to Socrates' irony, taking his utopia too literally, then certainly Strauss is prudent enough to read between the lines; yet his entire argument is based upon, or expresses, a peculiar understanding of irony, an analysis of which helps to account for his backhanded politics. He states at the beginning of his essay on the *Republic* that "it is one of Socrates' peculiarities that he was a master of irony."[35] Strauss then inquires into the significance of the fact that Plato uses an ironist--who professes ignorance--as his spokesman. "Could it be true that Plato, like his Socrates, the master of the knowledge of ignorance, did not assert anything, i.e., did not have a teaching?"[36] After a brief analysis of Socrates' "demonic gift," Strauss reaches the conclusion that "the assumption that the Platonic dialogues do not convey a teaching is absurd."[37] Strauss then stakes his interpretation of the *Republic* upon his understanding of irony: "Very much, not to say everything, seems to depend on what Socratic irony is."[38]

So Strauss turns at this point to Aristotle in order to divine the meaning of Socrates' irony (thus finding the key to Plato's "teaching"). Aristotle treats irony, Strauss tells us, as a kind of "dissimulation," or "untruthfulness." Thus it is primarily a "vice." But Strauss adds his own twist to Aristotle's treatment, claiming that if irony is a vice, it is a "graceful vice." And then he goes one step further: If irony is "properly used, it is not a vice at all."[39] Here Strauss has expanded upon--and wandered from--Aristotle's definition. For Aristotle gives faint and reluctant praise to irony, and he does so only in a direct comparison of irony with its antithesis, *alazoneia* (boastfulness). But Strauss uses this foot in the door to declare that irony implies--not ignorance in the least--but knowledge and "superiority" in the highest. "Irony is then the noble dissimulation of one's worth, of one's superiority. We may say, it is the humanity peculiar to the superior man: he spares the feelings of his inferiors by not displaying his superiority. The highest form of superiority is the superiority of wisdom. Irony in the highest sense will then be the dissimulation of one's wisdom, i.e., the dissimulation of one's wise thoughts."[40]

Moreover, irony is necessary, according to Strauss, because there is a "natural order of rank among men," and irony is a mode of communication that allows one to say different things to the different ranks of men: It is a shotgun approach. In *Persecution and the Art of Writing*, Strauss explains why this must be so. Irony is a mode of discourse one adopts when one fears persecution for one's independent beliefs. Plato couched his philosophic truths in a dramatic form out of fear of receiving the kind of reprisal that Socrates suffered at the hands of the Athenians. So, thanks to the Janus-faced ingenuity of irony, the boors will miss the point, the elect will see the light, and the philosopher will remain safely superior (if nobly patronizing as well).

For Strauss, then, irony is a particular manner of speaking or mode of writing. But it is not *simply* a rhetorical or dramatic technique, nor is it merely a form of artful dissimulation. Rather, irony seems to hold for Strauss epistemological ramifications. Irony for Strauss implies dissimulation of some superior trait--as if that superiority is some fact of nature--and he identifies this trait as wisdom. Hence, Strauss rejects out of hand Socrates' own profession of ignorance, declaring it to be a mere cover. For instance, in commenting upon Socrates' apparent inability to define justice in Book 1 of the *Republic*, Strauss flatly asserts that "surely Socrates is able to identify the what of a thing."[41] Later, Strauss describes the dissembling Socrates as "a man who pretends to be ignorant while in fact he knows things very well; far from being ignorant and innocent he is clever and tricky."[42] In short, irony is, for Strauss, a covert means of being authoritative, if not doctrinaire, in one's views, where one's authority would otherwise be disallowed. Thinking himself privy to the mechanics of irony, Strauss is able to draw certain unequivocal conclusions about the *Republic*. Strauss's professed ability to see through Socrates' ignorance allows Strauss to state confidently his own nonignorance with respect to the true meaning of the *Republic*, and also to the true meaning of politics in general.[43] For Strauss, the *Republic* is not fundamentally a philosophic quest but is an analytic jigsaw puzzle, to which he thinks he has found the single solution: "The *Republic* itself, properly read, supplies the answer to these questions."[44]

Stanley Rosen, in his rendition of Plato's use of irony,[45] exaggerates a theme that is already evident in Strauss's thought; and a comparison of the two is instructive for pinpointing what they view as ironic. Rosen retrospectively applies not Aristotle's, but Quintilian's definition of irony to the *Republic*, namely that irony is an expression in which the meaning is the "opposite" of what is said. Following this formula of substitution, Rosen not only discounts the seriousness of Plato's utopia as a viable political model but also rejects the literal text to the extent that he concludes that the entire book is a "kind of joke, a satire." Although Rosen neglects to differentiate among the various rhetorical and dramatic strategies of satire, comedy, irony, and humor, his flat equation of irony with satire betrays his understanding of irony as a total rejection of the literal in favor of its "opposite." This interpretive mechanism allows him, in turn, to draw the same political conclusions from his dramatic reading as Strauss does from his.[46]

Thus: Strauss takes Aristotle's definition of irony and twists it into a mechanism of reversal and substitution. Rosen furthers this argument by aligning the notion of irony with satire. Another frequent follower of Strauss, Arlene Saxonhouse, goes beyond Rosen to argue that the irony of the *Republic* must be read not as subtle satire but rather as outrageous comedy: "We cannot isolate the famous Socratic irony from Plato's own comic art."[47] In equating irony with comedy, Saxonhouse claims to have strengthened Strauss's original interpretation of the *Republic*, as a sham utopia that is to be taken as such. I contend, however, that the same questions that applied to Strauss's understanding of irony and to Rosen's understanding of satire apply to Saxonhouse's understanding of comedy.

Saxonhouse elaborates upon Strauss's occasional references to animal imagery in the *Republic* and upon his comment that Socrates' parallel between the city and the soul is "ludicrous." She carefully studies the references and allusions to animals in the *Republic* and argues that these animal images illustrate the book's connection to the comic world of Aristophanes. The comedy, moreover, is intended to undercut the ostensible perfection of Socrates' city, indicating the limitations of politics rather than its potentialities. For instance, whereas Okin read the passages on women *literally*, contending that Plato was advancing a bold argument for sexual equality, Saxonhouse contends that "in arguing for the equality of the sexes Socrates is presenting a notion so alien to Greek thought that it is fit only for the comic stage."[48] Socrates presents these ridiculous ideas, for example that men and women should exercise together,[49] so that they will be taken for what they are--absurd--and accordingly will be rejected. Saxonhouse contends further that the comedy of the *Republic* contributes overall to the view that social justice is "laughable" and that the point and purpose of the book is to orient the idea of justice away from social life and toward the private individual.

The problem with Saxonhouse's argument lies not in the evidence she cites but in her analysis of it via her concept of "comedy." She does not state a convincing case that comedy necessarily implies--or was supposed to imply, according to Plato--*rejection* and dismissal. First she needs to explain why animal images as applied to humans are (or were at the time) necessarily funny. She then needs to explain why humorous images are to be taken with disdain rather than with simple amusement. She tries to associate, to equate, the concept of comedy with repulsion by using intermediary words such as "ugly," "grotesque," "ridiculous," "laughable," and "absurd"; but one wonders why comedy could not equally be related to pleasure, entertainment, celebration, affirmation, and joy.

Saxonhouse tries to account for her overly pejorative view of comedy by invoking Aristophanes and thereby drawing a direct connection between the *Republic* and the *Birds*; but this explanation seems hasty at best.[50] For one thing, Aristophanes' work appears outwardly and forthrightly comedic and satirical. If Plato's intent in writing the *Republic* was so tied to the *Birds*, why did he couch his comedy in cryptic language and bury it in metaphors? Why not go straight to the punch line? In other words, Plato and Socrates make at least occasional concessions to serious matters, even if those shows of seriousness are mostly mock. Since Saxonhouse insists that Socrates' humor undercuts the ostensible idealism of the book, she needs additionally to explain why Socrates so often undercuts his own humor with pretenses of solemnity. Her basic line of reasoning--"If it is funny in Aristophanes, why isn't it funny in Plato?"[51]--ignores and hence fails to address the complex *interplay* of humor and seriousness that characterizes the dialogue throughout the *Republic*.

Finally, there appears to be an inconsistency between Saxonhouse's main argument and her conclusion. She states that Socrates' suggestion that citizens are animals undercuts politics. Saxonhouse's interpretation of the allegedly inherent opposition between animals and citizens is itself bizarre: "By turning human beings into animals as they participate in politics, Socrates takes away from them their humanity."[52] Apparently, their "humanity," according to Saxonhouse's interpretation of Plato, means that human beings are in their innermost essence nonanimals. The *Republic*, she explains, is an attempt to purge politics of the body and therefore is a ridiculous attempt because politics cannot in fact abstract from the body.[53] If it is somehow naturally true that "politics cannot abstract from the body," one might ask Saxonhouse, then what was so wrong with Plato's use of bodily and bestial imagery in the first place?

Evidently, what Saxonhouse really objects to is the mixing of metaphors, that is, the attempt to link mind and body or to relate philosophy and politics. For though Saxonhouse contends that the *Republic* makes philosophic notions look silly when they are applied to politics, she somehow at the end of her article redeems philosophical abstraction as a noble pursuit--but she reserves it as a virtue for the lone individual, not for the society at large. One wonders: If philosophic ideals and philosophic contemplation are ridiculous and grotesque for societies, why are they all right for individual philosophers? I confess that I cannot follow Saxonhouse's logic beyond this point. She reasons that since the *Republic* makes people into animals, it deprives them of their "potentialities": "It is only when human beings are allowed to recognize their deficiencies that philosophy is possible."[54] I think that what Saxonhouse is implying is that people can be thought capable of improvement only if the possibility is held in reserve that human beings can transcend their animallike existence. And politics, for her, defies and defeats transcendence. But then I am left utterly baffled by Saxonhouse's final remark: "True political activity occurs . . . [only] in the private discourse of a few individuals engaged in intellectual inquiry and philosophic endeavor, recognizing their deficiencies, their distance from perfection, as the animals of Socrates' city reenacting the comedies of Aristophanes do not and cannot."[55]

In their "dramatic" readings of the text, Strauss, Rosen, and Saxonhouse have not made an adequate case for the view that the ironic mode (and Plato's irony in particular) signifies an all-out rejection of what they consider the literal layer of the text.[56] First, they fail to account on aesthetic or philosophic grounds for Plato's use of irony. Instead, Strauss offers two extraneous reasons why Plato must "resort" to the ironic mode, one historical, the other ontological. According to the first reason, Plato employs irony in reaction to the historical fact of Socrates' execution. According to the second (which is related to the first), Plato employs irony in order to address men of different natures--which is to presume of course that men are in fact of different natures. In both cases irony serves as a cover over objectionable matters. Rosen and Saxonhouse are silent regarding the question of why one would turn comedic, perhaps because Strauss's explanation for irony--that one fears persecution--does not jibe well with comedy.

The problem with these readings is that they require a *total* rejection of the literal layer without explaining sufficiently why the author even bothered to state a literal case at all. The literal text, upon such a reading, becomes simply gratuitous (which presupposes, furthermore, that one can even identify and isolate the "literal layer" to be rejected). Popper may have taken the "political" argument in the *Republic* too literally, but the Straussians do not take it seriously enough. Why would Plato make a case for utopia if his real point is to make a case against utopia? If Plato's point is to reject visionary politics and instead to set limits to *Realpolitik*, then why do so tongue-in-cheek? That he feared persecution might account for his departure from the literal mode, but persecution alone would not account for his substantive presentation of a utopia, and this utopia in particular. How, exactly, would a book about a communistic, equalitarian state (as opposed to any of a multitude of other possible topics) provide Plato with a cover for his personal safety?

The Straussian school views irony as a simple reversal mechanism, a way of saying one thing and meaning the "opposite." This view of irony is problematic, however, because (1) it presumes that the reader is able to distinguish sharply between the "literal" layer and its "opposite," as if such distinct layers and such oppositions necessarily exist; and (2) it reduces the "literal" layer to mere subterfuge, thus committing the fallacy of explaining substantive meaning by analyzing an expression's rhetorical function. I pointed out that Strauss borrowed his definition of irony from Aristotle and that he twisted Aristotle's definition in a way that allowed him to extract certain political conclusions from his dramatic renderings of the text. But (to repeat) Strauss himself staked virtually his entire interpretation of the *Republic* upon his view of irony: "Very much, not to say everything, seems to depend on what Socratic irony is."[57] Hence, by Strauss's own admission, since his view of irony is dubious, then his entire argument must be considered suspect. If Plato was indeed a backhanded and closet supporter of Strauss's strong-arm version of democracy, then Plato certainly was circuitous in his approach--and the critical reader should demand more of a reason for this oddity than either Strauss or any of his followers has been able to give.

Although neither a member of the school of "dramatic" readers nor a Straussian, Werner Jaeger, in his *Paideia* books, articulates in a more sensible and straightforward fashion what Strauss attempted to formulate in his "transpolitical" argument.[58] Jaeger, too, claims that the arguments of the surface dialogue obscure the real meaning of the *Republic*. And he maintains that the central theme of the *Republic* is "about" justice as a personal virtue--as do the Straussians. But Jaeger does not regard the relationship between the state and (perfect) justice, between politics and *paideia*, as being essentially antagonistic as do Strauss and company. Jaeger begins his chapter on the *Republic*: "From the very start, Plato's thinking is aimed at solving the problem of the state."[59] Jaeger goes on to qualify this opening with the observation that what Plato meant by the "state" is not what is meant either by the state or by politics in a modern sense. The *Republic* is not concerned with constitutional law, nor with the art of governance, nor with legislation. Nor does Plato bind his considerations to any particular geographical setting. But the question of justice as personal virtue is for Jaeger, as he claims it is for Plato, related intimately to the constitution of the state. Jaeger reasons that Plato's "ultimate interest" is undoubtedly education and the "building of souls." But this enterprise is to take place in the "vivid, tangible form of the state," and the whole point of depicting justice as a virtue is to instill in the philosopher an inclination to return to his "true home," which is the city.

I will not press the details of Jaeger's lengthy exposition any further. For purposes here, it suffices to say that Jaeger presents a convincing case in support of the view that Plato's main theme in the *Republic* concerns the symbiotic relationship between politics and education. Yet if Strauss is too tendentious in his account of the interaction, or opposition rather, between the realms of the ideal and the real in the *Republic*, then perhaps Jaeger's version is too conciliatory.[60] Ernst Cassirer, in his *Myth of the State*, makes precisely that charge. He contends that Jaeger too easily resolves the question of whether the philosopher is inclined toward or summoned back to the political world. Cassirer points out two tendencies present in Plato's thought--one, to surpass the empirical world, and the other, to return to the empirical world. Jaeger smooths over the tension between the two (and thereby he undercuts the pathos and the profundity of the ambivalence in the book) by providing a straightforward albeit quasi-religious account of the education of the "soul." But the account exacts credulity. Jaeger is right, it seems to me, to assert the connection between *paideia* and politics, which helps to compensate for the oversights of the Platonic logicians and for the overstatements of the Straussians; but Cassirer is right to remind Jaeger of the unresolved tensions in Plato's thought and to alert us that Jaeger's account of the state and of the soul is self-consciously "mythical."[61]

If I may at this point--even after the somewhat discursive presentation of the above criticism--recover my implicit claim that the "dramatists" constitute a school of Platonic interpretation to be contrasted with the "literalists," then I will now interject a provisional comparison of the two. The literalists were distinctive in their singular or one-dimensional relation to the text: They felt that the *Republic* represented a unitary line of argumentation (or failed in its attempt to do so), and they translated and analyzed it accordingly. The dramatists differed from the literalists insofar as they perceived at least two interpretive layers present in the text and accordingly employed a comparative perspective in their commentary on the point and purpose of the book.[62] Substantively this meant that the dramatists regarded Plato's division between the logical and the dramatic, or between the utopian and the political, or between the "ideal" and the "real," as more complex than it would at first appear. Yet my criticism of the above dramatic theorists was that they analyzed the *Republic* according to a questionable strategy of drama or irony, which in turn allowed them to resolve the textual oppositions in favor of one side or another (again, as if the "sides" or "layers" could be clearly identified and juxtaposed). I suggested that their analyses were not only based upon a narrow definition of irony but had also failed to present convincing cases accounting for Plato's evident use of the ironic mode of presentation. Hence it is not so surprising that the self-proclaimed champions of strong-arm democracy, Strauss and Popper, should apply such radically different interpretive strategies to the book and arrive at such opposite conclusions, despite their similar political outlooks; for throughout they are of like mind regarding the basic terms of opposition between utopianism and liberal democracy, and they are eager to resolve the textual tensions completely in favor of the latter.

Historicists

I propose to define a third cluster of interpreters, a group whose members characteristically make general sense of the *Republic* by enforcing the interpretive distinction between the "historical" Socrates and the "Platonic" Socrates; in other words, the readers of this group recognize a marked discrepancy between the historical Socrates' teachings and Plato's philosophy. On record exists a good deal of historical and textual evidence justifying the respect for such a distinction. Scholars have grouped the dialogues according to style, and some have argued that the stylistic groupings correspond to the major periods in Plato's life. His works so arranged, Plato's views seem to have changed over the course of his fifty years of authorship. These periods have been identified roughly as: first, the period after Socrates' execution in 399 B.C., during which time Plato traveled to Cyrene, to Egypt, and possibly to Phoenicia; also during this time he served in the Athenian army; second, the period after the foundation of his academy (386-385 B.C.), which postdates a stay with a sect of the Pythagoreans around 388 as well as a trip to Sicily at the behest of Dion, brother-in-law of the tyrant of Syracuse, Dionysius I; third, the period after two more failed trips to Syracuse, in 367 and 361, up to his death in 347 B.C.[63]

Book 1 of the *Republic*, several commentators have contended, was written sometime during the "first period," after Socrates' death, while the rest of the *Republic* was written during the second period, probably around 375 B.C.[64] Obvious stylistic differences between Book 1 and the remaining books support the view that Plato wrote the *Republic* in two stages. Book 1 has Socrates primarily in the role of questioner, one who himself gives only short answers, and who never commits himself to any set position. Thereafter, the dialogue form all but drops out; he asks far fewer questions of his youthful opponents, and, in an uncharacteristic display, Socrates expatiates at length about his republic, committing himself to an elaborate and developed philosophical position.[65]

It is often argued further that these stylistic differences betray changes in Plato's own philosophical outlook and can be related to the circumstances of his biography. In the first period of his writing, Plato remains impressed by the martyred (or suicidal) Socrates. Hence Plato's presentation in Book 1 more accurately reflects the dialogue of the "historical" Socrates and is less the product of a creative Plato. The exchanges in Book 1 revolve around Socrates' primary concern with ethical--as opposed to political or philosophical--questions, in the pursuit of which a life of ongoing examination is more crucial than arriving at and formulating a set doctrine. Some Plato-watchers go on to speculate that after his exposure to the strange, mystical insights of the Pythagorean cult, and after founding his own academy for philosophical statesmen, Plato felt confident that he had found the answers to Socrates' persistent and incessant questions; and thus Plato became more a systematic philosopher, as opposed to a Socratic moralist and resident gadfly. It is alleged that further evidence of Plato's transformation, particularly concerning the Pythagorean influence in his thought, is to be found in his many later references to geometry, music, astronomy, dialectical logic, and the afterlife; and his experience at the academy is thought surely to have informed the middle chapters on the education of philosophers.

The foregoing thesis is not particularly heterodox--most Plato scholars accept some division between Socrates and Plato; the crucial difference from interpretation to interpretation, however, follows from the significance critics attach to or deduce from the division. Hegel, for one, interprets the division between Socrates and Plato as indicative of a decisive shift in the history of philosophical consciousness. Although Hegel, in his *History of Philosophy*, views Socrates and Plato as *jointly* combatting the influence of the sophists of their day as

well as the earlier nature philosophers (even though Hegel also claims
that both Plato and Socrates incorporated aspects of sophism and
naturalism into their philosophies),[66] Hegel reads Socrates' contribution to the development of philosophy as fundamentally distinct from
Plato's contribution.

The personage of Socrates represents for Hegel a moment in history
at which philosophy moved in the direction of the increased
"subjectivity" of thought. Whereas the sophists in their own way had
promoted consciousness of humanly negotiated standards of proper
conduct, Socrates refined their nascent anthropomorphism into an acute
consciousness of the subject, of the "I" that is separate from nature. The
Socratic "subjective morality," however, recognized the "spiritual
universal" within the particular I--man had the "outside" within him,
the objective was seen as located within the subject--and hence no
longer was man simply the measure of all things, as the sophists
taught. Socrates, according to Hegel, added ethics as a new conception
to philosophy. A student of the Socratic school was to act from deep
conviction, conviction based upon an "objective principle" within the
subject, and was not simply to conform to an external standard or law or
convention or moral precept, even if it was generally deemed proper.
But if this, the ethics of personal examination and conviction, was the
philosophical meaning of Socrates' historical dialogues, then,
according to Hegel, Socrates' "philosophy" must be viewed as "in a
piece with his life." The content of his philosophy directly informed
his method, a method namely of continual interpersonal conversation
and exchange. But this means that Socrates' philosophy, which was
indistinguishable from his philosophizing, cannot be abstracted or
displaced from the context of Athens, the site of those particular
conversations and dialogues. So considered, Socrates' philosophizing
must be criticized from a more developed standpoint of philosophy; and
a philosophy sufficiently self-conscious to be critical would render the
conclusion that Socrates' philosophical tendencies did not proceed from
the level of interpersonal dialogue to that of a science or a "system."

Hegel elaborates his analysis and critique of Socrates by examining
the irony in Socrates' method. According to Hegel, the point of
Socrates' pointed remarks was to inspire men to distrust their inherited
presuppositions and, in turn, to look for more principled ("objective")
guidance within themselves. He did this not primarily through a
twist of the logical screws but by presenting himself in an ironic manner.
To bring others to express their own presuppositions (so that they might
put them up for examination), Socrates frequently presented himself as
ignorant of conventional beliefs; he disingenuously put questions to his
opponents as if they were to instruct *him*, while in fact he was really

drawing common notions out of them for their sake. Hegel claims that this process was a form of *dialectics*, but was only a *subjective* form, i.e., it was an interpersonal--and not fully *logical*--give-and-take process. Irony is thus a manner of talking against *people*, but it fails to address what Hegel calls the "Idea itself."[67] Socrates' ironic manner drew out and broke the hold of established morality; and in Athens this entailed questioning one's traditional reliance upon Homer. Whereas Hegel views this process favorably--for in breaking the Athenians of their arrogance, Socrates helped them to think for themselves--Hegel is quick to remind his reader that Socrates' irony was an essentially *negative* development in the history of philosophy--even if it served as a goad toward greater philosophical accomplishment later on in the course of history.

Politically, Hegel regards irony as being especially insidious, for it is, he claims, detrimental to the existence of the state. The state depends for its existence upon the fact that certain notions are held in common by persons in their particularity: "But the State really rests on thought, and its existence depends on the sentiments of men, for it is a spiritual and not a physical kingdom."[68]

If the state is indeed a spiritual entity, then Socrates' irony was destructive of that spirit: That was its very aim in Athens. Hegel thus writes that Socrates' execution was justified from the particular political perspective of the Athenian court. Even the fact that Socratic morality and the related demise of Athens contributed, according to Hegel's long-run view of things, to the philosophical development of independent thought and to the realization of world spirit in the universal state does not seem to redeem irony in Hegel's mind. Irony, for Hegel, can only dissolve and can never construct, and thus it must not be valued in its own right, especially in political matters. Like the dialectic, irony "gives force to what is taken immediately" (just as Socrates gave the impression that he took seriously the examples of justice that his opponents presented to him), but irony takes something seriously only to promote its trivialization. At its best, irony, raised to the status of a system, systematically expresses a view of the "inherent irony of the world"--and thus of the triviality of the world and all endeavor.

But the problem is not irony's negativity per se; rather, the philosophical problem that irony poses for politics is that it sets the individual *against* the state permanently. Only the subjective consciousness maintains its validity after irony reveals the emptiness and vanity of the world. Hegel notes, however, that Socrates' own brand was not a satirical but a tragic irony: The terminus to his inquiries was a steadfast and lasting *opposition* of subjective reflection to conventional morality, a resistance that found its culmination in Socrates' own death. Yet this care for the self, Hegel maintains, was at the expense of the state. Socrates' integrity, his conviction that Athens's laws would be invalidated or jeopardized unless he upheld them in his person, *required* that he accept his death sentence--or, in grander language, Socrates' death attested to the sharp antagonism between philosophy and politics. For Hegel, Socrates' life and death are ultimately but negatively instructive in matters of politics.

Plato, however, went beyond the negativity of Socrates' teaching in his attempt to depict a polity in which philosophers and philosophy rule. In Hegel's terms, Plato aspired to a philosophical "system," as evidenced in his concern, for example in the *Republic*, with the question of the political feasibility of his ideal; for in examining the relation of philosophy to the state, Plato was addressing the issue of the relation of philosophy to "actuality." But although Hegel admires Plato's aspirations, he faults the effort for its shortcomings. The *Republic* gives us an *ideal* for the constitution of the state but the ideal remains, according to Hegel, *merely* an ideal--a "chimera" or a "utopia." It fails to be "self-producing," to become a concrete "idea"; in other Hegelian words, the Platonic ideal is too "abstract" because it "falls short of man's requirements": "The true ideal is not what ought to be real, but what is real, and the only real; if an ideal is held to be too good to exist, there must be some fault in the ideal itself, for which reality is too good."[69]

Plato goes astray, Hegel concludes, when he tried to solve Socrates' problem (of the relation between subjective morality and the state) by suppressing individuality in the republic altogether. Plato's philosophy remained too abstract when he excluded from the guardians in the ideal state the opportunities for private property, for family life, and for personal passion in politics. Rather, a fully developed and tenable political philosophy must meet the requirements, according to Hegel, of "recognizing" the individual and "combining him with the Idea." Hegel's critique of Plato, then, resembles Popper's at least in the charge of anti-individualism; but for Hegel the remedy is *more* philosophy, whereas for Popper, philosophy itself is the evil.

I want to couple, along with Hegel, in this "third school" of Platonic interpretation, another view that also carefully distinguishes between Socrates and Plato; this view, which could be called a "Wittgensteinian" interpretation of Plato, I find presented in Hanna Pitkin's book, *Wittgenstein and Justice*. Although the book is not primarily an attempt to interpret Plato, Pitkin makes certain important claims about Plato's work that need to be addressed in this survey.[70] Pitkin examines at length Socrates' exchange with the sophist Thrasymachus in Book 1 of the *Republic*. Though Socrates does not quite say what justice means, he seems to be advancing implicitly the position that because we (as his verbal opponents) seem to be able to make distinctions about what justice means, there is reason to remain committed to the position that justice is something common (in some way) and coherent (in some sense) to all of us. For purposes of argument, Pitkin attributes to Socrates the definition of justice as "giving each his due." She then opposes this definition of justice to that which Thrasymachus serves up instead, namely that "justice is in the interest of the stronger." Pitkin's analysis of this confrontation is brilliant. Both Socrates and Thrasymachus purport to be saying what justice *is*, though they clearly disagree about something. Pitkin clarifies their positions (for us, if not for them): Socrates is providing a definition of the "meaning" of justice, whereas Thrasymachus is presenting a "sociological" perspective on the "practice" of justice (which, as it turns out, is not really a definition of justice at all, according to Pitkin). If this is what they are doing, then what are they disputing, Pitkin asks. Might they even agree on some counts?

Pitkin recalls Robert Dahl's explication of the dilemma. Dahl writes that Socrates and Thrasymachus are really arguing past one another, that Socrates is presenting the "normative" definition of justice, while Thrasymachus offers an "empirical" description of the "facts" of justice in a particular society. Socrates is asserting what justice "ought" to be, Thrasymachus what it "is." Pitkin's response to this line of analysis is again stunning, holding the potential to subvert the *Weltanschauungen* of practicing political scientists everywhere. The "is-ought" distinction does not settle the dispute, for *both* Socrates and Thrasymachus (and not just Thrasymachus, as Dahl might think) are making claims about what justice "is." Pitkin further complicates the fine line between values and Dahl's facts, until finally she invokes Wittgenstein's concept of "grammar" (which she has discussed up to this point in the book) to extricate the reader from this conceptual quagmire. Mostly, Socrates is right about the *meaning* of justice, even if Thrasymachus may happen to be correct about the facts of what the Athenians *consider* just. But, she qualifies, the "meaning" of justice also depends upon the facts of the matter, not only the "facts of its grammar."[71] The concept of justice, or rather the "grammar" of justice, encompasses both sides of the issue, the Socratic and the sociological, and it inherently includes an inconsistency between what people consider just and what the word means. Nonetheless, even though both Socrates and Thrasymachus are partly right as well as partly wrong (for having "started from some grammatical truth" and for having "ignored others"[72]), Pitkin comes down on Socrates' side, for having proposed the more inclusive and substantive account of the meaning of justice. As she explains, "Empirical investigation presupposes conceptual definition."[73]

Generalizing from this example, Pitkin further explains that certain words or concepts include in their "grammar" similar tensions between the ideal meaning and their embodiment in social practice. Knowing this, one can draw from one's understanding of the dialectics of language certain implications for political theorizing. Pitkin associates the work of political theorists such as Hannah Arendt and Sheldon Wolin (she also names Eric Voegelin and Leo Strauss) with Socrates' view of justice. Arendt's and Wolin's quasi-Greek and quasi-performative[74] use of the concept of "the political" may seem "idealistic" to hard-minded political scientists, but, Pitkin concludes, their claims are not at all antiquated, nor are they speaking past their hard-minded colleagues. Further, a Wittgensteinian view of language holds implications for politics. *That* we come to share (and Pitkin addresses the complexities of this process) the "fixed regularities" in language along with the inherent inconsistencies and ambiguities says something about the public, democratic, collective, and participatory nature of language, which in turn implies something about politics. Just as (well not *exactly* as, Pitkin claims[75]) a Wittgensteinian view of language suggests that we must maintain an ongoing vigilance and continual reform of the relationship between the meaning and the use of our most cherished concepts, so too ought our politics be one of ongoing negotiation, exchange, critique, reform, adjustment, and renewal. We can embrace fully our ideals, even if they are imperfectly embodied in practice; yet we also need "to hold our concepts aloof."[76] Politics, Pitkin concludes, ought to provide room for *ad hoc*, pluralistic perspectives.[77] In contrast to such a vision of the relationship between theory and practice, Pitkin cites Plato's *Republic* (invoking albeit tacitly the distinction between Socrates and Plato), arguing that Plato's brand of theory, which she brands as "totalitarian," is an attempt "to theorize about the problem of order in the polity, that ultimately fails to address the political problem by eliminating politics; an attempt to theorize about justice that fails by eliminating the need for, and thus the real nature of, justice."[78]

At this point I want to comment upon Hegel and Pitkin jointly, for I think there is a contrast and comparison to be made between the two. I propose that they conceptualize similarly (despite differences) the relationship between the realms, as it were, of "the real" and "the ideal." Both authors wish to reconcile the alleged antagonism between ideality and reality, but they do so, finally, only by collapsing the distinction. To be sure, the reconciliations take different forms--Hegel is more adamant in his attempt logically to introduce ideality into worldly affairs; Pitkin, in contrast, invites us to see the rational standards of value already implicit in our conventions and institutions (so that we might commence a process of critique and reform).[79] But the logic behind the two approaches--namely that a unitary, all-encompassing logic informs and oversees practice (even in its diversity and plurality)--is remarkably similar. Hegel's penchant to posit that the world is better off when philosophic consciousness is heightened is more explicit: He asserts baldly (as we have seen) that the only true ideal is one that is real. Although this statement appears bewildering, Hegel contends that the prose itself contains its own solution: The infinitive "to be" conjoining "the ideal" and "the real" in the statement turns out, upon inspection, to be more than a mere copula. As we have learned from countless explications of Hegel's work,[80] what he means in that statement is that the actual contains a real, if implicit, ideal, precisely because the real nature of the actual tends toward its own completion or perfection. By thus loading the left- and right-hand terms of his equation, Hegel transforms the infinitive "to be" from a static into a moving verb. Hence he can retain at least the syntactical appearance of a distinction between the real and the ideal while drawing a logical bridge between the two. The ideal *becomes* actualized or, rather, actualizes itself: The idea bridges the ideal and the real and manifests itself in actuality. In short, Hegel preserves and yet "sublates" the ideal-real distinction by positing a logical bridge between the two, which, even though it does not manifest itself in the two-dimensionality of the sentence construction itself, allegedly will reveal itself in time through the logical movement of history.

While Pitkin states that Wittgenstein's concept of "grammar" resembles Kant's transcendentalism,[81] I want to suggest that her Wittgensteinian "applications" place her more in Hegel's idealist camp than in Kant's. First, there is more than a structural similarity between Hegel's *Geist* and Pitkin's treatment of grammar. Both *Geist* and grammar--whether mystically or naturally or rationally or however--seem to stand "aloof," to hover above, while still informing, worldly affairs. But more important than the imagery that Hegel and Pitkin similarly convey is the way in which both theorists use, or invoke, these categories to account for *implicitness*, postulating through them an unseen yet organic connection between worldly facts and higher values. For Pitkin, even if Thrasymachus-type characters may espouse a conventional or a sociological understanding of the nature of "our" values, implicit in their deeper understanding, and betrayed simply by their use of language, is a standard or rule or piece of grammar. Like it or not, we are implicated in a language system.[82] Now Pitkin is not entirely clear or consistent about this category, grammar. Early in the book she explains that grammar is "those regularities in language that go far beyond the element of meaning or sense that stays fixed regardless of context."[83] Yet later she wants to make these fixed regularities more adaptable to circumstance and change; somehow these "regularities" regularly allow for the "inconsistencies"[84] between meaning and use that were exemplified in the already mentioned case of justice. *Grammar* evidently is an "entity" or "structure" or "practice" or "category" (but not a "label"--one is tempted to say "spirit") that has vitally superintended all world-historical practice, that has overarched all historical epochs, that has traversed all boundaries. Unlike *Geist*, it allows for ultimate and ongoing differences of opinion and judgment; yet in similar fashion it seems to function theoretically for Pitkin, as *Geist* does for Hegel, as an explanatory catchall when the world doesn't quite measure up to our expectations. Pitkin distinguishes her "grammar" from Plato's "metaphysic,"[85] suggesting that grammar is something other than metaphysical; but I am not at all sure that the concept of grammar is not yet another version of *Geist* in less mystical garb, an even more secularized, academicized, and liberalized monotheism.

Pitkin's theory may be a more modest and democratic rendition than Hegel's, her politics less tendentious, but her theory and politics smack of Hegelianism nonetheless: The world is rationally coherent, more or less, and we can hold out the hope that an informed dialectic between logic and practice will lead toward a better world for all. In contrast to Hegel, Pitkin's outlook is less programmatic, her optimism more reserved and diffuse; but she banks her hopes for the future on reason, an investment she shares with Hegel.

If Hegel and Pitkin both complicate (in order to reconcile) the distinction between the real and the ideal, to the point of collapsing and effectively obscuring it, then the problem with their projects is that the world just doesn't always let them do what their theories say must be possible. Hegel's philosophy does not in fact show how a movement of logic translates into the actual movement of history. We encountered an example of this problem earlier in the discussion of Hegel's view of Socratic irony. Hegel does not, for instance, adequately explain how the negativity of Socrates' irony, or the subsequent fall of Athens for that matter, necessarily translates into the stuff of positive world history. If anything, one could say that Socrates' ironic refutations set the philosophical *preconditions* for political change in Athens, but that revealing contradictions in the logic of the Athenians did not alone provide the necessary and sufficient conditions for change, the real impetus. And more generally, even one who admires the subtleties and the sweeps of Hegel's system as a kind of poetry must admit that the twentieth-century possibility of world-wide nuclear war presents a prima facia rebuttal to Hegel's pronouncements of the progressive march of civil reason.

Similarly, Pitkin has difficulty, I think, in explaining, not only how linguistic analysis translates vitally into democratic sentiments, but also how democratic sentiments translate into democratic action and democratic action into political change. She ends her book endorsing obliquely a participatory politics that is to be finely distinguished from mere "philosophizing" (by which I presume she means an elitist, disengaging, solitary endeavor). Yet the connection between her alternative theoretical critique ("in the modes of life of human beings") and politics or political action is simply not well spelled out. Perhaps she feels she does not need to spell out this connection, or should not do so, lest she fall into the same trap of theoretical "totalitarianism" that Plato did; nonetheless I think there is a difficulty in her book. If indeed she avoids "platonizing" her theory, she does so only by placing us, her readers, in a psychological double bind vis-à-vis her work. Why we should live up to, embrace, and act upon the values and expectations that our concepts hold in reserve for us, concepts that Pitkin in her book explicates, is not automatically clear.

This difficulty, of the relation between theoretical knowledge and political action and change, is even more pronounced in the work of Hannah Arendt, whom Pitkin cites frequently and favorably. Arendt in the prologue to *The Human Condition*, for example, makes her well-known gloss, "What I propose, therefore, is very simple: it is nothing more than to think what we are doing."[86] Whereas this sentence suggests some separation between thinking and doing, by the end of the book Arendt has spun an elaborate argument to make a straight equation between thought and action: "For if no other test but the experience of being active, no other measure but the extent of sheer activity were to be applied to the various activities within the *vita activa*, it might well be that thinking as such would surpass them all."[87]

The equation seems mechanical and factitious; it would appear to defy common sense. Coming from someone who has written an open paean to the intrinsic meaning of freedom and natality, the uniquely human capacity to act spontaneously and independently, Arendt's theory seems oddly programmatic and definitive—an imposition upon us supposedly independent thinkers and actors. In both Pitkin and Arendt there is more than a trace of the problem that the prose becomes so rigid, literal, and successfully authoritative that it defeats the authors' self-professed purposes. They both know themselves to be writing about matters essentially spiritual;[88] yet the spirit-letter distinction is nevertheless applicable to their written works.

My intent, however, is not to disparage Pitkin and Arendt. Indeed, I do not mean to set myself at odds with them. They of all modern theorists directly address the problems of translating theory into practice, and they seek to articulate a theory that inherently takes others and others' perspectives into account. But I do mean to turn their critique of Plato back upon them. By suggesting that there is a discrepancy between the application of their theories and their own theoretical aspirations, I am proposing that they have not sufficiently taken Plato's perspective into account and have not really understood his *Republic*. But then again, in essence they perhaps have, and what I am really doing is trying to save Plato for them. They charge Plato with eliminating politics, for having favored theory over practice, in other words, with having chosen letter over spirit. But I think this conclusion is a result of their own theoretical procrusteanism, their own misappropriations of Plato's *Republic*. Careful readers though they are, Arendt and Pitkin, like Hegel, seem to overlook *Plato's* irony.

Ironists

In the foregoing I have dealt at some length with various schools of interpretation of the *Republic*. My main purpose in dwelling upon the secondary literature has been to lay the basis for yet another possible interpretation of the *Republic*, namely a claim to the effect that the *Republic* constitutes a philosophically ironic work. My analyses of the main schools of Platonic interpretation suggest that some readers have taken the *Republic* far too literally, missing the irony altogether, while others who are keen to the presence of irony in the book have misread the strategy of irony in favor of some alternative and incompatibly "unironic" conclusion. I have suggested all along that the various readings of *Republic* correspond to, or entail, various substantive positions regarding issues such as the relation of philosophy to politics or the state, the nature of justice, and the theoretical relation between the real and the ideal. Now that I have nearly reached the point in the chapter at which I will systematically present textual evidence in support of the claim that Plato writes ironically, I must mention still another interpretive view of the *Republic*, though one that is so closely related to my own reading that the two must be carefully distinguished.

The proposition that Socrates enlists irony as a rhetorical device in the *Republic*, or that he is on the whole an ironic character, has been known explicitly at least since Aristotle (only to have been forgotten, alas, by those with a dry, legalistic understanding of the "Socratic method"). Rhetoricians have traced the origins of the English word irony back to its introduction as *yronye* in 1502[89] from the Latin *ironia* and yet farther back to the Greek word *eironeia*. While the concept of irony surely existed prior to Socrates' time,[90] it is perhaps significant for our purposes that one of the very first extant recorded uses of the word *eironeia* is to be found in Plato's *Republic*.[91] The exact setting is in Book 1, shortly after Thrasymachus has confronted Socrates, demanding that he say what justice is. Socrates puts him off with a show of modesty and a backhanded compliment, to which Thrasymachus responds (laughing scornfully): "Ye gads! Here we have the famous irony of Socrates. I knew it, and I predicted to these fellows that you would refuse to answer, that you would be ironic and do anything rather than answer if someone asked you something" (337a).[92]

On the basis of this passage and a scant few other sources in Greek literature,[93] classicists conclude that *eironeia* generally had negative connotations. The *eiron*--who in Greek use was inseparably associated with Socrates' personality and influence[94]--was thought to be a deceptive fellow who deliberately misguided his friends, mocking them while he praised them sarcastically, and all the while managing to evade the central issues altogether. *Eironeia* in this sense was a sort of vulgar expression of reproach, a sly, deceptive pretense.[95]

Most rhetoricians credit Aristotle with being the first thinker to raise irony to a more dignified position, though his praise was reluctant and relative. For Aristotle, *eironeia* was a kind of artful dissimulation or self-depreciative concealment, which was one extreme on the spectrum of virtue that had at its opposite end *alazoneia*, or boastful exaggeration. In the mean of the two was truth. In the *Ethics*, Aristotle recommended *eironeia* over *alazoneia* as a guide to personal conduct, for if a person is unable to tell the precise truth, Aristotle explained, it is better for him to depreciate rather than to exaggerate his virtues. In his *Rhetoric*, Aristotle similarly measures his praise of *eironeia*, recommending it, though with some reproach, as a rhetorical weapon.

If classical rhetoricians are correct in their claim that *eironeia* was generally considered a disreputable mannerism in ancient Greece and that it gained some respect only with Aristotle, then surely Aristotle's ambivalent treatment of the term grew out of his ambivalent view of Socrates. Yet it should be noted that Aristotle limited the definition of *eironeia* to that of a rhetorical method, which in turn expressed one's personal virtue in relation to truth. Aristotle did not treat irony as a general mannerism or method, nor did he address the implicit philosophical paradoxes involved in Socrates' claim that he knew that he knew nothing.

Modern commentators, however, have read greater significance into Socrates' ironic disposition. G.G. Sedgewick, for instance, states, "I am confident that Socrates' irony contains the germs of all the newer ironies which have so afflicted the literature of the last century."[96] Norman Knox catalogues four distinct ironies that he has found associated with Socrates. First, Socrates repeatedly uses a limited figure of speech that scholars of later periods have called blame-by-praise and praise-by-blame. Second, Socrates' elaboration of the figure into a formal method, in order to expose ignorance and to pursue truth, has been labeled "dialectic" by some writers. Third, Knox notes Worcester's understanding of Socrates' whole way of life as ironic, his "deepening of self-depreciation and mocking sympathy into a pervasive manner of action toward people and ideas and events."[97] Finally, Socrates' genius at encompassing diverse elements in harmonious thought is often referred to as an "irony of detachment." Knox quickly qualifies this analysis with the claim that no one in the classical period associated Socrates' manner with the formal dialectical method. He further suggests that Sedgewick and others might be reading too many kinds of irony retrospectively into Socrates' life and character.

At issue here, I think, is really the aforementioned question of the relation between Socrates in Book 1 of the *Republic*, who supposedly represents more closely the "historical Socrates," and the Platonic Socrates of the later books. In other words, to attempt to extend the Socratic method from a simple rhetorical device or mannerism into a fully developed philosophical system is to seek a theoretical bridge between the historical Socrates and Plato. We have already encountered Hegel's answer to this issue: Socrates' musings and queries represent an immature version of Plato's dialectic (and Plato's dialectic represents only an immature form of Hegel's own dialectic).

This brings us to perhaps the main theorist of Socrates' irony, the Danish philosopher Søren Kierkegaard. Following Hegel and Schleiermacher, Kierkegaard distinguished between Socrates and Plato; but unlike the former authors, Kierkegaard endorsed the negativity of irony found in Book 1. As Hegel's critique of irony was that irony allows persons to be insufficiently philosophical, one can say that Kierkegaard viewed the problem the other way around; for he embraced irony precisely because it represented a moment in which philosophy *becomes* personal. Socrates' method might not have provided any positive results, but it established through the process of questioning and dialogue a kind of negative freedom for the individual. According to Kierkegaard, Socrates through his irony created an *essential* character, but his was an existence lying on a point "between the useful and the supernatural," between, as it were, Xenophon and Plato: "Irony oscillates between the ideal self and the empirical self; one would make Socrates a philosopher and the other a sophist."[98]

Kierkegaard also thought that Socrates' negative irony emancipated Socrates from the state. This was accomplished not only by granting him spiritual detachment but also by bonding him to individuals and individuality in such a way that the state became a superfluous abstraction. But if this was the effect of irony, then Plato's depiction of an ideal republic completely betrayed the spirit of Socrates' teachings. Hence Kierkegaard charged that Plato took seriously what Socrates meant only ironically.

With the mention of Kierkegaard's dissertation I can now refine, albeit in advance, my own argument, which is an extension of Kierkegaard's thesis, though modified. I am contending that Plato's writing can be distinguished from Socrates' teaching and that Plato sustains a level of irony *independent* of Socrates' ironic tendencies.[99]

In only a few works of secondary commentary have I come across a similar proposition--that Plato *writes* ironically--and one of these is to be found in Paul Friedländer's book *Plato*. Friedländer, in a wonderful chapter entitled "Irony," takes his cue from Goethe and asserts that Plato is a master of irony, that "one cannot approach Plato without taking into account what irony is and what it means in his work."[100] Friedländer presents a short description of the point of Socratic irony. If Socrates answered outright what justice *is*, as Thrasymachus demanded, then he would have yielded to an impossible request because "it demands one, and only one, already determined answer from a man for whom there is, as an answer, only continuous search." Hence he dissimulates himself, but, as Hegel shows, this ignorance turns back to an ultimate stage of wisdom.

While Friedländer admits that it is impossible to draw a sharp line of demarcation between Socratic and Platonic irony, he contends that we do as readers of Plato "gradually ascend to forms of irony for which Plato, the artist and thinker, alone is responsible."[101] Friedländer calls Plato's artistic design a "polyphonic structure of irony." In portraying Socrates' irony, posing as a simple reporter of the dialogue, Plato sets up various ironic tensions between Socrates' verbal jests and the more solemn direction of the dialogues. The parallelism of ironies and ironic tensions then point beyond Socrates, "straight to a metaphysical dimension, to the ultimate height to which it is raised by Plato, the ironic metaphysician."[102] The *Republic*, according to

Friedländer, follows this artistic scheme. The reader is led by Socrates' ironic negations to expect that the highest perfection eventually will be reached. But in the central part of the book, despite the tense expectations, the highest good is not reached, and a conditional account is accepted in its stead. This strategy underscores the ineffability of the highest Platonic vision, according to Friedländer. Socratic irony, then, "expresses the tension between ignorance--that is, the impossibility ultimately to put into words 'what justice is'--and the direct experience of the unknown, the existence of the just man, whom justice raises to the level of the divine."[103] Plato thus guides us beyond Socrates' ignorance and to a vision of the eternal forms, according to Friedländer.

Friedländer's analysis is insightful and probably comes closest to capturing in prose the magic of the *Republic*. But while I fully endorse his basic thesis that Plato's artistry contains layers of irony separate from Socrates' speech, I think he makes sense of the *Republic* by incorporating too comprehensively the later Platonic dialogues--and their doctrines of the forms--into this earlier work.[104] My own thesis is somewhat different:[105] Plato's irony in the *Republic* does not function to goad the reader toward the eternal forms but, like Socratic irony, sets up a dialogue of sorts between Plato and us (as Plato's audience) in order to prompt us toward further reflection regarding the nature of political justice; and therein Plato does remain true, albeit in a written rather than oral mode of expression, to Socrates' teachings.

I find a wealth of evidence in support of an "antimetaphysical" reading of Plato's irony in Jowett and Campbell's notes on the *Republic*.[106] Jowett and Campbell do not present their findings in a comprehensive essay,[107] but one can glean from their notes a remarkable and coherent interpretation of the book. In his notes, Jowett pays close attention to Socrates' ironic remarks and gestures throughout the dialogues of the *Republic*. Yet Jowett understands Socrates' irony not as an isolated figure of speech or method of argument but as a more general outlook upon the human condition. With respect to the use of *eironeia* in the book, Jowett comments, "The word gains a new association from the application of it to Socrates, who not only pretended ignorance with the view of gaining an advantage in argument, but sincerely believed it to be the natural condition of man."[108] Jowett's real focus, however, goes beyond even Socrates' outlook. With his sensitivity to the nuances of the Greek language, Jowett pays particular attention to Plato's *written* text. He comments frequently upon Plato's choice of grammar, syntax, verb tense, and word usage in particular passages, arguing that Plato's sometimes peculiar constructions necessarily betray and deliberately expose his authorial presence and intervention in the dialogues. Some of the constructions are purely dramatic and have little to do with irony; for instance, Jowett is keen to Plato's use of numerous metaphors and analogies (e.g., light, medicine, money, art, ships, waves, laughter, numbers, food, animals, sheep, dogs, pigs) that run throughout the book.[109] Jowett contends that these metaphors lend "continuity" to the book as a whole, providing threads of artistic connection that are not provided by the substantive logic of the running "argument" of the dialogues.[110]

But even greater is the attention Jowett gives to Plato's ironical plays upon words, separate from Socrates' ironic posturings. Jowett observes that, in certain passages, Plato's use of language is deliberately anomalous or in some way incongruous. Jowett hazards his own speculations as to whether Plato intends certain passages to be taken seriously (e.g., his references to the gods and to communism are probably earnest, according to Jowett[111]), not seriously (e.g., the passages on numbers[112]), or half-seriously (e.g., the passages on the education of the guardians[113]). But more often than not, Jowett claims that the interplay between irony and literalness yields not a definitive interpretation regarding Plato's intentions with respect to a certain point or passage but instead opens up the dialogue to further questioning (e.g., the passages on the banishment of certain modes of music and meters[114]). The point of the irony, Jowett suggests, is to call the surface dialogue into question, not to repudiate the "literal" argument altogether. For instance, Jowett offers a very different interpretation of the passages on communism than do the Straussians, who suggested that the comedy undercuts the literalness of the passages: "Is Plato serious in his scheme of communism? Modern readers would like to explain this part of the ideal commonwealth in a figure only; they might imagine themselves not far off a kingdom of heaven, 'in which they neither marry, nor are given in marriage.' But the particularity of the details forbids this: we seem rather to be entering on a 'new moral world'."[115] And further in Jowett: "The most extravagant and comical ideas often occur in the works of Plato. But the manner of saying them, which enhances the humour, does away with the feeling of bad taste and impropriety."[116]

Plato does not answer questions outright, says Jowett, and thus his ironical use of language is often a cause of "misapprehension"[117] or only raises further questions rather than putting any finally to rest. One of the book's central incongruities indicative of Plato's general irony is, according to Jowett, "Why . . . Plato, who is himself 'the last of the poets,' and the most poetical of prose writers, [should] be also the enemy of poetry?"[118] The reasons are "partly fanciful and partly real." But in general, Plato employs irony, understatement, certain qualifying

words, collocations, recurring phrases, and other *façons de parler* in
order to "avoid the appearance of dogmatism" by maintaining "the
resemblance to ordinary conversation" and by "keep[ing] before the
mind the pervading antithesis between the actual and the ideal."[119]
Plato is against the view of knowledge that can be "put into the
mind,"[120] and thus his difficulty is finding a mode of written
communication that facilitates independent inquiry and apprehension.
He therefore bases his writing upon conversation and dialogue--and
thus imitates the tragedians--but he wishes to find a mode of writing
that invites an examination of this imitation itself. In other words,
Plato wishes to carry on with his readers a more genuine conversation,
in writing, than that afforded by the poetry of the tragedians (a wish
he expresses openly in the *Phaedrus*[121]). The textual incongruities and
logical uncertainties constitute invitations[122] to the reader to pose questions of the text, as if one were involved in a dialogue with the author.
To skip to Jowett's main conclusion: The central question raised by the
book is not the question of the *nature* of justice but the question of
whether justice can be valued and pursued (even if its nature is not fully
known) for its own sake, independent of rewards and reputation. Jowett
contends that Plato, in addressing this question, is "not basing this life
upon another world."[123] Rather, the references in Books 6, 7, and 10 to
the doctrine of forms are, he contends, "merely illustrative."[124]

My own reading of the *Republic* is close to Jowett's--viz., that the
irony of the book provides a way of generating independent thought
from a lifeless text--but I will try to present the evidence for this
reading more systematically than he did in his scattered notes. My
correlative thesis is that such an ironic presentation entails a certain
philosophical outlook concerning the nature of justice, an outlook that
in turn holds political implications. I will defer to the end of the
chapter my final interpretation of the meaning of the irony of the
Republic, just as I will defer at least until Chapter 3 a detailed
program for identifying the presence of irony in particular passages.
This deference, encouraging a suspension of judgment vis-à-vis the text,
accords with the underlying structure of the book, which, I contend, is
written in a series of layers, allusions, loops, echoes, and imitations. In
keeping with the scheme of the book and its irony, I will first state the
evidence for my argument before I address the final point of the book.
To the *Republic*, then, I shall return at this time.

*   *   *

Descent and Return

Let us reconsider the first book of the *Republic*. I shall argue that the symbolic allusions and the dramatic play in the first book contain ironies, whether for immediate effect or in anticipation of later themes in the book, that are not attributable to Socrates' method and that, instead, indicate Plato's authorial presence.[125] These dramatic cues are the work distinctively of Plato's hand, in that they set up an implicit dialogue, parallel to the textual narrative, between Plato and us, his readers. The ironies are put there (and for now I defer the pedant's question of the epistemology of divining Plato's motives) unmistakably for *our* sake. Plato does not simply report the scene: Sometimes he mocks his own characters, engaging in private jests with us; sometimes he sides with them, reversing our expectations. As readers, we must be alert to this parallel layer of indirect discourse, for, while it is discernable from--because contained "within"--the "formal" or "literal" or "dramatic" layers of presentation, in some respect Plato's irony is detached from the surface text. I contend that in fact Plato's point in dropping dramatic cues is to invite us to think beyond the apparent logic of the text itself. Yet, while my reading casts doubt upon the surface narrative, inviting the suspicion that Plato is deliberately but indirectly advising us not to take Socrates' word sketches too literally, I also contend--contrary to Leo Strauss, for instance--that the doubt encouraged by the irony of the dialogues does not ultimately imply a definite and wholesale rejection of Socrates' visionary schemes. In Book 1, Plato's ironic commentary is most evident in his use of certain spatial and directional references, and other particularly *visual* devices.

"*I went down (kateben)*": A number of commentators suspect that this opening to the *Republic* holds hidden significance, but it remains unsettled why Plato begins with *kateben*. Eric Voegelin argues that the word *kateben* opens up a "symbolism of depth and descent" that recurs throughout the *Republic*. It recalls the "Heraclitean depth of the soul that cannot be measured by any wandering, as well as the Aeschylean dramatic descent that brings up the decision for Dike." But above all it deliberately recalls, according to Voegelin, "the Homer who lets his Odysseus tell Penelope of the day when 'I went down (*kateben*) to Hades to inquire about the return of myself and my friends'" (*Odyssey* 23.252-53).[126] Homer's tale of wandering, of the underworld, and of return will provide recurring motifs throughout the book (a point that provides strong evidence that there is a structural continuity between Book 1 and the remaining books); but at least for the duration of Book 1, the Piraeus symbolically becomes Hades. Voegelin finds further evidence for this interpretation in Plato's mention of the goddess Artemis-Bendis, to whom Socrates has been praying: She is understood by the Athenians as the chthonian Hecate, who attends to the souls on their way to the underworld.[127] The imagery of the underworld is then confirmed in the dialogue with the old Cephalus. Why, then, is Plato invoking Homer and Hades at the outset? Voegelin's answer is that Cephalus is moved to his reflections on justice by his impending descent to Hades, and that the netherworldly imagery of the scene indicates the profounder concern of Socrates, of the relationship between acting justly and the afterlife.

I suggest that the symbolism of Hades provides but the ominous *suggestion* that we are listening to the reflections of one on his way to Hades, and thus the symbolism functions as a preliminary disclaimer, alerting us that the scene is not what it seems to be. Plato provides us with an implicit contrast between Cephalus' sincere if shallow reflections upon justice and our privileged awareness of his eventual fate in the underworld. The contrast is ironic, if mildly so.[128] Plato sustains the irony of the scene by presenting to us, without explicit commentary, a Socrates who similarly gives a show of taking seriously the account of one who is going to hell.[129] Voegelin's analysis of the symbolism of this passage brings forth Plato's own staging of the scene; but Voegelin's quasi-theological conclusion--that the symbolism reflects Socrates' vested interest in the afterlife--seems overstated. Rather, the discussion appears to anticipate the issue in the book, later more explicitly posed, of whether justice brings rewards--and here worldly rewards (wealth) and otherworldly rewards (an afterlife) are considered jointly in the person of Cephalus. That the discussion rotates around the seemingly mundane issues of sex and money, and that the discussion as a whole takes on a lighthearted tone, produces a comedic effect that shades into a deeper irony when the reader considers the tragic consequences of Cephalus' complacent life.

Julia Annas notes a historical fact that complements Voegelin's symbolic analysis yet supports my view that the symbolism serves an irony that Plato has cast over the entire scene. Annas points out that Cephalus is not an Athenian citizen but a "resident alien" from Syracuse who has chosen to live outside the city, in the Piraeus (where trading and commercial activity take place). In other words, Cephalus has chosen moneymaking over citizenship, a life of self-interest with tangible consequences as opposed to politics. She writes that although it is often said that Plato's picture of Cephalus is sympathetic, portraying him as a dignified old man, the matter is not so simple. The *Republic* was written much later than the time it depicts, and Plato was writing for an audience that knew that the security based upon wealth that Cephalus was espousing was wholly illusory: "Only a few years later, Athens fell, the family [Cephalus'] was totally ruined, Polemarchus executed, and Lysias driven into exile."[130] Hence she contends that the contrast between Plato's apparently sympathetic presentation of Cephalus and his knowledge that the audience was privy to Cephalus' actual worldly fate reveals Plato's maliciousness toward, if not Cephalus personally, then moneymaking generally.[131]

The point is that Plato sets up a situational and dramatic irony in the reversal between Cephalus' security and his eventual fate, whether this fate be of worldly consequence (Annas's account) or of otherworldly consequence (Voegelin's account). Plato presents his situational irony through a dramatic contrast, by placing his sympathetic account against the background of the audience's awareness of Cephalus' downfall and against the symbolism of Hades. But these ironic reversals are for *our* purview and consideration, as readers of Plato; they run parallel to Socrates' ironic exchanges with the characters themselves. Plato's dramatic control of the scene is confirmed and so much as admitted at the very end, when Cephalus *bequeaths* (312d) the argument to the younger Polemarchus. The term reveals Plato's punning with the theme of inheritance (financial, familial, and poetic), and it appears to anticipate the later, more abstract discussions of the relationship between rewards and justice.[132] Whether this is a humorous or doleful juncture in the dialogue is debatable: Either way, the humor or the pathos is for our sake, a clue that Plato perhaps is attempting to engage us in dialogue.[133]

I wish to call attention to a few passages in Book 1 that anticipate later themes in the *Republic* as a whole and that, in contributing to the thematic continuity of the *Republic*, indicate Plato's own acknowledgment of his authorial control over the dialogues. Yet Plato plays off those moments in which he reveals his control or partial detachment from the text against passages in which he subordinates himself to the text, maintaining the pretense that he is simply a reporter of the speeches between Socrates and his fellows. The play between detachment and submission, in short Plato's ironic stance vis-à-vis his own book, runs parallel to Socrates' spoken ironies and, much like Socrates' method of questioning, invites a response from his audience.

1. Quizzing Polemarchus on the youth's poetic understanding of justice, Socrates steers the dialogue with the provisional, if ironic, conclusion: "Justice, then, can't be a very serious thing, if it's only useful when things aren't used" (333e).[134]

Of course, later in the book the question of the consequences and of the practicality of pursuing justice will be explored more directly, but this passage is a preliminary clue that Plato regards the question with complexity and ambivalence. Here, in an offhand fashion, Plato is suggesting that he is indeed "serious" about the question of the "usefulness" of justice. Or, if it is too soon to judge Plato's seriousness, and it probably is, at least the passage reveals Plato's anticipation of the charge that his republic to follow is simply a disembodied utopia (as some commentators have in fact claimed). By simply reporting Socrates' comment, Plato shows his awareness that justice will likely be evaluated with respect to its "usefulness." At the same time, Plato faithfully conveys Socrates' irony, thus undercutting and trivializing the content of Socrates' statement by presenting the remark as a casual concession to the opposite view, namely that maybe, indeed, justice isn't to be regarded completely seriously, precisely because it isn't "useful" (not, anyway, in the way Cephalus and Polemarchus might consider something as being useful).

2. Polemarchus' near concession that justice is akin to stealing (334b) contains a double irony that reflects Plato's ingenious hand. That Socrates has twisted Polemarchus' position into a defense of justice as thievery is ironic in view of Polemarchus' initial acceptance of his father's view of justice as respect for inheritance (or, in Simonides' words, justice as rendering to each his due). But the reversal is a challenge not only to the integrity of private property but also to the integrity of Polemarchus' entire system of beliefs. As Cephalus' son, Polemarchus inherited his father's argument with Socrates as well as his father's view of justice. His poetic defense of his father's mundane definition (returning what is borrowed) represents a mere recitation of Simonides' sayings, and Socrates' irony ("It is indeed difficult to disagree with Simonides" [331e]) underscores this uncritical dependence upon and imitation of the poet. Furthermore, Polemarchus likely acquired from Homer (334b) the view that justice is a kind of stealing. Though Polemarchus inherited the argument that his father "bequeathed" (331d) to him and accurately recites the words of the poets, in a sense he has stolen his views of justice from his father and from the poets, in that he has not arrived upon them independently. The implied direction of the passage--that justice requires independence of thought and conviction--is confirmed in a later passage (413d), in which Socrates warns that the guardians must not be forgetful or credulous. By "theft," Socrates explains, he means that persons can have their opinions in a sense stolen from them, or rather he says that such thievery is the process by which persons themselves relinquish their beliefs too easily, having them stripped from them by argument. The passage with Polemarchus of course raises the theme of Socrates' opposition to the sophists' superficial method of argumentation, based

upon externals. But more important, Plato seems to be making a comment upon the relationship between fathers and sons, disputing implicitly Cephalus' and Polemarchus' claim that family relations are analogous to matters of property; and Plato, through his irony, seems to be reserving a case for the need for independent, critical thought--as opposed to imitation and tradition--as regards the question of justice.

3. Plato invokes *mathematical* arguments, I contend, in order to give seemingly tangible substantiation to an (admittedly) elusive argument about the importance of pursuing justice. Recall that in Book 1 of the *Republic*, after Socrates has forced Polemarchus to take back all explanations of justice that Polemarchus has proposed (or parroted) up to that point, Thrasymachus breaks in and demands that Socrates say what justice is, with "none of this nonsense about benefit, profit, gain, duty, or advantage. I won't tolerate those barren vapidities" (337b).[135] Socrates at this point knows that Thrasymachus is "on" to Socrates' ironic ways, and his response to Thrasymachus can be taken as a kind of self-critique or confession: "You're a wise one, Thrasymachus. You know if you asked someone how much twelve is and said: 'None of this nonsense about two times six or three times four or four times three or six times two--I won't tolerate such foolishness!'--I think you know that no one could answer a question like that. So suppose he asked: 'How in the world do you want me to answer? Do I have to avoid the forbidden answer even if one of them is true? Shall I tell you a lie, or what?" (337b-c).[136]

In the past, I interpreted the above passage as evidence in support of a "Wittgensteinian"[137] reading of Socrates' exchange with Thrasymachus. It seemed to me that Socrates in the preceding discussion with Polemarchus was saying that there is something inherently contradictory about human reason when it directs itself toward questions like what is justice? but that, though persons cannot quite say what justice means, because they seem to be able to make certain distinctions about what justice is and is not, there is reason to suspect that justice has such coherent meaning. The above passage I read as the first time in which Socrates suggests that eliciting this meaning, if analytical methods prove wanting, may require a lie of some sort.

Such a view, I now think, makes too much sense of Socrates' efforts, a way of reading too much coherence into his lifelong examinations of justice. It settles too many counts by alluding to the quasi-objective meaning of the abstract notion of justice. Upon my second interpretation, I still think that the passage is a key moment in the *Republic*, but for different reasons. Noteworthy here is that Socrates puts the question of justice in numerical terms. If one cannot grasp the significance of justice in the abstract, then quantification helps. But

Socrates' ironic self-criticism suggests that the various examples will never "add up" to justice. The justice-by-numbers approach has limitations. Nonetheless, because Thrasymachus, in complaining sarcastically about Socrates' principled rejection of the various examples of justice given him, implicitly demands a definition of justice that accommodates Thrasymachus' concern for "benefit, profit, gain, duty, or advantage," Socrates will do his best to satisfy him, to provide a quantified answer to the question of justice. Socrates' admission to Thrasymachus of the difficulty in articulating the meaning of justice doubles as an admission by Plato, however, that explanations or depictions of justice henceforth in the text will necessarily be constructs. The passage anticipates Plato's recurring use of number analogies throughout the book and yet acts as a disclaimer towards all of these: We readers are not to take quantified versions of justice too literally! We will recall this passage later on; for now it serves as one of the bases of my assertion that there is a structural continuity between Book 1 and the remaining books. In this case, the continuity would confound the simple claim that Plato's later use of arithmetic models followed from his new-found reliance upon ethereal Pythagorean truths. The passage also anticipates the Big Lie[138] and its function: If number analogies fail to persuade you as to the significance of justice, you might require a direct falsehood of some sort. Teaching and convincing and committing one to act justly are the central issues here.

A subpoint might be made with respect to the above passage. The quantification of justice also represents a play upon the earlier money theme, which in turn adumbrates a more abstract version of the question, Does justice pay? Socrates' and Thrasymachus' philosophic opposition manifests itself in mundane terms in their rivalry over money. The sophist Thrasymachus expects compensation for his words, whereas the penurious Socrates is unaccepting of such favors. Thrasymachus demands a guarantee before he will spar verbally with Socrates; Socrates' friends vouch for him so that the match can begin. By the end of their tortuous exchange, Socrates has gained the advantage over Thrasymachus; at which point Plato steps into the dialogue to reveal that Thrasymachus has been doubly the victim of Socrates' irony, losing both the abstract as well as the mundane side to the argument: "And so, my dear Thrasymachus, injustice never pays better than justice" (354a).[139]

Desmond Lee, in his translation of the *Republic*, divides the book according to the rhythm and flow of the arguments, rather than into the classical ten-book form. He contends that the first "part" ends after Socrates' first encounters with Glaucon and Adeimantus. Jowett recognizes roughly the same divisions. Following Lee and Jowett, I will extend my preliminary observation to include these two discussions, as if they were intended to be thematically connected to Book 1.

4. Glaucon is not persuaded by Socrates' clever triumph over Thrasymachus, and he sets out to show Socrates that injustice actually pays better than justice. Glaucon employs visual imagery to this end, conjuring up the myth of Gyges[140] to state his case. Give Gyges' rings to a just man, allowing him the sweet temptation of becoming invisible at will, proposes Glaucon, and you also take away the visible threat of retribution for his ill actions and thus his incentive for acting justly. He will be led on by "self-interest" just like the unjust man, maintains Glaucon, and the just man will likewise seek the benefits that injustice pays: "This, it would be claimed, is strong evidence that no man is just of his own free will, but only under compulsion, and that no man thinks justice pays him personally, since he will always do wrong when he gets the chance" (360c-d).

At the end of Glaucon's discourse, Socrates replies, "I say, Glaucon, you're putting the finishing touches to your two pictures as vigorously as if you were getting them ready for an exhibition" (361d). Not only is Socrates teasing Glaucon here, but Plato is playing with us a bit. With ironic reserve he re-presents Glaucon's case: ironic (in some sense), because the book would not make any sense if Plato actually wished us to believe that injustice pays better; and the case that Glaucon makes-- that the just man must seek to *be* and not just to *appear* just--Plato surely wants us to consider seriously. But he waits until Book 10 to present to us his theory of art and the limitations of a Glaucon-type argument, and Socrates' ironic remarks at this juncture serve notice to us that we are to put Glaucon's argument on hold, that we are not to be taken in by pictorial presentations.

5. A similar exchange follows between Socrates and Adeimantus. Plato again sustains the irony of posing the rhetorical question (with all apparent seriousness), Why pursue justice, if not for the conse-quences? Unlike Glaucon's visual and worldly account, Adeimantus provides a poetic and otherworldly argument. If we can be unjust with impunity in this world, he reasons, then we need to consider what the gods will do to us. "But if there are no gods or if they care nothing for human affairs, why should we bother to deceive them . . . what argument, then, remains for preferring justice to the worst injustice, when both common men and great men agree that, provided it has a veneer of respectability, injustice will enable us, in this world and the next, to do as we like with gods and men?" (365e).

Thus Adeimantus asks for an argument, and the rest of the book counts as Socrates' explicit if measured response to that challenge. But Plato has given us plenty of clues--in and through the irony of his "straight" presentation of the ironic Socrates--that we are to take these arguments and what follows with a grain of salt. Plato's irony runs parallel to Socrates' irony, in the above cases serving us notice that we are to suspend judgment regarding the arguments of Thrasymachus, Glaucon, and Adeimantus, for there is something dubious in arguments that employ mathematical, visual, or poetic aids. And we have also been subtly forewarned that the arguments to come are tailored to the mathematical, visual, and poetic needs of these respondents. In the last book, our covert dialogue with Plato will be resumed, our suspicions will be confirmed. Glaucon's "visual" argument and Adeimantus' "poetic" argument will be recalled in Book 10, in the Theory of Art section; and the Gyges' myth and Homer's tale of an afterlife will be recalled in the last half of Book 10, in the Myth of Er. Thus the middle books--the political section--are bracketed by cross-relating books.[141] I shall argue that the Theory of Art and the Myth of Er both concern centrally the initial question, Why pursue justice? posed as it pertains to the self, to the individual. This becomes the next question on the agenda: If the individual cannot "see" for himself or herself the "larger" consequences of acting justly, then perhaps he or she will when viewing justice on a greater scale, in politics. This turn in the dialogue toward politics, however, is not simply for the sake of Socrates' fellows; in addition it is a comment, by Plato to us, upon his book itself. We turn to the larger topic of politics, says Socrates, because we are shortsighted men and the letters of politics are more legible. This reference seems to reflect Plato's extreme self-awareness of the written nature of his project, and our awareness of his awareness should influence our understanding of the relationship between Plato and Socrates.

Politics

So we turn to politics. As before, I wish to examine, in a running commentary, selected passages that are revealing of Plato's irony. Socrates' first proposal for organizing an ideal polity provides sufficient grist for the mill. Based on the premise that humans are interdependent beings, Socrates draws a very rough sketch of a very simple community in which basic needs are provided for. The argument seems commonsensical to begin with (a basic division of labor, etc.), but then Socrates' suggestions turn toward the humorous. He adds a "few luxuries" (372c) to the diet of these primitives: salt ("of course"), olive oil and cheese, different kinds of vegetables ("with which to make various country dishes"), some dessert, figs, peas, beans, myrtleberries, acorns ("to roast at the fire as they sip their wine"). And then Socrates delivers the overly modest conclusion: "So they will lead a peaceful and healthy life, and probably die at a ripe old age, bequeathing a similar way of life to their children" (372d).

Can Socrates be serious? Iris Murdoch says that this first minimalist political proposal is "surely not ironic,"[142] and Strauss claims that this "healthy city" is a depiction of the naturally just city "*par excellence*."[143] Desmond Lee notes, however, that the description has been regarded by some as an "ironic parody of the 'simple life' theories of Plato's day,"[144] and Jowett contends that many of the words in this section have ludicrous or facetious associations.[145] Glaucon immediately gives his own answer to the question of whether Socrates is serious: "Really, Socrates, that's just the fodder you would provide if you were founding a community of pigs" (372d).

Glaucon's reproach may only reflect the fact that he is a meat eater[146] and that his "endowments are too rich to find their fulfillment in the simple life,"[147] but Socrates does concede that he has been too miserly with life's comforts. To say that Socrates' first proposal is ironic, and that Plato's placement of Socrates' ironic proposal just prior to his "ideal state" reveals a parallel irony, is not to claim that Plato intends for the minimalist city to be rejected altogether. He notes in a tone of casual wisdom that there may be more than a grain of truth in leading the simple life, "For though the society we have described seems to me to be the true one, like a man in health, there's nothing to prevent us, if you wish, studying one in a fever" (372e).

If Plato is in control of the plot development at this point (rather than merely chronicling events as he saw them), then why does he have Socrates give a brief description of a primitive society just prior to the description of the enlarged republic? Why even mention that this is the "true" society, in a book that is devoted to a more elaborate description of the republic and entitled as such? I think that Socrates' irony, and Plato's parallel irony, are another indication to the reader that this first misstart functions as a partial disclaimer for the ensuing discussion. Plato is indicating to us, I suggest, that his "vision" to follow is not to be read credulously but with some critical perspective, some reserve, for he has undercut his own ideal before he has even begun--and that must mean something.[148] But what exactly this scheme of starts and misstarts means, whether Plato's modesty is affected or genuine, is, at this early juncture in the book, still too soon to determine.

A similar (ironic) tension--given by the juxtaposition of a comic disclaimer as the preface to an apparently serious presentation-- appears in the very next section, on education. Socrates describes how the guardian class must have certain natural qualities, and he likens the guardians to well-bred watchdogs (375a). Guardians must have the same keen perceptions, speed, and strength as dogs; and they must have the same courageous temperament, the same fearless spirit, as do dogs. But then Socrates claims that the guardians must have the same "philosophic" knowledge as do dogs, for dogs can distinguish the sight of a friend and a foe by their knowledge of the two. The Straussians recognize the elements of parody in this passage but then they actually take the connection between dogs and guardians quite literally, basing much of their interpretation of the political meaning of philosophy on it (distinguishing friend from foe).[149] Jowett, however, contends that "Socrates works the illustration with ironical gravity," and Sinclair argues that "we must not take Plato's little jokes seriously."[150] The suspicion that the passage is ironic is furthered by Socrates' introducing a play on words toward the end of the discussion. The two types of knowledge--*philosophos and philomathes*--both indicate love of learning; but the play on words--suggesting that the dog's knowledge indicates a great gift for the love of learning--only enforces the irony of the connection.   Surely the dog's life is not the exalted view of philosophy that Socrates--or even the Straussians--ultimately wish to depict (Adam interprets the passage as a parody of the Cynics[151]). It should also be noted that the whole discussion about philosophy here has been humorously unphilosophical, with Glaucon deferentially submitting to all of Socrates' barbs.

We come, then, to the famous theory of the censorship of the poets. I detect a whimsy in the argument, for I am not sure how gravely we are to treat Socrates' censorship of the "foul story" about Ouranos, the god who was castrated; a story that, we are told, should not be told, or if it must be told, it is to be told to a select few under an oath of secrecy, at which a rite should be required. And furthermore, at the rite they will sacrifice not a "mere pig" but something "large and difficult to get" (378b). That Socrates belabors the stories that are to be banned betrays his irony as well as Plato's ironic supervision.   When Adeimantus presses for more details, Socrates instructs him: "My dear Adeimantus, you and I are not engaged on writing stories but on founding a state" (379a). But then Socrates proceeds to describe in graphic detail the poets' passages that are to be censored.

Plato is clearly in control of the dialogue here, sustaining the irony of his presence by leaving his creative control unacknowledged, or rather, inexplicit.   But the reader must suspect that Plato is joshing when he has Socrates ban, in due seriousness, Homer's description of "Achilles, the son of a goddess," as "sometimes lying on his side, sometimes on his back, and then on his face," and then standing up and "wandering distraught along the shore of the unharvested sea," or "picking up the dark dust in both hands and pouring it on his head" (388b).

Plato's sense of humor is evident, at least through his use of Socrates as a straight man. What this technique indicates is that the "censorship" section is more complex than would appear, especially when Socrates says in all apparent earnestness: "For, my dear Adeimantus, if our young men listen to passages like these seriously and don't laugh at them as unworthy, they are hardly likely to think this sort of conduct unworthy of them as men, or to resist the temptation to similar words and actions. They will feel no shame and show no endurance, but break into complaints and laments at the slightest provocation" (388d).

So Plato invites us (as guardians *manqués*) to laugh, but then he has Socrates issue a check on laughter, stating that guardians are not to be too fond of it. I want to suggest that this passage is complicated, due to its apparently ironic presentation; but what *can* be concluded is that to accept it literally--as the Straussians do in their view that Plato banishes humor wholesale (so that we will reject his state)--is to be victimized, humorously enough, by the irony.[152]

Socrates shortly turns from content to form, from what is to be said (or what is not to be said) in educational matters, to how it is to be said and presented. He distinguishes between direct speech (or mimesis) and indirect speech (or narrative). Direct speech involves assimilating "oneself to another person" in order to "represent" the person; whereas indirect speech or narrative includes some of the "poet's words" between the dialogue. The second corresponds to Homer's form of writing. One might ask who employs the first form of speech. Desmond Lee, in his editorial notes, suggests that the first form (direct speech) applies to the Greek schoolboy, who was taught to recite Homer uncritically, with "imaginative identification."[153] But Socrates is talking not just about "reciters" but also "poets." And who would count as such a poet? "And so you will also understand that the opposite of this is when one omits the poet's words between the speeches and leaves only dialogue" (394b).

Surely the tragic poets, such as Sophocles and Aeschylus, would fall in this category; more generally, anyone who writes comedy or tragedy would employ the representational form of poetry (394b-c). But if one pays too much attention to the details of the discussion, one might overlook that Plato's *own dialogue* is very much cast in direct dialogue rather than in Homeric verse and narrative.[154] Plato seems to be tipping us off here, admitting his irony, by engaging in a kind of self-parody that is intended to establish a rapport, as well as distance, between the reader and him. The irony of this section would seem to be affirmed again shortly, when Socrates asks of Adeimantus: "It is unlikely therefore that anyone engaged on any worthwhile occupation will be able to give a variety of representations. For the same writers are incapable of equally good work even in two such closely allied forms of representation as comedy and tragedy. You did say these were both forms of representation, did you not?" Adeimantus replies: "Yes; and it's true that a man can't write both" (395a).

If Plato's dialogues are imitative, then the inquisitive reader almost has to ask whether the *Republic* represents tragedy or comedy. Saxonhouse contends that the book begins and ends with death and thus is framed by tragedy, but that comedy controls the central part of the dialogue.[155] Yet here in the discussion with Adeimantus, Socrates contends that one cannot write both tragedy and comedy. Thus the incongruity in the dialogue reflects back upon Plato and should make us suspicious about the entire book. The reader of Plato might recall that in the *Symposium*, the drunken Alcibiades, just before he falls under the table, suggests that there is a common genius of tragedy and comedy. One is tempted to declare that irony is this genius, but that declaration may be premature.[156] At any rate, Plato seems deliberately to be contradicting the rule laid down by Socrates, in that he goes back and forth between employing aspects of comedy and aspects of tragedy in his *Republic*; and the irony of his straight "representation" of Socrates denying this has the effect of forcing the reader to reflect upon the significance of the passage as a whole.

But to continue: Socrates embarks on an extended discussion of what is and what is not to be included in the ideal educational system. Again, I am unsure precisely how seriously we should regard this discussion (395c-412a).[157] If this is a serious book about such a serious topic as justice, then how literally are we to take Socrates' strictures against: certain *modes* of music and rhythm (398c-400c--this *could* be a parody of the Pythagoreans as much as a reflection of their beliefs);[158] sex with strangers (403c); certain foods (especially seasonings! [404c])? And one has to wonder whether Plato is intentionally pushing his case too far when he claims: "And if being so educated they follow on the same track in their physical training, they will, if they choose, succeed in never needing a doctor except in real necessity" (410b).

My answer at this point: It is unclear whether we are to take the educational scheme completely seriously, if only because there are occasional ruptures in Socrates' grave treatment of the topic.

The Big Lie

The discussion proceeds to the heart of the description of the "ideal state": the "Big Lie" and the role of the guardians. The logistics of the Big Lie have been analyzed numerous times by other commentators. Questions arise as to whether the lie, when put into practice, allows for individual mobility, accurate selection, and whether the lie would categorize individuals unfairly, manipulating them through myth and an illiberal educational program.

All of these questions are valid, assuming that one takes Socrates at this word in the passage. But I think that a narrow reading of Socrates' (and Plato's) purposes in proposing this mythic tale belies the greater significance of the tale. For an enlarged perspective on the passage, Eric Voegelin's views on the drama and the symbolism of the tale are again instructive. Voegelin notes that Socrates procrastinates (414d) in introducing the tale, because, Socrates says, the lie is so comprehensive and "big." The play on the word big (*gennaion*) reveals, says Voegelin, the satirical intention of the tale. The Big Lie, it turns out, is that all men are brothers. But the harmony of the polis requires that everyone mind his own business according to his natural gifts. Socrates has distinguished the nature of the rulers, guardians, and workers, and now he stresses that in spite of their differences, they are still equal, as brothers. Yet for Socrates, equality is the reality (*aletheia*) (414d), while the differences are dream images (*oneirata*). Voegelin reasons that, against the background of faction-ridden Athens, "The introduction of the supreme truth as an unbelievable Big Lie is one of the bitterest pages in a work that heaps so much bitter scorn on Athens."[159] The Athenians, Voegelin informs us, had an almost identical myth of their origin from the mother earth. Thus, the Big Lie's "heavy accent on the incredibility of brotherhood underlines the unbrotherliness of the Athenian brothers."[160]

But Voegelin contends that the meaning of the Phoenician tale goes beyond its satirical function. The word translated as "lie" is the Greek *pseudos*, which has more than one meaning. An occasional *pseudos* can be used for the benefit of the polis, for instance in the education of children, who are told myths or tales, even though they are literally untrue. Plato is playing with the paradox that an untruth (a *pseudos* embedded in a *mythos*) can turn out to convey truth (*aletheia*). The Phoenician tale, in particular, deliberately recalls Hesiod and his metal age. Voegelin contends that the point of recalling Hesiod's myth is to warn that the *eidos* of the good polis is not the product of historical development but rather is coexistent in the structure of the *politeia* (which means that justice is transcendental, not teleological).

Hence, the primary philosophical motive for the introduction of the myth is to suggest the ineffability of the equality of men. "The *pseudos* that begins as a Big Lie is subtly transformed into Great Truth," Voegelin concludes.[161]   Voegelin's insights are again brilliant but I question his analysis separating the "function" of the tale into "satire" versus "philosophy."   Instead, I would suggest that if we must distinguish between satire and philosophy, then the two should be seen as mutually reinforcing and held together in a sustained irony. Voegelin's strict bifurcating of historical satire and transcendental philosophy leads him to state that the higher purpose of the tale is that "the understanding of a universal humanity [which] originates in the experience of transcendence and the ineffable kinship of men under God revealed in the experience can immanently be expressed only through a myth of descent from a common mother or father."[162]

But take away Voegelin's invocation of God as a way to point to the absolute (and speakable) truth of brotherhood, and Socrates' truth becomes all the more elusive and, I would say, profound. The point, then, of mentioning the myth in the dialogue (the dialogue not so much between Socrates and his listeners as between Plato and us) would be to invite the reader to reflect upon these very weighty philosophical matters. The invitation takes the form of contrasts, incongruities, paradoxes, juxtapositions; of satire laced with (not divorced from) something resembling a "higher" truth. By the indirection of irony we are led to embrace the notion that all persons are (somehow) united (the Big Lie), even if different (myth of metals); but our insight now is not theological, nor even transcendental; it is the tenuous product of a kind of double perspective, between lies and truths, on the matter.

The Guardians

Upon completion of his discussion of the myth of metals, Socrates begins to lay out the working conditions for the philosopher-guardians. They are to lead Spartan lives: no private property beyond the essentials; no private quarters; food as the only wage. Jowett notes that "the slight exaggeration and comic formality of the language keeps up the humour of the passage."[163]   Adeimantus interrupts to voice the objection that Socrates is not making the guardians particularly happy (419a).   Socrates provides a provisional answer, stating that the purpose in founding their state was not to promote the happiness of any particular class but rather to promote the happiness of the whole community. But this straightforward answer is not very compelling, and Socrates presses on further to respond to Adeimantus' objections. But as Jowett observes, in much of this exchange with Adeimantus,

Socrates is being ironic and satirical, and Socrates in fact advises Adeimantus at one point not to view the guardians too harshly (426e)--which Jowett translates as "look at them not under a serious but under a comic aspect."[164] Socrates and Adeimantus proceed to review the various aspects of the state they have founded, and they rehearse their operational definitions of justice and injustice. But for all the labor that has gone into the discussion up to this point, Socrates warns, "Let's not be too emphatic about it just yet" (434d). And he suggests that they return to an examination of how justice applies to the individual. Socrates' comment seems to function as another Platonic disclaimer, a signal that the reader is to put his judgment in abeyance and is to regard the following material with still further critical reserve.[165]

The Individual

So the investigation returns to the individual. Again it would be well for interpreters, especially those who asseverate that the "individual" is the primary focus of the *Republic*, to note that Plato commences another major section with what I call a disclaimer. Socrates calls the inquiry "little" (435c), and though this word could refer simply to scale (which is just as probable as the earlier "big" of the Big Lie meaning no more than "large"), likely "little" includes negative connotations pushing it toward a translation such as "trifling." Even though Glaucon corrects him, Socrates expresses the view that they should not place too much credence in the present manner of argument (435d), a manner that has approached the question of justice, and the relationship between the city and the individual, in quantified terms (435a). Thus, though they continue on for a short while in the manner in which they have heretofore been examining justice, Socrates--and in effect Plato--forewarns us that shortly the dialogue will assume a qualitatively different method of presentation. Nonetheless they arrive at a definition of justice that "convinces" Glaucon, and their "dream come true" (443e), they proceed to reexamine the question of whether justice "pays." But for now Socrates puts the question in brackets, calling it "absurd" (445b). He promises to examine it nonetheless, yet first he responds to the demand of Adeimantus, who has not been convinced, to restate the argument about women.

Though this turn in the discussion appears to be a digression, the shift, viewed from a dramatic perspective, seems to have the function of underscoring the fact that the overwhelming question for Plato here is the issue of *convincing* persons about the virtue in pursuing justice. Glaucon has been too easily persuaded, having already given Socrates his vote of confidence in the republic (450a). Socrates admits immediately that he himself was not entirely committed to his own verbal description of the state, and he announces that he is glad that "no one questioned the description I had given" (450b)--as if he feels that he had earlier gotten away with something. And even while Socrates is about to embark on a second defense of the need for "communism" in matters of property and sex, he openly invites us to doubt the vision, both as a practical possibility *and* as an ideal.[166] This invitation may simply be ironic in the sense of modesty (the opposite of *alazoneia*), of understating the case as a way of luring us into greater commitment than we would otherwise have been willing to undertake. But I think the invitation offered by Plato is sincere: The point of the irony is to encourage us to entertain certain ideas while *at the same time* allowing us to hold countervailing viewpoints.

The discussion turns to an examination of the question of the "practical possibility" (471e) of realizing the state Socrates has been describing. Posing the question as a "practical possibility" is another, more abstract phrasing of the question: How are we to convince individuals to pursue "justice," an act that requires them to forgo immediate "pay-offs" such as spouses and property? Hence the discussion turns toward a focused investigation of the traits such an individual must possess: love of knowledge, self-control, generosity, lack of cowardice, a good memory, a sense of proportion, a sense of grace, and so on.

Though this discussion seems anything but ironic, it should be noted that Socrates began the section with another disclaimer (473c); and then Plato reinstates his ironic presence in having Socrates at the end restate the original question, now rhetorically: "Can you, then, possibly find fault with an occupation for the proper pursuit of which a man must combine in his nature good memory, readiness to learn, breadth of vision, and grace, and be a friend of truth, justice, courage, and self-control?" Glaucon's answer is telling: "Momus could find no fault there" (487b).

Momus, it will be remembered, is the god of criticism and mockery. Glaucon's response is further evidence of Plato's suggestive irony: Plato has broken his pretense of seriousness by his equally serious show of making a concession to Momus. And the contention that "Momus could find no fault there" is upstaged two sentences later by Adeimantus, who agrees with the logic of Socrates' argument but remains unconvinced. He calls the philosopher-guardians--who have just been deemed invulnerable to mockery--"odd birds" (487d). To say, as Saxonhouse says, that the entire section is one big joke to be laughed off[167] is to ignore Socrates' shows of seriousness. Likewise, to take the section completely literally is to overlook the significance of the humorous passages and comic disclaimers. Instead of advocating one side or the other, Plato, in switching between gravity and levity, suggestion and retraction, seems to be placing the burden of interpretation upon the reader. Whether he is leading the reader somewhere in particular is a matter about which it is too soon to conclude anything.

Socrates thus labors to perform some verbal trick that will win over the skeptical Adeimantus. He admits that to answer Adeimantus' question he, Socrates, must give him an "illustration" (487e). At this point Socrates presents his famous Allegory of the Ship. For our purposes, it should be noted that Plato has announced in advance that the imagery is to be taken as such, as imagery. We readers are privy to the allegory's representational shortcomings and thus are not surprised when the book does not end abruptly there. The allegory itself contains an allusion to Plato's difficulty in explaining the importance of philosophy: Socrates says that the other sailors on board will regard the true navigator as nothing but a useless "word-spinner" and "star-gazer" (498a). Adeimantus remains unswayed (498c); he is unconvinced that philosophy is the route to a happy destiny. Socrates' only response is to admit the problem, claiming that if the notion of philosophic rule is impossible, then "there would be some justification for laughing at us for day-dreaming" (499c).

At this point, the stakes of the discussion have been raised, and expectations have been heightened, for Socrates' credibility has been directly challenged. His case needs substantiation: Mere rhetoric or the elenchic method will not do. In a pivotal passage (500c), Socrates makes an analogy, if not an equation, between philosophers and artists; and shortly thereafter he refers to them as "philosophic-artists." The philosophic-artist will, as he works, "look frequently in both directions": at justice and beauty in their "true natures" and again in the "copy of them he is trying to make in human beings" (501b). The artist will sometimes erase and draw again, but he will go on "until he has made human nature as acceptable to God as may be."[168] Socrates asks whether this "beautiful picture" of the persevering artist--whom he now calls a "political artist" (501c)--might begin to persuade those who attacked the idea that philosophy might be reconciled with politics (473d-474a).[169] From here on, he introduces arguments that draw heavily upon visual imagery: the Simile of the Sun (507b-509c), the Divided Line Analogy (509c-511e),[170] and the Allegory of the Cave (514a-521c).

I want to propose--provisionally, for it is difficult to embark upon a full discussion of Plato's authorial role here until we have examined Book 10 and the Theory of Art--that once again Plato has given us readers sufficient forewarning that the ensuing arguments are not to be taken at full face value. We are to regard the "artworks" dramatically as Socrates' attempts to overcome Glaucon's and Adeimantus' resistance to Socrates' unstated but persistent injunction that they accept justice on its own terms; yet we are also to regard these verbal artworks as goads to our own self-examination in *our* philosophic exchange with Plato. Plato's self-conscious presence, his self-parody, his irony, invites us to question *him* and his book. We are not, as careful readers, simply to accept at face value the forthcoming myths and allegories.

The Sun and the Line

My treatment of the Simile of the Sun and the Divided Line Analogy will not be a full one, and what commentary I do care to offer will have to wait, for I think the images in themselves are presented in a straightforward, ostensibly serious manner, *as if* the ironic mode has been abandoned. Plato's retraction of the sun and the line images, of their literal significance, comes later in the book, though he does give a few hints to the effect that these sketches have been overdrawn. For instance, at one point (509c), Glaucon mocks sarcastically Socrates' "miraculously transcendent" image of the good. Socrates responds by dissimulating himself, putting up little defense on his own behalf: "Now, don't blame me, it was you who made me say what I thought about it" (509c).

The Allegory of the Cave

Much has been written about the Allegory of the Cave, in various efforts at interpretation. I will not discuss this mass of secondary literature; indeed, the allegory is rich enough to accommodate several interpretations. What I do want to do is to advance further the claim that Plato is playing with irony and that the allegory is part of his ironic presentation. To this end I wish to point to a few significant passages.

First, after his initial description of the cave (514a-c), Socrates responds to a remark that the allegory is an "odd picture." His response is that the picture is "drawn from life" (515a). Desmond Lee comments that this phrase (*homoious hemin*) means literally "like us," but he adds that the phrase has been a matter of controversy.[171] Lee concludes that there is a touch of caricature in this remark, that Plato is saying that "ordinary man is often very uncritical in his beliefs."[172] My reading of the passage is that it is more than mild caricature (how very many readers over the ages, enthralled by Plato's description of the shadows on the wall, have read those words, staring straight ahead at the page!).[173] Rather, the importance of Socrates' comment seems to emerge if one recalls that earlier Socrates likened the philosophers to artists, saying that such artists draw the state using a "divine pattern" (500e), though they also frequently look in the other "direction," namely at the copy found in human beings (501b). The issue of drawing according to a divine pattern or not will resurface in Book 10--thus it is here anticipatory as well as evocative--but for now I will limit my remarks to its latter function.

Again, Voegelin's analysis lends interpretive muscle. Voegelin's focus upon the symbolism of depth and descent leads him to notice a thread running from the opening Piraeus scene to the Allegory of the Cave to the Myth of Er: All three are *katabasis* scenes. In the first case (the opening), Plato recalls Homer's tale of Hades and thereby places the discussion in the Piraeus against the symbolic background of the underworld. Implicit in the logic of that imagery is that the Piraeus is the "underworld" to the political world of Athens, that locale from which Socrates initially walks down. Athens and Hades are the reference points for the logic of the symbolism. As such, the Athens that grants citizenship is the higherworld, in contrast to the moneymaking activity that is found in the harbor. Cephalus already has one foot in hell.

But Voegelin does not notice an inconsistency in the symbolic connection that he sees between the opening scene and the cave allegory. If the simple symbolism of depth and descent holds true, then symmetry would require that Hades, the Piraeus, and the Cave be grouped together as underworlds. Conversely, Athens and the source of light in the cave allegory should be symbolically related as "topsided" worlds. But this symmetry does not make interpretive sense. For the *political* world would in one case be on the topside, in the other case, on the lower side. However, the bright source of light in the cave allegory does not hail from a political world such as Athens, but from a world even farther beyond Hades and the underworld than is Athens. Nor, in retrospect, was Plato suggesting in the opening scene that Athens is a great source of enlightenment in contrast to the Piraeus.[174] Rather, something else must be going on, though there does seem to be a symbolic connection between the two scenes.

As Heidegger, Jaeger, and Voegelin have all proposed, the point of the cave allegory is that it states the essence of *paideia*, not that of philosophic truth. *Paideia* in this context, as Voegelin explains, means nothing more than a *turning around*, a turning away from the immediacies of existence. But therewith, the allegory also introduces the theme of *return*: One returns to the cave, once one has been philosophically enlightened. Voegelin claims that this means that the philosopher must return to Hades;[175] but I think otherwise.

If the cave allegory is an image "drawn from life" rather than from a "divine pattern," then the idea of ascension to the divine patterns is probably not to be taken literally, but heuristically, as is the pictorial contrast between a higher world and a lower world. More likely, we readers are to look as we read in the other "direction," at the copy "like us"; thus we can surmise that the theme of ascension is probably a setup for the main theme of *return (palin katabainein)*. Furthermore, if when the cave allegory enters the picture, the symmetrical logic that had established the Piraeus as Athens' Hades (as per Voegelin) breaks down, then we can probably conclude that Plato's ulterior point in both of these *katabasis* scenes is more to teach philosophic enlightenment than to convey the visual imagery of separate, disjunctive worlds. After reading the Allegory of the Cave, one realizes in retrospect that the significance of the opening scene now lies not so much in *katabasis* and the theme of depth and descent to the Piraeus but in the fact that Socrates has turned around, after the initial *katabasis*, and is *returning (apeini)* to cavelike Athens (having "seen the spectacle" in the Piraeus [327b]).[176] *Hence the space to which one returns in one's pursuit of justice is now, with these two "return" scenes in front of us, visually situated between higher and lower forms of self-interest--between moneygrubbing (the Piraeus) on the lower side and intellectual self-indulgence (beholding the light outside the cave) on the topside*:

> "Then our job as lawgivers is to compel the best minds to attain what we have called the highest form of knowledge, and to ascend to the vision of the good as we have described, and when they have achieved this and see well enough, prevent them behaving as they are now allowed to."
> "What do you mean by that?"
> "Remaining in the upper world, and refusing to return again to the prisoners in the cave below and share their labours and rewards, whether trivial or serious." (519d)

The Education of the Philosopher

If any section of the *Republic* poses great difficulty for me in advancing the claim that Plato writes with a sustained irony throughout the book, it is this one (519c-541b). The arguments appear very fixed, staid, and serious. Nonetheless, I think that there is strong evidence that the entire section has a double-edged or reflexive quality to it, such that part of *our* "philosophic education" with Plato will entail our learning to see through and beyond the rigid formality of this section. Again, most of my case will have to wait until I examine the Theory of Art, though even in this education section Plato gives plenty of clues to the effect that he regards arithmetic, plane geometry, solid geometry, astronomy, harmonics, and dialectics as part of the sensual arts and thus their abstract imagery is to be recognized as such (532b-534b). Socrates scolds Glaucon at one point for interpreting the metaphor of the mind's eye so literally (529a-b): Glaucon, thinking that his comment will please Socrates, praises astronomy for making the soul look upward, but Socrates instructs him that the mind looks "upward" only by studying "the real and the invisible." We ought, says Socrates, to treat the visible splendors of the sky, even though they appear constant and absolute, "just as one might treat a wonderful and carefully drawn design by Daedalus or any other artist or draughtsman" (529e). Socrates retreats from his seriousness in this education section, warning that he might be "slightly ridiculous" at one point. At Glaucon's request, he explains how: "I was forgetting that we are amusing ourselves with an imaginary sketch, and was getting too worked up. I had in mind as I spoke the unjust abuse which philosophy suffers, which annoyed me, and my anger at the critics made me speak more seriously than I should" (536c).

Imperfect Societies

This is another section from which it is difficult to draw definitive proof of Plato's irony. But I want to suggest that the reader, now suspicious of Plato's method, has to inquire into the possible irony of including an extended section on imperfect societies in a book supposedly about the "ideal state." Socrates seems to be begging certain questions up to this point, for he has yet to state the case convincingly that the "ideal" is even a practical possibility--and now he begins to prove how tenuous and fragile his ideal state is. The wry humor of this section should not be overlooked, or at least the political structures described and the scheme of historical decay should not be taken too strictly.[177] Why does the "perfect society" fail? The answer: The philosophers (whose ideal education we've been reading about in detail just up to this point) make a mistake--they miss the time for breeding.[178]

Even if one contends that Plato has abandoned a more obvious ironic "mode" in this section, his arguments are still fraught with subironies that have the effect of coloring the section as a whole as questionable. It should be observed in this regard that a series of ironic reversals are the cause for the successions of decay in the various political systems:

The mistake in the "ideal" turns into quarreling (the reverse of harmony) among the rulers, and the resultant (timocratic) state will fear having intelligent people hold public office. Timocratic men will, unlike philosophers, value money over intelligence, and they will pursue in the private sector their secretly held passion for wealth. But then this principle turns on itself, for the accumulation of wealth in private hands destroys timocracy; and oligarchy takes over. Unlike the timocrat, the oligarch lets his passions go unrestrained. This lack of restraint, then, is the principle of destruction that turns oligarchy into democracy. Unlike the oligarch, the democrat is free to pursue whatever he wishes; but this liberty for all ironically turns into tyranny and hence liberty for no one. And under tyranny, no one is safe or happy, Socrates concludes.

Cut to bare bones, the argument reveals a logic of ironic reversal clearly at work. But what or whom is Plato ironizing?--for now that his description of the "ideal state" is past, there would seem to be no reason to engage in mockery or self-parody, nor would there seem to be reason for Plato to clue his audience that they are to discount the seriousness of the ideal. The answer is given at the outset of the section. As Voegelin points outs, the entire "imperfect society" section is cast as a mock-Homeric appeal to the Muses: "Then how will change take place in our state? How will Auxiliaries and Rulers come to fall out with each other or among themselves? Shall we invoke the Muses, like Homer, and ask them to tell us 'how the quarrel first began'? Let us imagine that they are talking to us in a rather *dramatic, high-flown fashion, pretending to be very much in earnest, though they are really only teasing us* as if we were children" (545c--emphasis added).

Plato unmistakably admits the irony of this presentation, and the target of the irony is identified as Homer. The section follows closely the format of correlating political systems to their attendant character types; and thus as the argument degenerates to the unhappiness of tyrants, the question of the happiness of philosopher-kings reemerges, as a point of contrast. The "wickedest" and most "unjust" (576b) man will prove to be the unhappiest (576e). But even the enlarged perspective, the big picture, on the connection between individual happiness and politics fails to persuade: It does not follow from the proof of the unhappiness of the unjust man that the just man is happiest. Socrates has more talking to do (577a-592), until finally he more or less gives up on this point (592b). But before he does, Plato ties up some loose ends and, far from finishing the book at this point, prepares us for the finale, the last chapter.

In a key passage in Book 9 (587c-588a), Socrates attempts to describe "how much" unhappier the tyrant is than the philosopher-king. The dialogue takes on a heavily arithmetical tone. The tendency among readers, I suspect, is to take Socrates' calculations quite literally, and to some professional Platonic interpreters this means writing these passages off as the esoteric result of Plato's obscure venture into Pythagoreanism. One examines the number 729 for some special mystical significance and then routinely concludes that Plato has gone off the deep end. One commentator, M.A. Diès, has suggested, however, that the calculations in this passage are a *plaisanterie de mathématicien*.[179] They recall the mock-Homeric appeal to the Muses in the argument concerning the degeneration of the ideal society (546b-d). But I think they recall a passage even farther back in the book, in which Socrates explicitly connects human life (via human sexuality) and mathematics:

> [Socrates]: As law-giver, you have already picked your men Guardians. You must now pick women of as nearly similar natural capacities as possible to go with them. They will live and feed together, and have no private home or property. They will mix freely in their physical exercises and the rest of their training, and their natural instincts will necessarily lead them to have sexual intercourse. Or do you think necessity is too strong a term?
>
> [Glaucon]: The necessity will be sexual and not mathematical, but sex is perhaps more effective than mathematics when it comes to persuading or driving the common man to do anything. (458d-e)

The passage blends humor and seriousness in its dual reference to sexuality and mathematics as inducements for action. It is suggested in the passage that they differ because the motivation behind sexuality is bodyoriented and baser, whereas motivation on the basis of mathematics is intellectual and less self-centered. That human life itself is based and dependent upon a kind of "persuasion" is the source of both the humor and the seriousness of the passage.

Jowett gives the clearest explanation that I have encountered of the significance of the number 729. In Socrates' scheme of descending political orders and their representative figures (philosopher-king, timocrat, oligarch, democrat, tyrant), the oligarch is at third remove from the philosopher-king, and the tyrant is at third remove from the oligarch. Accordingly, the oligarch's happiness afforded by his wealth is an imitation at third remove from the happiness of the philosopher-king. And if wealth is but a shadow of real happiness (586c), then the tyrant's happiness is but a shadow of a shadow. A shadow, as a surface, can be represented (pseudo-) mathematically as 3 x 3 = 9. The 3s in this equation signify that the oligarch is thrice removed from the philosopher-king, and so on. To fathom the depth of the difference between the happiness of the philosopher-king and that of the tyrant, not 9, but 9 cubed (which equals 729), must be used to express the enormous interval. A cube expresses better than a surface the difference between a philosopher-king and a tyrant, for a cube represents the *depth* of the difference as well as the *solidity* of the just man's happiness. Plato switches from simple arithmetic to solid geometry, from two-dimensionality to three-dimensionality to make his point. The number 729, Socrates adds, conveniently corresponds to human life, because a year is supposed to consist of about 364 1/2 days and 364 1/2 nights, together which equal 729.[180]

Jowett remarks, "It should be remembered that Plato is only playing with numbers and must not be taken too seriously."[181] His testimony, Diès's analysis, and the other numerical references I have cited seem to indicate that the passage in question at the end of Book 9 is not to be taken literally as a mathematical proof. And toward the end of Socrates' calculations, Glaucon suggests that Socrates is being overly mathematical in his logic, when he responds to Socrates: "Obvious to a mathematician anyway!"

The remainder of the passage bears repeating here, for it has been overlooked (and mistranslated[182]) far too often:

> "Conversely, you will find, if you work out the cube, that the measure of the difference between the two in terms of true pleasure is that the philosopher king lives seven hundred and twenty-nine times more pleasantly than the tyrant, and the tyrant the same amount more painfully than the philosopher king."
>
> "What a terrific calculation," Glaucon exclaimed, "and all to show how much difference there is between the just and unjust man in terms of pleasure and pain!"
>
> "But it's quite correct," I replied, "and fits human life, if human life is measured by days and nights and months and years."
>
> "As of course it is."
>
> "And if the good and just man is so much superior to the bad and unjust man in terms of pleasure, will not his superiority be infinitely greater in terms of grace and beauty of life and of excellence?"
>
> "Infinitely greater," he replied emphatically. (587e–588b)

The question Socrates and company have been addressing all along, Socrates next reminds them, is whether injustice pays better, especially to the man who combines injustice with a reputation for justice. Hence the above passage harks back all the way to the beginning of the book; and I think this section especially recalls Socrates' first encounter with Thrasymachus. *For now Socrates has given a numerical answer to*

Thrasymachus, who originally asked for a definition of justice, according to Socrates, as if he were asking for a definition of twelve (337b). Putting the answer in terms of mathematical images explains in part Socrates' technical discussions such as the Divided Line Analogy. And the point here is similar to what Socrates was asserting in his opening exchange with Thrasymachus, in the divided line section, and throughout, at the points I would call Plato's ironic disclaimers. The question of justice is tricky not simply because it is difficult to conceptualize--difficult, because, as some commentators claim, invoking the logic of the Divided Line, our world and the world of the eternal forms (*eidos*) are so radically and literally separated. It is indeed difficult to conceive why one should pursue justice, but this is because the benefits--the personal "payments"--of pursuing political justice seem illusory and elusive. By claiming that the superiority of justice is *infinitely* greater than injustice, Socrates is saying that justice is qualitatively--and not just quantitatively--different, that the two, justice and injustice, are beyond comparison in terms of "payment."

The passage contains another admission that the arguments proposed and the language used have been proposed and used *ironically*. By irony I mean an understanding and use of language that self-consciously admits, and in some way indicates the admission, that language itself is inadequate as a mode of representation.[183] Plato in this passage reveals that all along he has not been trying *literally* to prove the happiness of philosophers--the language itself falls short of proving that--and yet the language contains a structure by which one can nonetheless glean the point Plato is trying, albeit indirectly, to convey. Even the humorous, whimsical side to Plato's language now shows itself deliberately ironic, a ruse, a cover for the more stirring, perhaps tragic, point Plato was suggesting: the calculation of 729 fits human life, *if* human life is measured by days and nights and months and years (as of course it is). The deliberately controlled quantification of the question of justice has been but a crutch for our ordinarily utilitarian and sophistic minds, minds that "measure" the value of existence or the value of action on a pain and pleasure calculus, in days and nights, in rewards and consequences. But Plato's irony here cannot "make" us think differently: it just presents options to us, by inviting us to be reflective vis-à-vis the text as we struggle to read the double-layered prose of irony.

Knowing this, we can reread with fresh insight the ending to this book (9), namely the famous passage:

> "I see what you mean," Glaucon said. "You mean that he [the just man] will do so in the society which we have been describing and

which we have theoretically founded; but I doubt if it will ever exist on earth."

"Perhaps [*isos*]," I said, "it is laid up as a pattern in heaven, where he who wishes can see it and found it in his own heart. But it doesn't matter [*diapherei de ouden*] whether it exists or ever will exist; in it alone, and in no other society, could he take part in public affairs." (592b)

Perhaps the pattern is laid up in heaven--*but no matter.* I take this sentiment to be indicative of the "double perspective" of irony, which should distinguish it from the traditional theological and traditional "Platonic" points of view. For now we will put this sentiment on hold, but we will return to this passage shortly.

Book 10

Annas declares that the main argument of the *Republic* ends with Book 9. She calls Book 10 an "excrescence" that appears "gratuitous," "clumsy," and which contains an "embarrassingly bad argument" as well as a "ragbag" section.[184] All in all, it is a "lame and messy ending." Though Book 10 seems to be particularly offensive to Annas, her views reflect a common complaint among Platonic commentators. Desmond Lee similarly writes that Book 10 has the appearance of an appendix or coda.

I want emphatically to take exception to such claims. Far from being a gratuitous appendix, Book 10 is, upon my reading, the kicker to the whole book--not the climax perhaps, but certainly an ending that is needed to make the book coherent. Plato has left too many dangling clues and too many loose ends along the way, all of which have only alluded to what he is up to. Why does Plato employ visual constructs or mathematical arguments while disclaiming them in part? Specifically he has not yet addressed (even ironically!) *why* he has written an ironic book. Hence the final book, I want to contend, is necessary for understanding *our* relation to Plato and Plato's relation to us as ironic educator. Therewith, we need to know how we are to take the book as a whole. To that end, Book 10 poses tacitly the question: What is this book, the *Republic*, representing? And if this book depicts a vision of an ideal republic and an ideal concept of justice, then how are we to follow these ideals? First we need to grasp the artistry of the book itself.

The Theory of Art

My interest in this section is not the same as that of those commentators engaged in the running debate about whether Socrates literally banishes part or all of representational poetry and whether his position on art in Book 10 is consistent with that in Book 2.[185] Suffice it to say that Socrates approaches art in more general fashion at the outset of Book 10 than he does in Book 2. His position is that artistic "creation" is not creation as such but is a form of re-presentation or mimicry. As re-presentation, it is at "third-order" remove from the idea it reflects or embodies. The discussion quickly switches from tables to justice: The point is, the artist cannot "create" justice, only gods can. Thus the discussion as a whole adumbrates another major retraction or disclaimer issued by Plato with regard to the ideal state, the "foundation" of which Socrates has just depicted in a "word sketch."

Yet if this discussion of art is the start of a disclaimer, the disclaimer soon assumes the form of an apparent diatribe against Homer (whereas in Book 3 Plato refrained from criticizing Homer, identifying his poetry as an example of the acceptable "mixed" type of speech). At first, Plato pulls his punches by couching his criticism of Homer in indirect language: "In all such cases, we should bear the following considerations in mind. When someone tells us that he has met someone who is a master of every craft and has a more exact understanding about all subjects than any individual expert, we must answer that he is a simpleminded fellow who seems to have been taken in by the work of a charlatan, whose apparent omniscience is due entirely to his own inability to distinguish knowledge, ignorance, and representation" (598d).

But immediately thereafter he identifies the culprit as Homer (598e). The problem with Homer and other tragedians is that they "fail to perceive that [their works] are representations at the third remove from reality" (599a). And when it comes to "matters of such importance as military strategy, political administration, and human education," we should have a right to cross-examine Homer. (The reader of Plato's *Phaedrus* might recall at this point Socrates' criticism of writing in general, namely that if one ever asks written words about what they say, from a desire to be instructed, the words go on repeating the same thing forever [275e].) So Socrates proceeds to pose certain rhetorical questions, ostensibly directed toward Homer; but what is remarkable is that the same questions could apply equally to Plato:

1. Socrates asks whether Homer has ever had any actual success in founding or reforming a state: "'My dear Homer,' we shall say, 'if our

definition of representation is wrong and you are not merely manufacturing copies at third remove from reality, but are a stage nearer the truth about human excellence, and really capable of judging what kind of conduct will make the individual or the community better or worse, tell us any state whose constitution you have reformed, as Lycurgus did at Sparta and others have done elsewhere on a larger or smaller scale." (599d).

The irony is that neither has Socrates had any "practical" political influence (and the practical effect of the *Republic* has been in doubt throughout the book). Socrates the pot is calling Homer the kettle black. And neverthless, Socrates and Plato both know that Homer's influence upon the Greek polity is firmly entrenched and widespread and that is precisely why they are combatting it.

2. Socrates belittles Homer for having no "followers": "Well, if he did no public service, do we hear of him founding a school of his own, where enthusiastic pupils came to hear him while he lived and to hand on a Homeric way of life to their successors? That was how Pythagoras got his great reputation, and his successors still talk of a Pythagorean way of life which distinguishes them in the eyes of the world from other people" (600b).

The irony here is that the gadfly Socrates also works solo (his only really enthusiastic "follower" being Plato himself--and if Plato is uncritically reporting Socrates' words, and especially if he is mimicking the Homeric mode of speech, then Plato is not really "following" Socrates). The talk of the Pythagoreans may be evidence that Plato's self-conscious use of "Pythagoreanism" throughout the book has been in ironic mockery, not mystical reverence.

3. Socrates chastises the "wandering" Homer for his faulty and unpopular educational methods: "Do you think, Glaucon, that if Homer had really been able to bring men the benefits of education, instead of merely representing it, he would not have had many enthusiastic followers and admirers? . . . Would the contemporaries of Homer and Hesiod have let them continue as wandering minstrels, if they had really been able to make them better men?" (600c-d).

Socrates should talk, having been sentenced to death for corrupting the youth. Of course, only Plato and his readers are in a position to know the irony of Socrates' remark (and this is a case of Plato writing ironically at Socrates' expense). Also Plato seems again to be raising the issue of being paid for one's pursuit of justice; and if Socrates berating Homer for having received no rewards is ironic, then this passage may actually be a backhanded defense of Homer against the sophists.

So what is the point? Why is Plato assuming the posture of directing an attack against Homer when the criticisms apply equally to Socrates or else to Plato himself? This central question--of why Plato poetically inveighs against the poets, or more specifically, why Plato uses a mock-Homeric mode to mock and mimic Homer--has been asked by a few commentators such as Jowett and Strauss but has been somehow ignored by the vast majority.

Eric Havelock, in his *Preface to Plato*, recognizes the paradox involved in Plato's poetic diatribe against the poets; but Havelock quickly dismisses the explanation that Plato is being ironic.[186] He calls an ironic reading of Plato reductionist and evasive, one that is based upon the assumption that "the *Republic* (so-called) is all about politics."[187] Instead, Havelock argues that by "poetry" and especially Homeric poetry, Plato means a vast social, cultural, and educational condition, a condition that was not nearly as narrow as our modern-day conceptions of "art" and "poetry." Furthermore, Havelock contends that Plato opposed Homeric poetry and culture because he was opposed to oral culture;[188] and he was opposed to oral culture because he viewed reality as "rational, scientific, and logical"[189] and felt that that reality must be presented in written prose, not spoken poetry.

My own view is that Havelock is basically correct in thinking that Plato is addressing a cultural condition far wider than what we might today understand as "art" or "literature" or "poetry" but that Havelock's own schematic categories--for instance his categoric opposition between "culture" or "education" and "politics"--seriously misconstrue the issues. His entire explanation is based upon the presumption that Plato necessarily opposed oral culture, and there is considerable evidence to the contrary in the *Republic* itself as well as the *Phaedrus*. If instead we try to understand Plato's prose as an attempt to extend certain aspects of oral culture into writing, then we must suspect Plato of taking a much more complex, rather than simply adversarial, stand toward Homer. Havelock misses the reflexive quality in Plato's writing, the extent to which his diatribe directed toward Homer is at the same time a self-critique;[190] and thus Havelock misses Plato's ambivalence toward Homer, and the irony of the book as a whole. He misses, for instance, the way Plato has bound the question of art to the question of politics: Plato does not want us simply to mimic the book, to "follow" his "utopia," the way in which one might recite and follow Homer. Havelock imputes to Plato his own narrow understanding of politics, namely as an artificial enterprise of passing legislation within boundaried areas, and thus he misses the possibility that a wider "artistic" reading of the book could be compatible with a "political" reading.

Plato himself in effect answers the question of why he is at once attacking and following Homer when he distinguishes between artists who understand that their art is representation, and those who do not. Plato's self-parody, his irony, is an indication to the reader of Plato's own awareness of his art *as* art. But the reason he conveys this awareness is not simply to draw attention to himself and his self-consciousness and his masterly control. Rather, the point seems to be to invite the reader to question the text for himself or herself, to regard the words as aspects of representative art, and as art to realize the book's inadequacies, namely that what Plato is trying to convey goes beyond (overlook the visual imagery) what is literally represented.

Plato then admits as much, that his text should be read critically, for he virtually tells the reader outright not to take his text too literally:

> "In the same way the poet can use words and phrases as a medium to paint a picture of any craftsman, though he knows nothing except how to represent him, and the metre and rhythm and music will persuade people who are as ignorant as he is, and *who judge merely from his words*, that he really has something to say about shoemaking or generalship or whatever it may be. So great is the natural magic of poetry. Strip it of its poetic coloring, reduce it to plain prose, and I think you know how little it amounts to." (601a-b--emphasis added)

If the reader misses the way in which the above references to metre, rhythm, and music reflect backward upon Plato's recurring motif of "harmony," then Plato clarifies himself so that the point will be grasped beyond doubt. Art, Socrates explains, appeals to the less rational part of our nature. Our minds are "liable to all sorts of confusions." Here Plato makes explicit his purposes in using mathematical language: "Measuring, counting, and weighing have happily been discovered to help us out of these difficulties, and to ensure that we should not be guided by apparent differences of size, quantity and heaviness, but by calculations of number, measurement, and weight" (602d).[191]

Allowing another glimpse into Plato's modus operandi, Socrates contends that just as one must not allow oneself to be carried away mindlessly by the pity that the tragic poets inspire, so must one resist more comedic forms of poetry. Naturally I am inclined to think that here Plato is referring to Socrates' (as well as his own) tendency to employ humor toward ironic ends: "Does not the same argument apply to laughter as to pity? For the effect is similar when you enjoy on the stage--or even in ordinary life--jokes that you would be ashamed to make yourself, instead of detesting their vulgarity. You are giving rein to your comic instinct, which your reason has restrained for fear you may seem to be playing the fool, and bad taste in the theatre may insensibly lead you into becoming a buffoon at home" (606c-d).

Thus runs Plato's "diatribe" against Homer. To be sure, one can cite other passages that reveal Plato's admiration for Homer.[192] What we can safely say, however, is that Plato's stance toward Homer is a complex one, perhaps one finally of ambivalence. But at least this reading of Plato's motives complicates the more straightforward reading of Plato's project as an attempt to substitute "philosophic" principles for Homeric poetic conventions (as Havelock argues). Surely Plato *is* doing something of the sort with respect to Homer, engaging in a kind of one-upmanship. Yet his view of the internality and independence of philosophic reasoning puts his "followers" in the situation of a psychological double bind (similar to Bentham's and Mill's sternly liberal tutoring of J.S. Mill). Put simply, the question is, How does an educator nourish (encourage, promote, facilitate, transmit, teach) independent thought? If Plato's point overall in the book is to introduce a new principle of *paideia*, then the following passage, which is dramatically highlighted by its placement at the end of the section on art, is written with an unmistakable irony in mind, which points to the difficulty of Plato's own task and indicates his awareness of the problem: "And so, Glaucon," I continued, "when you meet people who admire Homer as the educator of Greece, and who say that in the administration of human affairs and education we should study him and model our whole lives on his poetry, you must feel kindly towards them as good men within their limits, and you may agree with them that Homer is the best of poets and first of tragedians" (606e-607a).

The question remains, however, why Plato, though a confessed writer of representational poetry, insists that poetry must be repudiated in the ideal state. Whatever one has concluded up to this point on the issue of poetic banishment, one nonetheless has to take into account Plato's partial retraction of his argument at the end (607e-608b). He admits that poetry may prove to have high value and truth, but he advises his listeners to recite his argument "as a charm" (608a), that is, as an inner warning or a hedge against the possible ill effects of poetic rapture. The "argument" now becomes but a working hypothesis or a "theme": "Our theme shall be that such poetry has no serious value or claim to truth, and we shall warn its hearers to fear its effects on the constitution of their inner selves, and tell them to adopt the view of poetry we have described" (608b).

The section ends on the resonating theme of *choice*, that the personal ethics of becoming good or bad have greater consequences and that the pursuit of justice involves resisting certain temptations: "Yes, my dear Glaucon," I said, "because the issues at stake, the choice between becoming a good man or bad, are even greater than they appear, and neither honour nor wealth nor power, nor poetry itself, should tempt us to neglect the claims of justice and excellence of every kind" (608c).

The Myth of Er

Annas writes that the proof of the soul's immortality (in the section 608c-612, just prior to the Myth of Er) is introduced (608d) in a very "offhanded way," which "might make one wonder how seriously it was meant."[193] But she continues: "except--the irony seems pointless here." The "irony" appears pointless to her, I suggest, because she goes on to analyze the section and the myth following as straightforward argumentation and unironic prose. She even suspects as much, later apologizing: "Perhaps we are taking this myth too literally."[194] Her frustrations and confusions with the myth are not uncommon among serious students of the *Republic*. Why--after all the disparaging talk regarding representation--does Plato at the end resort to a superpoetic mythical account? Annas's answer: It just doesn't make sense and, moreover, it spoils the "unity" of the book.[195] Other interpreters speculate that the point of the myth is quasi-theological, that Plato is attempting to convey (not so subtly, I might add) the message that justice literally will be rewarded in an afterlife.[196]

I disagree with Annas on at least two counts (which is not to say that I agree with the theological interpretation). First, I believe that Plato sustains his irony all the way to the end, i.e., the Myth of Er is supremely and profoundly ironic; and second, that the irony does in fact have a point of sorts. Furthermore, I do not agree with the general lot of critics that the Myth of Er is a sloppy appendix or epilogue to the book. There is evidence for the myth's continuity with the rest of the book if only by virtue of its recollecting certain themes that are carried over from the "main" text. Some of these cross-references have already been mentioned. For instance, the theme of Gyges' ring is picked up from the beginning of Book 2 (or Lee's "Part 1"), and the point is reiterated: We are to pursue justice, Socrates explains, whatever the worldly consequences and the relative earthly "payoffs." And the nature and the respective order of Glaucon's and Adeimantus' concerns that were expressed in the early part of the book are preserved and carried over symmetrically into this ending. The Theory of Art section answers Glaucon's concern with visible, worldly consequences, and now, in the Myth of Er section, Socrates will examine the "otherworldly" implications of pursuing justice, in response to Adeimantus' concern for the invisible. It should be noted that this entire discussion is held to the main text by a symbolic extension--as Voegelin points out, the imagery of Hades is again invoked in the Myth of Er, recalling the scene in the Piraeus and the scene in the Allegory of the Cave.

But Voegelin takes the myth literally, as a straight statement of the inevitability of the coming of a day of reckoning for our souls. I should think that the symbolism needs to be further explored. As Voegelin notes, the opening of the *Republic--kateben*--immediately recalls Homer and the *Odyssey*. Now in the Myth of Er and *this* particular tale of descent and return, Socrates disavows the connection with Homer, stating, "What I have to tell won't be like Odysseus' tale to Alcinous" (614b). Plato *seems* to be disassociating himself as myth-teller from Homer--but the disassociation is tricky, fraught with ironies. As Desmond Lee points out, the next line (included below in italics), includes a play on words: "What I have to tell won't be like Odysseus' tale to Alcinous, *but the story of a brave man, Er.*"

Alci-noos means "stout-hearted," "brave," as Er was.[197] I want to suggest that this is *more* than a play on words. Alcinous himself is repeatedly referred to in the *Odyssey* as brave and hallow-hearted, but the reason for his bravery and hallow-heartedness is that he is "learned in designs from the gods" in how to rule over the Phaeacians.[198] But Er, we are told, is even braver. The suggestion--and I don't think I am reading too much into what must be a deliberate comparison--is that Er cannot rely upon "divine patterns" for making his choice whether to pursue justice. As Lachesis, maiden daughter of Necessity, tells the souls in the myth: "Souls of a day, here you must begin another round of mortal life whose end is death. No Guardian Spirit will be allotted to you; you shall choose your own. And he on whom the lot falls first shall be the first to choose the life which then shall of necessity be his. Excellence knows no master; a man shall have more or less of her according to the value he sets on her. The fault lies not with God, but with the soul that makes the choice" (617d-e).

As mentioned earlier, the difference between an artist's vision as "drawn from life" (515a) and one "drawn from divine patterns" (500e) forces a comparison of the two prior tales of descent, the Piraeus scene and the Allegory of the Cave.[199] Viewed from a perspective as "drawn from life," the two tales assume a common theme of returning to the political city, and that reading would seem to be reaffirmed here in Er's tale. The theme of choice, irrespective of personal consequences and independent of divine support, connects all three of these *katabasis* scenes.

But this insight now prompts a direct comparison of Plato's and Homer's respective artistry. Here in the Myth of Er we find a further connection to the main text, though by way of negative example. *For the first time* in the entire book--and the difference is striking--Plato (though still playing the reporter) writes in a narrative style ("indirect speech"), thus abandoning the pretext that he is directly reporting dialogue, with "no words between the speeches" (394b), for now he reports Socrates' report of Er's narrative. Hence Plato is conspicuously mimicking Homer (though still putting distance between Homer and himself), and there is some irony in that alone. But there is even greater irony in the point I think Plato is trying to get across through this layering technique, and it has to do with the self-conscious attitude invested and exhibited in the writing of a mock-Homeric presentation of a myth. According to Plato's own logic, his act of reproducing the Myth of Er is not even a straight example of re-presentational artistry but is a report of Socrates' account of the myth (as told to Socrates by Er). If anyone's counting, that means that Plato's writing constitutes a mode of art "at fifth remove" from the truth.

Clearly the myth is written ironically, in some sense. But the greater question remains: What is the point of the irony? Why present a "fifth order" myth, especially at the end of a book seemingly espousing independent philosophical inquiry?

First, the answer cannot be that in telling us a myth, Plato is hoping that we believe "what it says" on a literal level (namely that this character Er saw some souls judged, etc.). Second, that the myth is deliberately presented as fifth order myth (as opposed to a "straight" presentation of a myth, myth not embedded in layers of ironic relief) forecloses the interpretation that Plato is hoping for us merely to accept the simplest "message" of the myth, that he is sharing with us a difficult and esoteric vision of an "afterlife." Clearly, the theme of the afterlife is secondary to the central theme of the book, choosing to pursue justice; and the effect of a tale of an afterlife--ironically presented--begs only further the question of whether the pursuit of justice holds great rewards. Third, if, following the reasoning of the dialogue on representation, the point of the myth (as *pseudos*) is to convey the true (*aletheia*) message of pursuing justice, then it still needs to be explained why the myth is presented at fifth remove from the truth. Straight myth would have sufficed, and Plato would not have needed to add on the ironies involved in mimicking Homer. The answer must be more complex. What is Plato trying to accomplish?

The preliminary answer comes from an analysis of irony--irony as a representational strategy *and* as a philosophical outlook. To present a "fifth order" myth is to include an implicit mention, a tip-off or admission, that the myth is not *literally* true on the various possible levels of literalness, either as myth qua myth (Er's story) or as myth qua message (the reality of an afterlife). The admission counts as an indication to the reader that the literal mode is in some way *inadequate*. Language is viewed here as inadequate *not* because, as the standard Platonic interpretation goes, there exist eternal forms literally "outside" our perceived world, and our shadowy reality partakes only imperfectly of these higher truths. No, if anything, the book on the whole up to this point (e.g., in the Allegory of the Cave) holds out the suggestion or promise that we *can* be exposed to enlightenment. The problem is, the book further suggests, we have to do it mostly ourselves.[200] The book cannot just tell us what it is trying to tell us--for in a sense, an imitated thought is no thought at all.[201] On this score at least, irony is compatible with the *paideia* of the book. Irony requires an active involvement by the reader, to the extent that to recognize a phrase as ironic (without yet knowing the point of the irony), the reader must be able to question the validity of the literal text. The reader, then, "participates" in a kind of dialogue with the author as he or she faces the written text, doubting it and making guesses about when the author is being serious or literal with his words and when not (a situation very close to that suggested by Socrates in the *Phaedrus*[202]). However, as I have already suggested, irony does not entail a complete or outright rejection of the "literal" layer: The words and speeches presented are not simply gratuitous, nor are they simply place markers for their "opposite" meanings. For instance, part of what is involved in the irony of the Myth of Er is that Plato has presented this fifth-order myth as if it were "straight" myth. Perhaps we readers would not have read the myth seriously *had it not* been presented to us as myth (imagine if Socrates had attempted to argue the case for the intrinsic value of justice--a kind of value that by definition does not reveal itself in externalities--through a series of syllogisms). The literal text is retained at least in the form of a suggestion (otherwise why go through the bother of composing superfluous sentences?) here that justice does perhaps hold great rewards.

What the subliminal dialogue of irony does is to split the reader's attention, to suspend him between suggestions and retractions. Irony induces one to adopt a *double perspective* on things, a back-and-forth comparison between the literal and covert texts, between the different visions that they insinuate. The *strategy* of irony presupposes--and promotes--an intellectual outlook that is constantly checking, examining, criticizing, and comparing. But the point of the examination and the criticism is not, finally, simply to hold one in perpetual suspension between several alternating perspectives.[203] Rather, in allowing the competing perspectives or visions to undercut one another, the ironist (or one who is open to irony) gains a deeper appreciation for each vision. The back-and-forth process sharpens one's sense of the *difference* between such perspectives, yet the entire process presumes an overall *relation*, a connection, between the several layers of meaning. Irony as a rhetorical device is echo,[204] a kind of pretense or playfulness that, by virtue of its deliberate imitation of accepted language, poses a challenge to the validity of accepted language. Irony as a more general philosophical outlook is also a kind of pretense or playfulness but toward accepted reality, an embrace of a fiction that, for a moment anyway, challenges the validity of the prevailing view of the world.[205] Put in other terms, one can say that irony is a "sense of the difference and yet the relation between the realms of the actual and the ideal"[206] (one could substitute here the terms *appearance and reality* or *nature and convention* or *the absolute and the relative* and so on). But this "sense" is a thought process;[207] put briefly, irony presupposes, and cultivates, a capacity for open-ended, critical thinking.

The *Republic* is, to be sure, cast ostensibly as a utopia, but it is a utopia that is presented ironically. Upon my reading of irony, this means that although the specific terms of Plato's "ideal" state are not to be taken completely literally, neither is the vision to be rejected outright. Rather, it is to be retained, in thought and imagination, at least as a suggestive moment. As one writer on irony puts it, irony is a matter of "acting in the drama being played and yet looking on the play with an unmovable utopia in the back of the head";[208] the ironist is one who lives "in the world by playing the fool and not being one, by keeping utopia a city of the mind."[209] The irony of the *Republic* invites us into such a double perspective on things: Via a false show of modesty, we allow ourselves the indulgence of entertaining the idea of a higher, in some sense better, world; then we are brought back to our senses, our vision retracted and undercut as unreal; but finally we retain it, although with a deepened sense of the stakes involved. "Double perspective" is another way of saying that the *Republic* prompts us to look at ourselves from an enlarged point of view yet without losing sight of our very real limits: "And to see the souls choosing their lives was indeed a sight, Er said, a sight to move one to pity and laughter and wonder" (620a).

This is the comedy and tragedy and wonder of the *Republic*, when we realize that it is *we* who are those souls now, at every moment, choosing their lives (as we stare straight ahead at the page). This final vision in the Myth of Er turns on its head, in a strange ironic reversal, the exalted place that has been accorded to choice throughout the book.[210] Now we know: Even the promise of an afterlife has to be retracted, is subject to ironization. We must put even the choice to pursue justice in solemn perspective. Is irony so slippery that it paralyzes us into inaction? Hegel would be correct, then, that irony is essentially negative.

I disagree with Hegel. Irony is not, after all, a negative or destructive temperament and technique but instead gives way, I think, to a substantive, world-affirming ethos.[211] The questioning process presupposes (and cultivates) the value of life so examined: One is tempted to say that the ironic spirit provides its own justification. The spirit of irony is expressed in the choice to return to the finite world of politics, to act in and for such a world, even in the face of knowledge that puts that world and that activity into perspective.[212] Irony stands on its own; it does not truly invoke transcendentals or external constants for legitimation--hence an ironic reading of the *Republic* contravenes the standard, metaphysical reading of Plato and his ideational "system."[213] Nor does an ironic return to the polis imply that politics is necessarily an inherently meaningful enterprise; hence irony must be distinguished from an aesthetic view of political activity and from an Arendtian reading of the Greek polis. If, as the story of Oedipus suggests, we suffer and there is no reason for it, then there is also no reason to presume that politics, any more than art, science, religion, or philosophy, can "provide" justice.[214] There are no guarantees. Plato's point--and here I think he is closer to Nietzsche than the latter ever knew--is that without objective dispensations of justice, the temptation to be cynical, to seek power, to reap the immediate rewards of injustice, is great. Plato's response embodies the spirit of irony: Under such conditions, what can convince you to act otherwise? What would count as an argument? Perhaps a bald lie or a comforting myth would be easier to accept, but the question (and life itself) is more complex: Can you still affirm and act in a world the justice of which may be illusory (and not even conceptually "coherent"[215]), and the reasons for which may be based upon a lie? I read Plato's book as not merely an attempt to beg the question, hoping that we call his bluff, but as providing an answer of sorts: The philosopher is one who, knowing all of this, chooses[216] to return to the cave, nonetheless.[217] The function of presenting an explicit utopia is to provide a pedagogic crutch--for it is "hard to imagine a philosopher who loves justice not made mad and ridiculous by the world, unless he be an ironist."[218]

Yet my exposition of the inner workings of irony thus far sounds like an existential philosophy, when instead I think irony, or the spirit or the philosophy or the ethos that irony generates, holds essentially political implications. For the choice to return to the cave is a choice to return to a world with others, other finite human beings.[219] Irony as philosophy is not a program but an art, a way of constructing an enlarged perspective that puts human differences into perspective, lessening their importance. Irony thus generates or reflects an attitude by which persons can associate with each other even though they have nothing "naturally" in common. This is not some mawkishly catholic outlook, for irony deeply realizes that the relationships or the bonds or the community it seeks are initially, maybe even ultimately, based upon a Big Lie.[220] *Political communities are ironic communities.*

If this is the "answer," then I have violated it, I have not done it full justice; for the point of the book is that each individual must discover and choose to pursue this answer or an essentially similar answer for himself or herself.[221] The difficulty of writing and reading such a book is that the *paideia* of the book cannot be transmitted directly from one person to another (as Homer's poetry could be).[222] Hence the book wrestles with and embodies the logical paradox involved in any truly liberal education: How do you teach others the virtue of thinking for themselves? I want to suggest that Plato's "double bind" situation finds its resolution in irony. The book is about an "ideal" that Plato wants us in some way to follow, but in *simply* following, we would be mimicking it and thus would be failing the ideal itself, of independent inquiry, action, and interaction.[223] Therefore he writes poetry (or ironic prose) the subject of which is the evil of representational poetry; and the contradiction betrays Plato's detached perspective vis-à-vis his own text. The point is, the book is *art*, a construction, but the art contains, in and through irony, an *invitation* to question the text itself, to think beyond it, and ultimately to choose a path of justice independently of Plato's indirect encouragement. The best proof of Plato's logic is to be found in the fact that Plato does seem to establish a rapport, a kind of community, with his reader. That community, however, is not based upon nature but rather a shared pretense, upon the ironic artistry of the book itself (and a community of seekers *is* a community of sorts).

Hence, I do not think that Plato betrays Socrates' principle of leading an examined life. The irony of the book invites us to continue to question, to go on drawing distinctions, to criticize the book itself. (In this respect, the controversy surrounding the book demonstrates that the irony has not entirely failed, even if critics and commentators have said little about the overall irony of the book.) The book promotes not the mindless acceptance of the particular terms of the state it depicts, but rather opens up a substantive dialogue, the result of which is the cultivation of critical thinking. Yet the way in which the dialogue is carried out can possibly lead to the further result that something remotely resembling Plato's ideal is, ironically, created. Irony is a spiritual transmission. The political consequences of the book's *paideia* follow from the way it translates a solitary vision into a shared one that can be independently embraced and "followed" by others. Hence I do not think irony is destructive of politics or the state, as Hegel claimed (though I think irony would militate against the state as Hegel conceived it). And thus I also disagree with Karl Popper,[224] not only with his heavy-handed interpretation of Plato but also with his understanding of the function of "philosophy" or even "utopia" with respect to the politics of the state. My reading of Plato is one that is compatible with democracy ("excellence knows no master"[225]) and with an "open" society that respects individuals and encourages participation[226]--but this reading requires alternatively that one see the irony in the (literal) contradiction between Popper's liberal ideal and his illiberal, closed, even dogmatic theoretical approach. I think Thomas Mann is the modern writer who best expresses this paradoxical stance toward politics--though Mann credits Nietzsche rather than Plato for providing the inspiration--in his definition of "political irony," as "the self-betrayal of the intellect in favor of life."[227]

In conclusion, I repeat my claim that the *Republic* is a profoundly ironic work, not only in its strategy of presentation but also, in a more general sense, in the philosophical spirit that it expresses--namely, that justice is to be pursued for its own sake, independent of a concern for reward and reputation--and in the political ideal that it considers-- namely, that the pursuit of justice implies a return to the world of others, even if the notion of community may ultimately be but an enormous fiction. "Perhaps it is laid up as a pattern in heaven . . . but it doesn't matter" (592b).[228]

Notes

1. Other evidence of the prominence of ironic thought in ancient Greece can be found in Connop Thirlwall's "On the Irony of Sophocles," *The Philological Museum*, Vol. 2 (Cambridge: J. Smith, Printer, 1833), pp. 483-537; Annie F. Dekker, *Ironie in de Odyssee* (Leiden: E.J. Brill, 1965); Philip Vellacott, *Ironic Drama: A Study of Euripedes' Method and Meaning* (Cambridge: Cambridge University Press, 1975); and Helen P. Foley, *Ritual Irony: Poetry and Sacrifice in Euripedes* (Ithaca and London: Cornell University Press, 1985). Also, Schein contends that even though we read the *Iliad* as one of the earliest examples of Western literature, the book is actually an ironic meditation upon traditional themes. See Seth L. Schein, *The Mortal Hero: An Introduction to Homer's Iliad* (Berkeley: University of California Press, 1984).

2. E.g., Walter Pater notes in *Plato and Platonism* that there is "plenty of humor in [Plato] and something of irony" (London: Macmillan and Company, 1895), p. 209.

3. Allan Bloom's book, *The Closing of the American Mind*, which caused a stir one summer, is based on a particular reading of Plato, especially of the *Republic*. That Bloom has closed his mind to rival interpretations might suggest that the title of his book is a self-parody. Bloom, *The Closing of the American Mind* (New York: Simon and Schuster, 1987). See also: M.F. Burnyeat, "Sphinx Without a Secret," *New York Review of Books* (November 30, 1985); Martha Nussbaum, "Allan Bloom's 'American Mind,' " *New York Review of Books* (November 5, 1987); Gordon S. Wood, "The Fundamentalists and the Constitution," *New York Review of Books* (February 18, 1988).

4. Rorty explains that ironists read critics and cite numerous critics because they wish not to get trapped in the vocabulary of any single book. See Richard Rorty, *Contingency, Irony, and Solidarity* (Cambridge: Cambridge University Press, 1989), pp. 80-81.

5. Philip Merlan discusses the claim that Plato's works are "reports" in "Form and Content in Plato's Philosophy," *Journal of the History of Ideas* 8 (October, 1947), pp. 406-430.

6. Though I would exempt Vlastos's own works on Plato from this charge.

7. Karl J. Popper, *The Open Society and Its Enemies* (Princeton: Princeton University Press, 1950), p. 87.

8. Note that Wayne A.R. Leys presents an argument very close to Popper's and Wolin's in his "Was Plato Non-Political?" in *Plato II*, ed. Gregory Vlastos (Garden City, N.Y.: Anchor Books, 1971). Leys recites the argument that Plato did not like the "open" society; and he reasons that this is because Plato was "preoccupied with nonpolitical ideals," p. 171.

9. Susan Moller Okin, "Philosopher Queens and Private Wives: Plato on Women and the Family," in *The Family in Political Thought*, ed. Jean Bethke Elshtain (Amherst: University of Massachusetts Press, 1982), pp. 31-50. See also Okin, *Women in Western Political Thought* (Princeton: Princeton University Press, 1971).

10. Ronald Levinson levels precisely this charge at Popper, namely that he misses Socrates' irony. See *In Defense of Plato* (Cambridge: Harvard University Press, 1953), pp. 306-307.

11. Leo Strauss, *Persecution and the Art of Writing* (Glencoe, Illinois: Free Press, 1952), p. 30.

12. Leo Strauss, *The City and Man* (Chicago: University of Chicago Press, 1964), pp. 94-95.

13. *Ibid.*, pp. 111, 127.

14. *Idem, Persecution and the Art of Writing*, p. 24.

15. *Idem, The City and Man*, p. 24.

16. *Ibid.*, p. 74.

17. *Ibid.*, p. 8.

18. Strauss argues that the classics were not simply "abstract" in their philosophizing as are the moderns but that their philosophy related "directly"

to political life. *What Is Political Philosophy? and Other Studies* (Glencoe, Illinois: Free Press, 1959), pp. 28, 78.

19. *Idem, The City and Man*, p. 127.
20. *Ibid.*, pp. 117, 138.
21. *Ibid.*, p. 6.
22. *Ibid.*, p. 131.
23. *Ibid.*, p. 71.
24. *Ibid.*, p. 73.
25. *Ibid.*, p. 117.
26. *Ibid.*, p. 116.
27. *Ibid.*, p. 114.
28. *Ibid.*, p. 111.
29. *Ibid.*
30. *Ibid.*, p. 73.
31. *Ibid.*, p. 94.
32. *Ibid.*, p. 114.
33. *Ibid.*, p. 37.
34. See *Ibid.*, p. 111, and *idem, What Is Political Philosophy?* p. 222.
35. *Idem, The City and Man*, p. 50.
36. *Ibid.*, p. 51.
37. *Ibid.*
38. *Ibid.*
39. *Ibid.*
40. *Ibid.*
41. *Ibid.*
42. *Ibid.*, p. 77.
43. See *ibid.*, "Introduction."
44. *Ibid.*, p. 69.
45. Stanley Rosen, "The Role of Eros in Plato's *Republic*," in *Review of Metaphysics* 18 (March, 1965), pp. 452-475.
46. Rosen cites the following evidence in support of the view that the *Republic* is a "game or a joke"; but I fail to find the humor in many of these examples: 506c1, 509c7-10, 533a1, 536c1, 539b1, 544a1. Similarly, Strauss applies the word "joke" to Socrates' exchange with Thrasymachus, based on the passage 349a6-b1. Strauss, *The City and Man*, p. 5.
47. Arlene W. Saxonhouse, "Comedy in Callipolis: Animal Imagery in the *Republic*," in *American Political Science Review* (September, 1978), p. 890.
48. *Ibid.*, p. 896.
49. Jowett interprets the passage on the education of woman as a serious argument about the nature of convention. See B. Jowett, "Analysis," *The Republic of Plato: Two Volumes in One*, trans. B. Jowett (New York: Hearst's International Library, n.d.), p. 93.
50. The relationship between Plato's *Republic* and Aristophanes' comedies is one that draws much controversy. As mentioned above, the Straussians argue that the *Republic* actually suggests a comic reversal of the state it depicts. In response, Dale Hall writes: "Quite uncritically, [Strauss and

Bloom] just assume that Plato was trying to outdo Aristophanes in a comic satire of certain radical contemporary ideas, presupposing that Plato's purpose was in common with that of the dramatist." Hall mentions that Barker was sure that "Plato is seeking to meet the current satire on communism, including that of Aristophanes"; and he repeats Adam's contention that "Plato was probably dissatisfied with the comedians' travesty of views with which Plato had no little symphathy." Plato may have had Aristophanes' satire in mind, but this does not mean that Plato's purpose was similarly satirical. M.F. Burnyeat notes that the *Ecclesiazousae* must have been written in response to a shorter version of the *Republic*, and that the larger *Republic* we now have is Plato's counterattack. But Burnyeat claims that the jokes are at our expense and that Plato's ultimate point is to argue for the practicability of the absolute ideal. Paul Plass inquires into Socrates' nervousness at the outset of the section on women, and remarks: "The laughter which Socrates expects is ridicule from comic poets, whose response would be a combination of amusement and normal offended propriety, but Socrates does not meet criticism simply on this level with his practical argument about convention. He is ultimately intent upon the objective principle of what is best, and so he turns the issue into a sharp contrast between good and reason against evil and ignorance." H.D. Rankin argues that the *Republic* should be viewed as a satire, "but if we should do this, we would be at the advantage of not being compelled to try to harmonise its many contradictions and paradoxes. We should simply accept them as being there with the intention to stimulate and tease." For Rankin, the satire is more akin to Swift's "A Modest Proposal" than Aristophanes' utopia. See Dale Hall, "The *Republic* and the 'Limits of Politics' " *Political Theory* 5 (August, 1977), p. 296; M.F. Burnyeat, "The Practicability of Plato's Ideal City," Unpublished paper; Paul Plass, "Philosophic Anonymity and Irony in the Platonic Dialogues," *American Journal of Philology* 35 (1964), pp. 254-278; H.D. Rankin, "A Modest Proposal about the *Republic*," *Apeiron* 2 (1968), pp. 20-22. My own view, in brief, is that Plato's relation to the comic poets is analogous to his relation to the tragic poets: namely that he is at once mimicking and attacking the comedians as well as the tragedians, and that this ambivalence is for *our* purview, encouraging us to adopt a double perspective upon the text and ultimately upon political affairs.

51. Saxonhouse, "Comedy in Callipolis," p. 891.

52. *Ibid.*, p. 898.

53. *Ibid.*, p. 899.

54. *Ibid.*, p. 900.

55. *Ibid.*

56. J.H. Randall similarly adopts a view of irony such that irony entails a complete rejection of the literal layer: "Men have read the *Republic*, and imagined that Plato is urging a practical political program--they have been insensitive enough to Plato's irony to think, Socrates is taking the stump for the Perfect City Party in Athens. They have judged that Plato was himself eager to catch a king, and to train him into becoming a philosopher. It is really hard to understand that over the ages readers of the *Republic*, with its layer upon layer

of dramatic irony, have assumed, from the literal-minded Aristotle on, that Plato himself wanted or that any sane man in his senses could want, to *live* under such institutions as Socrates is made to elaborate--institutions so facinating to talk about, but so intolerable to have to endure." Randall, *Plato: Dramatist of the Life of Reason* (New York: Columbia University Press, 1970), p. 165.

57. Strauss, *The City and Man*, p. 51.

58. Jaeger's argument is really a variation upon Schleiermacher's essay on Plato, yet Schleiermacher was more suspecting of Plato's irony: "Is not an argument in favor of the supposition that he did by no means here construct his Republic as a mere scaffolding, afforded by the elaborate execution with which matters in it are discussed, which will bear no immediate application to justice? And if there is some ground for the supposition that this ideal state, even before Plato described it in the books we have, had been a subject of satirical allusion as sketches in his oral instruction, are we to believe that those oral sketches were in all respects so similar to the written works, that Plato in them also introduced the ideal of a Republic only as a scaffolding for his theory of virtue?" F.E.D. Schleiermacher, *Introduction to the Dialogues of Plato*, trans. William Dobson (New York: Arno Press, 1973), pp. 406-407.

59. Werner Jaeger, *Paideia: The Ideals of Greek Culture*, trans. Gilbert Highet (New York: Oxford University Press, 1943), Vol. 2, p. 198.

60. Jaeger mentions the "irony" of the book but says that it is for "artistic" purposes.

61. Although I think Cassirer's intentions and final conclusions are equally dubious--but I will not go into my reasons here. See Ernst Cassirer, "Plato's Republic," *The Myth of the State* (New Haven: Yale University Press, 1946), pp. 61-77.

62. For an analysis of dramatic elements in Plato's writing, see Dorothy Tarrant, "Plato as Dramatist," *Journal of Hellenic Studies* 55 (1955), pp. 82-89.

63. See A.E. Taylor, "The Life of Plato," *Plato: The Man and His Work* (London: Methuen and Co., 1926), pp. 1-10; Desmond Lee, "Introduction," *Plato: The Republic*, ed. Desmond Lee (New York: Penguin Books, 1974), pp. 11-22; see also Gregory Vlastos, "Socrates' Disavowal of Knowledge," *Philosophical Quarterly* 35 (January, 1985), p. 1n.

64. See B. Jowett, "On the Structure of Plato's Republic and its Relation to Other Dialogues," in *Plato's Republic: The Greek Text* Vol. 2, eds. B. Jowett and Lewis Campbell (Oxford: Clarendon Press, 1894); Lee, "Introduction"; and F.M. Cornford, "Plato's Commonwealth," *The Unwritten Philosophy and Other Essays* (Cambridge: Cambridge University Press, 1950), pp. 58-59.

65. See Jowett, "Analysis," p. 18.

66. G.W.F. Hegel, *Lectures on the History of Philosophy*, trans. E.S. Haldane and Frances H. Simson (London: Routledge and Kegan Paul, 1974), p. 307.

67. *Idem, The Philosophy of Right*, trans. T.M. Knox (Oxford: Clarendon Press, 1952), p. 101.

68. *Ibid.*, p. 439.

69. *Ibid.*, p. 95.

70. See Hanna Pitkin, *Wittgenstein and Justice* (Berkeley: University of California Press, 1972), esp. pp. 302-308. Pitkin explains that her interpretation "takes the *Republic* to be about exactly what the participants say it is about: the nature or meaning of justice" (p. 302). She distinguishes this "conceptual" reading from one that takes Plato's imaginary state literally as a political ideal (p. 303).

71. *Ibid.*, p. 178.

72. *Ibid.*, p. 187.

73. *Ibid.*, p. 178.

74. Pitkin explains the meaning of the term in her book and she uses it throughout.

75. Pitkin, *Wittgenstein and Justice*, p. 202.

76. *Ibid.*, p. 190.

77. *Ibid.*, p. 326.

78. *Ibid.*

79. An interjectory note here: Pitkin would probably deny that she is "reconciling" the distinction between reality and ideality because she contests the validity, or the absoluteness, of the distinction itself; yet her important insight that the fact-value distinction is not always useful or appropriate has the effect of favoring "Socratic meaning" over "Thrasymachean convention" when rivalries happen to arise or the issue is forced between the two.

80. E.g., Dieter Henrich, "Formen der Negation in Hegels Logik," in *Hegel-Jahrbuch* 1974 (Cologne: Pahl-Rugenstein, 1975), pp. 245-256.

81. Pitkin, *Wittgenstein and Justice*, p. 120.

82. See *ibid.*, p. 334.

83. *Ibid.*, p. 80.

84. *Ibid.*, p. 178.

85. *Ibid.*, p. 175.

86. Hannah Arendt, *The Human Condition* (Chicago: University of Chicago Press, 1958), p. 5. Arendt herself later retracted some of her views expressed in *The Human Condition* on the relationship between the *vita activa* and the *vita contemplativa*. See Melvyn A. Hill, ed., *Hannah Arendt: The Recovery of the Public World* (New York: St. Martin's Press, 1979), p. 305.

87. *Ibid.*, p. 325.

88. For instance, Pitkin starts out her book with the quote from Sophocles: "Speech too, and windswept thought He has taught himself, And the spirit that governs cities"; and the spirit of freedom out of which revolutions and acts of foundation spring is a recurring theme in Arendt's *On Revolution*.

89. Norman Knox, *The Word Irony and its Context, 1500-1755* (Durham, N.C.: Duke University Press, 1961), p. 15.

90. See Otto Ribbeck, "Über den Begriff des *Eiron*," *Rheinisches Museum* 31 (1876), pp. 381-400; D.C. Muecke, *Irony and the Ironic* (London and New York: Methuen, 1970), p. 15.

91. See G.G. Sedgewick, *Of Irony: Especially in Drama* (Toronto: University of Toronto Press, 1948), p. 11.

92. My translation.

93. See *ibid.* and Knox, *The Word Irony*, p. 3.

94. Knox., *The Word Irony*, p. 3.

95. *Ibid.*

96. Sedgewick, *Of Irony*, p. 13; also quoted in Knox, *The Word Irony*, p. 21.

97. Quoted in Knox, *The Word Irony*, p. 21. David Worcester, *The Art of Satire.* (Cambridge: Harvard University Press, 1940).

98. Søren Kierkegaard, *The Concept of Irony*, trans. Lee M. Capel (Bloomington: Indiana Univeristy Press, 1965), p. 158.

99. A number of writers in addition to Strauss, Friedländer, and Jowett have mentioned Plato's irony at least in passing. Randall, as I claimed above, treats irony as a reversal mechanism. Sesonske, as I mention below, considers the *Republic* an ironic *Apology*. Plass also attends carefully to Plato's particular irony. Hall mentions Plato's irony in his article on Strauss and Bloom, but he does not elaborate; and at the end of that article is a blurb that states that Hall is writing a work entitled "Irony in Plato's Philosophical Politics"--but I have not seen any subsequent mention of this work. Randall, *Plato*; Plass, "Philosophic Anonymity and Irony in the Platonic Dialogues"; Hall, "The *Republic* and the 'Limits of Politics'"; Alexander Sesonske, "Plato's Apology: *Republic* I," *Plato's Republic: Interpretation and Criticism*, ed. Alexander Sesonske (Belmont, Calif.: Wadsworth Publishing Co., 1966), pp. 40-47.

100. Paul Friedländer, *Plato: An Introduction*, trans. Hans Meyerhoff, Bollingen Series 14 (Princeton: Princeton University Press, 1958), p. 137.

101. *Ibid.*, p. 145.

102. *Ibid.*, p. 147.

103. *Ibid.*, p. 153.

104. Plass, following Friedländer, has, in my judgment, a very insightful view of the place of irony in Plato's writings; I am bothered, however, by his formulation--also resembling Friedländer's--that the negativity of irony also points to the "objective character of the *logos*," or that irony ultimately transcends ignorance. See Plass, "Philosophic Anonymity and Irony in the Platonic Dialogues."

105. Indeed, this could be a criticism of my work, that I make no attempt to extend my ironic reading of Plato's *Republic* to his later works, especially the *Laws*, the *Statesman*, and the disputed *7th Letter*. I do, however, make occasional references to the *Phaedrus*.

106. B. Jowett and Lewis Campbell, eds., *Plato's Republic: The Greek Text*, Vol. 3; hereafter I will refer to this work by Jowett's name only and the volume number.

107. Though Jowett mentions irony several times in his interpretive essays on the *Republic*. For instance, he writes of the *Republic*: "Nowhere in Plato is there a deeper irony or a greater wealth of humor or imagery, or more dramatic power." "Analysis," p. 1.

108. *Ibid.*, p. 26.

109. Jowett writes: "A real element of Socratic teaching, which is more prominent in the *Republic* than in any of the other Dialogues of Plato, is the use of example and illustration: 'Let us apply the test of common instances.' 'You,' says Adeimantus, ironically, in the sixth book, 'are so unaccustomed to speak in images.' And this use of examples or images, though truly Socratic in origin, is enlarged by the genius of Plato into the form of an allegory or parable, which embodies in the concrete what has been already described, or is about to be described, in the abstract. Thus the figure of the cave in Book VII is a recapitulation of the divisions of knowledge in Book VI. The composite animal in Book IX is an allegory of the parts of the soul. The noble captain and the ship and the true pilot in Book VI are a figure of the relation of the people to the philosophers in the State which has been described. Other figures, such as the dog in the second, third, and fourth books, or the marriage of the portionless maiden in the sixth book, or the drones and wasps in the eighth and ninth books, also form links of connection in a long passage, or are used to recall previous discussions." *Ibid.*, pp. 19-20.

110. *Idem*, Vol. 2, p. 10.

111. *Idem*, Vol. 3, pp. 176, 228.

112. *Ibid.*, p. 433.

113. *Ibid.*, p. 367.

114. *Ibid.*, p. 135.

115. *Ibid.*, p. 228.

116. *Ibid.*, p. 398.

117. *Idem*, Vol. 2, p. 251.

118. *Idem*, Vol. 3, p. 445.

119. *Idem*, Vol. 2, p. 251.

120. *Idem*, Vol. 3, p. 321.

121. 276a-b.

122. Plass writes: "In view of the frank portrayal of intellectual-erotic play in the dialogues one might expect philosophic anonymity to take the form of a seeming disinterest or shyness which is, in fact, intended to invite attention." "Philosophic Anonymity and Irony," p. 261. I have not included Stanley Fish's work on Plato (*Self-Consuming Artifacts*, chapter 1) in this survey. Though Fish is concerned with "strategies" of authors aimed at audiences and with the "act of reading" on the part of readers, I think he leaves it very unclear in his book how, or even whether, these two parties, authors and readers, interact. Fish pays particular attention to the experience of reading, though he is also concerned with how textual devices lead the reader; but he does not adequately explain how texts--even "self-consuming" ones--finally produce truly independent readings. In this regard, his reading of Plato's *Pheadrus*, coupling it with Christian homiletics, is too tendentious in my view; and his notion of conversion seems incompatible with my notion of irony. I will discuss further Fish's view of irony in the next chapter. Stanley E. Fish, *Self-Consuming Artifacts: The Experience of Seventeeth-Century Literature* (Berkeley: University of California Press, 1972).

123. Jowett, Vol. 3, p. 439.

124. *Idem*, Vol. 2, p. 17.

125. Alexander Sesonske similarly detects Plato's irony in the opening book of the *Republic*: "When we bring these remarks together we see, not only Plato's irony, but also the corrupted Athens which put Socrates to death." Sesonske's thesis is that the *Republic* represents an ironic *Apology*, that it is Plato's reply to the Athenian court that sentenced Socrates to death. See "Plato's Apology: *Republic* I," pp. 40-47.

126. Eric Voegelin, *Plato and Aristotle*, Vol. 3 of *Order and History* (Baton Rouge: Louisiana State University Press, 1966), p. 53.

127. Voegelin cites here K. Kérenyi in K. Kérenyi and C.G. Jung, *Essays on a Science of Mythology*, trans. R.F.C. Hull (New York: Pantheon Books, 1949), p. 164. See also Sesonske's reading of the significance of the goddess Bendis in this opening scene; "Plato's Apology," pp. 42-45.

128. Connop Thirlwall coined the phrase "dramatic irony" for this technique. See "On the Irony of Sophocles," *The Philological Museum* 2 (Cambridge: J. Smith, Printer, 1833), pp. 483-537.

129. I am using the term *hell* as loose substitute for *Hades* not in order to introduce the Christian conception of the afterlife but to convey the point that Plato was aware of the Orphic view of a judgment in the afterlife, with a scheme of rewards and punishments for one's actions in this world. There is considerable evidence in the *Republic* alone that Plato had been exposed to this view of the afterlife. He mentions the rewards and punishments that the poet Musaeus and his sons give for the blessed and the unjust, respectively (363c-e), and according to this account, the wicked clearly will receive a punishment "in some sort of mud in the underworld. " (see also 366a-b). Then, the poets' stories of terrors in the afterlife (386b) and the horrifying names in the underworld (387c) are to be banned as unsuitable for the guardians. Finally, the myth of Er is clearly a story of underworldly judgment, and the spirit that Er overhears even mentions Tartarus, a "place" in Hades where the unrighteous are punished (616a). In the *Gorgias*, Socrates explains that the righteous will go to the Isles of the Blessed, while the unrighteous are punished in Tartarus (523b). And in the *Gorgias*, Socrates contends that Homer bears out his stories of reward and retribution--for Homer represented those who suffer eternal punishment in Hades as not only kings and princes and the wickedest humans (Tantalus, Sisyphus, and Tityus) but also Thersites or any other private person who has done wrong (525e). That Plato was aware of these views of the afterlife and that he repeated them does not mean, however, that he subscribed to them; and my reading of the *Republic* furthers the case that he does not intend that his recitations be taken literally.

130. Julia Annas, *Introduction to Plato's Republic* (Oxford: Clarendon Press, 1981), p. 18.

131. And she underscores this last point by noting that Socrates was poor, that he taught for no money, and that this was a rub between the sophists and him.

132. The passage also anticipates and plays upon the theme of stealing (334b, 413d); and the implied direction of the ironic connection between justice and stealing is, I think, that the pursuit of justice requires an independence of thought and conviction--whereas Cephalus and Polemarchus have mindlessly mouthed the wisdom of the poets. All of this wonderfully complicates Plato's invocation of Homer.

133. Hanna Pitkin has suggested to me another way in which this juncture possibly indicates a separation between Socrates and Plato. The transfer of the argument from Cephalus to Polemarchus anticipates the later section on the decline of states (and therewith the entire generational question of *paideia*). Like Cephalus, Socrates will die for failing to solve the *political* questions of *paideia* and *dike*.

134. This and all subsequent quotations from the *Republic* are from Desmond Lee's translation, unless otherwise noted. Desmond Lee, ed. and trans., *Plato: The Republic*.

135. Translation from *The Republic*, trans. Raymond Larson (Arlington Heights, Ill.: AHM Publishing, 1979).

136. *Ibid.*

137. This was a reading inspired by Pitkin's *Wittgenstein and Justice* .

138. Voegelin notes that the translation of *gennaios* as "noble" when qualifying "lie" is a mistake. "Big" is better, he claims. *Plato and Aristotle*, p. 105n. I like to use his translation of *gennaion* as something "big" in order to draw attention to the visual imagery in the contrast between the big lie and the "little" inquiry into the individual (435c). This is not to suggest, however, that *gennaion* does not carry primarily connotations of nobility. For general purposes, "Great Lie" would be a happy compromise.

139. Regarding this exchange between Socrates and Thrasymachus, Jowett writes: "The satire on existing governments is heightened by the simple and apparently incidental manner in which the last remark (347d) is introduced. There is a similar irony in the argument that the governors of mankind do not like being in office, and that therefore they demand pay." "Analysis," p. 28.

140. The ring of Gyges tale is also a *katabaino* story (359d), as well as the discussion of the philosopher's dialectic in the section on the divided line (511b). So is story of the cap of Hades (612b), which is a reference to the *Iliad* (5.844f).

141. See Jowett, Vol. 2, especially "Essay 1," pp. 1-6.

142. Iris Murdoch, *The Fire and the Sun* (Oxford: Oxford University Press, 1977), p. 15.

143. Strauss, *The City and Man*, p. 95. Strauss completely misses what Jowett observes as the "charming" or facetious nature of this passage. In addition, Strauss does not attempt to explain, for instance, how "some desserts, figs, peas, beans, myrtleberries, etc." represent, as Strauss contends, "man's needs," or "the necessities of life." Strauss interprets the healthy city as a just city "in accordance with nature" but one that has eliminated the need for virtue.

144. Lee, "Introduction," p. 115.

145. Jowett, Vol. 3, pp. 82-83.

146. Strauss says that the first city is literally without pigs (*The City and Man*, p. 95), but in another sense, Glaucon is correct because the city is literally full of pigs, since pigs are not eaten.

147. Voegelin, *Plato and Aristotle*, p. 100.

148. One possible meaning is that the city of pigs allows Socrates to concede that you may not find justice there; it's *too good*, as it were, to need a concept of justice.

149. See Strauss, *The City and Man*, p. 97; Saxonhouse, "Comedy in Callipolis." Saxonhouse too acknowledges the argument (albeit in a footnote) that Plato might not be serious in likening guardians to dogs, but she seems to dismiss this reading, even though her article is about comedy in the *Republic*. Instead, she offers the curious interpretation that "Socrates goes so far in this analogy as to make dogs not only human, but even philosophic" (p. 894). This analogy, she argues, does not elevate the status of political dogs but rather brings down philosophy ("it is prostituted and made the possession of mere brutes"). I do not quite see how this interpretation is consistent with her claim that the *Republic* "is an attempt to purge politics of its attention to body" (p. 898). On the one hand she advocates that people recognize their deficiencies and brutishness so that they might commence with philosophizing; but she seems confused about the relationship between philosophizing and politics. Had she stuck more closely with Strauss's argument--that the *Republic* may be foremost about philosophy, individual justice, and personal virtue but that those matters in turn holds political implications in the form of limitations--I think her position would be more coherent. Bloom is more explicit in arguing that Socrates is partly serious and partly nonserious in drawing an analogy between guardians and dogs; but Bloom's interpretation is also peculiar. Socrates invokes the image of the dog, he contends, to show that the contrary characteristics of harshness and gentleness can in fact be found in a natural combination (i.e., the dog, who can distinguish friend from foe). But finally Bloom says that "this identification of dog-like affection for acquaintances with philosophy is, of course, not serious," for Plato's point is to heighten the difference between philosopher and warrior. Again, the question must be asked of Bloom as well as Saxonhouse why Socrates would introduce an analogy only to dismiss it. Allan Bloom, "Interpretive Essay," *The Republic of Plato* (New York: Basic Books, 1968), pp. 350-351.

150. Jowett, Vol. 3, p. 94. Thomas Sinclair also argues that "we must not take Plato's little jokes seriously." He reads the discussion of the philosophic dog, a parody of the "method of argument used by the 'nature' school of sophists, who advised that men should follow *physis* not *nomos*." "Plato's Philosophic Dog," *Classical Review* 62 (September, 1948): 61-62 (cited in Saxonhouse, p. 894n and p. 901, but incorrectly listed as *Classical Quarterly*).

151. James Adam, ed. *The Republic of Plato* (Cambridge: Cambridge University Press, 1902), Vol. 1, p. 108 (cited in Saxonhouse, p. 894n). On the relation between the *Republic* and the Cynics, see also Rankin, "A Modest Proposal about the *Republic*," p. 21.

152. Jowett asks us to take note of the following with respect to the section on education: "The constant appeal to the authority of Homer, whom, with grave irony, Plato, after the manner of his age, summons as a witness about ethics and psychology, as well as about diet and medicine; attempting to distinguish the better lesson from the worse, sometimes altering the text from design; more than once quoting or alluding to Homer inaccurately, after the manner of the early logographers turning the Iliad into prose, and delighting to draw far-fetched inferences from his words, or to make ludicrous applications of them. . . . These fanciful appeals to Homer add a charm to Plato's style, and at the same time they have the effect of a satire on the follies of Homeric interpretation. To us (and probably to himself), although they take the form of arguments, they are really figures of speech." "Analysis," p. 64.

153. Lee, "Introduction," p. 149; Lee credits Cornford with the idea of "imaginative identification."

154. Several commentators claim that the *Republic* is written clearly in the narrative form; but I do not think this claim fits Socrates' definition of narrative given in the *Republic*. He says that indirect speech or narrative includes some of the "poet's words" between the sections of direct dialogue. To be sure, the *Republic* is not entirely written in dialogue form. But clearly *Socrates* is presented as the ostensible narrator, not Plato. Plato rather subordinates himself completely to the person of Socrates, remaining ever the inscrutable "reporter" of Socrates' account. Thus the *Republic* is truly but an imitation of the Homeric form--and if anything, it more closely resembles mimesis than narrative. Tarrant, for instance, claims that "the *Republic* is purely narrative," but her reasoning seems to be that anything that is not entirely dramatic must be narrative. Again, the simple opposition between drama and narration misses the complexity of Plato's irony. See Tarrant, "Plato as Dramatist," p. 85. See also Eric A. Havelock's discussion of the relationship between Plato and Homer. Havelock's comment that Homer is the prototype of both imitative and narrative forms of poetry only adds, I think, to the complexity of Plato's irony vis-à-vis Homer. Havelock, *Preface to Plato* (Cambridge: Belknap Press, 1963), pp. 21-30.

155. Saxonhouse, "Comedy in Callipolis," p. 888.

156. Cf. Knox, *The Word Irony*, p. 140, and David Worcester, *The Art of Satire* (Cambridge: Harvard University Press, 1940), p. 90.

157. Tarrant argues that there are signs that Plato's condemnation of drama is not wholehearted, for room is left for positive work on right lines (401b). "This condition for toleration follows the passage (398a) prescribing a ceremonious dismissal of poets from the ideal city, and confirms the impression, given by its ironic and half-playful tone, that Plato is not, after all, entirely serious over this wholesale eviction." "Plato as Dramatist," p. 84.

158. Jowett writes that the section on music is written in a style of "affected ignorance." "Analysis," p. 73.

159. Voegelin, *Plato and Aristotle.*, p. 106.

160. *Ibid.*, pp. 106-107.

161. *Ibid.*, p. 107.

162. *Ibid.*

163. Jowett, Vol. 3, p. 160.

164. *Ibid.,* p. 175.

165. Other Jowett notes for this section from his "Analysis": "The humorous pictures of the lean dogs and the fatted sheep, of the light active boxer upsetting two stout gentlemen at least, of the 'charming' patients who are always making themselves worse; or again, the playful assumption that there is no State but our own; or the grave irony with which the statesman is excused who believes that he is six feet high because he is told so, and having nothing to measure with is to be pardoned for his ignorance—he is too amusing for us to be seriously angry with him" (pp. 79-80).

166. Jowett also suggests that the wave imagery is a Platonic invitation or tip-off: "First, there is the image of the waves, which serves for a sort of scheme or plan of the book. The first wave, the second wave, the third and greatest wave come rolling in, and we hear the roar of them. All that can be said of the extravagance of Plato's proposals [i.e., the community of property and of family, and the kingdom of philosophers] is anticipated by himself. Nothing is more admirable than the hesitation with which he proposes the solemn text, 'Until kings are philosophers,' &c.; or the reaction from the sublime to the ridiculous, when Glaucon describes the manner in which the new truth will be received by mankind." "Analysis," p. 103.

167. Saxonhouse, "Comedy in Callipolis," p. 890.

168. Compare this passage to 496b-e; the latter passage is very close to Strauss's interpretation of the political meaning of the book, yet Plato does not stop there, and the passage suggesting the political artist's determination would seem to undercut the passage in which the philosopher reconciles himself to political defeat.

169. The wave analogy also suggests the notion of striving or perseverance; but Kierkegaard seems to be the only writer who has pointed out that the point of the wave metaphor is to suggest that the waves must be ridden, despite the difficulty. He begins *The Concept of Irony* with the following passage (453d): "The problem is to be solved is anything but easy. Why yes, I said, but the fact is that when a man is out of his depth, whether he has fallen into a little swimming-bath or into mid ocean, he has to swim all the same. Very true. And must not we swim and try to reach the shore, while hoping that Arion's dolphin or some other miraculous help may save us?"

170. See Lee's notes on visual imagery of these passages. Lee, *The Republic*, pp. 312 n. 2, 314 n. 1, 315 n. 4.

171. *Ibid.,* p. 317n.

172. *Ibid.*

173. Cf. John Freccero's analysis of Canto III of Dante's *Inferno*, when the reader confronts the text in the same manner that Dante the pilgrim confronts the inscription above the gates of hell as he begins his *katabasis*. Freccero, "Infernal Irony: The Gates of Hell," *Dante: The Poetics of Conversion* (Cambridge: Harvard University Press, 1986), pp. 93-109.

174. Voegelin gets around this problem by ignoring that Athens is the "higher world" that sets the initial *katabasis* symbolism in motion; rather, Voegelin sees a transcendental "light of Truth" that leads Socrates upward out of the Pireaus-Hades. But then, one wonders, what is the difference between the Pireaus and Athens, if *both* are Hades, according to Plato's symbolism?

175. Voegelin, *Plato and Aristotle*, p. 117.

176. Voegelin talks about the duty of the philosopher to "return" to the polis, but he claims that this entails a return to a perfect polis only. What Voegelin does not explain is why Socrates *is* literally returning to Athens at the outset of the *Republic*. See Voegelin, *Plato and Aristotle*, p. 116.

177. Desmond Lee contends that Plato is concerned in this section with "moral degeneration" and thus the "historical framework should not be taken too literally," *The Republic*, p. 356; and Jowett contends that "the elaborate terminology of the section is not to be taken too seriously," Vol. 3, p. 367.

178. On the number in the ideal state, see Jowett, "Analysis," pp. 170-177. Jowett argues that there probably is some seriousness in Plato's discussion, but, on the other hand, "Plato himself indicates that he is not altogether serious, and in describing his number as a solemn jest of the Muses, he appears to imply some degree of satire on the symbolical use of number."

179. M.A. Diès, "Le Nombre Nuptial De Platon." *Mémoires à l'Académie Des Inscriptions et Belles-Lettres* 14 (1940); cited in Lee, p. 360.

180. Philolaus, a pre-Socratic philosopher of the Pythagorean school, counted 364 1/2 days in the year, though he also held that there is a great year of 729 months. See James Adam,ed.,*The Republic of Plato*, Vol. 2, p. 361.

181. Jowett, Vol. 3, p. 43.

182. Note that other translators have missed what Lee conveys--the idea of an unfathomable numeric calculation--in his "infinitely greater": Shorey renders it "surpass him inconceivably"; Bloom puts it "be greater to a prodigious degree"; Larson phrases it "a staggering amount"; and Grube chooses "an extraordinary calculation." Vaughan comes close to Lee with "incalculably more," and similarly Jowett renders it "immeasurably greater"; whereas Lindsay poses a rhetorical question with, "is it not incalculable?" ,

183. See also 588c-d, the comment that language is molded more easily than even wax or similar substances. Plass similarly comments that Plato writes powerfully but is also "aware of its inadequacy." See Plass, "Philosophic Anonymity and Irony in the Platonic Dialogues," p. 255.

184. Annas, *Introduction*, p. 335.

185. To name some of the names of those who have participated in this debate: Jowett, Croce, Bosanquet, Collingwood, Cavarnos, Murdoch, Havelock, Wilamowitz, Shorey, Cassirer, Pater, Sikes, Rosen, Greene, Tate, Grube, Webster, Cornford, Lodge, Verdenius.

186. Havelock, *Preface to Plato*, p. 6.

187. *Ibid.*, p. 7.

188. *Ibid.*, p. 201.

189. *Ibid.*, p. 25.

190. The same charge applies to Derrida and would undercut his entire argument concerning the *Republic* as well as his argument concerning Plato's view of the relation between the spoken and written word. I do not think that Plato is trying to achieve some kind of mastery by privileging speech over writing on the basis of certain inviolate oppositions. Derrida takes issue with Socrates' and Plato's "logocentric" presumptions and argues instead that the spoken word is never "purely present." But I disagree with his premise that Socrates and Plato held such a presumption. For instance, Philip Merlan seems already to have anticipated Derrida's counterinsights: "Now, certain utterances in Plato's writings seem to suggest that philosophical truth can be communicated better by oral teaching than by writing," and Merlan notes that *Phaedrus* 277a-d is usually interpreted in this way. But he adds, "To understand the true meaning of this passage we have to observe that Plato has in mind the 'inward' dialectic, the discourse of the soul with itself and not only the difference between the spoken and the written word. The word, whether inward or outward, may be living or dead. It is well known that Socrates insists that while he refutes others, he is at the same time refuting himself. *Euthyphro* 11e; *Meno* 80c-d." (Merlan, "Form and Content in Plato's Philosophy," p. 426.) In short, Derrida misses the inner dialectic or *"différance"* inherent in any Socratic utterance. He interprets the "living word" as an organism, but I really think this is a unfortunate metaphor. For Socrates and Plato, the word lives in *people* (if we must locate a site), not as some independent organism or abstract entity. If anything, Plato's writing is an attempt not to enforce but to bridge the difference between speech and writing, to encourage self-reflection even in one's outward relations. Derrida's "disseminations" suggest that the seeds of writing should be sown any and everywhere, but I think that Derrida's project itself is based upon a view of Plato that fails to take into account the reflexive quality of Plato's own works. See Jacques Derrida, "Plato's Pharmacy," *Disseminations*, trans. Barbara Johnson (Chicago: University of Chicago Press, 1981), pp. 61-172.

191. See also 603a.

192. Voegelin cites these passages—595b and 607a—as indicative of Plato's deep reverence for Homer. Voegelin, *Plato and Aristotle*, p. 131.

193. Annas, *Introduction*, p. 433.

194. *Ibid.*, p. 351.

195. *Ibid.*

196. E.g., see R.L. Nettleship, *The Theory of Education in Plato's Republic* (London: Oxford University Press, 1935), p. 364, and Strauss, *The City and Man*, p. 137.

197. See Bloom's note on Alcinous, *The Republic of Plato*, p. 471.

198. Homer, *The Odyssey of Homer*, trans. Richmond Lattimore (New York: Harper and Row, 1965), 6.12.

199. This theme of stars and patterns in the sky is touched upon in various places besides 500e and 515a; for instance, 489e mentions stargazers, 501b is the reference to the two directions of sight, 527d is the passage on astronomy and the mind's eye, and 592b is the famous pattern-in-the-sky passage. Jowett

argues that the philosopher of Book 6, who lets the storm rage past him (496d), strives to imitate the regular courses of the stars, a hope that is then answered by the "pattern in the sky" imagery in 592b. Jowett, Vol. 2, p. 18.

200. See 518c.

201. See Jacob Klein, *A Commentary on Plato's Meno* (Chapel Hill: University of North Carolina Press, 1965), p. 17.

202. See Friedländer, *Plato: An Introduction*, p. 20.

203. Though here I would like to distinguish between Plato's irony and that of Thomas More, as interpreted by Stephen J. Greenblatt. Greenblatt contends that More's role-playing is meant to confound the reader; and by making the task of interpretation so perplexing, More exerts power over his reader and vents his own monkish hostility. The more outrageous the fiction, then, the more impressive one's manifestation of authorial power. I suggest that Plato is much more respectful of his reader, his irony more self-conscious. See Greenblatt, *Renaissance Self-Fashioning: From More to Shakespeare* (Chicago: University of Chicago Press, 1980).

204. See Dan Sperber and Deirdre Wilson, "Irony and the Use-Mention Distinction," *Radical Pragmatics*, ed. Peter Cole (New York: Academic Press, 1981), pp. 295-318; and John Traugott, "The Yahoo in the Doll's House: *Gulliver's Travels* the Children's Classic," *The Yearbook of English Studies* 14 (London: Modern Humanities Research Association, 1984), pp. 127-150.

205. Rankin writes beautifully on the meaning of Plato's "satire," which is worth quoting at length: "Plato, like other great satirists, believes in every word and every idea,--or does so when he propounds it. And he puts forward suggestions which may be outrageous in some aspects, but are no more outrageous than ordinary experience. He makes his readers (or audience) look clearly at the absurdities in which they live through the medium of his scarifying scorn of it, and he proposes a solution which in some ways is no less absurd. But the heart of the joke is that he believes in his solution, whereas we are inclined not to take it seriously. He does not carry absurdity to its 'logical' conclusion, as the Cynics did in advocating incest, cannibalism and the like. He creates a social logic parallel to that which is accepted, and in which he believes, and the joke is on us when we regard his satire as mere satire. So with Swift: the outrageous suggestion in 'A Modest Proposal' that children in Ireland should be fattened for food is well known to be no more absurd and outrageous than the accepted treatment of children in that country at that time. I suspect the joke is that Swift really thinks his proposal would be better than the contemporary practice of starving and drowning etc." "A Modest Proposal about the *Republic*," p. 21.

206. John Traugott, "A Voyage to Nowhere with Thomas More and Jonathan Swift," reprinted in *Swift*, ed. Ernst Tuveson (Englewood Cliffs, N.J.: Prentice-Hall, 1964), p. 169.

207. Cf. Randolph Bourne, "The Life of Irony," *Youth and Life* (Cambridge: Riverside Press, 1913), p. 105.

208. Traugott, "A Voyage to Nowhere," p. 151.

209. *Ibid.*, p. 169.

210. Note Jowett's commentary on the Myth of Er: "Innocence and happiness in his previous life are not sufficient to sustain a man in the choice for the future: a severer probation or discipline is required, which is that of philosophy. And, suppose a man to have had the discipline, even the journey from one life to the other is a heavenly pilgrimage: and the return hither, if he have only moderate fortune in his opportunity of choice, is not unblessed. But most men are under the dominion of habit, and few know how to profit by experience." And he adds that Ajax is the twentieth soul to choose and Agamemnon the twenty-first "for the same reason that Atalanta is in the middle and Ulysses at the end of the series: that is to say, in order to heighten the effect of the narrative by the appearance of exactness, and to illustrate the working of the element of chance." The fate of Odysseus, finally, shows that he is unfortunate but remains superior to misfortune. Jowett, Vol. 3, pp. 481-2.

211. Thomas Mann writes that "art is intensely human, intensely humane, since it is the mediator between spirit and life, and nothing would be more erroneous than to regard its irony--the irony of all mediation--as a nihilistic escape from struggle and from human obligation." "Standards and Values," trans. Agnes Meyer, *New York Times*, Aug. 15, 1937; published as "Mass und Wert" in *Achtung Europa! Aufsatze zur Zeit* (Stockholm: Bermann-Fischer, 1938); quoted in Joseph Brennan,*Thomas Mann's World* (New York: Russell and Russell, 1962), p. 160.

212. Note that Lachesis tells the souls in the myth that a man will have more or less of excellence *according to the value he sets on her* (617d).

213. See Jowett, Vol. 2, p. 17; and Vol. 3, p. 439.

214. Connop Thirlwall saw a point of convergence between tragedy and irony, and he contended that tragedy, taken ironically, affirms rather than denigrates the human condition. See his "On the Irony of Sophocles." Nietzsche also tried to affirm the world through a reconsideration of tragedy, but not by way of irony. He was an open critic of irony--yet in late 1886, he retracted some of the deflationary views that he held in his youth; and when he wrote the second preface to *The Birth of Tragedy*, he included the suspicion or the admission that he might have fallen victim to Socrates' irony in supposing that Socrates was trying to transcend his own limitations through twists of logic: "And science itself, our science--indeed, what is the significance of all science, viewed as a symptom of life? For what--worse yet, *whence*--all science? How now? Is the resolve to be so scientific about everything perhaps a kind of fear of, an escape from, pessimism? A subtle last resort against--*truth*? And, morally speaking, a sort of cowardice and falseness? Amorally speaking, a ruse? O Socrates, Socrates, was that perhaps *your* secret? O enigmatic ironist, was that perhaps your--irony?" Nietzsche, *The Birth of Tragedy*, trans. Walter Kaufmann (New York: Vintage Books, 1967), p. 18.

215. "What is necessary is [the soul's] own coherence, its ability to judge a world in which evil is successful and the good are doomed; and in particular that while injustice may flourish, it cannot rest content. This, I take it, is what Plato's *Republic* is about. And it is an old theme of tragedy." Stanley Cavell,

Must We Mean What We Say? (Cambridge: Cambridge University Press, 1976), p. 309.

216. Hall contends that we should not conclude, on the basis of the passages that refer to the need to "compel" philosophers to rule, that the required undertaking is contrary to nature. As Hall points out, Socrates also talks of compelling philosophers to look toward the Good (519c, 540a). Hall wants to conclude in response to the Straussians that there is no opposition between philosophy and politics. I would not go that far in my interpretation of Plato, but I would suggest that compulsion (*anagkaxo*) can be inner as well as outward. Hall, "The *Republic* and the 'Limits of Politics,'" pp. 301-2.

217. "In this respect, the irony of a work of art corresponds to the ironic attitude which [Friedrich] Schlegel saw as mandatory in actual life. Only through irony could man achieve simultaneously a closeness to reality and a distance from it. Only the ironic attitude enabled man to commit himself wholly to finite reality and at the same time made him realize that the finite is trivial when viewed from the perspective of eternity." Peter Firchow, "Introduction," *Friedrich Schlegel's* Lucinde *and the Fragments* (Minneapolis: University of Minnesota Press, 1971), pp. 29-30.

218. Traugott, "A Voyage to Nowhere," p. 166.

219. It is frequently argued that the passage in Er's tale in which Odysseus chooses the lot of an ordinary man who "minds his own business" supports an antipolitical reading of the *Republic*. I think this conclusion is mistaken. As Plass argues, the Odyssean theme in the Myth of Er suggests that philosophy repudiates the concern for worldly greatness expressed in terms of reputation, status, and self-interest--in other words, the virtues of the political tyrant. But this is not to say that a nobler form of politics is a false ambition. Plass also attends to the Oedipal themes in the *Republic*: "In connection with the idea of losing one's self one naturally thinks of Oedipus. He begins as a successful man, notably self-assertive and proud of his wit, and when he comes to know his real self he undergoes a moral despair which breaks him into two selves; his former seeing (but morally blind) self and his new blind (but morally seeing) self. The split is dramatized when the blind Oedipus hears his own voice and wonders whether it *is* his. His new self cannot bear to recognize his old self as he embraces his humiliation and tries to wall himself in from the world. Oedipus has been interpreted as a symbol of Periclean Athens (Bernard Knox, *Oedipus at Thebes*), and if this is correct Plato and Sophocles both saw the moral problem facing their city and society at large as a problem of keeping human capabilities in their place. The anonymity and separation that Oedipus wants is sheer despair, while the philosopher hides behind his wall (*Rep*, 496d) to help preserve and ultimately extend the truth." Plass, "Philosophic Anonymity and Irony," pp. 261, 265. See also Gregory Vlastos' argument that the notion of "doing one's own" in the *Republic* corresponds to a view of social justice, not simply individual "righteousness." Vlastos, "The Theory of Social Justice in the *Polis* in Plato's *Republic*," in *Interpretations of Plato*, ed. Helen F. North (Leiden: E.J. Brill, 1977), pp. 1-40.

220. Allan Bloom writes: "The philosopher, of course, begins, as do all men, in the cave; and . . . he pays the strictest attention not only to particular or individual things but to their shadows. But the difference between him and other men is that he learns that they are only shadows—shadows which give us access to the truth--whereas they believe the shadows are the real things and are passionately committed to that belief. That is what cave-dwelling means. The cave must always remain cave, so the philosopher is the enemy of the prisoners since he cannot take the nonphilosopher's most cherished beliefs seriously. Similarly, Socrates does care for other men, but only to the extent that they, too, are capable of philosophy, which only a few are. This is an essential and qualitative difference, one that cannot be bridged and that causes fundamental differences of interest." Bloom, "Response to Hall," *Political Theory* 5 (August, 1977), p. 329. What Bloom apparently never considers is the possibility that the philosopher might fully understand that the shadows are shadows and *still* could remain committed to them and to this world.

221. I include this disclaimer in order to put distance between me and Strauss, who also claims to have found the "answer" to the *Republic*. Strauss, *The City and Man*, p. 69.

222. That the book represents an independent if backhanded affirmation of Homeric principles would seem to be suggested by Er's tale of his having seen Odysseus choose the lot of an ordinary man (620d). The worldliness of Odysseus's choice—which he makes in the memory of his former sufferings--is to be contrasted with the man who chooses first and chooses the greatest tyranny (619d-e). That first man, Er recounts, was one of the souls who had come from heaven, having lived his previous life in a well-governed state, but having not had the discipline of suffering. He blames his choice on fate and heaven and forgot that his misfortunes were his own fault.

223. This seems to be the point of the implied exhortations against a life of habit and patterned virtue (e.g., 619c-d). And it confirms the suspicion that Plato is not advocating a "well-governed state" that is based upon routine and custom.

224. Popper, *The Open Society and Its Enemies*.

225. 617e.

226. I find support for a democratic reading of Plato's Socrates in Gregory Vlastos's "The Historical Socrates and Athenian Democracy," *Political Theory* 11 (November, 1983), pp. 495-516.

227. See Thomas Mann, *Reflections of a Nonpolitical Man*, trans. Walter D. Morris (New York: Frederick Ungar Publishing Co., 1983).

228. In response to my final discounting the theme of ascension in favor of the theme of return, one could reasonably, i.e., literally, point to Socrates' final exhortation that we "hold ever to the upward way" (621c). But surely, after all the Odyssean references in the Myth of Er, the matter cannot be so simple as to mean that we are to pursue an arcane philosophy in relative isolation. Rather, Plato's final figurative point is probably consistent in some way with the

final drama of the dialogue--namely, now that Socrates is finished talking, he will most likely resume walking back to Athens.

3

Irony: A Politics of the Page

Like a modern city, he is totally dependent on a steady flow of supplies
from the outside world, and will be in danger of starvation, if the lines
of communication are interrupted. Without people and opinions for
his mind to play on, his irony withers and faints. . . . He lives in a world
of relations, and he must have a whole store of things to be related.
He has lost himself completely in this world he lives in. His ironical
interpretation of the world is his life, and this world is his nourishment.
--Randolph Bourne, "The Life of Irony"

What is irony? The word appears frequently around us, in the
press, in literature, in everyday conversation. Speakers of the language
seem to be reasonably "at home"[1] with the term, as a noun and as an
adjective, when they use such phrases as "My, isn't it ironic that . . ."
and "That's another of life's little ironies!" In such common usage, the
term seems to mean that the speaker has perceived that circumstances
have defeated certain expectations, that fate has repudiated
someone's intentions or labors in the face of that person's recklessness or
vanity. But ask someone who seems to have an intuitive command of
the word to *define* irony, or else to explain how one knows for certain
when someone is being ironic, and you will probably receive a confused
reply. Or ask a professional philologist to state succinctly what, say,
the exact relation between comedic and tragic forms of irony is, or what
the difference between satire and irony is, or what is meant by saying
that an author has adopted an ironic "voice" in his or her writing, and
again you will probably leave bedazzled. Trying to explain irony is
something like trying to explain why the sphinx was smiling when she
told her riddle to Oedipus.[2]

In this chapter I shall attempt what my better judgment tells me not to do: to outline a general *theory* of irony. Having declared that, I must forewarn that no general theory of irony can account fully for all the particular features of the various forms and applications of irony as it has been practiced. My designs here are not quite global, nor are they strict. Rather, I hope to piece together a conceptual analysis of the general workings of irony in much the same way that Max Weber construed all of modernity as Protestant: Call this an ideal-typical description of the "spirit" of irony. More specifically, I intend to reveal the "philosophical" character behind literary formulations of irony, and then to show the political implications of this character. My method relies heavily upon examining what other analysts of irony have had to say about irony, for these testimonials--which indicate how readers actually understand irony--will bear significantly upon what we finally decide irony is or is not.[3]

History of and Approaches to Irony

With some study, one soon discovers that the term *irony* has a long recorded rhetorical history.[4] Probing further, the student finds an extensive if somewhat obscure body of literature devoted to the analysis of irony.[5] Rhetoricians have defined the term innumerable times, mostly offering variations upon Cicero's *aliud dicere ac sentias*-- saying one thing and meaning another.[6] But then one can rest contented with these stock definitions for only a very short while, for one quickly realizes that there exist other figures of speech in which saying and meaning also fail to coincide: allegory, simile, metaphor, apologue, etc.[7] Thus it becomes difficult to find a single definition that clearly and distinctly differentiates irony from related expressions. Moreover, it is difficult to find a definition of irony that adequately comprehends the many varieties of irony: rhetorical irony, situational irony, dramatic irony, cosmic irony, irony of fate, irony of character, self-irony, *ingénu* irony, irony of manner, double irony, and so forth.[8] As one commentator has put it: "The difficulties about the word stem not from the fact that it has no definitions but from the fact that it has too many."[9]

Compounding the problem of definition, a seeker after irony learns that the varieties of irony can be broken down into further classifications and subdivisions: the "ironologist" D.C. Muecke, for instance, defines irony according to effect, medium, technique, function, object, practitioner, tone, and attitude. He organizes these various species into three basic "kinds"; he then identifies three basic "elements" within these kinds; and he further discovers three "grades" of irony and then four "modes" (which "cut across" the three grades). And then he lists twenty "forms" of one of these "modes" and even breaks down one of these forms into seven "types."[10] In a second book on irony, Muecke restrains his penchant for typologies and instead simply calls irony a "double natured quasi-mythological beast."[11] Muecke finally argues that the concept of irony is "vague, unstable and multiform,"[12] a position that had been advanced already in the eighteenth century by Pierre Richelet, who had declared that irony was impossible to define: "It is not possible to give a general idea of irony. There are so many different kinds and they are formed in so many manners that in order to describe it, one can only give a few examples."[13]

Otto Ribbeck maintains that irony can be understood as a single phenomonen but he calls that phenomonen *proteusartig*--in short, irony changes shape.[14] At the end of an entire book devoted to Thomas Mann's multiple moods of irony, Erich Heller writes (in obvious frustration):

> Deeply discouraged by even the best writers on the subject (with Hegel and Kierkegaard among them) as well as by Thomas Mann's extremely resourceful employment of the term, I have attempted neither a definition of it nor a catalogue of its varieties (which are such that it is impossible to grasp hold of the thing they vary). For like 'romantic', with which ever since Friedrich Schlegel 'irony' has enjoyed a firm and intriguing alliance, or like 'tragic', with which it has lived for an even longer time, it has maliciously provoked and invariably defeated hosts of definitions; and an earnest discussion of irony is likely to prove as incongruous and as tiresome as a dispassionate debate on love or a prosaic dissertation about poetry. Every attempt to define irony unambiguously is in itself ironical. It is wiser to speak about it ironically, and one good epigram may reveal more of its nature, if nature it has, than even Kierkegaard's profound thesis on the elusive phenomenon, written, as its title announces, "without ever losing sight of Socrates." For every assertion ever made about irony (unless what is meant is simply the figure of speech or the conversational pleasantry which goes by that name) is such that anyone might legitimately reply: "Ah, but that is not irony!"[15]

Indeed, the question of how even to study and to talk about irony has become a subject of inquiry unto itself.[16] The more we delve into the hidden recesses of irony, the more hopelessly, it seems, we become ensnarled.

To find some handhold on irony, commentators routinely review the rhetorical history and etymology of the term. Since this story has been rehashed in detail several times before,[17] I wish only to touch upon the highlights. In brief, the story goes as follows: In Greek antiquity, the word *eironeia* was largely associated with Socrates' character, indicating a self-deprecating verbal manner. Aristotle refined the notion of *eironeia* into a particular rhetorical method, to be contrasted with *alazoneia*, or boastfulness. Cicero distinguished between irony as a mere figure of speech and irony as a pervasive habit of discourse, and Quintilian refined the distinction, differentiating between irony as a "trope" and as a "schema."[18] Both Cicero and Quintilian defined irony (i.e., *ironia*) basically as saying one thing and meaning another, and this definition stuck with rhetoricians for fifteen centuries.[19] Later introduced into English (as *yronye*), irony was understood as a rhetorical device by which one praises-by-blame or blames-by-praise.[20] Throughout the English classical period irony was associated with mockery and derision, and not until the early eighteenth century, with the introduction of the satiric literature of Swift, Defoe, Fielding, and others, did irony become associated with a certain humorous voice that characterized entire works of literature. In the nineteenth century, mainly in Germany, the term (i.e., its German equivalent, *Ironie*) was applied to more than verbal phenomenon, now extending to events, dramas, and fate itself. So applied, irony eventually signified an entire philosophical outlook, a particular way of recognizing contradictions and disparities, not just in sentences, but somehow in the world at large. Finally, in the hands of us moderns and postmoderns (according to these general surveys), irony indicates a paradoxical philosophical position whereby one recognizes that all philosophic interpretation can be subverted, whereby, in other words, one finds meaning, in sentences and in life itself, by accepting and by making a game out of the world's inherent meaninglessness.[21]

A main issue raised by these historical surveys (if I may treat them collectively) is whether irony is best considered a "term" or a "concept," in other words whether it should be defined narrowly or broadly, as an isolated, or even an "extended," verbal phenomenon or else as an extensive worldview. Some commentators force the issue: A.R. Thompson, for instance, claims that irony means little more than a "dry mock";[22] Arthur Wright pleads for a far wider application.[23] A few commentators have tried to show a relation between "verbal" irony and "philosophic" irony, arguing that there is more than merely a historical continuity between the two. G.G. Sedgewick explains that in the Romantic period, irony represented "not a mere clash of speech with meaning, or of apparent situation with real situation, but the mental attitude of a being, divine or human, who beholds such things."[24] The evolution of irony, then, from the classical to the

Romantic period represented a shift of emphasis from words as objects to speakers as subjects. Sedgewick lets the matter rest with the assertion that there is "an objective and a subjective side" to the concept of irony: "first, the clash between appearance and reality in events or language; and second, the *sense* of this clash as felt by a dramatist or a spectator."[25]

Muecke offers a fuller account of irony's evolution from being viewed as a word play to being viewed as an elaborate philosophical orientation. He argues that irony became "universalized" in the late eighteenth century, beginning as a "simple verbal phenomenon" and then developing into a "situational" phenomenon and finally expanding into a "general" view of the cosmos. Before the German Romantics seized it, irony had been viewed essentially as *intentional* and *instrumental*, in other words as a rhetorical device that an author employed in order to state his case, to mock a victim, to suggest moral correctives. The German theorists of irony made it possible to think of irony as something unintentional, as occurring in nature with no discernable author, as something observable and therefore represent-able in art. The focus of irony thus shifted from the active to the passive, from the intentional ironist to the victim of events. An irony of events now signified a certain kind of reversal taking place over time, whereas the former verbal irony signified a semantic inversion. The notion of ironies over time opened the way to other mental juxtapositions, for instance in literature, wherein scenes could undercut one another, thus producing certain tensions and reversals between entire situations. The next stage, according to Muecke, was a universal-ization of these local ironies, the elevation of dramatic ironies to metaphysical dignity. Muecke summarizes his account thus:

> We have seen the concept of irony enlarged in this Romantic period beyond Instrumental Irony (someone being ironical) to include what I shall call Observable Irony (things seen or presented as ironic). These Observable Ironies--whether ironies of events, of character (self-ignorance, self-betrayal), of situation, or of ideas (for example, the unseen inner contradictions of a philosophical system such as Marxism)--could be seen as local or universal. They were all major developments, not least the development of the concept of *Welt-Ironie*, Cosmic Irony or General Irony, the irony of the universe with man or the individual as victim.[26]

Irony developed one step further, according to Muecke. The irony of events turned back toward a consideration of man as an author, for a general world-irony posed the question of man's ability to comprehend such a world and to act within it. Friedrich Schlegel was the principal figure in this development. His interest in irony grew out of his studies of art, in particular his comparisons of ancient Greek art and Shakespeare's work. He began to reflect upon the status of the artist vis-à-vis his creation: Whereas the Greeks seemed to achieve a perfect idealization in the art work, modern artists seemed never to attain anything in their art beyond their own personal affectations. Shakespeare, however, was one "modern" who defied the dichotomy between "objective" and "interested" forms of artistic creation.[27] Shakespeare's personality was inscrutable in his works and yet it seemed to pervade all of his creations. Schlegel surmised that Shakespeare's success had something to do with his personal stance vis-à-vis his own work. He deliberately suppressed his own personality, never explicitly acknowledging within his works his role as playwright; yet he arranged his materials in such a way that his presence is perceived by the spectator nonetheless. Hence, irony for Schlegel reveals itself in the formal structure of works, yet the term actually refers to the artist's mental stance with respect to his own creations, the fact that he is fully aware of the ironies inherent in the very fact of being an artist. Muecke writes:

> The artist is in an ironic position for several reasons: in order to write well he must be both creative and critical, subjective and objective, enthusiastic and realistic, emotional and rational, unconsciously inspired and a conscious artist; his work purports to be about the world and yet is fiction; he feels an obligation to give a true or complete account of reality but he knows this is impossible, reality being incomprehensibly vast, full of contradictions, and in a continual state of becoming, so that even a true account would be immediately falsified as soon as it was completed. The only possibility open for a real artist is to stand apart from his work and at the same time incorporate this awareness of his ironic position into the work itself and so create something which will, if a novel, not simply be a story but rather the telling of a story complete with the author and the narrating, the reader and the reading, the style and the choosing of the style, the fiction and its distance from fact, so that we shall regard it as being ambivalently both art and life.[28]

This last "type" of irony is the most complicated and the most difficult to analyze. It is difficult to analyze because, as Muecke and Sedgewick suggest, it has both "an objective and a subjective side" (Sedgewick), or, as Muecke says, the ironic artist "stand[s] apart from his work and at the same time *incorporate[s] this awareness of his ironic position into the work itself*" (italics added). Thus a historical account alone will not suffice to answer the question What is irony?, for the dichotomies that such accounts encourage--between "narrow" and "broad" forms of irony, between "verbal" irony and "philosophical" irony, between irony as a "term" and irony as a "concept"--are perhaps false, misconceived. Schlegel's concept of irony (which he claimed was nothing more than Socratic irony) brings to bear a point about irony that the rhetoricians begged or obscured for centuries: Irony is not simply an "objective" phenomenon, nor is it simply "subjective."[29] I want to say in preliminary fashion: Somehow it is both--persons interacting with words.

As with the historical reviews of irony as a trope, I find many contemporary treatments of irony in the field of literary criticism to be problematic. The reason is the same. Many modernist and even poststructuralist critics, like the classical rhetoricians, privilege the written text, taking it as their first priority. With irony in particular, I will argue, this is a trap. It is a trap, to give a preview, because irony entails a particular relationship among authors, readers, *and* texts but one in which the text is diminished in importance; indeed irony is a communicative relationship in which the very validity of the written word is implicitly called into question. To use (advisedly) an old distinction: If irony is a form of communication that favors "spirit" over "letter," then it will do little good to give exclusive or primary emphasis to the importance of letters and texts.

Rhetoricians and literary critics generally transform the question What is irony? into Where is it located? The reason for this shift has to do, I suppose, with occupational pressures for critical verification. If a literary figure cannot be "verified" according to "objective" interpretive categories, it allegedly cannot be said properly to exist.[30] The concern for location and "presence" then supplants the question of a thing's "nature." The search for placement reintroduces the subject-object dichotomy: Does irony reside in the "mind" of an author or a reader or is it located "in the text"? If I can speculatively reconstruct this line of thinking, I think the next step is to link the verifiable with the visible, the observable. Only textual structures, textual criteria, are visible, admitting of "ocular proof,"[31] and thus only textual formulations of irony are presumed verifiable. The "intentionalist" argument is fallacious, for we cannot observe what an author is thinking.[32] Notions like "the sublime" are subjective; and if irony is akin to "sublimity," then it cannot serve as a tool of critical analysis.[33]

I do not want to caricature or overgeneralize. Many of the textual formulations found in contemporary criticism are very revealing. But they are frequently plagued by the imperative of verification, which proceeds from the commonsensical insight that only the text is visible and thus only textual evidence--regular "criteria," "structures," "patterns," and discernable "strategies"--are verifiable. Hence Cleanth Brooks yokes irony to the entire structure or "context" of poetry.[34] Hence Wayne C. Booth provides a step-by-step approach to the reading of "stable irony."[35] Even the postmodernist followers of Jacques Derrida, who implicate the concept of irony in their deconstructive readings,[36] seem to spend a great deal of time scrutinizing texts (though such textual engagement is supposedly beyond logocentrism).[37]

Surely visibility is integral to the act of reading and the business of interpretation: The written word is seen. But I think more is involved in the concern for visible "structures" or stable "criteria" than simply the basics of anatomy. The concern for objectivity, verification, and criticalness, as "impersonal" and detached from strictly "human" considerations as these aims may seem, is no less than a concern for universality among human beings, for commonality.[38] Seeing is what readers have in common (disregarding for the present those versed in braille). I think the reasoning of many literary theorists is that commonality must first be established before one can forward a coherent argument about the language of texts. For commonality is presumedly the basis of communication. As David Simpson writes: "This question of communicability is not simply an argument about language; it is also an argument about mind, as we should perhaps expect within a predominantly nominalistic context. How can there be said to be a common or universal mind when different individuals project different readings into the same text? And of what value is the notion of a normative psychology in standardising or controlling the limits of interpretation which the same text can give rise to?"[39]

Consider the following proposition (posed a bit extravagantly): that "irony" is a mode of communication that somehow does not presuppose or require "commonality"--in the sense of a preexisting, naturally valid community among readers and writers--as its basis. If true, then the interpretive obsession with the independent text has been misplaced all along. We would need to rethink the whole enterprise of reading irony. Simpson argues that indeed this is the case and that the theorists of Romantic irony brought this to bear: "It is not the case that Romanticism simply has no place for the idea of general nature; but it is an argument which becomes much more difficult to maintain as an explanation of how art functions. The legacy of the enlightenment was, crudely put, that 'all men are partakers of the common faculty, reason; and may be supposed to have some communication with the common instructor, truth' (Godwin, *Enquiry*, I, 215)".[40]

The Romantics, Simpson continues, had not given up entirely on epistemology and the faculty of reason.[41] But they harbored deep reservations that divine revelation, or universal mind, or categoric mental structures, or common psychological mechanisms, or organic social processes, or enduring conventions could provide that shared foundation which would necessarily guarantee the meanings of language. According to Simpson, they realized, if inchoately, that the search for an epistemological foundation was a search for an outside authority to govern human discourse; and they rebelled against such legacies from the Enlightenment. Romantic irony, instead, was an attempt to *create* meanings, through a commitment to an ongoing process of interaction between writers and readers, artists and audience members. Readers and writers would have to forge their own ties; they could not rely upon some preestablished "authority," or some metalanguage, to guarantee that they would understand each other. Romantic irony "eroded the potential gap between comment and metacomment, and between subject and predicate, which is the *sine qua non* of authoritarian discourse."[42]

Having called into question both the historical and the formalist approaches to irony, we can begin to consider irony anew. I wish to address irony as a *general* phenomenon, as a concept, which is to suggest that my account will borrow heavily from the Romantic period. But my affinity for the Romantics does not mean that I have necessarily taken sides in the debate over whether irony is a "trope" or a "philosophy."[43] Instead, I contest the opposition. I do diminish the importance of the text and shift my focus to authors and readers and to their experiences of writing and reading and interacting; and this does eclipse the view of irony as a "trope" or a "figure" or an identifiable and determinate verbal phenomenon. But I shall not attempt to subsume all the varieties and instances of verbal irony under some comprehensive theory.[44] Rather, I will present an account of irony that seeks to defy the "subject-object" dichotomy.[45] What irony as an "it" is, I will argue, is primarily an outlook, a worldview, a mode of consciousness, a way of thinking. Indeed, one could argue that "irony" is not even a thing but is a complex, interactive process and that the term in noun form belies its elusive nature, that it invites reification and reductionism.

My shift in emphasis from the "text" to authors and readers, from the "objective" side of irony to its "subjective" side does not mean, however, that irony is *simply* subjective, *simply* a "way of thinking."[46] Rather, I shall argue that the ironic stance necessarily entails an orientation toward representational *forms*, toward "objective" expression, that, as it were, the ironist is under inner obligation to manifest his irony. The problem is, the ironic stance is in tension with any of its particular formal expressions, for irony in general militates against the formulas of language; thus irony's "nature" is never fully revealed in any specific instance of irony.[47] The upshot of this idiosyncrasy is truly remarkable for literary analysis: Irony cannot be "defined" on the basis of its particular forms, even though in practice it necessarily assumes some form.[48] And, as already mentioned, the forms of irony are many. That "irony" has an elusive, manifold, and antiformulaic character was a point stressed by Kierkegaard: "Irony is an existential determination, and nothing is more ridiculous than to suppose that it consists in the use of a certain phraseology, or when an author congratulates himself upon succeeding in expressing himself ironically. Whoever has essential irony has it all day long, not bound to any specific form, because it is the infinite within him."[49]

Let us be clear about this passage: When Kierkegaard used the term irony, he was *not* referring above all to *a way of writing*. Similarly, when Goethe, Schlegel, Hegel, Solgar, Heine, Marx, and others in the Romantic period used the term "irony," they did not mean first and foremost a certain mode of presentation. I, too, am interested in this broad, general sense of irony--irony as a sensibility--and I am afraid that a rhetorical analysis of irony, in emphasizing outward expression, tends to miss irony's underlying complexity, and thus its real essence. Were I to rewrite the rhetorical history of irony, I would argue that Aristotle, in classifying Socratic irony primarily as a *rhetorical method*, elided the meaning of Socrates' exchanges; and that all those rhetoricians who for centuries followed Quintilian, who followed Aristotle, in their definitions of irony, likewise misconstrued the term. To the extent that many modern linguists base their understanding of irony (as a strict figure of speech) upon the conventional rhetorical history of irony, then I think that their use of the term has wandered too far from its Greek origins. Instead, I suggest that we look for a way to repair this apparent discrepancy between current conventional usage and irony's broader character.

To accomplish that goal, I will try to draw a connection between the Platonic theme of "return" and the rhetorical approaches to irony. But I shall proceed from the text outward, in an attempt to reveal the philosophical spirit *behind* literary instances of irony. In brief, I propose that an analogy can be drawn between Plato's ironic return to the political world and that moment in which readers and writers of (what is conventionally labeled as) irony choose to return to the text. Irony's character, however, is complex, for the return to the text presupposes an initial distancing, a detachment, from the text. If, finally, we can reach a *general* understanding of irony's odd disposition relative to texts--that it is not beholden to any specific form but finds expression in some form nonetheless--then perhaps we can catch a panoramic glimpse of why so many moods, effects, types, strategies, and voices have been attributed to irony.

An Either/Or Modest Proposal

A conceptual analysis of irony cannot follow standard analytical procedure: a terse statement or hypothesis defining the nature of the phenomenon to be explained; followed by supporting evidence and argumentation; followed by a confirmation of the original hypothesis, with an appropriate conclusion in elaboration thereof. The problem, as suggested above, is that irony, as part of its "nature," defies formulaic descriptions of itself.[50]

Hence we will adopt an "experiential" approach to irony. We will begin by considering irony from the perspective of a reader as she confronts an ironic passage (defined for now as such by fiat). The account is anecdotal and provisional; I am not laying down rules for the successful identification of irony. Thus I am avoiding Wayne C. Booth's distinction between the "ideal" or "implied" and "actual" reader.[51] Mine is not the "ideal" reader, for I am not contending that if certain procedures are carefully observed, a reader will necessarily be able to spot irony. Nor am I excluding the possibility that some "actual" readers will misinterpret irony, as Stanley Fish has worried about and warned against.[52] In other words, though I am beginning the account from the perspective of the reader, I am not leaving the business of irony fully up to the reader, nor am I locating irony exclusively "in the text" as a kind of mechanism that readers merely trigger. I am leaving open the possibility that irony may involve other variables: the talents of the writer, the literary conventions available in certain periods, or certain sociological or psychological or cultural preconditions that may affect the way readers read.[53] I am also leaving open the possibilities that irony may be misinterpreted or overlooked, or that it may be discovered even centuries later, or that it may be attributed improperly. If anything, I am arguing that one should approach irony *tentatively* and not with hard-and-fast rules; that the activity of reading irony involves considerable guesswork, questioning, risk, and doubt.

Suppose a reader faces for the first time Jonathan Swift's "A Modest Proposal for preventing the Children of Poor People from being a Burthen to their Parents or Country, and for making them Beneficial to the Publick,"[54] or, to cite another example, Søren Kierkegaard's opening to *Either/Or*: "Dear Reader: I wonder if you may not sometimes have felt inclined to doubt a little the correctness of the familiar philosophic maxim that the external is the internal, and the internal the external."[55]

In both cases, something probably strikes him or her as odd. Swift's title is longer than modesty would seem to dictate, and the idea that children might be a burden to their parents, financial considerations aside, takes a stab at civilized sensibilities. Victor Eremita, Kierkegaard's pseudonym, seems overly cautious in asking his reader to challenge what seems to be a glaring contradiction in terms in Hegelian philosophy (that the external is the internal, etc.). The reading of irony typically begins, it seems, with the awareness that something is awry in normal discourse, that something is unusual. Commentators have frequently mentioned that irony begins with a signal of sorts, leading to an awareness of textual oppositions, contradictions, incongruities, and incompatibilities.[56] Spoken ironies may involve a clue to the listener by way of some change in intonation or manner, some twist of logic, or perhaps through a wink of the eye or a nudge of the elbow.[57] Written ironies may include some factual inconsistency, some bit of stylistic exaggeration or anomalous arrangement, something out of whack, off-key, out of tune.[58] Booth devotes an entire chapter to the proper identification of such signals,[59] but I don't want to press the point too far.[60] Beda Allemann argues, rightly I think, that irony need leave no telltale signs at all:

> Literary irony is the more ironic, the more it is able to renounce the signs of irony--without losing its clarity. This fact entails the consequence that an adequate, purely formal definition of irony cannot be given for literature. Where the signals are missing, where indeed the inadequacy of the signals is precisely the precondition of the highest degree of irony, then we must necessarily give up hopes of a purely formal analysis, for the entirely negative signal can no longer be differentiated.[61]

Perhaps then we will need to modify our account already, to the effect that the reader's contribution consists not primarily in her picking up upon textual cues and spotting signals (for this formulation would require that such signals need always exist) but in her awareness that something *might* be awry with the workaday reading of a passage. In this modified version, it is more important that the reader be on guard and critical, that she be ready to question the "literal" layer of signification.

My argument thus far is not dependent upon an implicit view of the stability of the "literal" layer. I am not contending that there necessarily exist determinate "literal" and "covert" or "figurative" levels of meaning. I am more concerned with the reader's stance toward the text than with the ontological status of the "text itself." All my account thus requires is that the reader be suspicious that the text is open to simultaneously competing and perhaps undercutting interpretations, that she be attentive to the possibility of "otherness" of meaning (*allos*) with respect to the implied direction of a passage.

Along similar lines I oppose the view of irony as a reversal mechanism, a rhetorical device that "inverts" or substitutes X for Y. For instance, the Oxford English Dictionary defines irony as "a figure of speech in which the intended meaning is the opposite of that expressed in the words used."[62] It first can be objected that there are many kinds of figures of reversal (antiphrasis, allegory, metaphor, litotes, etc.) and that these figures are not synonymous or formally coincidental with irony.[63]

But worse, such formulations, by suggesting that ideas and passages have necessary complements or antinomies, shift the burden of interpretation from the reader and locate it instead within the text. Irony becomes then a textual mechanism that somehow inherently and automatically reverses itself, if only the reader will take notice. Even if we modify these formulations from the position that irony involves "opposites" or "contraries" (substituting Not-X for X)[64] into a more open version of substitution (some Y for X), we still encounter problems. For any substitution formula still carries the presumption that irony in and of itself yields definitive statements.[65]

But does, for instance, "A Modest Proposal" lead the reader to some interpretive resting point? Wright, in an otherwise insightful article on irony, attempts to force the distinction between "rhetorical irony" and the "ironic view" by invoking "A Modest Proposal": "In 'A Modest Proposal,' the whole sense must be completely reversed; no ambiguities lurk in the background; this is a piece of satire, one of the weapons of which is rhetorical irony."[66] Granting for the moment that Swift's piece exemplifies merely rhetorical irony, let's ask the question: Is it so clear that Swift is intending the "opposite" (presumably that the children *not* be eaten) of what he is proposing? It seems to me that it is not automatically clear that Swift's proposal is to be rejected out of hand. *The key to Swift's irony is that he has proposed his policy in a way that indeed makes some sense.* To be sure, the reader will probably discern the satirical intention of the piece; she most likely will not take Swift's advice literally.[67] But whatever Swift's ultimate purposes, for our purposes it should be emphasized that Swift at least has "played it straight," sustaining the appearance that he is presenting a rational and plausible policy for alleviating the plight of the poor.[68]

I propose that we take seriously the extent to which irony requires that the reader *not* simply reject the "literal" layer out of hand. Irony is not simply reversal, or inversion, or substitution, or negation, because the meaning of the "words expressed" is not simply gratuitous, nor is this meaning merely the function of some reverse proposition. The "literal layer" is not simply gratuitous if only because, typically, the ironist apparently has gone to some length to state his case. To be sure, this literal meaning--for instance, that children should be eaten--may be a foil for an alternative sensibility, but I contend that it is not simply a rhetorical setup. Irony is not the same as satire or caricature: Satire and caricature characteristically employ more obvious signals, such as distortion or exaggeration, that virtually compel the reader to acknowledge that meanings are being altered (in the event of which the reader stands merely as a witness). But irony typically involves the suppression of such signals; the author feigns innocence, or parrots without commentary, or acts as impersonal narrator. Thus the reader's experience in confronting irony is not as simple as substituting Y for X. We must therefore explore irony further.

Though irony is not some substitution mechanism, I do think irony involves some sense of doubleness, some notion of undercutting perspectives, some contrast between projected and implied meanings; that irony involves some sense of a declination from the presumed "straight" reading of a text. For instance, in the above example from *Either/Or*, the reader is likely to realize that to doubt Hegel "more than a little" suggests an alternative position, namely to doubt Hegel quite a lot. Some contrast, between modest and radical doubt, is being implied. But the contrast is not simply a substitition of the latter position for the former, nor do modest and radical forms of doubt constitute "opposites."

The key to the sense of doubleness in irony, I contend, is that the integrity of the "literal" layer is retained to some extent: It is not to be rejected altogether (as it might be in satire or sarcasm). The straight reading of "A Modest Proposal" has some ring of validity to it. The point can be furthered by considering a particular analysis of irony by Dan Sperber and Deirdre Wilson.[69] Sperber and Wilson reject substitution and reversal mechanisms as descriptions of irony, and they argue instead that irony can be understood as a semantic shift from "use" to "mention."[70] In particular, irony constitutes a case of implicit or "echoic" mention--in short, that somebody's words are being mentioned without direct attribution to that person.

Sperber and Wilson's argument is cogent, and I think it can be used to support my contention that the "literal" layer of signification is in some sense retained, for the ironist has left at least a trace of a suggestion that the "mentioned" words are to be taken seriously, if only because they have been carefully "echoed" and reproduced faithfully. (For example, Swift's argumentation echoes the economic reasoning of the English landlords.) The validity here is similar to the sense in which imitation is the sincerest form of flattery: Such "flattery" may be merely a backhanded compliment, but the point is that the imitation is not overt mockery, it is not an obvious setup for eventual rejection. But while their notion of "echo" conveys the element of imitation in irony, Sperber and Wilson do not go far enough, I think, to explain the element of *pretense* in irony. If irony represents a semantic switch from use to mention, as they claim, then it needs to be explained why the ironist removes the quotation marks from the proposition he is "mentioning" instead of "using," thus transforming his passage into *implicit* mention or echo.[71] The key question is not whether the author has echoed but why he has echoed (if echo it is) without explicitly acknowledging it.

The notion of echo helps explain the partial retention of the literal layer, but echo cannot account fully for the complex character of the ironic posture, for the notion of pretense behind these seemingly semantic shifts. What, then, is the nature of the sense of doubleness in irony, due to the partial retention of the literal layer, if irony is not echo, inversion, substitution, negation, or reversal?

The key is to be found in the reader's reasons for *not* being able to reject completely the literal layer, even though the text seems to contain incongruities inviting such rejection. The reason is precisely that the reader has no clear authorization from the author or "the text" to make that rejection.[72] The author has not given any explicit go-ahead signal that his expressed meaning should be reversed or rejected. Nor will the text perform the reversal for the reader. The reader has ample cause to doubt Kierkegaard's modesty or to question Swift's sincerity, but she cannot jump to the conclusion that Kierkegaard is necessarily refuting Hegel or that Swift expects his proposal inevitably to be regarded as patently absurd.

The reason the reader cannot automatically reject the validity of the literal text on the basis of textual signals and apparent oddities is related to the fact that the author has apparently sustained a pretense, assumed a cover, remained virtually inscrutable. This point brings to the fore another crucial aspect of irony: that the reader "participates" in the text. The main reason the oddities and incongruities are odd and incongruous is because the reader has "discovered" them herself. The author has not explicitly acknowledged the discrepancies in his work. But the reader's "participation" in the text, the nature of this engagement, is not the same as when an attentive reader notices that a text contains factual contradictions, grammatical errors, or scholarly oversights, or that the text is open to several, equally plausible interpretations. No, the oddities and incongruities in irony appear especially odd and incongruous because they seem *deliberate*, calculated, and planted and yet have not been explicitly acknowledged. The reader is caught between conflicting layers of signification, between suggestion and retraction, because on the one hand she notices certain inconsistencies and yet on the other hand cannot find explicit authorial confirmation of them though they seem deliberate. Swift nowhere, for instance, comes out and admits that his title is perhaps too long.

Simpson nicely describes how the reader's participation in the text leads to a kind of ambivalence or paradox:

> I must, however, explain briefly what I mean by "irony" in what follows. I do not mean that if a writer says "X" we are to understand that he means "Y"; this would be the stable notion of irony, irony as definitive statement, which does not seem to me to have much place in Romanticism. The situation as I see it is that, if a writer says "X," then we question the meaning of what he says both as we receive it into our own codes and canons of significance and as it relates to the context of the rest of his utterances, their moods and voices. This double focus is likely to produce a paradox of the hermeneutic sort; how are we to be sure where one begins and the other ends? This is Romantic irony.[73]

But is this all there is to irony? Many commentators think so, that irony ends in ambivalence and paradox, that its final teaching is dualism or subversion.[74] Angus Fletcher, for instance, contends that the ironic method helps us to live with irony but that "the ironies remain."[75] Haakon Chevalier, however, views irony not as a curative but as a symptom of schizophrenia, "a mode of escape from the fundamental problems and responsibilities of life."[76] But the ironist, according to Chevalier, enjoys his schizophrenia: "Irony characterizes the attitude of one who, when confronted with the choice of two things that are mutually exclusive, chooses both. Which is but another way of saying that he chooses neither. He cannot bring himself to give up one for the other, and he gives up both. But he reserves the right to derive from each the greatest possible passive enjoyment. And this enjoyment is Irony."[77] In an only slightly different vein, Paul de Man writes: "Irony is unrelieved *vertige*, dizziness to the point of madness."[78]

I do not agree with these accounts, but I can understand why some persons regard irony so (and I think my view of irony can account for such interpretations). I do not believe that irony (regarded as a general concept) necessarily ends in doubleness, ambivalence, paradox, or incompletion. To be sure, neither the text nor the author provides the reader with an obvious reconciliation to the suggested incongruities and tensions. Simpson is again very good in his explanation of this problem:

> Any employment of the strategy of "voices" asks questions about the authority of the subjectivities which they enunciate, and there is no sure concept of an ultimate truth whose articulation they might be working towards. When meanings are presented within overtly or implicitly signified spoken voices, we have to estimate, not just *what* is said, but also by and for whom, and on what particular occasion it is said. This makes for a necessarily unstable structure whose complete meaning is probably unattainable, and whose partial meanings themselves demand large contributions from the reading mind, disposed according to its own needs and convictions.
>
> This is an important part of what I want to call "irony." Allemann (*Ironie und Dichtung*, p. 16) regards "literary irony" as involving a tension between what the speaker appears to *say* and what the reader/hearer deduces that he really *means*; but, in the Romantic context, the qualification must be made that the deduction about what is really "meant" *cannot be accomplished on the evidence of the text alone* italics added]; the reader must intrude, even manipulate, in his own person, and often constitute something of a different order from what is before him.[79]

This may in a sense be true in all reading of any text. But irony, we might say, places an especially heavy burden of interpretation on the reader. She is confronted with textual tensions and oddities that cannot be reconciled or resolved on the basis of textual evidence alone. I am sympathetic with readers of ironic texts who quit at this point, for they may feel puzzled and frustrated, and an opportunity to take leave of those texts presents itself. But I believe irony dangles a carrot in front of the nose of the reader, inviting her to continue. I agree with Simpson that the deduction of meaning at this stage cannot be accomplished on the evidence of the text alone. But I do think the reader has recourse to more than simply that which is provided by her reading mind, "its own needs and convictions." Namely, a shift of focus takes place. The reader is invited to enter into a kind of silent dialogue with the author, in a medium parallel to the text itself. This sounds a bit mystical and metaphorical, but I think the point can in fact be substantiated on the basis of "the text." I am not contending that the reader attempts somehow to read the author's "mind" in order to recover the "intended" meaning of the passages in question. No, I am suggesting that at some point in the reader's experience the author becomes conspicuous by his absence, that he draws (i.e., seems to draw) attention to himself, inviting the reader to reflect upon the author's activity as author in general (and not simply as author of this or that particular passage).[80] The reason the reader is drawn beyond the text, even after textual analysis has been virtually exhausted, is that a momentum of sorts has been building. The author has suppressed his presence and yet the textual incongruities seem to attest to his authorial control. But the point is that the author has maintained the pretense that nothing is wrong with this arrangement, that his apparent authorial detachment and his apparent authorial control are not mutually incompatible. Thus it is the element of *pretense* in irony that leads the reader on, encouraging her to believe that reconcilation can be attained, that the textual tensions are not to be accepted as normal, that answers are possible. Socrates was a master of this technique in spoken form.

At this point in the experience of reading irony, the reader must shift her focus away from the text almost completely and instead attempt to draw inferences about the author. This is a natural shift in the process of reading irony--natural though not easy and certainly not inevitable. Some readers may pass beyond this watershed and others not; and that fact helps to explain why irony lends itself to so many radically different interpretations. It may also help explain why a study of the rhetorical history of irony reveals a division between those who regard irony as a textual phenomenon and those who regard it as a philosophical stance.[81] If the reader presses on, however, it seems likely that she will be drawn to inquire: What is the author of irony really up to?

The question requires a certain abstraction from the text. Instead of asking what the author *means*, what message he is trying to convey, it becomes necessary to examine his entire *method* of communication, his way of using language. Irony, if pursued far enough, leads to an investigation of language itself. Specifically, we are interested in the author's tendency toward *pretense*.

This line of inquiry has already been taken up in the history of irony, namely by the Romantics and their critics. Several Romantic theorists of irony dwelled upon the ironist's ability to *detach* from the text, to adopt a distanced, skeptical stance vis-à-vis the work.[82] The Schlegel brothers, Goethe, and other admirers of irony celebrated the element of detachment as a moment of liberation and freedom for the individual (a topic later taken up more centrally by Kierkegaard). Hegel and the critics of irony viewed the aspect of detachment as the artist's self-aggrandizement at the expense of the rest of humanity.

The ironist disengages himself, but his act of liberation entails simultaneously the belittling of the text and the belittling of others; hence irony represents little more than the ironist's attempt to glorify himself. These charges against irony have not been put to rest. The ironist, it is still claimed,[83] may achieve a certain perspective upon the text but his is the height of arrogance; hence irony reflects the ironist's self-delusion rather than true philosophic knowledge. The ironist flaunts his superiority, but only by mocking others. He provides a critique of the human condition, but only by hypocritically exempting himself from the human race. His "objectivity" is therefore no more than an orgiastic display of "subjectivity."[84]

But the criticisms of irony based upon the aspect of detachment do not really go to the heart of the matter, because the ironist's stance consists of more than detachment. Detachment does not explain why the ironist writes at all, why he even uses language. If we carry the idea of detachment to its logical conclusion, we would have to ask why the ironist does not detach completely, why he does not sever all ties and instead choose simply not to write anything. Silent superiority would be the ultimate snub. Yet what is interesting about irony is not simply the element of detachment, but that irony reveals a combination of detachment and implication: The fact (as shown by the sheer existence of the "text") is that the ironist writes, even though he may be partially disengaged from, not fully committed to, his own activity. As Friedrich Schlegel contended, the ironist may think of his role as godlike, but he does not choose the option of "divine idleness."[85] Rather, he actively participates in the human world, employing the human conventions of language even though he may not fully respect them.[86] Hence, just as irony is not synonymous with paradox and skepticism, neither is it simply equivalent to nihilism, fatalism, absurdism, and cynicism--"isms" that are typically linked with a detached perspective.

Irony's interplay between detachment and implication can perhaps be best introduced by way of a discussion of representational art. Here Friedrich Schlegel's theories are most relevant.[87] The self-aware artist, Schlegel contended, realizes that his art can never fully portray the world. The world is infinite and dynamic; works of art are finite and static. But by *accepting* his limitations, the artist can in a way overcome them. The artist incorporates his awareness of the discrepancy between art and the world into his work: He includes a "criticism" or "mockery" of his work as an aspect of the work itself. Schlegel called this technique "transcendental buffoonery"--and he equated it with irony itself.[88] The self-aware artist reveals his detached presence behind the work, calling attention to his creative role and thus to the fictional nature of the work; and thereby he undermines the credibility of the work as dramatic illusion (which at the same time undermines any illusion of godlike creativity). But by making the admission that his work is indeed fiction, by admitting art's representational limitations (and by admitting that he is indeed a "buffoon" and not a god), the ironic artist creates the dramatic space for his art to unfold as a valid activity in its own terms. His "mockery" enables art to exist against the background of skepticism. Hence a work of art reveals a combination of detachment *and* affirmation. A "negative" sets the stage for a "positive."[89] In short, revealed *pretense* is the key ingredient in the strategy of ironic representation.

Let me illustrate Schlegel's notion of artistic irony with an example of my own. Consider, say, the Vietnam War monument in Washington, D.C., and ask the question: How does a stone monument, cold, straight, dark, and solemn, stand as a testimony to the horrors of that particular war? The answer, by default, is that a monument to a human holocaust does not *literally* portray the grotesqueness of war: The monument "itself" is not grotesque. Its black color and flat surfaces do not directly signify red blood, foul odors, and painful screams. There is an obvious discrepancy between the monument's starkness and the war's true-to-life horrors. By making this discrepancy so poignant, the monument (i.e., the artist who created it) in effect includes a tacit admission that it does not even attempt to represent the visual, tactile, and auditory horrors of warfare. By acknowledging its limitations, its representational shortcomings, the monument *alludes* to such horrors. It embodies a strategy of indirection: By its very straightness, its starkness, its solemnness, the monument conveys the sentiment that the war was a grisly abomination.[90] Many observers have described the monument as "powerful," but the curiosity should be noted that the aesthetic "power" of the monument is due precisely to the suppression of overt representational signals: It is through an artistic strategy of irony that silence can be deafening, that solemnness can speak volumes.

It is perhaps a mistake, however, to suggest that the primary function of ironic art is representational, that is, that works of art reproduce particular images or convey particular *messages*. For I think that Schlegel's point was that the artist's "transcendental buffoonery," his combination of detachment and implication, his *pretense*, establishes the *context* of art, the validity of fiction. The realm of art or fiction becomes a distinctive *medium* for a particular kind of interaction between artists and spectators. Art becomes viewed, then, as an experience, an activity for persons, not simply an instrument for relaying direct messages. In admitting the representational inadequacies of the finite work--but *by proceeding nonetheless, in the face of this disclosure*--the artist extends an invitation to his audience, thereby hoping to establish a kind of silent rapport with them.[91] The artist diminishes--perhaps to the point of mocking--the literal or "nonfictional" status of the work, but in the process he or she creates a context for a different form of interactive experience, valid now on its own terms.

Perhaps now we can return to the written word to consider how the strategy of irony, as a form of pretense, operates in verbal contexts. G.G. Sedgewick points out that Arthur Sidgwick took for granted that the meaning of irony is "the consciousness of the inadequacy of language." He quotes the latter:

> If we attempt to use only the language which appears to be adequate, we overshoot the mark. . . . We give the idea not of a really deep and sustained feeling, but of a paroxysm, a momentary fury, an extravagance. . . . As in the vision of Elijah, the sign of an Almighty Presence is the still small voice; and so it is with human spirits, in their degree. . . . Thus it often comes about that while the lower stages of feeling can be expressed, the higher stages must be suggested. In the ascent the full truth will do; but the climax can only be reached by irony.[92]

Understatement, Sedgewick explains, is the "true nature" of irony; irony is "language mocking itself." He interprets this self-mockery as a recognition of discrepancy: "For the thing as stated, the Appearance, falls so far short of the thing itself, the Reality, as to be for all practical purposes a different entity."[93]

Though this explanation is somewhat formulaic and too neat, I basically concur with Sedgewick's and Sidgwick's notion of irony as consciousness of the inadequacy of language. The strategy is similar to Schlegel's analysis of art.[94] By mocking or partially disclaiming one's own discourse, one disrupts the convention that implicitly holds that words carry intrinsic import;[95] and by making this admission an aspect of one's use of language, one can consciously manipulate words to make a point, nonetheless. Irony, then, might be defined at this point as an understanding and use of language that admits, and somehow conveys the admission, that language itself is inadequate as a mode of representation. But then again, this formulation is deceptive, for it seems to endorse the presumption that the function of writing is representational, and it begs the question of why language might be viewed as inadequate. As with Schlegel's view of art, I think the point about admitting inadequacies can be extended to written discourse: Irony breaks the appearance of intrinsic meaning in order to create a context for interactive communication between authors and readers. Rhetorical irony, I propose, is actually an attempt to use pretense, to use words consciously as mere media,[96] to lay the basis for a kind of indirect human interaction and engagement.

We need to explore this point. Why is written language inadequate for human interaction, for communication? I think this insight, if insight rather than extrapolation it is, issues partly from an implicit, invidious comparison of written language with spoken language, and by extension, with human interaction in general.[97] Because the written word is static and finite, the result of little squiggles and scratches on a flat surface, while the world is three-dimensional and dynamic, the word cannot literally represent the fully rounded, multifaceted, technicolor qualities of experience itself; nor can it measure up even to the experience of spoken interaction. This is not a wholesale condemnation of written language itself, as a learned activity, as a "part" of the world, an experience unto itself (the point of which is not simply to reflect the world[98]). But, if pressed, one surely must concede that there exists a discrepancy between the representational import of the written word and "life" in its many configurations; and this discrepancy becomes especially salient when one compares the experience of spoken discourse with the experience of reading written discourse. Spoken intercourse gives the impression of greater immediacy, of direct engagement with one's other; written interaction is by comparison more removed, more abstract. I do not want to press these comparisons too far: I am not well versed in the art of phenomenological description. The point really is this: The written word has at least the *appearance* of permanence, of fixed meanings and absolute ties of communication. Words *seem* not to change. These appearances can lull one into complacency, into the presumption that written language holds intrinsic meanings, that it necessarily bridges the distance between individuals. The spoken word does not seem to encourage such pretensions: Spoken discourse involves innumerable qualifications, improvisations, clarifications, nuances, equivocations, intonations, and so forth.[99] Spoken interaction, to press these somewhat contrived distinctions further, is more evidently an "experience" rather than a "mode" of representation.

But to recover our train of thought: The ironist attempts to transform the written text from a "mode" into an "experience" (or more precisely, to make the reader aware of reading particularly as an experience, a kind of human interaction). He does this by disclaiming, through covert signals, that the text is adequate as a form of representation and yet continues to employ the text *as if* it were a straightforward mode of expression. In short, the ironist may inwardly harbor no pretensions about language, but he maintains appearances to the contrary.

Perhaps our discussion may seem to have become somewhat overblown, yet I think it is necessary to discuss irony in broad and general terms, if only because irony has been applied, not merely to several authors and their different "voices," but to entire fields of endeavor: the visual arts,[100] poetry,[101] novels,[102] music,[103] mathematics,[104] science,[105] prayer,[106] and confession.[107] Some commentators, wishing to retain irony as a coherent and delimited "term" of literary criticism, lament these larger applications of the word,[108] but I think there is indeed a connection that needs to be pursued between irony as a textual phenomenon and irony as a more general stance. The key to that connection is in the element of pretense. Why does an author use language that he regards as inadequate?

Let us take a look at one of the "broader" applications of irony. Cleanth Brooks achieved a certain notoriety in critical circles for having made the sweeping statement that irony is the principle of all poetry (and especially of modern poetry).[109] How could a self-respecting thinker be so undiscriminating? In a follow-up explanation, Brooks asked, if a poet wants to "say" something, why doesn't he say it directly and forthrightly?[110] Why say it obscurely and partially, through the use of metaphor? Why use poetry at all? To summarize Brooks's argument: Direct statement leads to abstraction, goes straight to the "universal" and thus takes us out of the field of poetry, which deals with particulars and details. Poetry dwells upon particulars because its purpose is not to make statements but to create an entire experience of sorts:

> For the theme in a genuine poem does not confront us as abstraction--that is, as one man's generalization from the relevant particulars. Finding its proper symbol, defined and refined by the participating metaphors, the theme becomes a part of the reality in which we live--an insight, rooted in and growing out of concrete experience, many-sided, three-dimensional. Even the resistance to generalization has its part in this process--even the drag of the particulars away from the universal--even the tension of opposing themes--play their parts. The kite properly loaded, tension maintained along the kite string, rises steadily *against* the thrust of the wind.[111]

Poetry creates an experience, according to Brooks, not by direct imitation but by indirection and connotation. But these metaphors and connotations are not released from a statement until its meaning is "warped" or "loaded"[112] from the pressures of the context, in other words, through an acknowledgment of the poetic form itself (hence the "principle of structure" in poetry in his title). Brooks calls the warping of a statement by the context "ironical," and "irony" as the acknowledgment of the pressures of context.

So Brooks believes he has defined the "context" of poetry, has identified the "structure" of poetry. But his use of irony--as the acknowledgment of the pressures of context--suggests far wider applications. He asks, what "would be a statement wholly devoid of an ironic potential--a statement that did not show any qualification of the context"? He cites as an example propositions like "Two plus two equals four." In a footnote, he qualifies this. He admits, "This is not to say, of course, that such statements are not related to a particular 'universe of discourse.'" But he wishes to distinguish, he explains, between a "universe of discourse" and a "context."[113]

If it were only so simple! But, as R.S. Crane suggests,[114] even mathematical propositions are "warped" on the basis of context and thus, according to Brooks's formulation, reveal an element of irony in their usage. It would seem that every use of language presupposes a particular "context"--which is not so easily distinguishable from the "universe of discourse."

The notion of context provides a springboard for making a leap from the "term" irony to the "philosophy" behind irony. Brooks is right, I think, to associate irony with the acknowledgment of contexts--this formulation is very close to Schlegel's, Sidgwick's, and Sedgewick's idea that irony involves an implicit acknowledgment of limitations. But Schlegel et al. contended that the limitations acknowledged were uniquely *human* limitations, and Brooks contends that irony is a "structural" principle. Moreover, Brooks's identifying the structural context of poetry seems to be based upon a dubious distinction between a "universe of discourse" and a "context"--as if the "context" of poetry could simply be posited as such, as if it were a "natural" category. Thus it would seem that Brooks's notion of contexts need not be confined to the context of poetry, and we are left with Crane's sarcastic suggestion that all language might be considered ironical if we give Brooks his way. We might resolve this problem as follows. In poetry, the textual "signals" of the context are fairly obvious; it is usually clear from rhythmic pattern, spacing, and so on, that statements are being "warped" by context.[115] Hence it is easier to talk about poetic contexts as "structural" than it might be in applications in which the acknowledgment of contexts is less forthright. But there is a very general sense in which the acknowledgment of contexts applies to many more linguistic formations than simply poetry and in a way that relates the notion directly to human affairs. Put crudely but simply:

Words are used by human beings, their most general "context" is that of human life, human interaction.[116] The problem is that humans tend to forget that words have contexts, that they are human constructs; the words, their meanings, seem to crystallize, to detach from human usage. To be sure, it can be argued that words must be afforded some independence from human manipulation, otherwise they will possess no constancy, and thus no coherent meaning, at all. But we are concerned now with the other extreme, the extent to which words sometimes seem to lose all connections to human contexts, all vitality, can become irrelevant and clichéd, can become *too* abstracted from use. The problem might be said to stem from an inherent, phenomenological tension between language and human life. Words--especially written words--have the appearance of permanence and fixity; whereas human life and human interaction are, on most counts, fluid, fleeting, and finite.[117]

The ironist, we might declare, is one who is keenly aware of these inherent tensions between language and human life;[118] that language is meaningful only in a human context, is thus conditioned and limited by the limitations of human beings, and yet has, and necessarily must have in order to function, an element of relative fixity and permanence. Words often purport to form, and perhaps do indeed form, a permanent bond between humans, withstanding the fragility of human exchange, rendering some semblance of stability and permanence--in a word, meaning--to their lives. But the ironist, ever mindful of the relation and yet tension between language and life, plays the two off against one another, now considering and comparing the permanence of language with the the frailty of human existence, now comparing the inadequacy of language with the deeper, often ineffably profound moments of human exchange.

This mental juxtaposition, of the mechanics of language and the dynamism of human existence, informs the textual strategy of irony. The lure, the motor, of the ironic strategy is in the suggestion that there might indeed be persons on the other side of texts, that readers will actually read one's works with sensitivity and intelligence or that real, live writers might actually have been responsible for the arrangement of those squiggles on the page. The reader is drawn to reflect upon the text, to inquire after the author, because the element of pretense, the apparent contradiction between the author's detachment and his authorial control, leaves the suggestion that the squiggles are *deliberate*, even if ambiguous.[119] The ironic author drops the hint, then, that the text may well be superfluous to the task of human communication, for an invisible, almost telepathic form of exchange is alluded to, seems possible, more real even than that provided by ordinary discourse.

One could propose in sweeping fashion that an element of irony is the principle of intelligibility in any text: that there must be humans on either side.[120] But, in the hope of keeping reasonably close to the more conventional understandings of irony, I suggest that we limit the term to those examples in which readers and writers are actively conscious of, actively in search of, the presence of human deliberation in texts (and hence irony may represent more a difference of degree, than of kind, from unironic discourse). On this score, we could say that the strategy of irony is to prompt writers and readers to pursue each other, to confront one another very generally as human beings, rather than to consider one another simply as authors or readers of this or that particular passage. For instance, we can see this principle at work especially in the most rarefied forms of irony, i.e., those examples in which the "signals" are the fewest, the subtlest, the vaguest. In these instances, we must discover why, as Allemann has contended, the fewer the signals, the "better" the irony. The reason has to do, I think, with taking *risks* within linguistic contexts.[121] If the ironic author need not explicitly admit his presence, if he can remain for the most part inscrutable--and yet can be "found out" anyway; and if the reader inquires after a phantom and catches him; in other words, if an ironic transmission nevertheless "works," then part of the exhilaration, the meaning of the experience, is that the parties concerned have taken a risk, have defied ordinary language, and won. The key to this strategy of indirection seems to be that a heightened interactive experience has been effected even though language has been tacitly acknowledged as inadequate. The "human side" of language wins out, despite appearances to the contrary. The appeal of such an approach seems to be that if we, as authors and readers, take risks, if we make concessions to the validity of the "literal layer," if we make a show of accepting the appearance of the permanence of language, and yet if we in actuality can defy that formal structure and overcome those risks, finally confronting each other as the humans behind the texts, then it is as if we have forged a bond even more durable than language, that we have achieved a "higher" form of communication.[122] Having made concessions to language and yet having admitted its inadequacy seems to reinforce the validity of our silent exchange. The exhilaration, the intrigue of irony is that human interaction, in all its supposed ambiguity and frailty, is pitted directed against the supposed permanence of language and somehow prevails, against the odds.

Irony, then, involves a sense of doubleness but the doubleness is not due simply to "a clash of speech and meaning" (because the "literal layer" is not rejected outright in favor of a "figurative" or an alternative "intended" meaning). Nor is the sense of doubleness due to a straightforward clash of "appearance" and "reality." As Wright writes: "[The divided vision of irony] has led some to feel that 'the basic feature of every irony is a contrast between a reality and an appearance.' But the matter is not so simple: the ironist is not sure which is and which merely seems."[123] I have suggested that the doubleness, the tension in irony, is best described as a clash between a view of language as contextual and a view of language as representational. Like Wright, I think that irony confounds rather than resolves the distinction between appearance and reality--irony plays back and forth between big falsehoods and little verities.[124] But I have also contended that irony does not end in paradox: It has a direction, it has a resolution of sorts.[125] As I have described this contest, the contextual side wins out. The resolution, however, is a "backhanded" one, an affirmation of human exchange by indirection. Put differently: Irony involves a deflationary stance toward ordinary language, but the meaning of this deflationary stance, this admission of inadequacy, is not some thoroughgoing skepticism. Rather, irony is the use of language, *in spite of* one's skeptical presumptions. In short, ironic *pretense* is doubleness but not *duplicity*, for the pretense of irony reveals a certain kind of commitment, the value of the exchange for it own sake, which is for the sake of a kind of remote contact with other human beings.[126]

Irony circumvents the representational appearances of language in order to reclaim the value of subliminal dialogue, as an integrating experience unto itself. While I question Brooks's flat association of poetry with irony, I agree with his claim that irony attempts to "create" an actual experience, or a heightened awareness of that experience, between humans (as poetry attempts to "create" the experience of flying a kite). Why is this remarkable? Simpson claims that Romantic irony grew out of a philosophical milieu in which persons had serious doubts about whether language is necessarily underwritten by some metalinguistic guarantee, some transhuman authority, or some general conception of human nature. Similarly we might now propose: Irony is a form of communication that is not based upon a presumption of human commonality; it is rather one that "creates" its own common ground, its own context, for interactive communication. And paradoxically, the acknowledgment of surrounding contexts is what creates the specific context for irony. This is a very unconventional interpretation of the workings of irony, not to mention the workings of language in general. For instance, Booth contends that irony rests ultimately upon a common set of (preexisting) human values. In reply, Fish argues that irony rests upon a common set of assumptions relative to a particular reading "community." Both Booth and Fish attempt to reconstruct the "human side" to the reading experience, but they remain too attached to the importance of the text as a necessary point of commonality, a natural intersection. To my mind, irony is a way of bringing readers and authors together by using the text as a pretext. The issue, then, is why one wishes to engage with others at all, especially when one is skeptical about the whole enterprise. We might say: The key variable that determines the formal character of irony is how widely the context is initially defined, how many and what kind of readers the author is trying to reach. The author's choice to proceed, to manifest his ironic sensibility, is what in turn "informs" the selection of particular signals, e.g., whether to be very obscure, less so, and so forth.[127]

We need to pursue how exactly the element of *pretense* works to extend the subliminal human dialogue of irony, to create the "context" for indirect communication. Perhaps we can approach the answer itself by indirection, by examining again the arguments of irony's detractors. The critics of irony claim that the element of pretense is just a cover for arrogance, a ruse to set up a victim for ridicule, thus inflating the ironist's sickly ego. Upon this reading, irony is merely self-conceit, and as such represents an escape from responsibilities, from commitment.[128] Those critics who observe, however, that irony has an "intersubjective" dimension beyond the ironist's sickly self-indulgence modify their case somewhat. Irony may include, they concede, an "experience of interaction" of sorts, but this experience is simply an extension of the ironist's snobbery. The ironist draws up "sides": Either you are with him or against him. If irony erects bonds of social cohesion, engages in a kind of community building, it does so only by exclusion, by drawing invidious comparisons.[129] Benjamin DeMott, for instance, contends that irony binds people simply by virtue of quickness, the fast exchange of sallies:

> The ironist steps forth as a self-protecting man; fearing quick assessment he seeks a manner that will convey that he is more complicated than any words he utters can suggest. Exchanging conversational coin with him means entering a secret relation, accepting membership in an exclusive community, marking yourself off from fools. For the ironist's talk constantly posits two listeners: one who is witless, hence capable of understanding nothing except the public, dictionary meanings of the words said; another who is quick enough to comprehend that the words spoken add up to more (or less) than their public significance. As this implies, quickness alone can be a bond that creates the community.[130]

But DeMott is even more damning: "It is not necessary that quickness be accompanied by faith in the good and the true." An ironic community is not based on moral principles but is the artificial product of a social posture, a "mere gesture of knowingness."[131] Having no solid moral foundation, this community cannot sustain itself:

> It must begin in gestures that create an elite group; it must end not in positions but in universal hostility--hostility to all positive assertion, rejection of any lines of intelligence available to ordinary men. The one truth the new irony has to tell is that the man who uses it has no place to stand except in momentary community with those who seek to express a comparable alienation from other groups. The one conviction it expresses is that there are really no sides left: no virtue to oppose to corruption, no wisdom to oppose to cant. The one standard it accepts is that on which the simple man--the untutored nonironist who fancies (in his dolthood) that he knows what good and bad should mean--is registered as the hero of our world, a cipher worth nothing but uninterrupted contempt.[132]

"If this is true," DeMott asks, "if the sicknik is ultimately the man who knows nothing, why has he attracted the highbrow attention mentioned before?" DeMott seems still to be reviewing the minutes of the Athenian court case against Socrates, imagining himself in the role of prosecutor. It is a difficult role: How does one prove positive guilt when the accused is someone who pleads ignorance, that he knows nothing? DeMott does little more than to beg the question of moral principle and moral certainty: If the traditional notion of community is without foundation, all is lost.[133]

Several commentators have attempted to argue that an implicit notion of epistemic exclusion, of snobbery and victimization, must be included as a variable in any formal analysis of irony,[134] but I don't think that these analyses can hold up under sustained investigation. This characterization of irony seems to hold for examples of irony as an isolated trope, as blame-by-praise or praise-by-blame. But as we reach more complex forms of irony, it becomes increasingly difficult to identify the victims, as opposed to the perpetrators. Some commentators modify this account by employing the notions of "self-victimizing irony," "self-parodying irony," "self-irony," or "double-irony";[135] but then they have obscured the distinction between snob and victim until it is meaningless. The modern association of irony with snobbery grows out of irony's historical connection with "raillery" and the "dry mock," but I think the element of irony in such applications inheres not so much in the mockery but the "dryness"--in short, in the element of pretense.

Again, we should not simply rehearse the charge again and again that Socrates corrupts the youth; we need to explain why Socrates uses language at all when he harbors deep reservations about its epistemological basis. The *ad hominem* attack upon his arrogance doesn't get us very far. The charges of snobbery, arrogance, and exclusivity can be explained in part, it seems to me, by the apparent fact that the ironist, in doubting the basis of language, eschews shibboleths, refuses clichés, and shatters traditional pieties. For this alone he may encounter resistance and provoke animosity. His method may also antagonize his opponents because it requires that they actively "participate" in the exchange; the heavy burden of interpretation required by irony may itself cause some discomfiture for those who would prefer to receive guidance and moral instruction passively or else to receive nothing at all.

Schlegel's response to the charge of arrogance has already been mentioned: Irony is actually a form of self-limitation, an informed type of buffoonery or self-parody that applies equally to others.[136] Kenneth Burke has also suggested that irony issues not from arrogance but from modesty. In fact, he flatly equates irony with a democratic and inclusive concept of "humility": "True irony, humble irony, is based upon a sense of fundamental kinship with the enemy, as one *needs* him, is *indebted* to him, is not merely outside him as an observer but contains him *within*, being consubstantial with him."[137]

Similarly, Randolph Bourne called the ironist a "friend" to his supposed enemies, for irony is "the truest sympathy,"[138] "founded in the common democratic experience of all men": "The ironical mind is the only truly modest mind, for its point of view is ever outside itself."[139] And Wright distinguishes between the "pretended humility" of Pascal, who used irony as a weapon, and Socrates' "real humility," which was based upon a "recognition of contradictions in human experience." In other words, Socrates identified with others; he was trying to reach out to others with his verbal jabs. On this view, ironic pretenses do not constitute an insult to others but count rather as a backhanded compliment of sorts.

Irony's critics see only the backhandedness. They view the be-all and end-all of irony as subversion, negation, demolition, corrosion.[140] But they miss the most important and most paradoxical aspect of irony, the return. Schlegel, Thirlwall, Bourne, Burke, Muecke, Jankélévitch, Mellor, and Wright have stressed that, appearances to the contrary notwithstanding, irony is a positive, constructive, affirmative stance toward others, though a stance that is presented in the form of a backhanded compliment. The reason the ironist pays his compliments with such circumlocution is that he holds countervailing sentiments, harbors deep reservations, remains fundamentally skeptical in his attitude toward others. And he does not compromise these sentiments, though he may labor against them. He is neither quite a skeptic nor a romantic (if by romanticism we mean an attempt to overcome skepticism).

I cannot, however, give a good, straightforward reason why the ironist writes, why he plays it straight, why he pretends not to doubt the validity of language when he seriously entertains thoughts to the contrary. Schematically, we might say that the ironist detaches even from his detachment, that irony contains an inner imperative to turn upon itself, which in turn requires that the ironist return to the text, that he implicate himself.[141] But schematic designs do not get to the heart of the matter. In a sense, the spirit of irony has to do with doing the unexpected, with the fact that there is no good and precise "reason" for returning to the text, for seeking out others.

I am tempted to supply a formula at this point to make sense of the ironist's odd behavior. Simpson suggests one: "The process becomes the product." His explanation is intriguing:

> The world is a text, but no longer in the sense that it is the book of God; the act of reading is one of imaginative self-confrontation, setting up a framework of interdetermination from which there is no escape. But at the same time there is a kind of freedom within this system. Within this inclosure, where the reader is at times so isolated that he is conscious of having to "invent" the author as his proxy, this reader can also be aware of having to make decisions about himself through his near-total responsibility for the "meaning" of the text. If there is no sure way of articulating the degree to which the reader is forming the text and the text forming the reader, then one possible response becomes the "leap of faith," the decision about which priorities will be adopted being taken despite the refusal of the text to satisfy them completely.[142]

Can this be? Does the experience of reading irony really come down to a decision about priorities? If I read him correctly, Simpson is saying that because one cannot really be sure what another person is saying or writing (a skepticism encouraged by the theorists of irony in the Romantic period), because one doubts that there exist metalinguistic "guarantees"[143] that underwrite the reading experience, it is only the commitment to continue reading itself, to go on pursuing the text's and the author's meanings, that makes the "ironic form" of communication possible. Irony is really a commitment, not a form. "Irony is duty,"

Schlegel contended, drawing cryptically upon Kant.[144] And I think in similar fashion, Kierkegaard labeled the "confine" between the aesthetic and the ethical stages on life's way as the confine of irony. Irony, according to Kierkegaard, tricks and teases us out of the purely aesthetic stance--which is irresponsible--and prompts us toward ethics, toward a morally responsible outlook.[145]

Simpson's explanation for the ironic reader seems to make sense for the author as well: that irony comes down to a conscious commitment, a choice made amidst great skepticism. The decision to write ironically, to return to the text, to pretend that language matters after all, seems to be based on nothing more than an conscious decision about priorities, a choice to seek out the reader rather than not, a belief apparently that it is better to try to communicate with others--even though one remains highly skeptical--than not.[146] It is a commitment that seems to be based upon a backhanded affirmation, something like living the life of examination because the unexamined life is not worth living. "One would say that Swift manages to fulfil nothingness, complete the void, vanish himself, and abandon the reader in utter paralysis, except that against all logic the feeling of his end-games is one of vitality."[147]

The strange result of it all, the real irony behind irony, is that the author's mere *pretense* about language breathes life once again into sentences that have gone stale, that have been emptied of meaning. Now they mean something because they *might* mean something. Irony engages authors and readers in a cat-and-mouse routine: Can you spot the other? But this mutual orientation toward one another--the mere suspicion that there exist real, live authors or real, live readers on the other side of the page--tends to be mutually reinforcing: Writers trying to write ironically and readers on the look out for irony end up pondering each other (at the slightest textual provocation), wondering whether there is indeed a figure behind the shadow. If the pondering is mutual, then, and if there were a judge somehow above the fray, he could declare that the act of ironic intercourse had been performed successfully. But I think the term *irony* should be applied to the pondering itself, to the reader's and writer's orientations toward the text, and not be reserved solely for those instances when it clearly "succeeds."[148] (We use the term *fishing*, for instance, to describe the activity of one who drops his line into the water and waits, and our use of the word *fishing* does not depend upon whether that person actually catches a fish on that particular expedition. Reading and writing irony are, in this regard, something like fishing.)

Irony is a certain kind of pondering, a certain intellectual orientation, a mode of consciousness. For those who want such stances defined and located, we would have to say that irony begins with the individual, the writer or the reader. But this is not to say that irony is simply "subjective," that it is merely an "attitude" or even "worldview."[149] For it is an attitude that entails implication, that virtually requires expression. Thus I maintain that it is best to regard "irony" finally as an interactive experience--even if that interaction is oblique and indirect.[150] And it is contagious: Suspicion breeds suspicion, examination examination. From the reader's perspective, she finds reason to doubt the text; this leads her to "participate" in the text, to investigate further. Perhaps the author has sent out clear signals, perhaps only nudges, perhaps nothing much to go on at all. But what is truly remarkable about irony is that this complex stance *can* be provoked and nourished in readers; the quality *can* be cultivated. The author's irony consists of a combination of detachment and implication vis-à-vis the text, and he encourages this same combination, this double posture, in his reader. The reader doubts, distances herself, but then returns to the text, examining further. The lines of communication in irony may be very remote, the engagement very indirect; but there does seem to be a point of contact.[151] Simpson writes: "Few writers are more eloquent than Coleridge about the obligation which an author must place upon his reader, that of 'kindling his own torch.' . . . The reader must be free to 'create' his own meaning, but the author must not cease to exercise some level of control over the limits within which such meanings can be formulated."[152]

Irony, then, is best understood as a give-and-take between author and reader, a process that requires, on both of their parts, a play between critical detachment and engaged participation.[153] It is a back-and-forth, a process of constant checking, guessing, criticizing, examining, and judging. Randolph Bourne called it the "science of comparative experience," an experience that "compares things not with an established standard but with each other, and the values that slowly emerge from the process, values that emerge from one's own vivid reactions, are constantly revised, corrected, and refined by that same sense of contrast."[154] Simpson contends that irony is the antidote to "authoritarian discourse" whereby the meanings of language are assumed to issue from an outside authority. But ironic communication, according to Simpson, functions reciprocally between author and reader; they "invent" their own meanings, with help from one another, almost out of thin air.[155] A commitment to communication generates the thing itself.

Mellor writes, "Romantic irony, in sum, is a mode of consciousness or way of thinking about the world that finds a corresponding literary mode."[156] I have claimed that the expression in forms, that participation in the text, is not inevitable, but, like Mellor, I find the most significant aspect of irony to be in its constructive potential, not in its deconstructive presumptions.

Yet although irony entails at least partially a positive orientation toward texts, it cannot be defined as a textual phenomenon. Wayne C. Booth as well as the Derrideans view irony as a characteristic of texts (whether as a resident property or, by default, as a malleable form), though Booth and the Derrideans derive very different results from this premise. The Derrideans regard textual irony as self-subverting and playful,[157] whereas Booth claims that irony can be stable. I think both accounts miss the crux of irony, namely that decisive moment in which an author decides to write despite his or her reservations and in which a reader continues to read despite his or her confusions. Irony is rather a way of thinking about texts that produces an oblique form of human interaction; and though this human dialogue may be refracted "through" the text, the "text itself" is of secondary importance.[158]

The best formal analyses of irony that I have read fail to capture the essence of irony. Sperber and Wilson's notion of "echoic mention" is an excellent semantic analysis of irony, but it does not hold up under review (even though they intend their semantic analysis to be coupled with a "pragmatic" analysis). As I mentioned earlier, Sperber and Wilson do not address why the ironist *manqué* removes the quotation marks from his example of "mention," transforming it from a case of explicit to indirect or echoic mention (i.e., why does he camouflage his act of mentioning?). I argued that Sperber and Wilson thus could not account for the element of pretense in irony.[159] But what this is saying is that Sperber and Wilson's notion of echoic mention cannot account for the uniquely ironic consciousness that informs the various textual instances of irony.[160]

I realized this point in observing the style of some born-again evangelicals who were preaching on Sproul Plaza at the University of California, Berkeley campus. They employed a distinctively self-mocking posture, exaggerating the stereotypical evangelical gestures, feigning the traditional fire-and-brimstone sermon. They even invited ridicule from the audience as they played it straight. The point of the seemingly self-disparaging technique, I decided, was that they were not just puppets of God; their self-mockery was meant to convey their underlying self-awareness. They may have been mouthing old formulas, but they were not simply rehearsing the Word. According to the analysis of "echoic mention," they were employing irony, being ironical, echoing formulas (even though they may actually subscribe to them). But I realized that there was a vast difference between what they were doing and what, say, Jonathan Swift was doing. Swift's pretenses reflected a moral or affirmative outlook that accommodated, even while it withstood, his countervailing misanthropic sentiments. The pretense of the evangelicals, I suspected, was little more than rhetorical; it seemed to be merely a technique to forward the cause, an instrument to further the mission. As proponents of a dogma that precludes radical doubt, they were at best, I am inclined to say, "feigning irony." And the difference between "feigned irony" and "genuine irony" is not a formal difference but is attitudinal.[161] Irony is not simply a technique, not just echo, not mere mouthing, not just tongue-in-cheek: In real irony, when one mouths, one must mean it; when one pretends, one must be serious about not taking oneself too seriously.[162] "Irony is no joking matter," said Friedrich Schlegel. Irony is no joking matter because behind the sphinxlike smile is a keen understanding of the depths humanly possible in disbelief and skepticism.

Prolegomenon to Politics

Why is this crazy, complex form of speech, or way of thinking about speech and language, relevant for politics? Isn't irony too cryptic and covert to be of any significance for politics, which for the most part is public and open and not cryptic and covert? Wasn't Aristotle referring to "ordinary language" when he made a connection between language and politics? We might begin to respond to these questions by noting that ordinary language can also corrupt, enforce barriers, propagate falsehoods; that, in other words, it may encourage disengagement from politics as much as it may serve politics. We cannot presume a natural connection between language and politics because we cannot take it for granted that human beings will naturally talk to one another or that, even if they do, speech will necessarily bind them. I should hasten to add, however, that these negative comments about ordinary language need not imply that ordinary language and ironic discourse are necessary rivals, are mutually exclusive, or even that much divides them.[163]

In preliminary and general terms, we could say that irony is important for politics insofar as it is a way of using language that exhibits and induces a high awareness of human contexts and human limitations, and that, despite these limiting conditions, nonetheless assumes positive expression. We might add that irony is a way of communicating across barriers, a way of extending dialogue where there has been no firm basis. It is a way of forming remote ties of interaction, of building communities of sorts, where natural "commonality" may be in question. In irony, persons seek out and recognize each other on the basis of little more than a shared pretense. Perhaps we can take this affirmation of the importance of textual interaction and expand it into a *general* affirmation of the importance of human dialogue and interaction. For the ironic outlook is in a sense blind: Oedipus, in the end, is our ironic guide.[164] And the blindness of irony may hold implications for politics, for an expansive political vision; for a blind affirmation means that one need not see one's opponent *physically* in order to acknowledge his human existence, to "see" him morally and *politically*.

Simpson contends that irony provides a model for reciprocating and participatory communication, as opposed to "authoritarian discourse." As such, irony might be a way of generating participation and commitment out of ambivalence and detachment--not a search for transcendence but a return to the text and to one's other.[165] Charles Glicksburg categorizes irony as a philosophical expression of "subjective idealism,"[166] by which he means a view of free individuality that provides the intellectual detachment necessary for action.[167] I question that formulation, for irony may begin with the individual, but it consists fundamentally in an orientation toward others, in an "intersubjectivity." And I question the use of the term "idealism," for the ironic orientation, despite its detached demeanor, contains in the author an inner imperative to manifest itself in "objective" and very "real" forms of textual expression.[168] But irony does seem to have much in common with politics itself: a combination of distance and engagement that leans finally in favor of the latter; an extension of human dialogue as the precondition for interaction. Irony is very close to politics if we define politics in broadest terms as a process through which interpersonal contexts are defined and created.

That language is public and thus holds important implications for politics is a commonplace among political theorists, especially those who read and recite Aristotle. But what is often overlooked is that language is also the bridge between the public and the private, the impersonal and the personal; indeed, it is the very medium through which such distinctions are concocted, broached, and affirmed. Language, then, is mostly public but it is not simply public, for it possesses, because it presupposes, a silent, nonpublic dimension, a moment of repose before any words are even uttered. We must ask why persons break silence, before we can understand "ordinary language," and well before we can understand full-fledged political activity. Thomas Mann called the problem of irony "without exception the profoundest and most fascinating in the world," because it held the answer to why "spirit" would allow itself to succumb to "nature": "In this peculiarly absolute judgment of values resides the ironic god, resides Eros."[169] Irony, for Mann, was a mood of erotic (i.e., life-affirming) "self-surrender," of interaction, of compromise, of talking rather than not. Like Mann, I believe politics requires earnest commitment and thus may be at odds with irony's ambivalence; but this commitment may also rest upon a pretense of sorts, about which the serious politician may be able to learn a great deal from the enigmatic ironist.

Ironic Political Communities

In the foregoing, I have attempted, if discursively, to present a general theory of irony as reversal and return. To summarize that theory: Upon inspection, all modes of irony reveal a logic of reversal at work. This reversal may be strictly rhetorical, or it may be attributed to protracted dramas and events at large. The character of the reversal, whether isolated or extended, rhetorical or conceptual, partial or complete, and the site of the reversal, whether stylistic or cosmic, observed or received, and so forth, account for the major "variables" in the compositions of the many ironies analysts have tracked and catalogued. But I have also insisted that irony, unlike many forms of satire as well as outright lying, cannot be understood entirely as a reversal or substitution mechanism. The "literal" layer of significance is never completely subverted, for it is retained at least to provide a sense of the stakes or expectations involved in the act of subversion. To the extent that an exoteric or literal layer is retained (and irony in general suggests a spectrum of possibilities here), the effect of "double-voicing" is created, for now covert and literal layers play off one another.[170] The resultant ambiguity of ironic double-voicing prompts the reader to look outside the text for resolution, which eventually draws the reader's attention to questions of authorial presence and context. Upon analysis, the textual double-voicing betrays a doubleness of authorial sensibility, a detachment from, as well as commitment to, the text. Thus I have proposed, as have other commentators, that irony traces to an attitude behind and toward the text, that it is a stance finally of thought, not words.[171] This attitude is one of detachment, but not *simply* detachment. The ironist's commitment to write, in spite of his skeptical presumptions, I have likened to the Platonic theme of "return." As with Plato's philosopher, what is finally significant about the ironic stance toward texts is indeed the act of returning to them, not the initial withholding and distancing. And this freely affirmative pose, apparently little more than a pretense that it all matters, would seem to hold important implications for politics.

Irony is usually not associated with politics. If anything, irony is associated with a nonpolitical or even an antipolitical stance.[172] The ironist, it is contended, is a fence-sitter; he is committedly uncommitted about important issues and stakes his integrity precisely upon his ability to deflate false moral presumptions and grandiose political claims (Flaubert is frequently cited in this regard). If the ironist does venture to make a political statement, it can be only an indirect and negative one.[173] Hence some commentators recommend irony as a tool against all political ideology.[174] At most what one can say (they say) is that irony preserves a negative freedom for the lone individual, he who exalts aesthetics but remains irresolute otherwise.[175]

With respect to this tricky matter of the relation between irony and politics, however, I want to reiterate a point made above. Irony is not simply a mechanism for reversal, but rather *an ironic reversal is one that recognizes it own parasitism upon that which is being reversed.* The precise political implications of this definition can brought to the fore by exploring two other schools of thought, the Straussians and the Derrideans, both of which employ "nonparasitic" versions of ironic reversal but which nevertheless try to develop constructive political communities out of irony, as I do.   I shall try to clarify my notion of an ironic political community by comparing it with the respective political visions of the Straussians and the Derrideans.

As explained in the previous chapter, central to the Straussian project is a notion of irony as a straight reversal and substitution mechanism, a way of privileging the "esoteric" subtext over the "exoteric" text. The Straussians derive this understanding of irony from their readings of Plato and Socrates, both of whom, they contend, were dissembling their superior natures and superior intellectual virtues when they were feigning ignorance or proposing utopias. Hence the Straussians find political import in irony's tendency to draw together a secret society of superior readers, an elite who can see through Plato's designs and are able to conclude that what Plato actually intends is for philosophers to reject his republic.   But the Straussian notion of political community presupposes (1) a view of irony as *complete* subversion and (2) a natural hierarchy of virtues among humans, which cannot be bridged by any means.

By contrast, though irony, even my notion of irony, may be open to charges of elitism and invidiousness, nothing I have said necessarily requires a natural disparity of talents or insights among humans at large. Irony's parasitic character does not mean that an ironic tie can be forged only at the expense of some rival group of persons.   If ironic political community has a basis in "nature" behind all its poses and pretenses, its foundational premise begins with the fact that all humans are subject to a shared victimization by death, and politics, therefore, is vulnerable to a similar victimization. That insight need not be exclusive, can be shared, and in fact would seem to invite collectivist or democratic conclusions.

Another school of brokers in irony, which I will call loosely the Derrideans, view irony as anything but successful substitution and re-privileging. Instead, this school emphasizes irony's double-edged quality, to such an extent that the doubleness allegedly collapses upon itself, resulting in complete indeterminacy and the forfeiture of any notion of resolution or closure. Irony thus understood is touted as the appropriate trope for the entire postmodern condition,[176] the period of living in the aftermath of the deaths of God, Hegel, and Nietzsche: For all now (it is coyly contended) is perspective, randomness, phenomena, difference, contingency, pretense, and veils. Though Paul de Man happened to view irony as infinitely *corrosive*, certain followers of Barthes, Bakhtin, and especially Derrida celebrate the *affirmative* side to postmodern ironization, despite all the subversion. A postmodernist now accepts playfully and joyfully the breakdown of determinate meanings, the loss of certainty, the deconstruction of critical dichotomies and differences; he/she can then learn to live nontragically with polyvalence, multiplicity, perspectivism, discordance, language, otherness, and so forth.[177] If the postmodernist ventures into the political realm, he/she usually advocates, if obliquely, a revitalized pluralism of respect and accommodation. We are to reject false unities and universals, but in the meanwhile, the postmodernist advises us, we are to recognize the universal multiplicity of being.

If pressed, however, the postmodernists, in a spirit of rejecting all aporias as nostalgic, will not give us *reasons* why we *should* accept our fragmentary language or our divided world as they have described it. And then I might ask them: Why should I respect the life of the Other, simply or seemingly because an analysis of language yields the conclusion that all subjectivities are merely enforced linguistic illusions or that the "self" is already penetrated by Otherness?[178] That is to say, the postmodern pluralists seem to subscribe to a new foundationalism, a new naturalism and functionalism, now based on the workings of language--though they do not admit this foundationalism as such. They are quick to pronounce themselves graduated from foundations and metanarratives, beyond good and evil, past the need for justifications and reasons, ready to play and eager to deconstruct. They claim to have liberated themselves from all parasitism upon old, shopworn dualisms: appearance versus reality, surface versus depth, difference versus unity, signifier versus signified, and so forth.[179] But actually they sneak an ethics into language analysis while they deny precisely that that is what they are doing--which is not merely disingenuous, nor can it be credited with a deliciously self-conscious irony. Postmodernism, as applied to politics, only begs or defers or "problematizes" important questions of human relations, and thus it offers and can offer, truly, no resolutions and no politically viable schemata.

A notion of irony as aware of its own parasitism upon old forms and yet proceeding in spite of them represents not some throwback to a bygone humanism, a view that behind every text is a human being, from whose intentions all textual meanings follow; a view that only humans can and probably will repair a disordered world; a view that recognizes tragedy but heroically redeems the idea of redemption.[180] No, the turn away from textual formulations of irony, as neither inherently subversive nor inherently indeterminate, may suggest a return to emphasizing authors and readers, but it does not represent a return to an erstwhile humanist project. Rather, the ironist's initial shift away from the text represents a concession that one cannot provide discursive justifications for postmodern political practices; and the return to the text suggests that though no "arguments" are possible, one must proceed nonetheless, if only by indirection. Yes, the ironist seems to hold out the promise that reconcilation and resolution are ultimately possible; thus he lures his reader on. But finally the ironist reveals that his affirmation of the text and of Other is not, and cannot, be based on natural categories. There is no good reason for seeking out the Other, let alone affirming his or her existence. And one cannot simply ignore or collapse the differences among humans to which we/they so often subscribe. Only a pretense, a choice, a whim, a leap--that it all matters, especially in the face of death--is the ironist's way of bridging these supposed differences.

For the political ironist, then, the world is still tragic in this post-God period, even if irony makes it a little more livable. But the world matters only if we accept that proposition provisionally, as a partial fiction, the partiality of which depends upon our still distinguishing between fiction and nonfiction (even if we contest that distinction along the way). We ironists cannot simply jump to the facile conclusion that "all is now fiction, hence anything is possible." To be an ironic mock-hero does not mean that one mocks completely the old notion of epic heroism, nor that one adopts altogether a new antiheroic pose.

Goethe, that old bird, once claimed that Kant's transcendental deduction was actually, unbeknownst to Kant himself, an exercise in ironic projection. Goethe's own *Faust* must be understood in a similar vein. Goethe in the end "saves" Faust, but this denouement was not a desperate act of rearguard romanticism (as Nietzsche thought it was). The Dantesque machinery at the end of the play suggests at most a mock-redemption, and the mock character of this ending should prevent us from seeing in it any sort of literal return to Dante or to Christianity in general (though a redemption in some loose sense it is). Still, Goethe seemed to believe that even mock-redemptions in the modern world would need to be parasitic upon the old forms of heroism; and whatever affirmations and lesser redemptions such ironics contain, they will also need to be parasitic upon old and enduring notions of tragedy.

*   *   *

The crucial question in this attempt to implicate politics with irony is whether persons will take action upon their ironic sensibilities--or rather, whether they will extend their "textual" activity and subliminal interaction into the world at large. Simpson ends his book proposing that the ironic consciousness is the appropriate mode for "the making of meaning through history."[181] Mellor ends hers declaring that (Romantic) irony "can potentially free individuals and even entire cultures from totalitarian modes of thought and behavior."[182] I am intrigued by these suggestions but must caution that since irony is so risky, so unstable, so covert, its "successes" cannot be considered inevitable, nor can they always be clearly identified. Irony cannot be considered a "sure thing" for politics. It is a difficult pose to strike and one even more difficult to maintain, this "pretense without pretensions" (a formulation that suggests the proximity of Schlegel's transcendental buffoonery to Kant's transcendental aesthetic, the ethos of a "purposiveness without purpose"). Still, the possibilities are enticing. In the next chapter, I will examine the relation between irony and political action, approaching the issue by indirection with the question: Why did irony fail to make a full transition from art to politics in the nineteenth century?

Notes

1. "We cannot use language maturely until we are spontaneously at home in irony." Kenneth Burke; quoted in Wayne C. Booth, *A Rhetoric of Irony* (Chicago: University of Chicago Press, 1974), p. xvi.

2. I borrow this image from J.A.K. Thomson's *Irony: An Historical Introduction* (London: George Allen and Unwin, 1926), p. 235. Friedrich Schlegel alerted his reader to the difficulties involved in trying to explain irony to the uninitiated: "To a person who hasn't got [irony], it will remain a riddle even after it is openly confessed." *Critical Fragments* #108. And Kierkegaard issued a similar caveat: "The ironic figure of speech also contains an attribute characteristic of all forms of irony, namely, a certain exclusiveness deriving

from the fact that although it is understood, it is not directly understood." *The Concept of Irony*, trans. Lee M. Capel (Bloomington: Indiana University Press, 1965), p. 265.

3. Alford laments that analyses of other analyses of irony so often resemble the *via negativa* of medieval theology. Steven A. Alford, *Irony and the Logic of the Romantic Imagination* (New York and Berne: Peter Lang, 1984), p. 9.

4. Kierkegaard's words are pertinent here: "While these considerations sufficiently orient us with reference to the history of this concept, this is not to say that a conception of this concept, insofar as it seeks confirmation and support in the foregoing, does not involve difficulties. To the extent that one seeks a complete and coherent discussion of the concept, one will soon convince himself that it has a problematic history, or to be more precise, no history at all." Kierkegaard,*The Concept of Irony*, pp. 260-261.

5. See my bibliography; for additional sources, including foreign language sources, see the bibliographies in Vladimir R. Rossman, *Perspectives of Irony in Medieval French Literature* (The Hague: Mouton, 1975); Uwe Japp, *Theorie der Ironie* (Frankfurt am Main: Vittorio Klostermann, 1983); Norman Knox, *The Word Irony and Its Context, 1500-1755* (Durham, N.C.: Duke University Press, 1961); D.C. Muecke, *The Compass of Irony* (London: Methuen and Company, 1969); Hans-Egon Hass, *Ironie als Literarische Phänomen* (Cologne, 1973); Booth, *A Rhetoric of Irony*; S.J.E. Dikkers, *Ironie als Vorm van Communicatie* (The Hague: Kruseman, n.d.); Helmut Prang, *Die Romantische Ironie* (Darmstadt: Wissenschaftliche Buchgesellschaft, 1972); John Vignauz Smyth, *A Question of Eros: Irony in Sterne, Kierkegaard, and Barthes* (Tallahassee: Florida State University Press, 1984); and Ingrid Strohschneider-Kohrs, *Die romantische Ironie in Theorie und Gestaltung* (Tübingen: Max Niemeyer Verlag, 1977).

6. See G.G. Sedgewick, *Of Irony: Especially in Drama* (Toronto: University of Toronto Press, 1948), p. 5; phrase adopted from *De oratore* 2. 269, and *Academica* 2. 15.

7. Knox mentions also: metonymy, synecdoche, asteismus, micterismus, charientismus, preterition, banter, raillery, burlesque, paronomiasia. One might add old-fashioned lying to this list (of expressions in which speech and meaning are in some way at odds). See Knox, *The Word Irony*, pp. 34-37.

8. See Muecke, "Basic Classifications," *The Compass of Irony*, pp. 40-63.

9. Andrew H. Wright, "Irony and Fiction," *A Journal of Aesthetics and Art Criticism* 12 (September, 1953), p. 111.

10. Muecke, *The Compass of Irony*, passim.

11. *Idem, Irony and the Ironic* (London: Methuen and Company, 1982), p. 13.

12. *Ibid.*, p. 7.

13. Pierre Richelet, *Dictionnaire de la langue française ancienne et moderne: Nouvelle édition augmentée d'un très-grand nombre d'articles* (Lyons: Frères Duplain, 1759), 2, p. 473. Translated by Rossman in *Perspectives of Irony*, p. 10. A.E. Dyson makes a similar statement against generalizing

about irony in *The Crazy Fabric: Essays in Irony* (London: Macmillan and Co., 1959), pp. 220-221. Richard Howey nicely puts these frustrations into perspective, with his opening comment: "Someone--a Socrates perhaps--might find it ironic that irony is not a definable term." "Some Reflections on Irony in Nietzsche." *Nietzsche-Studien* 4 (1975), p. 36.

14. See Sedgewick, *Of Irony*, p. 4; from Otto Ribbeck, "Über den Begriff des *Eiron*," *Rheinisches Museum* 31 (1876), pp. 381ff.

15. Erich Heller, *The Ironic German: A Study of Thomas Mann* (Boston: Little, Brown and Company, 1958), p. 235. In fairness to Kierkegaard, it should be noted that Kierkegaard made a similar complaint about treatments of irony: "In the period after Fichte where [irony] was particularly important, one finds it mentioned again and again, suggested again and again, presupposed again and again. But if one searches for a lucid discussion one searches in vain. Solgar complains that A.W. Schlegel in his *Vorlesungen über dramatische Kunst und Literatur*, where one would certainly expect to find an adequate exposition of it, mentions it only briefly in a single passage. Hegel complains that the same is true of Solger, and finds it no better with Tieck. And now since all complain, why should not I also complain?" Kierkegaard, *The Concept of Irony*, p. 261.

16. For instance, Dikkers in *Ironie als Vorm van Communicatie* (English summary, pp. 147-152) reviews and criticizes four methods of defining irony: analytic, synthetic (intentional, typological, functional, etymological), linguistic, and by examples. See also Norman Knox, "On the Classification of Ironies," *Modern Philology* (August, 1972), pp. 53-62. One wants to agree with D.J. Enright's view of the whole genre of commentary about irony: "The critic's stance is all wrong; the more earnest he is, the more likely to slip on a succession of banana skins." *The Alluring Problem: An Essay on Irony* (Oxford and New York: Oxford University Press, 1986), p. 3.

17. See Ernst Behler, *Klassische Ironie, Romantische Ironie, Tragische Ironie* (Darmstadt: Wissenschaftliche Buchgesellschaft, 1972); William A. Becker, "Concepts of Irony with Special Reference to Applications in the Visual Arts" (Dissertation, Columbia University, 1970), part I; Mary A. Grant, "The Ancient Rhetorical Theories of the Laughable," University of Wisconsin Studies in Language and Literature 21 (Madison, 1924); Norman Knox, "Irony," *Dictionary of the History of Ideas* Vol. 11 (New York: Charles Scribner's Sons, 1973), pp. 626-634; *idem, The Word Irony*; Muecke, *Irony and the Ironic*, chap. 2; Sedgewick, *Of Irony*; Thomson, *Irony: An Historical Introduction*; Rossman, *Perspectives of Irony in Medieval French Literature*; Eugene Zumwalt, "Divine and Diabolic Irony: The Growth of a Tudor Dramatic Sense" (Dissertation, University of California, Berkeley, 1956), esp. Appendix 1; Lilian R. Furst, *Fictions of Romantic Irony* (Cambridge: Harvard University Press, 1984), pp. 1-48.

18. See Knox, *Irony and Its Context*, p. 5.

19. *Ibid.*, p. 6.

20. *Ibid.*, p. 15.

21. Charles Glicksberg in *The Ironic Vision in Modern Literature* (The Hague: Martinus Nijhoff, 1969) quotes Alexander Blok: "All the most lively and sensitive children of our century are stricken by a disease unknown to doctors and pyschiatrists. It is related to the disorders of the soul and might be called 'irony.' Its symptoms are fits of an exhausting laughter which starts with a diabolical mockery and a provocative smile and ends as rebellion and sacrilege." Glicksberg adds: "Life is a meaningless dance, a whirlwind of mechanical energy, a game that follows no comprehensible rules and that can never be won, a joke, a thing of sound and fury signifying nothing. All distinctions are confounded: good and evil, comedy and tragedy, heaven and hell, spirit and flesh, mind and body" (p. 3). Similarly, Northrop Frye linked irony with a sense of the apocalyptic, and Kenneth Burke made irony synonymous with fatality, the inevitability of defeat and reversal. See Frye, *Anatomy of Criticism* (Princeton: Princeton University Press, 1957), p. 224; Kenneth Burke, *A Grammar of Motives* (New York: George Braziller, 1955), pp. 511-517, and *The Philosophy of Literary Form* (Berkeley: University of California Press, 1973), pp. 418-421. Samuel Hynes contends that twentieth-century irony is "a view of life which recognized that experience is open to multiple interpretations, of which no *one* is simply right, and that the co-existence of incongruities is part of the structure of existence." *The Pattern of Hardy's Poetry* (Chapel Hill: University of North Carolina Press, 1961), pp. 41-42; quoted in Muecke, *Irony and the Ironic*, p. 31.

22. Alan Reynolds Thompson, *The Dry Mock* (Berkeley: University of California Press, 1948), see pp. 247-258.

23. Andrew H. Wright, "Irony and Fiction," *A Journal of Aesthetics and Art Criticism* 12 (September, 1953), p. 111.

24. Sedgewick, *Of Irony*, p. 18.

25. *Ibid.*, p. 26.

26. Muecke, *Irony and the Ironic*, pp. 22-23.

27. In his early studies of the Greeks, Friedrich Schlegel used the terms *objectiv* and *interessant* to distinguish between ancient art and modern art. Schlegel admired the Greek artists for refraining from admitting any trace of their own personalities in their works, whereas he looked with disdain upon modern artists, whose works, Schlegel contended, contain so much of the author's personality that the reader cannot distinguish between creator and creation. Shakespeare, however, was one modern who was *objectiv* and *interessant* at the same time, according to Schlegel. David Worcester *The Art of Satire* (Cambridge: Harvard University Press, 1940), pp. 122-126; and Oskar Walzel, *German Romanticism*, trans. Alma Lussky (New York: G.P. Putnam's, 1932), pp. 34-41.

28. Muecke, *Irony* (London: Methuen, 1970), pp. 20-21; also see Worcester *The Art of Satire*, pp. 122-126; René Wellek, "The Romantic Age," *A History of Modern Criticism: 1750-1950* Vol. 2 (New Haven: Yale University Press, 1955), pp. 5-73; Anne K. Mellor, *English Romantic Irony* (Cambridge: Harvard University Press, 1980), pp. 3-30; and *idem*, "On Romantic Irony, Symbolism

and Allegory," *Criticism* 21 (Summer, 1979), pp. 217-229; Beda Allemann, *Ironie und Dichtung* (Stuttgart: Neske Pfullingen, 1956); Walzel, *German Romanticism*; Ernst Behler, "Friedrich Schlegel und Hegel," *Hegel-Studien* 2 (Bonn: H. Bouvier und Co., 1963), pp. 203-250; Prang, *Die Romantische Ironie*, pp. 8-16; Alford, *Irony and the Logic of the Romantic Imagination*, pp. 16-104.

29. See Raymond Immerwahr, "The Subjectivity or Objectivity of Friedrich Schlegel's Poetic Irony," *Germanic Review* 26 (October, 1951), pp. 173-191.

30. For instance, Rossman writes: "In order to establish sufficiency, I have therefore tried opposition and incompatibility in as many forms and on as many people as I could. I am now convinced that opposition and incompatibility are both necessary and sufficient. Moreover, the advantage of these criteria is that irony thus defined does not depend on the reader's individual value judgments (for the text usually provides its own), but can be objectively analyzed by readers of any epoch, nationality, or cultural background." *Perspectives of Irony*, p. 32.

31. Stanley Cavell, *The Claim of Reason* (Oxford: Clarendon Press, 1979), p. 496.

32. Note John Searle's criticism of those who oppose "intentionality" to "verifiability": "Equally positivistic is the insistence that concepts that apply to language and literature, if they are to be truly valid, must admit of some mechanical procedure of verification. Thus, for example, if one attempts to characterize the role of intention in language, many literary critics immediately demand some mechanical criterion for ascertaining the presence and content of intentions. But, of course, there are no such criteria. How do we tell what a person's intentions are? The answer is, in all sorts of ways, and we may even get it wrong in the apparently most favorable cases. But such facts as these--that there is no mechanical decision procedure for identifying an author's intentions, or for determining whether or not a work is a work of fiction or whether an expression is used metaphorically--in no way undermines the concepts of intention, fiction, and metaphor." "The Word Turned Upside Down" (Review of *On Deconstruction*, by Jonathan Culler) *New York Review of Books* 30 (October 27, 1983), pp. 78-79.

33. Muecke warns: "It is not inconceivable that 'irony,' now a key concept in literary criticism, will follow into limbo the concept of 'sublimity,' so indispensible to earlier centuries." *Irony and the Ironic*, p. 13. Similarly, in *The Compass of Irony*, he writes: "We cannot go on meaningfully saying that *Don Juan* and *Psalm 23* are both ironical. 'Ironical' without distinguishing qualifications is now in danger of being as uninformative a term in literary criticism as 'realistic'" (p. 13). Eleanor N. Hutchens seems to concur: "Few terms in modern criticism are more useful than 'irony,' and few are in more danger of losing their usefulness through indiscriminate application." "The Identification of Irony," *ELH* 27 (Baltimore: Johns Hopkins Press, 1960), p. 352. Wayne Booth, A.R. Thompson, and Norman Knox all argue that the use of irony should be defined and limited (see Booth, *The Rhetoric of Irony*, p. ix, Thompson, *The Dry Mock*, p. 247, and Knox, "On the Classification of Ironies," p. 62.

34. Cleanth Brooks, "Irony as a Principle of Structure," *Literary Opinion in America*, ed. Morton Zabel (New York: Harper and Brothers, 1951), and *The Well Wrought Urn* (London: Dennis Dobson, 1949).

35. Booth, *The Rhetoric of Irony*.

36. See Paul de Man, "The Rhetoric of Temporality," in *Interpretation: Theory and Practice*, ed. Charles S. Singleton (Baltimore: Johns Hopkins University Press, 1969); Jonathan Culler, *Structuralist Poetics* (London:" Routledge & Kegan Paul, 1975), pp. 154-159; Cyrus Hamlin, "The Temporality of Selfhood: Metaphor and Romantic Poetry," *New Literary History* 6 (1974); Harold Bloom, ed., et al., *Deconstruction and Criticism* (New York: Seabury Press, 1979); for criticisms of the deconstructionist argument, see Mellor, "On Romantic Irony, Symbolism and Allegory," and *English Romantic Irony*, pp. 22-24; Muecke, *Irony and the Ironic*, pp. 31, 101; and Susan Suleiman, "Interpreting Ironies," *diacritics* (Summer, 1976), pp. 15-21.

37. John Searle makes the point that deconstruction actually betrays a rather crude understanding of reading, according to which there are supposedly "mechanical criteria" for ascertaining the presence of intentionality (which the critic then deconstructs). "The Word Turned Upside Down" (review of Jonathan Culler, *On Deconstruction*), *The New York Review of Books* XXX (October 27, 1983), pp. 78-79.

38. This charge may seem misplaced with respect to the postmodernists, that is at least with respect to their stated intentions; but I shall argue below that the postmodernists are attempting to find a new "commonality," though now a commonality that partakes heavily of differences, otherness, discordance, plurality, and diversity.

39. David Simpson, *Irony and Authority in Romantic Poetry* (London: Macmillan Press, 1979), p. 172.

40. *Ibid.*, p. 173.

41. *Ibid.*, p. 178.

42. *Ibid.*, p. 193.

43. As Simpson writes: "I must now try to gather the evidence for the utility of the term 'irony' as a description of those features of the Romantic discourse which I have emphasized in this account. . . . It would not be practical to try to acknowledge all previous discussions of the subject of irony; in fact, surprisingly few of them seem to treat the concept in the way it has been treated here, though of course almost all of them have something in common with, and something to say about, what has been described as the Romantic situation. I shall try to indicate the most important connections and relations as they seem significant; but it will be clear by now that I am less interested in the historical usages of a particular word than in the delineation of a concept, or a series of interrelated concepts, dominant in the Romantic period even if not unique to it." *Ibid.*, p. 188.

44. I.e., I will not attempt what Kierkegaard claimed for himself: "But as the concept of irony has so often acquired a different meaning, it is essential that one does not come to use it consciously or unconsciously in a wholly arbitrary fashion. To the extent that one subscribes to the ordinary use of

language, therefore, it is essential for one to see that the various meanings it has acquired in the course of time can all be accommodated here." *The Concept of Irony*, p. 262.

45. See Steven E. Alford's discussion of the irrelevance of subject-object dichotomies with respect to irony, in *Irony and the Logic of the Romantic Imagination*, pp. 30ff.

46. D.C. Muecke contends, for instance, that "Irony, like beauty, is in the eye of the beholder and is not a quality inherent in any remark, event, or situation." *The Compass of Irony*, p. 14.

47. The disparity between concept and instance is particularly acute in the case of irony, for the ironist uses language, knowing that a literal reading of his assertions will miss his ulterior designs. He is *deliberately* withholding--which is quite different from a simple awareness that language falls short of conveying one's full meanings.

48. Though I greatly respect Muecke's ear for examples, I question his taxonomical approach to irony, for his account attempts in vain to extract a theory of irony from historical applications of the word. Knox also wishes to produce a "general theory" based upon the analysis of examples, but this seems to follow a recipe approach to language, namely that concepts have certain set ingredients ("variables"), and that different applications of the same concept represent a different mix of the same ingredients, though with different measures of each. See Knox, "On the Classification of Ironies."

49. Søren Kierkegaard, *Concluding Unscientific Postscript*, trans. David F. Swenson and Walter Lowrie (Princeton: Princeton University Press, 1941), p. 449.

50. Friedrich Schlegel noted an "irony of irony" in the attempt to speak of irony without using it: even when we try to speak unironically of irony, "what we want this irony to mean in the first place is something that happens in more ways than one." "On Incomprehensibility," *Friedrich Schlegel's* Lucinde *and the Fragments*, trans. Peter Firchow (Minneapolis: University of Minnesota Press, 1971), p. 267. And Julias remarks to Lorenzo in the fragments for the proposed continuation of *Lucinde*: "The final irony, I think, is to be found rather in that it seems to be becoming impossible for you to talk about irony without being ironic." *Ibid.*, p. 133.

51. See Wayne C. Booth, *The Rhetoric of Fiction* (Chicago: University of Chicago Press, 1961).

52. See Stanley Fish, "Short People Got No Reason to Live: Reading Irony," *Daedalus* 112 (Winter, 1983), pp. 175-191; and Booth, "A New Strategy for Establishing a Truly Democratic Criticism," *Daedalus* 112 (Winter, 1983), pp. 193-214. Since I am not endorsing Booth's view of "stable irony," Fish's criticisms are beside the point for me. But neither am I placing as much emphasis upon the reader as Fish does. His contention that an interpretive strategy "produces the object of its attention" (p. 189) seems to me perilously close to a literary solipsism in which the readers are the authors as well. In other words, his distinction between irony as the "property of texts" and irony as a "reading strategy" seems to me overdrawn (a distinction that he should

dispute as much as he disputes the distinction between "stable" and "unstable" ironies--p. 191 n. 8).

53. For instance, Fish discusses the sociological assumptions that may affect and contribute to interpretive strategies; see "Short People Got No Reason to Live." Muecke also discusses the need for a sociological approach to irony (*Irony and the Ironic*, pp. 1-2). He mentions, for instance, William Empson's claim that no Japanese can understand irony, whereas the Chinese use it all the time ("The Voice of the Underdog," *New York Review of Books* 12 [June, 1975], p. 37). Richard Howey argues for a cultural approach to irony: "In attempting to unravel the dialectics of irony it is crucial that we keep constantly in mind that irony is a *cultural* phenomenon and its efficacy frequently depends upon a knowledge of the allusions that serve as its objects. Sometimes these allusions are types or institutions that have more or less universal significance, but the ironic thrust almost always depends upon quite specific cultural, and at times even personal, characteristics that invest a given allusion with concrete immediacy. An ironic statement which has become abstract has lost its cutting edge. This is not to say that irony must limit itself to dubious and contemporaneous allusions, thereby reducing itself to an aspect of popular culture; rather, the most important forms of irony already presuppose an awareness of cultural and institutional traditions." Howey, "Some Reflections on Irony in Nietzsche," p. 47. In discussing the origins of Irish irony, Conor Cruise O'Brien discounts the idea of an "Irish mind" in favor of an Irish "predicament" in the eighteen and nineteen centuries, which was congenial to the nature of irony. O'Brien, *Writers and Politics* (New York: Pantheon, 1955), pp. 104-5. William Becker uses a modestly psychoanalytic approach to irony: "Once we recognize, however, that irony is not just an exercise in stylistics but is a reflection of ulterior drives and can itself be functional beyond being a rather inefficient means of communication, we are prepared to see that one of the principal aims of even the simplest verbal irony is the detachment of the ironist from some specific reality." "Concepts of Irony," p. 39. He also mentions Theodor Reik's analysis of Anatole France's irony. Reik, following Freud's association of irony with humor, attempts to find the origins of France's irony in an experience of embitterment with something he once loved, i.e., the Church. See Reik, "Saint Irony," *The Secret Self: Psychoanalytical Experiences in Life and Literature* (New York: Farrar, Straus, and Young, 1952), pp. 161-183. Finally, Eugene Zumwalt's main thesis in *Divine and Diabolic Irony* is that "irony can be studied as a cultural manifestation and that the ironic achievements of authors and arts in given periods and places can be distinguished from each other" (p. 341). The irony of ancient Judaic scripture is not the same, contends Zumwalt, as that of medieval-Christian scriptural plays.

54. "A Modest Proposal (1729)," in *The Prose Works of Jonathan Swift, D.D.*, ed. Temple Scott, Vol. 7, (London: George Bell and Sons, 1905), pp. 205-216.

55. Søren Kierkegaard, *Either/Or*, trans. David and Lillian Swenson (Princeton: Princeton University Press, 1944), p. 3. (I borrow this example from Muecke, *Irony and the Ironic*, p. 60).

56. See Muecke, *Irony and the Ironic*, pp. 19-20. Muecke is responsible for describing irony as a "two-story" phenomenon, a figure that involves fundamentally two levels of signification, though one that is not simply a clash of contraries. Sedgewick, Booth, and Haakon M. Chevalier, *The Ironic Temper: Anatole France and his Time* (New York: Oxford University Press, 1932), have all made similar statements attesting to irony's oppositional nature. Knox defines the sense of opposition as a clash of appearance and reality, which he proposes can be plotted on a spectrum, ranging from "the slightest of differences to diametrical opposites." He contends that this variable--the "degree of conflict"--is one of four crucial variables (field of observation, agents and actors, and other aspects) in the composition of irony. See his "Irony" and "On the Classification of Ironies."

57. Booth, *A Rhetoric of Irony*, p. 53.

58. "The ironist hears the formulas of speech others cannot hear, and if they ring upon his ear as symbolic of a posture he does not like, he echoes them back at those who mouth them, but echoes them somehow inappropriately, off key, at the wrong place or time, with absurd exfoliations." John Traugott, "The Yahoo in the Doll's House: *Gulliver's Travels* the Children's Classic," *The Yearbook of English Studies* 14 (1984), p. 145.

59. Booth, *A Rhetoric of Irony*, pp. 46-86. See also Hutchens, "The Identification of Irony."

60. Susan Suleiman's review of Booth ("Interpreting Ironies") is pertinent here. She argues that Booth tries to combine three interpretive approaches in his attempt to identify irony on the basis of signals--a stylistic-semiotic approach, a phenomenological approach, and a traditional approach. She contends that he fails on his own terms. First he looks for stylistic clues in the language of the text; then he draws upon the *reader's* expectations in the reconstruction process; finally he seeks to uncover the *author's* meanings and intentions. The first two approaches are markedly separate from the third, for "the notion of authorial intention is at best superfluous to the stylistician and the phenomenologist" (p. 19). Booth himself does *not* confine himself to stylistic clues when he *in fact* interprets the ironies of particular texts. Instead, he draws upon "outside" information, which he claims draws upon the "common experience" of an informed English reader.

61. Beda Allemann, "Ironie als literarisches Prinzip," *Ironie und Dichtung* (Stuttgart: Neske Pfullingen, 1969), p. 20; quoted in Simpson, *Irony and Authority*, pp. 22-23. Wilson O. Clough, in a review of *L'Ironie* by Vladimir Jankélévitch, underscores this point by noting that irony prefers to suggest, and may even employ silence, like Socrates' silence before his accusers. "Irony: A French Approach," *Sewanee Review* 47 (April-June, 1939), pp. 180-181. Guido Almansi seems to overstate this aspect of irony when he declares that the truly ironic is the ambiguously ironic. *L'Ironie de l'ironie* (Urbino: Centro Internazionale di Semiotica e di Linguistica, 1979).

62. For the full entry from the OED *and* an analysis of same, see Hutchens, "The Identification of Irony," p. 352. For the stock dictionary

definitions through the ages, see Knox, *The Word Irony*, pp. 38-98; and Zumwalt, "Divine and Diabolic Irony," pp. 348-370.

63. Paul Grice attempts to provide a semantic analysis of irony that does not make reference to "figurative meaning" as the opposite of literal meaning. See "Presupposition and Conversational Implicature," *Radical Pragmatics*, ed. Peter Cole (New York: Academic Press, 1981), pp. 183-198.

64. See *ibid.*, pp. 187-191.

65. Both Grice and his opponents, Dan Sperber and Deirdre Wilson, assume that irony consists of *propositions*, in one case "implicated," the other, "mentioned." See Dan Sperber and Deirdre Wilson, "Irony and the Use-Mention Distinction," *Radical Pragmatics*, ed. Peter Cole (New York: Academic Press, 1981: 295-318), p. 311.

66. Wright, "Irony and Fiction," p. 118.

67. See Suleiman's discussion of this. She contends that one does not have to *believe* that eating children is inhuman in order to grasp the irony of "A Modest Proposal," whereas Wayne Booth thinks that irony hinges upon common values. According to Suleiman, the "only way to make belief a necessary factor in determining understanding would be to define belief as an epistemological phenomenon, akin to what Foucault calls *episteme*. She concedes, however, that the distinction between belief and understanding may be artificial but that the criticisms of Booth still apply. "Interpreting Ironies," p. 20.

68. Frye recognizes this point: "The argument of Swift's *Modest Proposal* has a brain-softening plausibility about it: one is almost led to feel that the narrator is not only reasonable but even humane; yet the "almost" can never drop out of any sane man's reaction, and as long as it remains there the modest proposal will be both fantastic and immoral." *Anatomy of Criticism*, p. 224. Muecke concurs: "Interpreting Swift's 'A Modest Proposal' is not a process that entails discarding the literal meaning; it is still there in all its plausibility." *Irony and the Ironic*, p. 45. And Muecke argues that the difference between appearances and reality is not so clear in this case, for "Swift is advising the Irish to do in reality what so far they have done only metaphorically and in part. . . . Swift is pointing out that there is *not* all the difference in the world between killing and allowing to die (and from the sufferer's point of view particularly) and he implies as well that those in power, who are so deficient in conscience as to allow people to die, are scarcely in a position to object to their being killed, especially since they can be killed at a profit, profit being a motive for such people where pity is none." *The Compass of Irony*, p. 84.

69. Sperber and Wilson, "Irony and the Use-Mention Distinction."

70. Sperber and Wilson emphasize that the difference between "use" and "mention" is a "logical" one, and that in "natural language" it is often difficult to differentiate between the two. Nonetheless, here is a way to illustrate this distinction: In the statement, "These examples are rare and marginal," the word "marginal" is being used, whereas in, " 'Marginal' is a technical term" and "Who had the nerve to call my examples marginal?" the word *marginal* is being mentioned. This becomes more obscure in cases of indirect speech, for

often the "mention" proposition is not being *reported* but is only *implicitly* mentioned (e.g., "Oh, you've got a toothache" in response to "I've got a toothache"). Often the reference proposition is from the distant past or is in anticipation of future propositions. Sperber and Wilson label these cases of implicit mention as "echoic mention."

71. Thus Sperber and Wilson fail to do precisely what they accuse Grice of failing to do: "Grice's account, like the traditional one, fails to explain why an ironical utterance should ever be preferred to its literal counterpart" (p. 297). Sperber and Wilson fail to explain why a speaker would shift from use to echoic mention, because they fail to account for the removal of quotation marks. But this is to say that the entire distinction between use and mention in irony is dubious, that unless an explanation for the removal of quotation marks is given, the distinction is useless. Sperber and Wilson's problem is that they accept Grice's Russellian premise that ironic propositions have literal "counterparts," that irony yields definitive "statements." The same critique would apply to *Spy Magazine's* wonderfully hip analysis of *irony* as an act of "air quoting." Paul Rudnick and Kurt Andersen, "The Irony Epidemic," *Spy Magazine* (March, 1989), pp. 93-101.

72. If I may be allowed to "operationalize": I believe this point, that the "literal layer" is not completely discarded in irony, was expressed in a different, more formal way by various members of the New Critics school. For instance, I.A. Richards defined irony in *Principles of Literary Criticism* (New York: Harcourt, Brace and Company, 1952) as the "bringing in of the opposite, the complementary impulses" (p. 250). Irony was not simply a reflection of the author's mind but was an inherent quality "in" a work, a balanced "poise" or "sense of equilibrium" between competing views (Muecke traces this idea to A.W. Schlegel, who noted how Shakespeare anticipated the audience's "tacit objections" to idealizations; *Irony and the Ironic*, p. 26). Robert Penn Warren later substituted "tensions" for Richards' notion of "oppositions," thus allowing a further extension of irony to various formal aspects of all writing. Cleanth Brooks carried this extension even further, with the claim that all poetry exhibits a kind of irony, simply by virtue of the formal arrangement of one part of a poem to another. Finally, we can see this desire to reconcile oppositions in Kenneth Burke's notion of irony. Metaphor, metonymy, and synecdoche differ from irony, according to Burke, because their "motives" remain on the level of comparing term for term. Irony, however, is a trope in which the terms "interact" to produce a "development," which creates "subperspectives." None of the participating subperspectives can be treated as the main perspective; rather the "ironic perspective" views the subperspectives as contributory to an overall view according to which no single perspective stands out. Burke ends, however, by asserting that irony contains an "over-all formula" which he reveals as "what goes forth as A returns as non-A." Burke, *A Grammar of Motives*, pp. 511-517. Bert O. States summarizes Burke's argument as a claim that irony is not a "presence" in a work (as the New Critics proposed) but is a "perspective" upon the work that can however be inferred from the "work itself." See States,

Irony and Drama: A Poetics (Ithaca and London: Cornell University Press, 1971), pp. 9-16.

73. Simpson, *Irony and Authority*, p. xii.

74. Stanley Hopper quotes Schopenhauer's phrase, "Irony is the pathos of the middle." Hopper, "Irony--The Pathos of the Middle," *Cross Currents* 12 (Winter, 1962), p. 31.

75. Angus Fletcher, *Allegory: The Theory of a Symbolic Mode* (Ithaca: Cornell University Press, 1964), p. 232. Similarly, René Wellek, writing in reference to F. Schlegel, contends that irony is the "recognition of the fact that the world in its essence is paradoxical and that an ambivalent attitude alone can grasp its contradictory totality." *A History of Modern Criticism* Vol. 2, p. 14.

76. Chevalier, *The Ironic Temper*, p. 42.

77. *Ibid.*, p. 79; quoted in Wright, "Irony and Fiction," p. 113.

78. de Man, "The Rhetoric of Temporality," p. 198.

79. Simpson, *Irony and Authority*, pp. 97-98.

80. See Paul Plass's discussion of the relation between irony and authorial self-assertion. "Philosophic Anonymity and Irony in the Platonic Dialogues," *American Journal of Philology* 35 (1964), esp. pp. 261-263.

81. This distinction recalls Kierkegaard's distinction between "executive" and "contemplative" irony. See *The Concept of Irony*, pp. 271-275.

82. Paul de Man cites Peter Szondi's commentary on the ironic consciousness in Friedrich Schlegel: "The subject of romantic irony is the isolated, alienated man who has become the object of his own reflection and whose consciousness has deprived him of his ability to act. He nostalgically aspires toward unity and infinity; the world appears to him divided and finite. What he calls irony is his attempt to bear up under his critical predicament, to change his situation by achieving distance toward it." de Man, "The Rhetoric of Temporality," p. 201.

83. To name names of some of the critics and near-critics: Irving Babbitt (*Rousseau and Romanticism*), Chevalier (*The Ironic Temper*), Benjamin DeMott ("The New Irony: Sickniks and Others"), Glicksberg (*The Ironic Vision in Modern Literature*), Norman Holland (*Dynamics of Literary Response*), May Sarton ("The Shield of Irony"), John D. Schaeffer ("Ironic Discourse and the Creation of Secularity"), Thompson (*The Dry Mock*), Leonard P. Wessell, Jr. (*Karl Marx, Romantic Irony, and the Proletariat*).

84. Certainly this corresponds with Chevalier's analysis of Anatole France. See Chevalier, *The Ironic Temper*.

85. See Muecke, *The Compass of Irony*, p. 198, and *Irony*, p. 20; Mellor, *English Romantic Irony*, p. 14; Connop Thirlwall also emphasized the poet's godlike, and yet limited, role: "The dramatic poet is the creator of a little world, in which he rules with absolute sway, and may shape the destinies of the imaginary beings to whom he gives life and breath according to any plan that he may choose. Since however they are men whose actions he represents, and since it is human sympathy that he claims, he will, if he understands his art, make his administration conform to the laws by which he conceives the course of mortal life to be really governed." Connop Thirlwall, "On the Irony of

Sophocles," *The Philological Museum* Vol. 2 (Cambridge: J. Smith, Printer, 1833), pp. 490-491.

86. Plass describes Plato's simultaneous reliance upon the written word and awareness of its inadequacy. See "Philosophic Anonymity and Irony in the Platonic Dialogues," p. 255. And Howey claims that an aspect of "philosophic irony" in the writings of Nietzsche is the awareness that "philosophy *must* use language and yet that language again and again brings us up against its own limit points." Howey, "Some Reflections on Irony in Nietzsche," p. 40.

87. In thinking about Schlegel's aphoristic writings as constituting theories, I have found the works of Alford, Furst, Handwerk, Mellor, Muecke, Wellek, Worcester, Eichner, Behler, and Immerwahl to be quite helpful.

88. Schlegel, "Critical Fragments," ed. Firchow, p. 148. See Muecke, *The Compass of Irony*, p. 198.

89. See especially Mellor's description of this phenomenon. *English Romantic Irony*, pp. 1-30. Knox, on the other hand, emphasizes that irony does not always represent a constructive, affirmative stance, as Mellor seems to argue. He takes Glicksberg to task on similar grounds: "This philosophical stance is consonant with quite a wide range of tones, but one tone we should not expect to find is that of final defeat, which requires the broad philosophical stance that says either, "Not Yes, No!" or, "Yes and Yes equal No because they cancel each other out." Such a stance is not essentially paradoxical, for it settles on a final, negative truth. The paradox Glicksberg makes so much of, that nihilistic artists go on living and creating works of art, is paradoxical indeed, but it is clearly subordinate to or submerged by the dominant note of defeat. Surely there is enough difference between saying "Yes and No" and saying primarily "No," that we need separate classes here." Knox, "On the Classification of Ironies," p. 60.

90. Of course one could argue that *any* monumental art is ironic. For instance, under pressure from various veterans' groups, the National Park Service agreed to place an additional monument to the Vietnam War in the general location of the first monument. The second monument is more "graphic," a portrayal of three soldiers looking off into the distance. Clearly the second monument follows aspects of my description of ironic representation, but by the same measure it certainly is less "ironic" than the first. Thus we must recognize "degrees" of irony. Furthermore, in my description of the monument, I have deliberately left from my account any mention of the presense of words--namely the names of the dead--inscribed on the monument. A fuller account of the irony of the monument would need to incorporate a discussion of these words as part of the monumentality of the monument. Finally, in light of the above discussion we might place as a contrast to Schlegel's view of art that which was expressed in the Hebraic stricture against pictures and likenesses of Yahwe; the ancient Hebrews--at least in matters of art--seem to have lacked the sense of pretense required for ironic representation.

91. A.W. Schlegel described irony as a "surreptitious exchange."

92. Arthur Sidgwick, "On Some Forms of Irony in Literature," *Cornhill Magazine*, 3d ser., 22 (1907); quoted in Sedgewick, *Of Irony*, p. 9.

93. Sedgewick, *Of Irony*, p. 9.

94. Schlegel himself extended irony to written language. See Mellor's discussion, *English Romantic Irony*, pp. 10-11; and Muecke, *The Compass of Irony*, pp. 196-7.

95. A.W. Schlegel called irony "a sort of confession interwoven into the representation itself." *Lectures on Dramatic Art and Literature*, trans. John Black (New York: AMS Press, 1965), p. 369.

96. "The *dédoublement* [of irony] thus designates the activity of a consciousness by which a man differentiates himself from the non-human world. The capacity for such duplication is rare, says Baudelaire, but belongs specifically to those who, like artists or philosophers, deal in language. His emphasis on a professional vocabulary, on "*se faire un métier*," stresses the technicality of their action, the fact that language is their material, just as leather is the material of the cobbler or wood is that of the carpenter. In everyday, common existence, this is not how language usually operates; there it functions much more as does the cobbler's or the carpenter's hammer, not as the material itself, but as a tool by means of which the heterogeneous material of experience is more-or-less adequately made to fit. The reflective disjunction not only occurs *by means* of language as a privileged category, but it transfers the self out of the empirical world into a world constituted out of, and in language--a language that it finds in the world like one entity among others, but that remains unique in being the only entity by means of which it can differentiate itself from the world. Language thus conceived divides the subject into an empirical self, immersed in the world, and a self that becomes like a sign in its attempt at differentiation and self-definition." de Man, "The Rhetoric of Temporality," pp. 195-196.

97. I've avoided invoking Derrida's *différance* in this discussion, but his writings on the relation between writing and speaking are pertinent here. See Jacques Derrida, *Disseminations*, trans. Barbara Johnson (Chicago: University of Chicago Press, 1981).

98. I've included this qualification, but for the most part this discussion is written "specifically for someone who is in the grip of conceptual puzzlement." See Hanna Pitkin, *Wittgenstein and Justice* (Berkeley: University of California Press, 1972), p. 84.

99. Simpson quotes a wonderful passage from Rousseau to support this idea: "Writing, which would seem to crystallize language, is precisely what alters it. It changes not the words but the spirit, substituting exactitude for expressiveness. Feelings are expressed in speaking, ideas in writing. In writing, one is forced to use all the words according to their conventional meaning. But in speaking, one varies the meaning by varying one's tone of voice. . . . There really is an equivocation which would be eliminated by a vocative mark. The same equivocation is found in irony, when it is not made manifest by accent." Jean-Jacques Rousseau, *Essay on the Origin of Language*, trans. John H. Moran and Alexander Gode (Chicago: Chicago University Press,

1986), pp. 21-22. Passage quoted in Simpson, *Irony and Authority*, p. 218n. Also see Robert Darnton, "Readers Respond to Rousseau: The Fabrication of Romantic Sensitivity," *The Great Cat Massacre and Other Episodes in French Cultural History* (New York: Basic Books, 1984), pp. 215-256.

100. See Becker, "Concepts of Irony with Special Reference to Applications in the Visual Arts"; José Ortega y Gasset, *The Dehumanization of the Arts and Notes on the Novel*, trans. Helene Weyl (Princeton: Princeton University Press, 1948), p. 48; Muecke, *Irony*, pp. 5-6.

101. See Brooks, "Irony as a Principle of Structure"; Gasset, *The Dehumanization of the Arts*.

102. Georg Lukács, *The Theory of the Novel*, trans. Anna Bostock (Cambridge: MIT Press, 1973).

103. See Jankélévitch, *L'Ironie*; Muecke, *Irony*, pp. 5-6.

104. R.S. Crane contended that if one accepts Cleanth Brooks's criterion for poetic "structure," then one must view even mathematical equations as ironical (and not simply "abstract"). In fact, he called $E=mc^2$ "the greatest 'ironical' poem written so far in the twentieth century." "The Critical Monism of Cleanth Brooks," *Critics and Criticism: Ancient and Modern*, ed. R.S. Crane (Chicago: University of Chicago Press, 1952), pp. 104-105.

105. According to Goethe, one must have a sense of irony to be a good scientist. Muecke quotes Eugenio d'Ors: "Science is irony: science is in a sense aesthetic like art. At every point of its progress, science accepts implicitly, notes in its own margin, the possibility of contradiction, the progress to come. It defines, it cannot dogmatize." See Muecke, *The Compass of Irony*, p. 129-131. Muecke also quotes the hero of Svevo's *Confessions of Zeno*: "Accountants are by nature a race of animals much inclined to irony." *Irony and the Ironic*, p. 1. And Arthur Miller writes, in reference to Heisenberg's Principle of Indeterminacy, that it is "dialectical irony that the measurement itself changes the particle being measured." "Introduction to the Collected Plays," *Arthur Miller's Collected Plays* (New York: Viking Press, 1957), p. 54 (quoted in Knox, "Irony," p. 634).

106. Kierkegaard contended that Solgar viewed irony as a kind of "contemplative prayer." *The Concept of Irony*, p. 323.

107. Schlegel, *Lectures on Dramatic Art and Literature*, p. 369.

108. Thompson and Hutchens belong to this category.

109. Cleanth Brooks, "Irony and 'Ironic' Poetry," *College English 9* (February, 1948), pp. 231-37.

110. *Idem*, "Irony as a Principle of Structure," p. 729.

111. *Ibid.*, pp. 740-741.

112. *Ibid.*, p. 730.

113. *Ibid.*, p. 731n.

114. Crane, "The Critical Monism of Cleanth Brooks," pp. 83-107.

115. This is oversimplified, of course. One would really need to examine the sociological history of poetry in order to determine all that is involved in the identification of the "context" of poetry.

116. Furst adroitly attends to the important of contexts in ironic transmissions, but she seems to regard culture as the most expansive definition of context: "In this particular instance the key to correct understanding lies in the cultural context. Our perception of irony depends on a series of cultural norms shared by the speaker and his interlocutor. Since no sentence is in itself ironic, and conversely any sentence can be ironic, the cultural context often plays a vital role in making us decide whether irony is present, and if so, to what extent." *Fictions of Romantic Irony*, pp. 15-16.

117. See Mellor, *English Romantic Irony*, pp. 10-12, "On Romantic Irony," p. 228; Muecke, *Irony and the Ironic*, p. 23.

118. See Kierkegaard, *The Concept of Irony*, pp. 118, 333.

119. Freud classified irony as a species of the comic (Knox contends that Freud was thinking exclusively of verbal and satiric irony--"Irony," p. 634). But what is often overlooked is the main point of Freud's discussion about irony, namely that while irony comes very close to joking, it can be understood without any need for bringing in the unconscious; whereas jokes relate to the unconscious. "A comparison like this between jokes and a closely related type of the comic [i.e., irony] may confirm our assumption that what is peculiar to jokes is their relation to the unconscious and that this may perhaps distinguish them from the comic as well." Sigmund Freud, *Jokes and the Relation to the Unconscious*, trans. J. Strachey (New York: W.W. Norton, 1960), p. 174. Only a few commentators have discussed irony with respect to psychoanalysis, but they seem to ignore Freud's main point. See Brian Moloney, "Psychoanalysis and Irony in 'La Coscienza di Zeno,'" *Modern Language Review* 67 (April, 1972), pp. 309-318; Holland, *Dynamics of Literary Response*; Reik, *The Secret Self*. Also see Muecke, who likens the processes of writing and reading irony to "Witzarbeit." *Irony and the Ironic*, p. 41.

120. My argument about reading irony seems close to Cavell's comments on behalf of "ordinary language": "This is all that 'ordinary' in the phrase 'ordinary language philosophy' means, or ought to mean. It does not refer to particular words of wide use, nor to particular sorts of men. It reminds us that whatever words are said and meant are said and meant by particular men, and that to understand what they (the words) mean you must understand what they (whoever is using them) mean, and that sometimes men do not see what they mean, that usually they cannot say what they mean, that for various reasons they may not know what they mean, and that when they are forced to recognize this they feel they do not, and perhaps cannot, mean anything, and they are struck dumb. . . . Not more than normally, however, because there are any number of (specific) ways in which and occasions on which one's words do not say what one means. Because the connection between using a word and meaning what it says is not inevitable or automatic, one may wish to call it a matter of convention. But then one must not suppose that it is a convention we would know how to forgo." Stanley Cavell, *Must We Mean What We Say?* (Cambridge: Cambridge University Press, 1969), pp. 270-271. Wayne Booth remarks that irony is one language game that Wittgenstein did not investigate; similarly, I think Cavell does not pay sufficient attention to irony, a case in

which authors and readers are looking for unconventional, extraordinary, and deliberate disruptions between speech and meaning. I am not at all sure whether we can classify irony within the confines of "ordinary" language: though it is a widely used means of discourse, irony seems to be an attempt precisely to *defy* ordinary formulas. For someone asking "Must we mean what we say?" and who looks for a relationship between skepticism and romanticism, Cavell seems to have consistently committed a glaring omission by overlooking irony.

121. Furst is very good at explaining the importance of doubt and ambivalence in ironic exchanges: "There are thus a number of ways whereby an ironic countermeaning or subtext within the discourse may be detected. None of them is infallible, for irony must always retain its quintessential ambivalence." *Fictions of Romantic Irony*, p. 20.

122. Perhaps Nietzsche's assertion that Socrates married *ironically*, just to demonstrate that philosophers abhor marriage, is relevant here. *On the Geneology of Morals*, trans. Walter Kaufmann (New York: Vintage Books, 1969), p. 107. We can only speculate whether Nietzsche would have viewed Socrates' marriage as "malicious" had he read Kierkegaard's comments on philosophy, love, and irony, e.g., "Naturally it goes without saying that the love affair existing between Socrates and Alcibiades was intellectual. But if we ask what was there in Socrates that made such a relationship not only possible but necessary (for Alcibiades is correct when he says that he is not the only one bound to Socrates in this way, but almost everyone who associated with him), then I have nothing to reply except that it was Socrates' irony." Kierkegaard, *The Concept of Irony*, p. 85.

123. Wright, "Irony and Fiction," p. 113.

124. Chevalier, Sedgewick, Knox, and others have argued that the clash between appearance and reality is a necessary variable in the operation of irony, but, as Wright contends, irony seems more to confound the distinction than to employ it. F. Schlegel meant by "transcendental" (as in "transcendental buffoonery") a hovering between the ideal and real (see Mellor, "On Romantic Poetry," p. 227), and Muecke asserts something similar when he writes: "Placing these two pictures side by side we get a composite image of man as infinite and free in imagination and reflection but finite and limited in understanding and action. In other words, we see the real ironizing the ideal, or more precisely, the ineluctable realities of life ironizing man's compelling need to reach towards perfection (and this can be recognized and expressed with bitter or despairing irony); but conversely, the ideal can ironize the real, that is man can express his spirit's independence of the word with disdainful or insouciant irony. Muecke, *The Compass of Irony*, p. 192.

125. I think this is the sense behind Schlegel's remarks that the oppositions of irony are reconciled, but not by synthesis. See also, *Athenaeum Fragments*, #53, #121, *Lyceum Fragments*, #108, and *Literary Notebooks*, #802. See Mellor, *English Romantic Irony*, pp. 11-12.

126. Kierkegaard distinguishes between mere dissemblance and irony: "Dissemblance, insofar as one wishes to relate it to the subject, has a purpose,

an external purpose foreign to dissemblance itself. Irony, on the other hand, has no purpose, its purpose is immanent in itself, a metaphysical purpose. The purpose is none other than irony itself. . . . Irony has, therefore, no external purpose but is self-purposive." Kierkegaard,*The Concept of Irony*, p. 273.

127. Knox discerns four separate "variables" in irony, but I think they are more interrelated than his scheme allows. As I have explained it, his variables of "appearance/reality" and "field of observation" have to do with the initial choice of how far to extend dialogue.

128. See Thompson, Chevalier, Reik, Holland.

129. DeMott overlooks completely Kierkegaard's distinction between a "society" of ironists and a "community" formed by irony: "Insofar as the higher circles . . . speak ironically . . . to this extent irony is in the process of isolating itself, for it does not generally wish to be understood. Here the irony does not cancel itself. It is, furthermore, merely an inferior form of the ironic conceit which desires witnesses in order to convince and reassure itself, for it is merely an inconsistency which irony has in common with every negative standpoint that while according to its concept it is isolation, it nevertheless seeks to constitute a society, and, when it cannot elevate itself to the Idea of community, seeks to realize itself in conventicles. But there is as little social unity in a coterie of ironists as there is truly honesty among a band of thieves. If we now disregard that aspect of irony which it opens to the conspirators and consider it in relation to the uninitiated, in relation to those against whom its polemic is directed, in relation to the existence it conceives ironically, then it usually expresses itself in two ways. Either the ironist identifies himself with the nuisance he wishes to attack, or he enters into a relation of opposition to it, but in such a way, of course, that he is always conscious that his appearance is the opposite of what he himself subscribes to, and that he experiences a satisfaction in this disparity." Kierkegaard, *The Concept of Irony*, p. 266.

130. Benjamin DeMott, "The New Irony: Sickniks and Others," *American Scholar* 31 (Winter, 1961-62), p. 11.

131. *Ibid.*, p. 115.

132. *Ibid.*, pp. 115-116.

133. John Schaeffer makes a very similar case, arguing that irony artificially creates secular community only by denying religion. "Ironic Discourse and the Creation of Secularity," *Soundings* 66 (Fall, 1983), pp. 319-330.

134. See Knox, "Irony," p. 627, and Dikkers, *Ironie als Vorm van Communicatie*, p. 150.

135. See Dikkers, *Ironie als Vorm van Communicatie*, p. 151; John B. McKee, *Literary Irony and the Literary Audience* (Amsterdam: Rodopi N.V., 1974).

136. Simpson writes with respect to the Romantics: "The poet cannot be accused of intruding in his own person if he has no sense of selfhood upon which to base such an intrusion; the erasing of the selfhood thus becomes one way of dodging the intentionality problem, and the poet can thus avoid having to dramatise his own presence in the text. . . . This question of aloofness is

possible because there is a corresponding elision of the question of personal identity. If the artist chooses to confront his selfhood as an issue, then he is also compelled to assess it as it intends or modifies his presentation of things outside him, objects or characters." Simpson, *Irony and Authority*, pp. 184-5.

137. Burke, *A Grammar of Motives*, p. 514.

138. Randolph Bourne, "The Life of Irony," *Youth and Life* (Cambridge: Riverside Press, 1913), p. 107.

139. *Ibid.*, pp. 109, 127.

140. Of course the view of irony as subversion is held not only by irony's critics. Several commentators have embraced the playfulness of irony's supposedly subversive nature. See Henry S. Kariel, "Affirming a Politics of Inconsequence," *Polity* 17 (Fall, 1984), pp. 145-160 (though Kariel does not use the word *irony* in this article); John S. Nelson, "Political Theory as Political Rhetoric," *What Should Political Theory Be Now?* ed. John S. Nelson (Albany: State University of New York Press, 1983), pp. 169-240; and Richard Rorty, *Consequences of Pragmatism* (Minneapolis: University of Minnesota Press, 1982).

141. Paul de Man mentions E.T.A. Hoffmann's longing for an ironic reconciliation with, a "return" to, the world; but de Man argues in response that the ironist can never overcome his alienated condition, his "permanent parabasis." De Man contends that when the ironist attempts to act on an "intersubjective level," he betrays the ironic mode. I suggest that irony indeed can turn upon itself, but that this betrayal often represents--ironically--more of an extension than disjunction with the original ironic character. See de Man, "The Rhetoric of Temporality," pp. 199-200.

142. Simpson, *Irony and Authority*, p. 180. Compare this to Fish's thoughts on reading: "By making literary and ironic readings equally the products of interpretation, I may have seemed to undermine stability altogether, because if interpretation covers the field, there is nothing on which a particular interpretation can rest. But what I have been trying to show is that interpretations rest on other interpretations, or, more precisely, on assumptions--about what is possible, necessary, telling, essential, and so on--so deeply held that they are not thought of as assumptions at all; and because they are not thought of as assumptions, the activities they make possible and the facts they entail seem not to be matters of opinion or debate, but a part of the world." Stanley B. Fish, "Short People Got No Reason to Live," p. 190. See also Fish, *Self-Consuming Artifacts: The Experience of Seventeenth-Century Literature* (Berkeley: University of California Press, 1972), pp. 425-6. Simpson talks of inventions and leaps of meaning, whereas Fish belabors the reader's background assumptions, as if these necessarily provide a foundation for interpretation. Simpson writes of *creating* interpretive communities, Fish writes about finding ones that already exist.

143. Simpson, *Irony and Authority*, p. 169.

144. Japp begins his book *Theorie der Ironie* with this epigram from Schlegel.

145. Kierkegaard, *Concluding Unscientific Postscript*, pp. 448-451; see also Hopper, "Irony--The Pathos of the Middle," p. 35.

146. Nothing I have said absolutely prevents an author, so equipped with the requisites of the ironic outlook, to return to the text and write in a way that completely renounces all indications of his irony. We might then be inclined to say that such an author was not "writing ironically," for his writing, as judged from the "text itself," would not seem to correspond to any of the forms of irony that we conventionally associate with the term *irony*--unless of course we were fully expecting this author to write in an openly ironic mode (perhaps because we at that time are living in an age of much irony or because we know the author from his past works), in which case the author's understated style might still seem to be an ironic commentary upon the more forthcoming forms of irony of his age. But I have contended in this chapter that generally it behooves the ironist to manifest his irony, for the "return to the text" is above all not a return to the squiggles and scratches on a surface of papyrus but is a return to the world of others. As such, the return entails an attempt to engage with others. Yet this commitment to others runs up against the ironist's basic skepticism, an overcoming of which virtually requires a strategy of ironic pretense. Again, the reason the ironic author sustains his pretense has to do with with the dilemma of being committed to language on the one hand and yet being aware of the inadequacies of language on the other: he cannot just say what he wants to say (as I am attempting here) without violating his original skepticism. To be sure, an ironist can probably carry on his everyday written correspondence (laundry lists, etc.) in an altogether unironic fashion; but in writing that really matters, when the point is specifically to engage others in a philosophic fashion that is true to the tenets of irony, I think an ironist who refrains entirely from what we would generally designate an "ironic mode" is rare indeed.

147. Traugott, "The Yahoo in the Doll's House," pp. 147-8.

148. I am sympathetic with Booth's claim (and his reply to Fish) that he is interested in those moments when persons do in fact seem to "share" ironies; but Fish has a point, that one can never be sure. I should think, however, that their dispute need not be posed so severely as a contest between certainty and skepticism.

149. Mellor also contends that irony does not represent a form of "existentialism." See *English Romantic Irony*, p. 184.

150. Note Muecke: "I have taken being ironical to mean transmitting a literal message in such a way or in such a context as to challenge a response in the form of a correct interpretation of one's intent, the transliteral meaning. In brief (Instrumental) Irony is an act, not simply a significance." *Irony and the Ironic*, p. 100.

151. "As there is something forbidding about irony, so also it has some extraordinarily seductive and enchanting moments. The disguise and mysteriousness which it entails, the telegraphic communication which it initiates, inasmuch as the ironist must always be understood at a distance, the infinite sympathy it assumes, the elusive and ineffable moment of

understanding immediately displaced by the anxiety of misunderstanding--all this captivates with indissoluble bonds." Kierkegaard, *The Concept of Irony*, p. 85.

152. Simpson, *Irony and Authority*, p. 167.

153. "I have a suspicion that some of the most conscious artists of earlier times are still carrying on ironically, hundreds of years after their deaths, with their most faithful followers and admirers." Friedrich Schlegel, "On Incomprehensibility," *Friedrich Schlegel's* Lucinde *and the Fragments*, p. 267.

154. Bourne, "The Life of Irony," p. 105.

155. "I have played down moral and religious positions thought to do us good, or at least to elevate Swift in our estimation, in favour of the play of the mind that makes for consciousness, which, I argue, is what the ironist, inviting us to make something of nothing, has to offer, and which, in the Platonic scheme to which Swift was attracted, is everything." Traugott, "The Yahoo in the Doll's House," p. 150.

156. Mellor, "On Romantic Irony," p. 229.

157. It should be noted that the Derrideans would probably take issue with this account of their views of "textual irony," attributing such tendencies instead purely to readerly strategies. But even in defining the text as but a template of sorts, they are, I am suggesting, making a claim as much about the nature of texts as about readers and interpretive strategies. For them, irony is an ever present possibility lurking in texts, a negative aspect but an aspect nonetheless, which is there to be worked upon, interpreted, deconstructed, and so forth by the enterprising analyst.

158. Perhaps this is why Schlegel, Heller, and others have felt that any attempt to speak unironically of irony is bound to fail.

159. Sperber and Wilson's idea of "echoic mention" seems to be a semantic formulation for what Sedgewick referred to as the dramatic senses of "Reminiscence" and "Anticipation." In Sedgewick's account, however, these are extensions of consciousness, of sympathy, and not semantic techniques. *Of Irony*, p. 53.

160. There are other, interrelated problems with Sperber and Wilson's analysis of irony ("Irony and the Use-Mention Distinction") that might be mentioned. First, they credit their notion of echoic mention with the advantage of facilitating the analysis of an author's evocation of attitudes and images without having to make reference to the notion of figurative meaning; yet they do not consider *what* this attitude or attitudes might be. They presume that the ironic attitude is limited to an   attitude that casts aspersions upon the proposition "mentioned." They say, for instance, that the speaker may think the proposition untrue, inappropriate, or irrelevant (p. 307), but beyond these suggestions, they give few clues. They fail to consider that an author may not be adopting a deflationary attitude toward the proposition he "echoes." In short, Sperber and Wilson treat irony mainly as an isolated verbal phenomenon, and specifically as an instance of "dry mockery" or satire. Thus their notion of echoic mention is not very helpful in analyzing the more paradoxical and ambivalent forms of irony. What, after all, is being

"mentioned" in Beckett's plays, and how does one distinguish between "mention" and "use" in such examples? Furthermore, echoic mention is not very helpful in analyzing the notion of irony as a voice that an author sustains throughout a work. Again, the distinction between use and mention is difficult to maintain when it is applied to a entire work. In addition, echoic mention is not able to explain cases wherein an author seems to mock himself, or when he slips in and out of his own irony. Finally, echoic mention does not lend itself to nonverbal applications of irony. Instead, I suggest that the notion of pretense, of detachment and implication, can encompass these expanded applications of irony; whereas Sperber and Wilson's echoic mention is limited in being confined to the realm of semantics.

161. My forcing this distinction undermines, I think, Muecke's distinction between "Closed" and "Open" ironies, the difference between mere "rhetorical" irony and those with the ironical "vision." See Muecke, *Irony and the Ironic*, p. 49. Also note that F. Schlegel claimed that one could not even feign irony. "Lyceum Fragments," #108, *Friedrich Schlegel's* Lucinde *and the Fragments*, p. 155.

162. Wright argues that although the ironist entertains a profound dualism, he is not "uncommitting": "No ironist can be doctrinaire--as the examples just adduced must show. None of them sees a clear and present answer. There is vigor, there is humility, there is sympathy, in the ironist's search, there is judgement finally--but never serene certainty. Irony comes as the result of the quest for meaning in the universe, as the result of human experience; it is not a piece of equipment, like an entrenching tool, with which a man starts out. And this result is the true divided vision--that of Chaucer, Cervantes, Swift, and Jane Austen." Wright, "Irony and Fiction," p. 114.

163. One writer who I think has overstated the opposition between "literal" and "ironic" forms of writing is Richard Rorty. But my differences with Rorty on this score begin with his reading of Plato. See Rorty, *The Consequences of Pragmatism*, pp. 136-137. And see the response to Rorty by Michael Fischer, "Redefining Philosophy as Literature: Richard Rorty's 'Defense' of Literary Culture," *Soundings* 67 (Fall, 1984), pp. 312-324.

164. To reiterate a point that I made in Chapter 2: The story of Oedipus is not necessarily "tragic," at least not in our sense of the tragic as life-deprecating. See Thirlwall's "On the Irony of Sophocles."

165. Glicksberg contends that irony represents a "search for transcendence," *The Ironic Vision*, p. 260; but Becker asserts that "the figure of Odysseus on his return to Ithaca is a perfect prototype of the Aristotelian ironist." "Concepts of Irony," p. 12.

166. Glicksberg, *The Ironic Vision*, p. 5.

167. Several commentators have contended that irony represents a concern for intellectual freedom. Anthony A. Collins writes: "The great Concern is and ought to be, that *the Liberty of examining into the Truth of Things should be kept up*, that Men may have some Sense and Knowledge, and not be the *Dupe* of *Cheats* and *Imposters*, or of those who would keep them in the dark, and let them receive nothing but thro' their Hands. If that be secur'd to

us by Authority, I, for my part, am very ready to sacrifice the Privilege of *Irony*, tho so much in fashion among all Men; being persuaded, that a great Part of the *Irony* complain'd of, has its rise from the *want of Liberty to examine into the Truth of Things*; and that if that *Liberty* was prevalent, it would, without a Law, prevent all that *Irony* which Men are driven into for want of Liberty to speak plainly, and to protect themselves from the Attacks of those who would take the Advantage to ruin them for direct Assertions." Collins, *A Discourse Concerning Ridicule and Irony in Writing* (London: J. Brotherton, Printer, 1729), pp. 23-24. Similarly, Thirlwall contended that "the highest triumph of irony consists not in refutation and demolition. It requires that, while the fallacy is exposed and overthrown by the admissions which it has itself demanded, the truth should be set in the clearest light, and on the most solid ground, by the attempts made to suppress and overwhelm it." Thirlwall, "On the Irony of Sophocles," pp. 484-5. And Thompson quotes Georges Palante, who quotes Proudhon (*Confessions d'un Révolutionnaire*) thus: "Liberty, like reason, exists and manifests itself only in the incessant disdain of its own works; it perishes when it admires itself. This is why irony has always been the character of philosophical and liberal genius, the seal of the human spirit, the irresistible instrument of progress. Static folk are always solemn folk; the man of the people who laughs is a thousand times nearer reason and liberty than the anchorite who prays or the philosopher who argues. Irony, true liberty! it is thou who deliverest me from the ambition of power, from the servitude of parties, from the respect for routine, from the pedantry of science, from the admiration of great persons, from the mystifications of politics, from the fanaticism of reformers, from the superstition of this great universe, and from self-adoration." Thompson,*The Dry Mock*, pp. 250-251.

168. Kierkegaard stressed that "it must be remembered that irony is essentially practical," *The Concept of Irony*, p. 274.

169. Thomas Mann, "Goethe and Tolstoy," *Essays of Three Decades*, trans. H.T. Lowe-Porter (New York: Alfred A. Knopf, 1948), pp. 122-123.

170. Even the most complex forms of irony reveal a reversal of sorts. John Freccero associates irony with a poetic strategy that turns on a notion of fiction that seemingly denies its own fictionality. One wants to say that this treatment of fiction requires an initial context for fiction, or an acknowledgment of fiction *as* fictional, the expectation for which is then reversed or undermined by a claim to literalness. See John Freccero, *Dante: The Poetics of Conversion* (Cambridge: Harvard University Press, 1986), pp. 101ff. Furst's final "theory" or definition of irony also reveals a logic of reversal at work in the ironist's play upon the distinction between fiction and nonfiction: "What is ultimately at issue in romantic irony is nothing other than the authority of the invented fictional world both unto itself and in relation to the world of our experience. The authenticity of the self-contained illusion remains intact in traditional irony, whereas it is incessantly undermined and questioned in romantic irony. A progressive deconstruction of illusion takes place: first it is broken within the fiction by the impulse to self-representation in mirror images and in those labyrinthine arabesques so favoured by Romantic and modern narrators. The

illusion become controversial at a second level through the continual arousal of the reader's awareness of the text's standing as fiction. This has a strangely contradictory impact: for the pretence of realism is heightened when the contingencies of the known world appear to be faithfully noted as they beset the narrative; but at the same time the sense of artifice is strongly reinforced through the reader's realisation of the games that are being played." Furst, *Fictions of Romantic Irony*, p. 239.

171. See Marianne Shapiro, "The Status of Irony," *Stanford Literature Review* 2, No. 1 (Spring, 1985), p. 10.

172. See, for instance, Enright, *The Alluring Problem*, pp. 108ff.

173. On irony's indirect approach to moral instruction, see David L. Hall's *Eros and Irony: A Prelude to Philosophical Anarchism* (Albany: State University of New York Press, 1982); and Shapiro, "The Status of Irony," p. 13.

174. "Irony's guns face in every direction; it is committedly uncommitted, in its essence anti-political, or anti-ideological, whatever the ideology. Politicians of all shades dislike it rather more than they dislike the opposition parties; it doesn't go in for 'pairing' or other mutual arrangements; it is sneaky." Enright, *The Alluring Problem*, p. 110.

175. Rorty cites Derrida to support him in the belief that irony and politics are best kept apart. Richard Rorty, *Contingency, Irony, and Solidarity* (Cambridge: Cambridge University Press, 1989), esp. pp. 122ff.

176. Cf. Handwerk, Simpson, Smyth, Culler, Wilde, Lang.

177. Lang introduces and clarifies a much-needed distinction between "irony" and the French notion of "humor," a distinction she borrows from Gilles Deleuze, Jean-François Lyotard, Roland Barthes, and Louis Marin. Irony properly understood, she contends, is "modernist," whereas "humor" is "postmodernist." The former requires a search for the intender behind the text, as well as a basic understanding of language as something separate from thought. Humor does, or needs, none of this. For Lang, the significance of the distinction is key, for she wants to affirm the affirmative side of postmodernism, which necessitates a view of the text from a "humorous" perspective, rather than from an ironic one. Candace D. Lang, *Irony/Humor: Critical Paradigms* (Baltimore and London: Johns Hopkins University Press, 1988).

178. Handwerk's book is an extended exploration of the possible relation between Schlegelian irony and Lacanian selfhood. Gary J. Handwerk, *Irony and Ethics in Narrative: From Schlegel to Lacan* (New Haven and London: Yale University Press, 1985).

179. "Barthesian humor--the affirmation of a self constituted in and out of language--is not a choice of appearance *instead* of reality, signifier *instead* of signified. . . . It is quite simply the assumption of a critical paradigm within which the dichotomies that ground the classical concept of irony have no pertinence. . . . For [Deleuze and Lyotard], theorizing from the standpoint of humor entails an attempt to think negativity as such (Derridean *différance*), rather than as an absence of positivity, as well as the affirmation of the inherent

otherness of the self and, with it, the elaboration of a non-thetic, non-teleological mode of critical discourse." Lang, *Irony/Humor*, p. 61.

180. Wilde contends that the modernist enterprise is (or was) essentially humanistic and heroic, whereas the postmodernist vision accepts randomness and antiheroism. Alan Wilde, *Horizons of Assent: Modernism, Postmodernism, and the Ironic Imagination* (Baltimore and London: Johns Hopkins University Press, 1981). Enright devotes a fair amount of space in his book to ironizing Wilde, among many others.

181. Simpson, *Irony and Authority*, p. 200.

182. Mellor, *English Romantic Irony*, p. 188.

4

Art, Irony, and Politics in the Nineteenth Century

> If Hegel had written the whole of his *Logic* and then said . . . that it was merely an experiment in thought . . . then he would certainly have been the greatest thinker who had ever lived. As it is, he is merely comic.
>
> --Kierkegaard, *Journals*

Ironic theory enjoyed a renaissance in the nineteenth century. The Schlegel brothers, Friedrich and August, were the prime movers in this renaissance of Greek thought, together promoting a version of irony as a complex aesthetic or philosophical stance, a new *Weltanschauung*, as it were. Friedrich Schlegel's turn to irony began in the field of aesthetics. He used the term *irony* to describe a quality of "doubleness" that he perceived in Shakespeare's art. Shakespeare as a writer seemed to be simultaneously *distanced* from his own plots and characters as well as *invested* in them: He was both "objective" and "interested" in his works, to repeat Schlegel's words. This doubleness toward one's works became, under the Schlegels' joint guidance, a metaphor for a possible attitude toward all of life: One could be simultaneously distanced and engaged, even towards oneself; self-critical and yet very much involved. Yet, however much Friedrich Schlegel might have been intrigued by this stance of self-aware ambivalence, eventually he abandoned all hopes for the ironic renewal of German culture that he at one time entertained. Indeed, Schlegel in the latter part of his career apparently acquiesced to the anti-irony view of his major critic, G.W.F. Hegel.

What is more, though theories of irony became prominent in the nineteenth century, Hegel's general critique of the beast--namely that irony does not transfer successfully from the realm of art to that of politics--eventually won the day. In order then to advance the present countervailing thesis--that irony can indeed serve politics--we need to reexamine these nineteenth-century debates over irony, perhaps to alert ourselves in advance to the possible failings of an ironic politics. In the sections that follow, the works of four of leading nineteenth-century theorists of irony--Schlegel, Hegel, Kierkegaard, and Marx--shall be reviewed, organized with respect to the working premise that, informed as to its dangers and shortcomings, we can still take the ironic theory of the nineteenth century as thematically, if negatively, instructive for our overall project.

Schlegel and Transcendental Buffoonery

We begin with the leading theorist of irony in the nineteenth century, Friedrich Schlegel, whose thought and life we will briefly examine in the hope of gaining some insight into the question of why irony went astray. Schlegel's influence upon the course of nineteenth century thought has been vastly underestimated, perhaps because his writings were unsystematic, eclectic, and somewhat reckless; and consequently his influence now seems obscure in relation to the monumental thinkers of his times. Despite such disparaging commentary, he has been recognized as the originator of hermeneutics and the theory of "understanding," which was later formulated by Schleiermacher, August Boeckh, and Otfried Müller and which influenced the historical method developed by Dilthey, Scherer, Julian Schmidt, Mommsen, and Treitschke.[1] He was the first to sense the dark background of Greek life, in anticipation of Nietzsche's discovery of the "Dionysian" element.[2] He has been credited with being the first to introduce the "aphoristic" method into philosophic writing, bringing it from French writing into German.[3] Hegel attended his lectures on transcendental philosophy at the University of Jena from October, 1800, to March, 1801; and though he eventually turned against Schlegelian irony, Hegel's development of his dialectics certainly was indebted to Schlegel in many respects.[4] Schlegel's sometimes extreme ideas also figured directly in the writings of Solgar, Tieck, Novalis, Jean Paul, Adam Müller, Heine, Marx, Kierkegaard, and eventually Thomas Mann. Finally, it is of some note that even his writings on Indic philology and Oriental philosophy are considered by some scholars to have been pioneering in these fields.[5]

But mostly Friedrich Schlegel is known, to the extent that he is known, for his contributions on two subjects, namely irony and Romanticism.[6] Indeed, many commentators lump the two terms together in writing about Schlegel, employing the phrase "Romantic irony" in connection with Schlegel--though it is questionable whether Schlegel ever actually used the two in combination.[7] Yet Schlegel's thought underwent so many twists and turns--indeed, radical transformations-- that commentators should not presume that his major concepts, such as "irony," "poetry," and "Romanticism," all belonged to a consistent or even developing worldview. We need to draw a few distinctions.

The problem in studying Schlegel is that he was such an experimenter and dabbler that it is hard to find one work that is representative of the whole, if there is a whole. He wrote no systematic theory, and he began several projects, large and small, and frequently left them unfinished. Making matters of interpretation even more difficult, Schlegel wrote in several formats over the course of his life, trying his hand at aphorisms, essays, plays, novels, poetry, in addition to his longer discursive pieces.

Commentators seem to make sense of Schlegel by looking to his friends. The standard interpretation of the corpus of his writings is that first Schlegel was looking for an answer to Kant, was in turn influenced by Winckelmann and Schiller, then found an answer in Fichte, was further influenced by Schelling and Goethe, and later was steered toward religion by Novalis, Schleiermacher, and Lessing.[8] Apparently Schlegel was easily swayed, if we are to believe these accounts, and the question of interpretation is a matter of putting the pieces in proper order. One supposedly finds the proper order by discovering an overall theme, an ulterior motive, that led Schlegel to this thinker or that one.

Leonard P. Wessell, Jr., is one commentator who has attempted to reconstruct Schlegel's ulterior motives. In one article he declares, "The objective of this study is to investigate the philosophical foundation underlying and determining the nature of Schlegel's synthesis of *das Romantische* and *das Klassische* into what is now called his "romanticism."[9] Schlegel's underlying concern, according to Wessell, is "metaphysical," specifically an attempt to provide an answer to Kant's "antinomic" view of the universe, which was based upon a view that man can experience only the finite. In short, Schlegel according to Wessell resolves the dualism of Kantian philosophy by adopting Schiller's aesthetic categories, and he uses Fichte's transcendental Ego to overcome Kantian limitations. The solution, then, is that the notion of *becoming* overcomes the limitations placed upon the static notion of *being*. In a process of becoming, "all is reconciled," most important the gap between finiteness and infinity. Yet this solution, according to Wessell, leads to eternal frustration, because man is defined as infinitely longing, never satisfied with any finite goal.

In a book-length study of this phenomenon, Wessell goes into greater detail.[10] Now we learn that Schlegel's quest for infinity was not simply some abstract revolt against Kant but was fundamentally religious in inspiration. Schlegel, the son of a Protestant minister, was another captive of German Idealism, which promised a secular eschatology but could not deliver what it promised. According to Wessell, Novalis and Schlegel teamed up[11] to found a progressive and universal poetry, which cast its eschatological imperatives in a "mythopoetic" form. The bottom line, for Wessell, is that romantic irony cannot achieve immortality, and, unlike religion, which makes similar promises, can lead to very destructive worldly consequences. Wessell's eventual thesis is that Marxism was originally inspired by Schlegelian romanticism.

Of little concern to Wessell is the complication to his thesis that Schlegel wrote: "Whoever is not, in the consciousness of his infinite power, pervaded with the feeling of his insignificance, must be a little shortsighted."[12] Wessell instead suggests that Schlegelianism stems from a deep-seated vanity, a foolhardy attempt to overcome one's human imperfections. Wessell, especially in his attempt to link the "evils" of Marxism with Schlegel's "romantic irony," wants to ignore the differences between the baby and the bathwater so that he can throw out one with the other. Let us consider a few points about Schlegel that Wessell apparently overlooks.

Hans Eichner notes a few important complications to the theory that Schlegel's irony was the product of a modified Fichteanism. First, Eichner locates Schlegel's concern with Fichte against the background of the rise of empiricism and materialism, which Schlegel felt posed a threat to the dignity of man. In 1796, Schlegel expressed his "ulterior motive" thus: "From the point of view of the consistent empiricist, everything divine, dignified, sacred, great, sublime etc. is *nonsense*. All this is really *mystical*."[13] He added that "It is really the mystics from whom we must learn philosophy. . . . The *nature* and starting point [of mysticism] is the arbitrary positing of the absolute." And then he identified Fichte as one of these mystics: "Spinoza is the best mystic known to us before Fichte." Eichner contends that Fichte would have been appalled had he known that he figured in Schlegel's mind as a mystic, but Eichner adds that the term implies criticism as well as praise as Schlegel used it. Schlegel embraced Fichte's philosophy because it repudiated the rational empiricism of the mechanists and materialists:

If they tended to believe in the primacy of matter, Fichte denied that it had any reality; if they attempted to found all knowledge on empirical evidence, Fichte strove to erect a system that was purely deductive; if they based science on the concept of strict causation, his key concept was Freedom; and if at least some of them managed to combine the mechanical philosophy with theist beliefs, Fichte evolve a form of ethical pantheism that rigidly excluded the possibility of a personal God. Thus, Schlegel found in his philosophy a magnificent vindication of the dignity of man, the intellectual courage and honesty that seemed lacking to him in almost every other quarter.[14]

Yet Schlegel did not, according to Eichner, subscribe *tout à fait* to Fichte's philosophy. Fichte seemed to deny the independence and variety of nature, and Schlegel respected its "infinite plenitude" as much as he himself might "thirst for the infinite." In addition, Eichner notes that though Schlegel in the 1790s was attracted to Fichte's ideas, later Schlegel would explicitly criticize Fichte's philosophy for producing nothing but "empty concepts and dead abstractions."[15] Whereas Wessell faults Schlegel for his Fichtean presumptions, Eichner points out that Schlegel, in 1806, accused Fichte's philosophy of solipsism: "What is most frightening to man is *absolute loneliness*. But Idealism is the very system in which the mind is completely isolated, bereft of everything that relates him to the ordinary would, so that it stands alone and completely deprived."[16]

There exist other ruptures in Schlegel's career that demand investigation and that contravene the view that Schlegel's thought represented, more or less, a continuous pattern leading to an identification of irony with romanticism. The first rupture has to do with his religious inclinations. Early on, Goethe wrote to Schlegel, inquiring, "Of what religion are you?" Schlegel replied, "I haven't decided yet." But by 1808 Schlegel had made a firm decision, having converted (along with his Jewish wife) to Catholicism, and to his death he remained a dedicated and outspoken follower of the Church. The turn to institutional religion must have been a drastic change. Earlier Schlegel had written, "Every God whose concept is not *made*, i.e., fully produced, by a man for himself, but is given to him, is--however sublime this concept may be--a mere idol. . . . Religion is a matter of arbitrary choice."[17] And in 1800 he published what he originally intended as "a new Bible," an example from which is the following passage: "The understanding, says the author of the *Speeches on Religion*, knows only of the Universe; let the imagination rule, and you have a God. Quite right! The imagination is man's organ for the

Godhead."[18] The "later" Schlegel certainly would have considered such a passage blasphemous.

Not only did Schlegel's religious tendencies change in mid-course, but his political sentiments also reversed themselves. In the 1790s he had been an ardent partisan of the French Revolution,[19] but by 1803 he had lost all faith in it; and later in his life he identified the revolution as part of the "false theories and pernicious systems of the eighteenth century."[20] After his religious conversion, Schlegel became a political conservative, first advocating a return to the old order before the Revolution, and eventually promoting the idea of a multinational state, modeled after the Holy Roman Empire and under the joint rule of the pope and emperor (though not Napoleon).[21] Eventually Metternich appointed him to a diplomatic position, but his religious extremism embarrassed the Austrian government in Frankfurt. Friedrich Gentz wrote that Schlegel "never had any talent for practical matters," and that his "religious, or rather, ecclesiastical frenzy had turned him into an utter fool."[22]

These ruptures suggest that it is a mistake to presume that Schlegel's life and work can be plotted along a single axis. I want to propose that this presumption is especially misplaced where his idea of irony is concerned. Commentators such as Wessell read irony into every corner of Schlegel's life, but it seems rather to have occupied only a bracketed period in the course of his writings, roughly from 1795 to 1799.[23] For instance, irony cannot be automatically associated with Schlegel's early quest for Greek ideality. Eichner points to the "Lyceums-Fragmente" to demonstrate that Schlegel's literary views had changed since 1795: "My essay on the study of Greek poetry is a mannered hymn in prose on objectivity in poetry. The worst feature of this essay seems to me its total lack of that *sine qua non*, irony."[24]

After 1800, the concept of irony dropped out of Schlegel's formal writings. The problem for some interpreters, however, is that his concept of romantic poetry pressed on. Schlegel used the notion of romantic poetry to prop up his vision of a progressive Christianity,[25] but the question is whether irony can be implicated in Schlegel's later zeal for poetic salvation.

Raymond Immerwahl has argued persuasively that Schlegel's notion of romantic poetry was not synonymous with his concept of irony. In brief, Immerwahl's argument is that the two are commonly confused because Schlegel referred to irony as transcendental buffoonery in the 42nd *Lyceum Fragment*, and he used the term "transcendental poetry" in the 238th and 247th *Athenaeum Fragments*. But Immerwahl argues that the term "transcendental" derived in Schlegel's thought as much from Schiller as from Fichte and thus contains two essential elements:

the philosophical concern for the relationship of the real and the ideal, and the reflection upon one's own process of thought or poetic expression. Insofar as it derived from Schiller, irony can apply to "naïve" poetry as well as to "transcendental" poetry. Schlegel's concept of irony then, according to Immerwahl, was not simply the destruction of the dramatic illusion associated with the romantics but also included a textual reflection of the author's ironic conception of human experience and character:

> These two contradictory attempts to reduce Schlegel's irony to a rigid formula exemplify an error that has plagued criticism of the subject for over a century: the insistence upon some special "romantic irony" of Friedrich Schlegel only remotely connected with irony as it is ordinarily understood. I have found no instance of this unhappy phrase in Friedrich Schlegel himself. He injected new subtlety and something of his own personal philosophy into the word, but he still meant *irony*, and his application of the concept was not even restricted to what he called "romantic" poets.[26]

If we can distinguish, therefore, Schlegel's concept of irony from his romantic and religious yearnings, then we might better understand his irony on its own terms. Indeed, though Wessel interprets Schlegelian irony as an eschatological imperative, it would seem that irony as "transcendental buffoonery" was fundamentally at odds with Schlegel's later Catholicism; and irony as "self-limitation" and "self-parody" was even at odds with Fichte's self-centering ego.

What we perhaps can say about Schlegel's personal bout with irony is that it fizzled out, that Schlegel himself became increasingly *unironical* after 1800. Can we make sense of Schlegel's irony, then, as a practical failure? Eichner provides us, I think, with a possible starting point for investigating this question. Schlegel was attracted to Fichte, Eichner contends, because Fichte's *Theory of Science* seemed to provide the answer to a problem that Kant had failed to solve, namely how to withstand the increasing threat of materialism in the wake of the rise of science. Schlegel was concerned not with some vague notion of religious immortality but rather, contends Eichner, with "the dignity of man." *This* theme, if any, was a constant preoccupation of Schlegel's from his early writings onward. Schlegel was impressed with the Greek's ability to achieve objective ideality in artworks, but his interest in the Greeks was not simply a quest--as some commentators have claimed--for ultimate perfection.[27] Such interpretations miss the extent to which nineteenth-century writers such as Schlegel recognized a fundamental difference between art and religion. Art, unlike religion, was viewed as a distinctly *human* sphere, the artist as a human creator. Yet art attains ideals, a higher form of communion, above ordinary discourse and human interaction. Schlegel defined the artist as a "spokesman of God," but as Eichner argues, "God" here contains no specifically Christian connotations. Artworks are plastic and worldly; they are, in Schlegel's words, "organic." In other words, if art achieves some form of perfection, it is an ideality that is located precisely within the world of actuality. In a passage that Schlegel claimed was completely "unironical," he confesses that he considers "art to be the heart of humanity."[28] I am tempted to aver that what Schlegel was really seeking in art was not communion with nature nor worldly immortality but a communion with *others*--and the plasticity of art lent the appearance of objectivity and a sense of firmness to such an intangible enterprise.

Such an interpretation will have to pass as conjecture, for the incontrovertible evidence backing such speculations cannot be drawn from Schlegel's scattered writings. Nevertheless, I suggest that throughout most of his life Schlegel sought objective expression, some observable documentation, for human dignity. But the one period in which he seemed to suspend this need was his ironical period. Eichner recounts Schlegel's reaction to Kant's *Critique of Judgment*. Kant had declared that there are no laws of beauty, and that therefore aesthetic judgments are not subject to proof. At first Schlegel resisted this view, espousing instead the neoclassical position that there must be objective rules of taste. But after 1796, Schlegel abandoned neoclassicism, now asking himself the question: How does criticism operate if there are no rules of taste? In brief, he responded with his theory of irony. Now it was "just as fatal for a thinker to have a system as not to have one. He will therefore have to make up his mind to combine the two."[29] Irony was a choice to proceed in the absence of rules and standards; it was born from "a feeling of indissoluble antagonism between the absolute and the relative, between the impossibility and the necessity of complete communication."[30] Now was the time in which Schlegel announced that the concept of God would have to be created. I propose that Schlegel, in his ironical period, was contending that the dignity of humankind rested upon a choice.

Such a position does not sit easily. If human dignity is based upon a choice rather than external rules and forces, then how does one argue against the rationalists, who have all the externalities to their advantage? Irony is a difficult pose to sustain because it does not lend itself well to argumentative validation and to external confirmation; and for this reason, it seems, Schlegel gave up on it. Instead he again looked for human dignity, some higher spiritual interaction, in various "forms": in poetry, in the novel, in physical sexuality, in religion, finally in nature. In 1800 he wrote his "Gespräch Über die Poesie," in which he called for a "New Myth," a kind of pantheism, that would unite humanity. His eventual turn to religion was prompted by Lessing's *Erziehung des Menschenge-schlechts*, which suggested to Schlegel "the notion of a 'progressive' Christianity that would culminate in a third revelation, supplanting traditional Christian ethics with its motivation through rewards and punishments by an ethic based on moral virtue as an end in itself."[31] Eichner writes about Schlegel's "conversion" thus: "To put matters differently, he came to realize that his doctrine of poetry as a source of knowledge depended on an external sanction--that 'inspiration' presupposes a 'spirit,' that 'enthusiasm' presupposes a 'theos.' In the end, as he gradually came to see, one could not avoid the necessity of deciding between the alternatives of a purely secular world of relative, uncertain, man-made values, and a world of faith and divine sanctions."[32]

By 1802 Schlegel began to accept a God given to man rather than one created. A concern for institutional religion had replaced Schlegel's ironic tendencies. "With so many failures and disappointments weighing on his mind, his dream of an imminent rejuvenation of mankind dissolved, and with it his faith in the self-reliance of man. The time to search for external support, for a different meaning to life, for supernatural sanctions and reassurances had come, and it so happened that all his major activities and experiences in Paris combined to guide this search in the same direction."[33]

We will return, in our discussion of Marx, to the question of why irony seems to require objective expression, and why it lends itself to mythic formulations. For now we can conclude that Schlegel abandoned, or betrayed, his own irony. Before and after his ironic period Schlegel tried in vain to look for solid foundations for the spiritual ties that he sought among humans, searching first in art, then in myth, then in religion, and eventually in nature. His irony left him frustrated, until he finally called out, "What gods will rescue us from all these ironies?"[34] Schlegel himself never quite made the conversion from ironic art to ironic politics, but he left behind backhanded suggestions that there may indeed be such a connection. For instance, we can perhaps discern such unwitting suggestiveness in Schlegel's apparently unironical injunction: "Don't waste your faith and love on the political world."[35]

Hegel and Determinate Negation

Hegel took issue with Schlegel's notion of irony. Though Hegel's view of irony derived in part from his reading of Schlegel, a reconstruction of their "debate" reveals important differences between the two. An understanding of these differences will, I believe, advance and refine the eventual case concerning the relation of irony to politics.

In the introduction to *The Phenomenology of Spirit*, Hegel distinguishes between two kinds of skepticism.[36] One kind of skepticism is that which doubts but doubts as an inquiry into truth. The other is one that, as it were, just doubts and doubts everything. In Hegel's terminology, the former has a "content" to its process and progress, for it "negates" in order to "determine"--it is a "determinate negation."[37] The latter sees only "pure nothingness in its result"; it is at best conscious of its nothingness, and thus has as a "content" only a "determinate nothingness." Progressive negation, on the other hand, has a "goal" (rather than "nothing") fixed for itself. But to work toward this goal, determinate negation (or philosophical consciousness, he eventually calls it) must be "something that goes beyond limits, and since these limits are its own, it is something that goes beyond itself."

Let us skip now to the back of the book. In his essay on "culture," Hegel essentially addresses the skepticism of his age (or rather, of the generation of his predecessors) and advances an argument that their "alienated consciousness," rather than proving the spiritual bankruptcy of the day, held positive or "determinate" implications. As has been noted before,[38] the background text to the chapter is Diderot's *Rameau's Nephew*. Though there now exists strong evidence that Diderot did not intend the exchange between Moi and Lui to be read as a simple morality play between virtue and vice,[39] Hegel seems to have taken this simple opposition as Diderot's own position; and Hegel thought that he was presenting an interpretation contrary to Diderot. Whereas Diderot seems, according to Hegel, to be siding with the morally consistent Moi, Hegel himself rejects Moi as an "honest soul" in favor of Lui as an "alienated self." The alienation of self is really a demand for a "still higher consciousness,"[40] which for Hegel is a constructive imperative, even if the alienated self calls for the dissolution of the "whole world of perversion." To be sure, the ability of the self to detach in consciousness from widespread conditions betrays, writes Hegel, a kind of vanity as much as it reveals a kind of integrity or independence. But the self-centered self that is vain enough to repudiate the rest of the world as being itself vain *rises above its own vanity*, for its object is the "beyond of this world."[41] The alienated self directs its gaze in a "double reflection": On the one hand, it is negative and critical, on the other, it projects beyond itself, presuming that a positive goal lies beyond its own negative judgments. Seeing the vanity of all things, it becomes serious.

Is the real difference between the two forms of skepticism, then, only a matter of *outlook*, the one pessimistic and the other (implicitly) hopeful?[42] I am not at all sure that such a question can be answered by reference to the *Phenomenology* alone. We can, however, gain a better sense of the importance of the distinction between the two forms of skepticism by examining what Hegel says regarding the aesthetics of *irony* in his later lectures.

In his introduction to his *Aesthetics* (a work pieced together posthumously), Hegel explains that he is attempting to determine the philosophical significance of art. He begins with a historical survey of post-Kantian philosophers who address aesthetic phenomena, and he quickly seizes upon the name of Friedrich von Schlegel. The Schlegel brothers, he explains, were "greedy for novelty in the search for the distinctive and extraordinary"; and though their natures were essentially "nonphilosophical" and "uncritical," the Schlegels did, Hegel concedes, appropriate and advance the "Idea" of philosophy. Hegel's basic contention is that Schlegel, like Schelling, applied Fichte's philosophy to art and eventually developed it in his own way. The importance of Fichte's philosophy for Schlegel, explains Hegel, was: (1) that the abstract *ego* is posited as the principle of all knowledge; and (2) that since everything is subordinated to the knowing ego, all "objective" matters are deemed valuable only in relation to the ego ("nothing is treated *in and for itself* as valuable in itself, but only as produced by the subjectivity of the *ego*"[43]). Finally, the third aspect of Schlegel's aesthetic Fichteanism is that the ego is an *active* individual and attempts to make its individuality real in its own eyes. To do this one attempts to form one's life artistically, but even as an artist, one must negate or belittle even one's own art works. ("In that case, I am not really in *earnest*, either with this content or, generally, with its expression and actualization."[44])

These three principles constitute the general meaning of Schlegel's irony, but the philosophy of irony, according to Hegel, develops yet further. The next form of irony negates everything "factual, moral, and of intrinsic worth," declaring the objective world to be vain and null. The *ego* may remain immune at this point from its own criticism; but eventually, Hegel suggests, the ego itself will fail to find satisfaction in self-enjoyment, "so that it now feels a craving for the solid and the substantial, for specific and essential interests."[45] But at this stage the ironic ego has painted itself into a corner. It longs for truth and objectivity, but it cannot renounce its own isolation. In this final stage of irony, the ego is attacked by yearning and is reduced to "quiescence and impotence."[46] Irony, in other words, is a self-destructive impulse, but the ego's own tragic downfall is conditioned by its own representation as null of all that "has worth and dignity for mankind." For Hegel, irony's cul-de-sac is philosophically unacceptable: "This then implies that not only is there to be no seriousness about law, morals, and truth, but that there is nothing in what is lofty and best, since, in its appearance in individuals, characters, and actions, it contradicts and destroys itself and so is ironical about itself."[47]

Yet Hegel's argument is woefully incomplete at this stage, I think, for he has not explained precisely how irony is *detrimental* to the march of philosophy. If the ironist wishes to be a "Diogenes in a tub,"[48] then what does it matter to the rest of us? Even if we consider his analysis of the aesthetics of irony as an elaboration upon the purely negative form of skepticism, Hegel still has not really explained the difference between the two modes of skepticism, the two essentially negative forms of consciousness; he has only asserted that one is serious and the other not. Both forms of consciousness detach from the conditions of immediate reality, but irony posits, according to Hegel, a nothingness beyond itself, whereas the "determinate negation" is expectantly posed toward the future.

The answer becomes clearer in a section on the "ideal" of art. Hegel at the end of the section addresses the relation of tears and laughter to art's "ideal." For the most part, art is joyful and pleasurable, and the joy promotes self-awareness. But, in music for instance, "Even in suffering, the sweet tone of lament must sound through the griefs and alleviate them, so that it seems to us worth the while so to suffer as to understand this lament. This is the sweet melody, the song in all art."[49]

Hegel explains that irony claims to have this same justification, but the problem with irony is that it ends in *"mere heartfelt longing"* instead of in acting and doing."[50] "[Irony] is a longing which will not let itself go in actual action and production, because it is frightened of being polluted by contact with finitude, although all the same it has a sense of the deficiency of this abstraction."[51] In short, irony as a mode of philosophical consciousness presents no basis for *action*, whereas Lui's longing and alienated consciousness implied an eventual resolution and thus provided him with a reason to orient himself actively and earnestly toward the future.

Why does this discussion matter? I submit that both Schlegel and Hegel were struggling with an epistemological problem inherent in political theorizing, namely, how can one claim a logical basis for being simultaneously a *critic* and a *visionary*, and then act deliberately on the basis of one's ambivalence? Both Schlegel and Hegel were attempting to postulate an "organic" basis for higher values, an organic bridge between present reality and imagined ideality, and I have proposed that art holds a special appeal or promise to those addressing this conceptual dilemma; for the sensuousness, the plasticity, the worldliness of art and artistic activity seem to reconcile the discrepancy between thought and world, subject and object, ideality and reality. As for the debate between Schlegel and Hegel, I will leave aside for now Hegel's charge of Fichteanism against Schlegel. As mentioned above, there are sufficient reasons to believe that Hegel misread Schlegel and overemphasized his Fichtean side.[52] But a "non-Fichtean" reading of Schlegel's irony, in which the plasticity of art is emphasized over the subjective stance of the creative ego, complicates the debate between Hegel and Schlegel, for if anything, a non-Fichtean Schlegel brings Schlegel's irony *closer* to Hegel's "serious" skepticism. With such modifications, the comparison of Hegel's and Schlegel's notions of irony becomes more refined and more interesting; for now we need to regard Schlegel's irony as *less* cynical and condescending than Hegel made it out to be, but we must also regard it as *more* reserved vis-à-vis the future than Hegel's determinate negation. Now comparing the two, I think it becomes clear that Hegel has a legitimate point with regard even to a modified Schlegelian irony, namely that irony *has* a tendency to detach itself, to reserve commitment, that it is a mode of consciousness that does not translate readily into "action." But that conclusion is drawn only from the comparative perspective of Hegel's progressive dialectic, and before we accept this standpoint as a final conclusion, perhaps we should shift the burden of proof back upon Hegel.

Kierkegaard and Ironic Individuality

Søren Kierkegaard provides us with a ready-made critique of Hegel from the perspective of irony. I will not go into Kierkegaard's entire argument, for it is somewhat extraneous to my main project. It should be noted, however, that Kierkegaard accepts Hegel's charge of "Fichteanism" brought against Schlegel;[53] thus his defense of irony rests upon his distinguishing Socrates' irony from post-Fichtean irony and upon his insistence that Socratic irony is the true one.[54] Granting those points, we can jump to his final, cryptic chapter, which is entitled "The Truth of Irony." "Irony," Kierkegaard says, "is like the negative way, not the truth but the way." The passage, the editor points out,[55] refers to John 14:6, a reference that Kierkegaard has mentioned earlier in the book. Christ had said, "I am the way, the truth, and the life." These words presented a tangible reality to the apostles, for Christ was immediately visible to them and could be taken at his word. But Socrates, Kierkegaard notes, was "invisible" to his age, and he was only to be misunderstood through his words.[56] In explanation of the above epigram, Kierkegaard says that the method of irony is "not the way whereby one who imagines himself to have a result comes to possess it, but the way whereby *the result forsakes him.*"[57] The reference is clearly to Hegel and Hegelianism. Hegel's assertive skepticism requires that the skeptic come to "possess" the result he imagines. Thus Hegel must assume the burden of proof: "Hence when philosophy teaches that actuality has absolute validity, it is essential that it in truth acquire validity."[58] One would presume, Kierkegaard argues, that if philosophy bears this requirement, then in one's own lifetime one could hope to see "this abundant actuality in truth become visible." But he notes, in an obvious allusion to the Hegelian outlook: "There is a different tendency in our age that exhibits an enormous enthusiasm, and curiously enough, what excites it seems to be enormously little. How beneficial irony could be here. There is an impatience that would reap before it has sown. By all means let irony chasten it."[59]

The difference between irony and Hegelianism is that irony "teaches us to actualize actuality," and it does so, according to Kierkegaard, by placing an emphasis upon the here-and-now, upon actuality. Yet this emphasis upon actuality, he adds, must not mean that one "idolizes" actuality, nor that human beings necessarily long for "a higher and more perfect." Rather, the "content of life" must be connected to, must become "a meaningful moment in," the "higher actuality" that the soul desires. Actuality then, says Kierkegaard, *acquires* its validity--not as a "purgatory"--but "as a history wherein consciousness successively outlives itself." Romantic tendencies may prompt us toward something higher, "but man shall not put asunder what God has put together, so neither shall man join together what God has put asunder." In short, Kierkegaard contends that "actuality acquires its validity through action." But the action, he adds, "must not degenerate into a kind of stupid perseverance, but must have an apriority in itself so as not to become lost in a vacuous infinity."[60]

Thus Kierkegaard contends that it is irony (properly understood) and *not* Hegelianism (as determinate negation) that truly contains an imperative and inner drive toward self-validating and progressive action. Kierkegaard makes this case by shifting the burden of proof back upon Hegel, implying that Hegel's "determinate negation" does not represent a mode of consciousness viably posed for action, for it simply does not produce the goal that it imagines for itself. Hegelianism, as a mode of action, thus becomes either "stupid perseverance" or else perpetual deferral, an unending carrot-and-stick enterprise. The ironist, in contrast, can approach the truth by admitting that the truth forsakes him, and yet this admission does not require that he know the truth fully in advance or that he repudiate the validity of the present. Further, it "rescues us from the prolixity which holds that to give an account of world history, for example, would require as much time as the world has taken to live through it."[61] Irony, for Kierkegaard, bridges conceptually the present and future in such a way that it promotes positive action.

Kierkegaard does not prove that the ironist will necessarily take action or that the action will be taken responsibly. For his purposes, it is sufficient to make room for irony for the "authentic individual," and he leaves it at that. Irony itself is not the truth, but the way. Yet Kierkegaard does state a strong case that action oriented toward the future cannot be based wholly upon positive criteria, and thus he reveals a confusion in Hegelianism in its attempt to extract a "determinateness" out of a negation. Action does not always admit of identifiable goals. But we must ask the question: Kierkegaard has made a strong case for irony as regards the authentic individual, but can entire communities really be formed on the basis of truly negative, i.e., ironic, propositions?[62]

Marx and Ironic Deviations

It may be stretching matters to say that Karl Marx was struggling precisely with the problem of ironic communities, but a case could be made that the relation of irony to intersubjective action was of central concern to Marx. Marx, it is known, was well acquainted with the nineteenth-century movement now sometimes known as "Romantic irony." In fact, "well acquainted" is too weak a description; Marx was immersed in or at least surrounded by the ironic movement of his day. Marx's early confrontation with Hegel is legendary, but the Schlegel-Hegel nexus in that saga has not been well remembered. Among some of his other odd accomplishments, Friedrich Schlegel was Hegel's first instructor of transcendental philosophy, the latter having attended Schlegel's lectures at the University of Jena in 1800. Hegel's development of the dialectic begins with a discussion of irony, though Hegel thereafter seized almost every opportunity he could to vilify the Schlegels and their irony.[63] Hegel eventually contended, for one thing, that irony was destructive of the spirit necessary for the formation of the political state.[64]

Marx, the university student, took two of his ten courses at Bonn from A.W. Schlegel, and Schlegel sat on the committee that read

Marx's dissertation.[65] The foreword to that dissertation begins with a discussion of Socratic irony, and Marx mentions in passing Friedrich Schlegel and his doctrine of irony. Seldom, however, has this foreword been discussed in secondary literature,[66] perhaps because it was dropped in the English translation and published only separately, as part of Marx's doctoral notebooks.[67] Althusser and others have dismissed Marx's dissertation as hasty and schoolboyish,[68] but here it is that Marx novelly addresses the problems of theorizing after Hegel. That discussion comes in the foreword to the dissertation, in the seemingly obscure analysis of irony. I suggest that we examine carefully the foreword--as well as the relationship between the foreword and the dissertation itself--for together they reveal the extent to which Marx understands himself to be an *ironic* post-Hegelian theorist. This story about Marx, as far as I know, has not yet been told.

Margaret Rose almost tells it, in her book *Reading the Young Marx and Engels.*[69] Her mistake, I think, is to focus on *parody* instead of *irony* (more on this distinction later); but her story about parody in Marx's writings is very instructive, and I'd like to review it as a point of departure for my claim about irony.

Rose follows Althusser in his project of periodization, similarly attempting to distinguish "early" from "late" Marx and to mark the date of Marx's basic self-reversal. Rose identifies Marx's crucial break by monitoring his apparent attitude toward parody, which he deployed as a method of counterargument against the "young Hegelians" of his day. The young Hegelians themselves parodied their opponents, mainly, contends Rose, out of a need to smuggle such leftist sentiments past the Prussian censors of the 1830s and 1840s. Their "esoteric" readings of Hegel attracted Marx for a time, but eventually Marx realized that he must break from Hegel altogether, even "leftist" Hegelianism (and once the practice of censorship was lifted, Rose surmises, Marx saw little reason to continue such a restricted form of debate).

Rose notices a change in Marx's attitude toward parody, beginning with *The German Ideology*. There Marx parodies the young Hegelians' use of parody, but the direction of Marx's parody is now to attack, for instance, Bruno Bauer's *overuse* of parody. Parody, Marx now thinks, according to Rose, is not only elitist but is also symptomatic of the whole problem of Hegelianism: the young Hegelians are nothing more than "phrase-fighters" themselves, just like those pious Hegelians whom they criticize; and hence their parodic criticism never really quits the realm of speculative philosophy. Rose discovers moments in *The German Ideology* in which Marx abandons parody and "speaks directly,"[70] using "more effective"[71] language instead. At these junctures, according to Rose, Marx is on the verge of breaking with idealism in favor of "the science of historical materialism"; and thereafter, increasingly, he employs "facts and figures" instead of metaphors, symbols, and parodies. By 1852, Rose concludes, the exiled Marx has fully rejected parodic techniques in favor of scientific methods of criticism.

Rose's analysis of Marx's bout with Hegelianism is astute, for she realizes that *Marx* realizes that breaking with Hegel, and "young Hegelianism" in particular, is no easy matter: "The dilemma facing Marx, of how to use parody to break from a past which included the use of parody [was] the central stylistic and epistemological problem facing Marx in *The German Ideology*."[72] But she doesn't go far enough, and her treatment of Marx's "solution" is too neat.[73] She mentions that Marx's introduction to *The German Ideology* includes the comment that language is "inseparably linked to the material life of society and the labour process of men";[74] and she rightly explains that Marx criticises Bauer and others for fighting only against *ideas*, and thus for reducing their battles to mere words and phrases, even though these young Hegelians believe that they are advancing the spirit of Hegel through their negations of the master. "Not criticism but revolution is the driving force of history," Marx responds and Rose repeats. Rose finds a frankness and a corresponding lack of parody in Marx's criticisms of these "critical critics." But does speaking "clearly" and "directly" (even in espousal of "materialism"[75]) settle matters? Surely Marx must realize that he is himself engaging in "criticism," not revolution, as he writes those charges. Surely Marx must realize that he is himself using but words, phrases, and ideas to attack the words, phrases, and ideas of the young Hegelians. Surely Marx must understand the complications involved in his attacking the language and philosophy of a group of critics on the grounds that they limit their criticism to the realm of language and philosophy, *though they presume otherwise*. So, too, must Marx realize, if we pause to think about it, that when he writes, "Philosophers have only interpreted the world, in various ways; the point, however, is to change it," he is following Feuerbach's *very own* philosophical method of debunking philosophers. Marx must know that the eleventh thesis is (on the face of it) yet another example of the tendency of German philosophers to heap criticism upon criticism.

Parody is not the issue here. Nor is science. Irony is.

I propose that Marx's dissertation cannot be fully understood without its original foreword, and that the discussion of *irony* is crucial for indicating Marx's ulterior purposes in the main work. This joint reading of the foreword and the dissertation will show, I believe, that Marx's treatment of the problem of philosophizing after Hegel was much more "mature," more complex, than commentators have hitherto realized. The "Hegel-question" that Margaret Rose finds resolved for the first time in *The German Ideology* had already been anticipated and answered in the dissertation. Marx at this time is not just another "young Hegelian," who pays homage to Hegel by rhetorically attacking him. Furthermore, I want to suggest that only by recognizing Marx's awareness of the "irony" of his writings can we finally make sense of his subsequent "Feuerbachian" phase and his subsequent critique of Feuerbach. Finally, if this rereading of Marx's ironic period alters our understanding of Marx's early relation to Hegelianism, then perhaps we shall need to reconsider the conventional view of the "later" Marx as well. Did he remain an "ironist"? Let us first examine those student writings of Marx.

Part 1: The Foreword

Marx begins the foreword to the dissertation with the comment that at certain "nodal points" in history, philosophy apprehends abstract principles in a totality, but he adds that at other moments, "philosophy turns its eyes to the external world, and no longer apprehends it, but, as a practical person, weaves, as it were, intrigues with the world, emerges from the transparent kingdom of Amenthes and throws itself on the breast of the worldly Siren."[76] Philosophy is then a carnival, and it is essential in these latter moments that philosophy should "wear character masks."

Marx takes up the question of how it is at all possible to philosophize after Hegel's "total triumph." Times following total philosophical triumphs are "unhappy and iron epochs, for their gods have died and the new goddess still reveals the dark aspect of fate, of pure light or of pure darkness. She still lacks the colours of day."[77] But Marx advises that all is not lost, even though what is unfortunate in such times is that it is impossible "to recognize any reality" that is not just an extension of the present. Fortunately, however, "subjective consciousness," the subjective form of philosophy, can break with reality. And only from a later philosophical vantage point, as Hegel suggests, can we understand the *curriculum vitae* of these subjective beginnings.

Next Marx labors to "define the subjective form of Platonic philosophy." To do this he compares the respective starting points of Socrates and Christ. Marx denies that there is any easy analogy between Socrates and Christ, because they are as different, he says, as are philosophy and religion. He adds that the contradiction is even greater between Christ's grace and Socrates' form of midwifery, namely *irony*: "Socratic irony . . . namely as the dialectic trap through which human common sense is precipitated out of its motley ossification, not into self-complacent knowing-better, *but into the truth immanent in human common sense itself*, this irony is nothing but the form of philosophy in its subjective attitude to common consciousness."[78]

But irony has an "objective content," Marx claims, for "Heraclitus, who also not only despised, but hated human common sense, is just as much an ironist [as Socrates], so is even Thales, who taught that everything is water, though every Greek knew that no one could live on water, so is Fichte, with his world-creating *ego*, despite which even Nicolai realised that he could not create any world, and so is any philosopher *who asserts immanence in opposition to the empirical person*."[79] Irony has an "objective content" in its ability to abstract from existing reality and empirical conditions. Religious grace differs from irony, Marx explains, because it depends entirely upon "empirical persons."

Marx turns the discussion in a different direction to stress an unexpected point. If Socrates and Christ are analogous characters, it is because they personify, respectively, philosophy and religion. But that *analogy* is as vacuous, he contends, as the analogous *division* between their historical personalities and their philosophies or religions. Marx cites as an example the supposed division between Socrates' brainchild--the *Republic*--and the general idea of the *Republic* that has since been promoted. Marx plays with what today might be called "structural" comparisons and contrasts. If Hegel is correct in distinguishing between *Plato* and *Socrates*, contending that the former asserted a positive version of "Greek subjectivity" against the latter's "corrupting principle of subjectivity," then Plato is "diametrically" opposed to Christ, he says, for Christ asserted subjectivity against the existing state, whereas Plato did the reverse. Furthermore, *this* is the real difference between Plato and Christ, *not* the fact that Plato's *Republic* remained historically an ideal while the Christian church achieved worldly reality. Thus, according to Marx, it is more correct to say that there are Platonic elements in Christianity, rather than Christian elements in Plato. In short, Christianity is more *political* than Platonism is *eschatological*.

Thus Marx discounts the view that Platonic philosophy is *religious*. This is not to overlook, he says, the fact that Plato's teaching may bear certain *marks* of religion, or that it achieved a cultist, pseudoreligious quality. Marx compares this aspect of Platonism to the philosophies of other philosophers, namely Aristotle, Spinoza, and Hegel. The latters' theories take on a more general form, are "less steeped in empirical feeling," are "moreover, more beneficial to a mind with more general education," and therefore "the inspiration of Plato culminates in ecstasy while that of the others burns on as the pure ideal of science; that is why the former was only a hot-water bottle for individual minds, while the latter is the *animating spirit of world-historical developments*."[80]

Thus Platonic philosophy resembles religion because it assumes a "subjective form," but this fact should be no reason, according to Marx, for mistaking it for religion. Furthermore, Marx adds that "Plato's pronouncements on the salvation of the soul, etc. prove nothing at all," for these were only the philosopher's attempt to "free the soul from its empirical limitation" and again should not be mistaken for religion. The real question is, says Marx, why Plato desired to "provide a positive, above all mythical, basis for what is cognized by philosophy." He adds that such a desire is astonishing, because it means that Plato could not find an "objective force" in his system itself, in the "external power of the Idea."

The initial answer, claims Marx, can be found in *irony*, the "subjective form of the Platonic system." Plato turns to mythologizing because "what is the pronouncement of an individual and is asserted as such *in opposition to opinions or individuals needs some support through which the subjective certainty becomes objective truth*."[81] A further question, says Marx, is why Plato mythologizes only in those dialogues which expound moral and religious truths (whereas the "purely metaphysical" *Parmenides* is free from mythologizing). Why, in other words, is the "positive" basis for morals a mythical one?

Marx's answer is that a negative expression of the "Absolute" as regards questions of morals and so forth is not sufficient: "Where the Absolute stands on one side, and limited positive reality on the other, and the positive must all the same be preserved, there this positive becomes the medium through which absolute light shines, the absolute light breaks up into a fabulous play of colours, and the finite, the positive, points to something other than itself, has in it a soul, to which this husk is an object of wonder; *the whole world has become a world of myths*."[82]

Plato employs myths and allegories, concludes Marx, as a positive expression of the Absolute, in order to present a philosophy of transcendence, though a transcendence "which at the same time has an essential relation to immanence."[83] Plato's positive expression does not negate Socrates' negative teachings--they are connected in a "dialectic," which is "the inner, simple light, the piercing eye of love, the inner soul which is not crushed by the body of material division, the inner abode of the spirit."[84]

Part 2: The Dissertation

We must bear in mind that this foreword is to serve as the introduction to Marx's dissertation, "On the Difference Between the Democritean and Epicurean Philosophy of Nature." Let us turn briefly to the subject of the dissertation so that we might consider the relationship between the foreword and the body of the dissertation. The dissertation itself is a fascinating piece of writing, which needs to be read, I propose, as a sustained allegory. Ostensibly it is about natural physics, but Marx eventually reveals that his true subject is not simply physical science but rather pertains directly to human affairs.

Traditional scholarship has it, Marx begins, that Epicurean physics was more or less a direct extension of Democritean atomism. After reviewing several accounts that accuse Epicurus of imitating and even plagiarizing Democritus, Marx observes that as theorists, Epicurus and Democritus stood diametrically opposed "in all that concerns truth, certainty, application of this science, and all that refers to the relationship between thought and reality in general."[85] Democritus was a skeptic; Epicurus was an avowed dogmatist. Democritus was an empiricist, who, dissatisfied with philosophy, traveled in search of knowledge. Epicurus had "nothing but contempt for the positive sciences," was "blissful in philosophy," and left "his garden in Athens scarcely two or three times." These separate tendencies in the two men reflected differences, Marx contends, in "practical energy" and "theoretical consciousness."[86] Democritus used *necessity* as a form of reflection of reality, whereas Epicurus thought that *chance*, not necessity, was the way of the world.[87] Yet this difference corresponded to a difference in the way individual physical phenomena were to be explained. *Necessity* appears in finite nature as *relative* necessity, hence as determinism;[88] and thus Democritus was concerned only with "real possibilities." *Chance*, however, suggests that reality is *only* possibility, but the possibility is now "abstract" rather than "real." "Real possibility seeks to explain the necessity and reality of its object; abstract possibility is not interested in the object which is explained, but in the subject which does the explaining. The object need only be possible, conceivable."[89] Marx contends, then, that Epicurus proceeded with "boundless nonchalance" and unfettered imagination in explaining physical phenomena, whereas Democritus restricted his focus to the confines drawn by the "intellect."

The task then, according to Marx, is to comprehend why Epicureanism has appeared to scholars to be consistent with Democritean physics, when actually these theories stood diametrically opposed. Marx wishes to account, in other words, for the *relation*, as well as *difference*, between Democriteanism and Epicureanism.

Marx proceeds to examine in detail the difference between Democritus' and Epicurus' explanations of physical phenomena. Democritus and Epicurus both agree on two principles of the motion of atoms: falling in a straight line, and repulsion. But Epicurus endorses an additional third principle, namely the "deviation of the atom from the straight line." Marx examines Cicero's and Bayle's reflections upon Epicurus' "declination" principle and finds contradictions in the logic of these two commentators. Epicurus invokes the idea of deviation or declination from a straight line in order to explain why atoms *meet*. According to Epicurus, atoms make a very tiny swerve from their straight, downward paths of motion. From this swerve arises all the complex combinations and adhesions of the atoms with one another. But Cicero faults Epicurus for not explaining the *cause* of the swerve. Cicero contends that Epicurus invoked the idea of declination in order to allow the atom to escape from complete determinism and thus to account for *repulsion*. Bayle contends that Epicurus invoked declination to account for the *freedom* of atoms. Marx contends that neither of these reviews does justice to Epicurean physics:

> Epicurus is supposed to have assumed a declination of the atom in order to explain the repulsion on one occasion, and on another freedom. But if atoms do *not* meet without declination, then declination as an explanation of freedom is superfluous; for the opposite of freedom begins, as we see in *Lucretius*, only with the deterministic and forced meeting of atoms. But if the atoms meet *without* declination, then this is superfluous for explaining repulsion.[90]

Marx then turns to consider "the declination itself." I suggest that this section is crucial for understanding Marx's early relation to Hegel and Hegelianism. When an atom is falling in a straight line, the atom's "specific quality" as an individual atom does not matter, says Marx; the atom's individual existence is subordinate to the line's composition. But when the atom swerves, it distinguishes itself from the line. The line no longer "determines" the form of existence for the individual atom, and now the atom can be considered to exist separate from the line. Hence it can be said that the swerving "negates" the line, for the swerving motion has nullified the downward motion. Epicurus was reproached, says Marx, for not assigning a "cause" to the swerving effect; instead, Epicurus contended that the motion of declination was self-initiated, that, in Marx's words, "something in its breast" makes the atom "fight back and resist." Cicero objected to this explanation, however, contending that Epicurus ascribed two contradictory motions to the individual atom, that of downward fall and of oblique declination. Marx replies that Epicurus was well aware of this contradiction and thus endeavored to represent the declination as "being as *imperceptible* as possible *to the senses*."[91]   Bayle wanted Epicurus to attribute an independent spirituality to the atom, but Marx defends Epicurus by asserting that declination represents the "real soul" of the atom, even though "the concept of abstract individuality"[92] remains attached to the existence of the line as a whole.

Marx elaborates on this last point. The atom achieves its "abstract individuality," its existence as an atom, only by abstracting from the straight line.   The concepts of "self-sufficiency" and "abstract individuality," Marx contends, are pure abstractions from "immediate being": "As a matter of fact, abstract individuality can make its concept, its form-determination, the pure being-for-itself, the independence from immediate being, the negation of all relativity, effective only by *abstracting from the being that confronts it*; for in order truly to overcome it, abstract individuality had to idealise it, a thing only generality can accomplish."[93]

The consequence of the declination of the atom, according to Marx, is that, on the one hand, the concept of the atom is a negative one, a relation to something else; yet on the other hand, this negation must be "positively established."   Marx contends that the concept of the individually swerving atom can be positively established "only if the being to which it relates itself is none other than itself, hence equally an atom, and since it itself is directly determined, many atoms."[94] And the way to express positively the idea of self-same swerving atoms, Marx reasons, is precisely through the principle of repulsion.

Thus Marx accounts for the relation, as well as difference, between Democritus and Epicurus. Epicurus was interested in chance, in possibilities, in the individual atom, in swerving; but to account for the swerve--a negative and relative notion--he ultimately had to express it in positive terms.   Hence he endorsed the principle of material repulsion as the positive consequence of declination from a straight line. Thus Epicurean physics *looks* like Democritean atomism, but the former includes a crucial intermediary step. "*Democritus*, in contrast to Epicurus, transforms into an enforced motion, into an act of blind necessity, that which to Epicurus is the realisation of the concept of the atom."[95] Democritus, writes Marx, "considers the vortex resulting from the repulsion and collision of the atoms to be the substance of necessity. He therefore sees in the repulsion only the material side, the fragmentation, the change, and not the ideal side, according to which all relation to something else is negated and the motion is established as self-determination."[96]

Epicurus may *look* like a materialist and a determinist, but "the declination of the atom thus changed the whole inner structure of the domain of the atoms. . . . Epicurus was therefore the first to grasp the essence of the repulsion--even if only in sensuous form, whereas Democritus only knew of its material existence."[97] *Repulsion*, then, is the "positive" or "material" expression of the identity and relation of individually swerving atoms among one another. Marx inserts the following paragraph at the end of the section on declination: "Hence we find also more concrete forms of the repulsion applied by Epicurus. In the political domain here is the *covenant*, in the social domain *friendship*, which is praised as the highest good."[98]

The externalized, material form of the atom always belies its inner essence, as a freely deviating abstract individual. In the remainder of the dissertation, Marx shows how steadfastly Epicurus adheres to the absolute freedom of the atom, even when his atomic theories directly contradict prevailing theories of astronomy. Epicurus is willing, in effect, to adjust the theories of the heavens in order to accommodate his deviating atom.[99]

Analysis

We now must repeat the question: What relation does the foreword to the dissertation bear to the dissertation itself? Why, in other words, does Marx's talk in the foreword about irony, about Hegel's "total triumph," and about the relation of Plato to Socrates hold significance with respect to the "difference" between Democritus and Epicurus? Why, we might inquire more pointedly, does *Plato* figure so prominently in a discussion about post-Aristotelean physics?

Irony, Marx says in the foreword, is the "subjective" and "practical" form of philosophy, a mode of consciousness that can break with existing reality, that can recognize realities that are not just extensions of the present. Clearly Marx is drawing here an analogy between Socrates' irony and Epicurus' swerving atom. But Marx's point in the foreword is more about *Plato* than Socrates. Plato did *not* betray Socrates' irony, Marx contends, even though Plato cloaked his philosophy in myths and religious symbols. Platonic philosophy, then, is analogous to the "consequence" of the declination of the atom, namely that "subjective" and apparently "negative" concepts seem to require "objective" or "positive" expression. But Marx stresses a similar point in both the foreword and the dissertation: Platonic philosophy is *not* the same as religion, and Epicureanism is *not* the same as Democritean determinism.

The most important analogy that Marx implicitly draws between the foreword and the dissertation, however, is between himself and Epicurus, which parallels an analogy drawn between Hegel and Democritus. The foreword begins with the question of how it is at all possible to philosophize after Hegel's total triumph, how, as it were, one can "swerve" from Hegelianism. Traditionally, scholars have interpreted the young Marx as still enraptured at this time with Hegel and Hegelianism, and they have read Marx's dissertation as an attempt "to fill in lacunae in Hegel's system,"[100] or else to find a way to put Hegelianism into practice (as a benign resolution to his schoolboy Oedipalism). I suggest, however, that a careful reading of the foreword along with the dissertation reveals that Marx is thoroughly distancing himself from Hegel while at the same time he is informing us that his alternative stance will nonetheless *resemble* Hegelianism in outward form: a double stance, which cannot be reduced to the epigonal anxiety of the typical young Hegelian.

Some of the Hegelians "understand our master wrongly," Marx writes (with obvious sarcasm), for they think that "mediocrity" is the normal manifestation of the absolute spirit.[101] They recommend that we simply wait for Hegel's philosophy to realize itself. The consciousness of such persons, Marx adds, is "sated in itself," and "is not allowed to recognize any reality which has come to being without it."[102] The "fortunate thing" in such unfortunate times is the "subjective form" of philosophy, e.g., Socrates' irony and Epicureanism.[103] Yet while Marx defends Plato from those who accuse him of being a religious zealot, and while he labors to prove the *difference* between Epicurus and Democritus, the force of his narrative leads in still another direction. In particular, Marx wishes to show why, in the wake of totalizing philosophies, it is necessary for the subjective form of philosophy to wear "disguises" and "character masks";[104] why Plato employs myths and Epicurus endorses the principle of repulsion; and why, by extention, Marx will *apparently* embrace Hegelianism. He advises that "one must not let oneself be misled by this storm which follows a great philosophy, a world philosophy." But he adds, "Ordinary harps play under any fingers, Aeolian harps only when struck by the storm."[105]

In other words, in order to philosophize after Hegel, in order to "live at all after a total philosophy,"[106] Marx is saying that we need "ironists," or those who are able to break with totalizing views of reality, and then can act on their own, like the self-initiating motion of Epicurus' swerving atom. But because Hegel's triumph is so encompassing, according to Marx, post-Hegelian ironists will need to couch their subjective philosophies in Hegelian terminology, nonetheless. "What formerly appeared as growth is now determination, what was negativity existing in itself has now become negation."[107] Parroting Hegel, though with an irony so subtle that it remains virtually undetectable, may be the only effective way of breaking Hegel's *spiritual* hold on his followers: the "cry" of Epicurus, Marx remarks in a passage that would seem to be directed against the "atheistic" young Hegelians, is "not the man who denies the gods worshipped by the multitude, but he who affirms of the gods what the multitude believes about them, is truly impious."[108]

I find this entire section extremely startling, and a little eerie. The issue of the dissertation is so clearly, even if tacitly posed, that it is almost as if Marx is announcing in advance that we are not to read his subsequent writings entirely literally. It is almost as if Marx is anticipating, and denying in advance, the contemporary distinction between the "early Marx" and the "late Marx," between the young idealist-humanist and the mature scientist-dialectician. It is almost as if Marx is informing us from the outset of his career that his subsequent works will assume an "objective" form of expression, that his philosophy will *resemble* Platonic myth, Christian eschatology, Hegelian determinism, Democritean materialism, and Epicurean "repulsion." But the point of disclosing the *difference* between Democritus and Epicurus is that Marx's real concern is with "practical" matters--how philosophy achieves its "transubstantiation into flesh and blood,"[109] how post-Hegelian individuals may truly *break* with their master and take deviating action, how atoms swerve of their own accord (and Marx remarked in a letter many years later that his early interest in Epicurus was "political" rather than "philosophical").[110] Marxism will only *resemble* Hegelianism, and there will be as much difference between Marx and Hegel as there was between Epicurus and Democritus. Epicurus (even more than Prometheus[111]) is apparently Marx's early hero, but this means that the young Marx was centrally and self-consciously concerned with the intricately problematic relationship between "idealism" and "materialism" as it pertains to theorists who hope to instigate worldly change that is altogether new.

What are we to make of all of this? I should think that Marx's flirtation with irony would make the young Marx a much more interesting writer and thinker than we might otherwise suppose. Commentators such as Leonard Wessell, Jr., reject Marxism because of these early "mythopoetic" yearnings, but a careful reading of the dissertation shows that Marx was *deliberately* engaging in and consciously in control of his own mythproduction. He was attempting to transform his "subjective philosophy," his ironic sensibilities, into a principle of action, and he in effect announces that his action-oriented theorizing will necessarily resemble aspects of Platonism, Democriteanism, and Hegelianism.

No one, I should think, who reads the dissertation together with the foreword can blithely accuse the young Marx of "determinism," of being in any way programmatically "Hegelian." Marx's fascination with atoms that swerve of their own accord runs throughout the dissertation and throughout his doctoral notebooks. Yet the fascination with self-swerving atoms is always connected to the question of how self-swerving atoms meet, relate, and configure with one another, without, as Cicero suggests, giving them "definite assignments beforehand."[112] The young Marx, upon my reading, is neither a burning "idealist" nor a budding "materialist"; rather he is interested--and very self-consciously--in both theoretical outlooks, in how human beings think and act on their own as individuals, and in how they relate fundamentally to each other as human beings. Hegel, too, was interested in closing the gap between "idealism" and "materialism"-- and precisely for this reason the leftist Hegelians were attracted to his "philosophy"--but Hegel's total theoretical triumph was won at the expense of inhibiting possibly self-activating individuals; and Marx in the dissertation promotes irony as a form of philosophy that represents a key moment of individual deviation away from Hegel. Moreover, the deviating individual is quite aware of his apparent contradictions in theory[113]--which would seem to suggest that Marx already in his dissertation has distanced himself inwardly from the young Hegelians who piously criticize a pious rendering of Hegel, who religiously promote the seemingly irreligious stance of Hegelianism. (Engels, by the way, confirmed this early break with Hegel, contending that Marx in the dissertation "showed complete independence of Hegel."[114])

Hence, the dissertation suggests that an ironic sensibility lurks under the cover of Marx's own Hegelianism, even though the dissertation also attests to the limitations of an ironic outlook. That Marx gave such importance to irony in the foreword to his dissertation should make us suspicious about the rest of his writings; and we cannot immediately dismiss his irony as a youthful indulgence, if only because Marx announces the importance of irony so assuredly: "Any philosopher who asserts immanence in opposition to the empirical person" is an ironist, he declares.[115] Was Marx being "ironic," then, when he later advocated hand-to-hand combat, when he wrote of a revolutionary proletariat, when he envisioned a communist state? And if not, why did Marx's irony get dropped by the wayside?

Before we jump to any conclusions, a caveat on the risks of reading irony is in order. If Marx is indeed being "ironic" in his writings after the dissertation, we cannot expect to find firm textual "proof" of the presence of this irony. Irony is always cryptic, and at best we might be able to produce telltale, roundabout evidence. But compounding the problem of discovering Marx's "ironic" outlook is that Marx would be, according to his dissertation, an ironist *on the sly*, a writer who *conceals* his ironic view of things. Is all hope lost of pinning Marx down?

I suggest that we can discern Marx's "irony" by indirection, by disclosing its deep presence through elimination, by smoking it out of hiding: For *unless* we attribute a buried form of irony to Marx's language, we cannot make complete sense of his "early" writings. Or to put it more positively: Only by crediting Marx with an ironic, self-critical, partially detached, performative understanding of the function of his own language can we provide an answer to the questions left over from Rose's analysis of *The German Ideology*. This latter work begs several questions, all of which revolve around the problem of *self-reference*, of Marx's theoretical relation to his own works: If ideas reflect the dominant material relationships and reflect the interests of the ruling class;[116] if change comes about as a result of certain developments of productive forces;[117] if liberation is a historical, not a mental act;[118] if communism is not an "ideal" to which reality must adjust but is actually the "real" movement now operative;[119] why, oh why, then, is Marx writing at all? Similarly, if the historical process Marx describes in *The Communist Manifesto* leads so certainly, so inevitably, to communist overthrow, if the bourgeoisie have sown the seeds of their own destruction, then why is Marx, as a theorist, exhorting the workers onward? What is the status of Marx's writing in relation to that hard history? Why is he writing?

Conceivably one could answer that Marx is claiming epistemo-logical exemption for himself (after all, he is not really a member of the working class); or that Marx is being a hypocrite; or that he is simply ignoring or missing the problems of self-reference. But these answers are facile, for surely we have a preponderance of evidence suggesting that Marx is a theorist who thinks about the relationship between a theorist and his theory (e.g., Democritus was a skeptic, Epicurus was an avowed dogmatist). The dissertation suggests a more interesting answer, one that would settle the apparent problems of self-reference: namely, that Marx was *deliberately* overstating his case in using language that made his historical scheme *seem* inevitable, language that went beyond wishfulness or exhortation to the point that it sounds predictive. Marx knowingly used such language, one might infer further, because he had concluded that the general lot of persons need to see themselves as part of a larger, objectified historical whole before they will commit themselves to truly novel forms of action--but the point for us is that Marx, the crypto-ironist, would be well aware that his historical scheme is but a ploy.

Attributing an element, a continuous thread, of irony to Marx's self-understanding of his status as a post-Hegelian theorist would also dispel some of the textual inconsistencies perceived by commentators such as Alvin Gouldner and Marshall Berman. Gouldner notices "dissonances," "anomalies," and "internal contradictions" throughout Marx's writings. He accounts for these apparent disparities by claiming that a fundamental tension, between voluntarism and determinism, permeates Marx's project. In fact, there are really "two" Marxes, according to Gouldner: the moral critic, and the scientist. Gouldner notes, for instance, that the eleventh thesis betrays this fundamental tension, for Marx dismisses idealism and yet idealistically calls for change.[120] Marshall Berman attests to a similarly contradictory attitude displayed in *The Communist Manifesto*, wherein Marx reveals his dual concern with "solid" matters on the one hand, and the emphemeral, fragile side to human affairs on the other hand. Both of these readings require that Marx be incapable of ironic self-reference: With Gouldner we are left with a schizophrenic Marx, and with Berman we are left with a Marx who is the unwitting victim of his own irony.

Dominick LaCapra takes note of Marx's textual "ambivalence," but he is one commentator who suspects that Marx is being, in some sense, deeply ironic. In fact, he detects a strain of irony as late as the writing of *Capital*:

> But if one moves to *Capital*--the *locus classicus* of the "mature" Marx for many commentators, even for those who would reinterpret it in the context of the *Grundrisse*--one has what is probably the most crying case of a canonical text in need of rereading rather than straightforward, literal reading geared to a putatively unitary authorial voice. Here the readings of both Althusser and his opponents may have been more dogmatic than Marx's writing. The issue that should, I think, guide a rereading is that of "double voicing" in the argument of *Capital*. Of the utmost pertinence would be a set of related questions circulating around Marx's indecision--at times calculated and at times seemingly blind--between a "positivistic" assertion of theses and a critical problematization of them. Among these questions would be the following: To what extent is Marx putting forth certain propositions in his own voice (for example a labor theory of value) and to what extent does he furnish an ironic deconstruction of

the system of classical economics and the capitalist practice it subtended (including the assumption of a labor theory of value)? Does Marx himself simply have a labor theory of value or is it part and parcel of the system he is criticizing?[121]

Though he sees evidence of an "ironic countervoice"[122] in sections of *Capital*, LaCapra contends that Marx's tactic of "double voicing" is most noticeable in *The Eighteenth Brumaire*. In that work Marx contrasts his own project with those of writers who were the ironic victims of their own texts.[123] Why is that disclaimer important? Marx in *The Eighteenth Brumaire* finds himself, ironically, in a historical position similar to one once occupied by Hegel: that of a theorist trying to explain why a revolution has failed to live up to its theoretical promise. LaCapra suggests that Marx's ambivalent rhetoric here cannot be identified with "false consciousness,"[124] for Marx's "carnivalesque" language would seem to imply that his use of language throughout has been "performative" rather than "representational," a deliberate ploy intended to affect the course of events, not merely depict and predict them.

Generally *The Eighteenth Brumaire* has been read as Marx's attempt to substitute his own "materialist" view of history for Hegel's mystified dialectic, but the matter cannot be so simple. On the one hand Marx seems to be furthering Hegel's project by pointing out an omission ("[Hegel] forgot to add: the first time as tragedy, the second time as farce."[125]); yet Marx's mockingly indifferent attitude toward his authority ("Hegel remarks somewhere...") would seem in effect to undermine the authority of his own text. The main point of *The Eighteenth Brumaire* is to raise the issue of historical innovation, and Marx's ironic alignment with Hegel's outdated theory would seem to invite the question of how far, or in what sense, Marx wants us to accept his own new scheme of things.[126] Could the Marx who tells us in his dissertation not to take Plato's eschatology literally be telling us something similar about his own writing at the outset of *The Eighteenth Brumaire*?

I realize that any attempt to read irony into Marx's later writings will meet with resistance, for most commentators perceive some kind of hardening of Marx's heart after 1848. If he ever was an "ironist," it might be said, then he appears to have gotten carried away with his own language. Any theorist who demands that absolutely "no concessions" be made in theory has probably lost touch with his erstwhile irony.[127]

But if Marx indeed abandoned his underlying ironic sensibility in his later years, the dissertation foreshadows that development.

Marx's explanation of why irony is so difficult to sustain is telling. The irony that inspired Platonism, he writes in the foreword to his dissertation, is only "a hot-water bottle for individual minds" while "the pure ideal of science" is the "animating spirit of world-historical developments."[128] Irony lacks an "objective force in the system itself" and thus looks for external support. Just as the "abstract individuality" of the atom is achieved only in negative relation to the line, so does "the pronouncement of an individual [which] is asserted as such in opposition to opinions or individuals need some support through which the subjective certainty becomes objective truth."[129] What I think Marx is saying is that it is difficult to garner widespread support for action, to justify action, on the basis of what seem to be negative ideals. The problem is especially acute in the aftermath of totalizing philosophies, for then any deviation from the norm will seem *purely* negative. Irony, the "subjective form of philosophy," represents the ability of individuals to deviate, to abstract from normal conditions; but while that deviation may itself contain an "objective content," may in other words represent an intrinsic freedom for the individual, it will be difficult to promote action upon such abstract possibilities. Epicurus' solution was to make the principle of declination, of self-initiated motion, into an "objective principle" that extended to all atoms, namely the principle of repulsion. Similarly, Marx will make "repulsion" the "material principle" in human affairs; a Hegelian "myth" will become the "positive basis for morals."

Marx thus points to a problem in irony: Irony represents "subjective philosophy," the intellectual expression of freedom, but irony does not lend itself readily to collective action, to, as it were, the swerving of *many* atoms on their own. Irony needs the support of myth, some expression as an "objective" or "material" force, in order to become "the animating spirit of world-historical movements." The lesson from Marx's dissertation seems to be: Individuals are more likely to swerve, to meet, and thus to form new configurations, if you tell them that they are driven by outside forces, by a principle of repulsion, rather than if you tell them that they can initiate action by themselves, can swerve of their own accord.

Still, we do know that Marx continued to pay homage to Epicurus throughout his lifetime. In *The German Ideology*, Marx calls Epicurus "the true radical Enlightener of antiquity," and Marx contends that "the idea that the state rests on the mutual agreement of people, on a *contrat social*, is found for the first time in Epicurus."[130] Even in several places in *Capital*, Marx refers to "the gods of Epicurus," who live freely in "the space between worlds,"[131] evidently defying the laws of those worlds. And the best bit of evidence for uncovering the continued importance of the dissertation is to be found in a series of letters Marx wrote to Ferdinand Lassalle in 1857-1858. Lassalle had sent Marx a book on Heraclitus, which received Marx's strong approval. Marx, it should be remembered, had referred to Heraclitus in the dissertation as an "objective ironist," one who, like Plato, is as much an ironist as Socrates, though his formal philosophy appears otherwise. In one of the letters to Lassalle, Marx recalls that eighteen years earlier Marx himself had written about ancient philosophy, and in distinguishing Epicurus' atomism from that of Democritus, Marx had come to a conclusion to which he still held. His summary of that conclusion is as follows: "Even with philosophers who give their works a systematic form, for instance Spinoza, the true inner structure of the system is totally different from the form in which the philosopher consciously presents it. "[132] That summary comes remarkably close to a restatement of Marx's original testimonial to irony, and should probably suggest to us that we read Marx's writings aware of his distinction between outward presentation and "true inner structure" (*der wirkliche innere Bau*).

The above reconsideration of Marx's dissertation lends support to LaCapra's implicit contention that we have systematically misread all of Marx, that we have read him far too literally, that we have failed to see how and why Marx meets his opponents on their own territory by adopting their own terms.[133] I never cease to be amazed at how often I hear the old saws repeated in criticism of Marxism--that it represents "economic determinism," "scientism," "utopianism," "secular eschatology"--when precisely those excesses were the charges that *Marx* leveled against his opponents, the bourgeois capitalists, the political economists, the young Hegelians, the utopian socialists, the mystic anarchists. f one listens carefully, one can almost still hear an ironic ring to Marx's use of the term "materialist" in his interpretation of history, as if he were echoing the rules and rhetoric of the "capitalist materialists," while turning their own supposedly immutable laws against them. To think that Marx is now constantly accused of being the one preoccupied with economic matters! Perhaps we have been, or have allowed ourselves to be, victimized by Marx's irony.

Finally, Marx's use of irony can be tied directly into our general discussion concerning the relation of ironic art to politics in the nineteenth century. In two places in his dissertation notebooks Marx speaks of art as an objective expression of "subjective philosophy," but he claims that art tends toward ossification. Where "abstract individuality" appears in its "highest freedom and independence, in its totality," he writes, there the being that is swerved from is "all being," and "for this reason, the gods [of art] swerve away from the world, do not bother with it and live outside it."[134]   "These gods of Epicurus have often been ridiculed, these gods who, like human beings, dwell in the inter-mundia of the real world, have no body but a quasi-body, no blood but quasi-blood, and, content to abide in blissful peace, lend no ear to any supplication, are unconcerned with us and the world, are honoured because of their beauty, their majesty and their superior nature, and not for any gain."[135]

These gods were no fiction of Epicurus, says Marx. They did exist, as the plastic gods of Greek art.[136]   The ideals of art can abstract so far from being that eventually they inspire no action. "What is best has no need of action, for it is its own end," Marx quotes Aristotle. In his foreword, Marx suggests that imitative art can even function as an escape from productive action.   The centuries following totalizing philosophies "set about moulding in wax, plastic and copper what sprang from Carrara marble like Pallas Athena out of the head of Zeus, the father of the gods."[137]   Such are "unhappy and iron epochs," for their gods have died and the new goddess has yet to appear. We can almost hear Marx saying: Art may embody and prefigure a kind of free activity, but if relied upon too heavily, especially in political affairs, it can become an opiate of the people.

Political Implications of Nineteenth-Century Irony

The foregoing material has been organized and presented according to the thesis that irony failed in the nineteenth century to make a full transition from the realm of art to the realm of politics. The writers whose works I have briefly discussed--Schlegel, Hegel, Kierkegaard, and Marx--toyed with the idea that irony somehow has applications for political action; yet none of these thinkers was ultimately successful in extending irony, whether in theory or in practice, into the political world.   Surely the original thesis, however, is in need of refinement. In present form it suggests that irony is a neutral "technique" that can be simply lifted and transferred from one "realm" to another, from art to politics.   We need to explore further the relation between irony and action, and perhaps we need to reexamine the distinction itself between art and politics as it pertains to irony.

I suggest that the story of irony in the nineteenth century can be approached from another direction, namely that the century really came down to a contest between the Hegel and the "ironists": Schlegel, Kierkegaard, Marx, and Nietzsche.[138]   Kierkegaard and Marx, for instance, presented similar critiques of Hegel and Hegelianism. Both took issue with Hegel's notion of negation as a principle of action. Both questioned, in effect, Hegel's notion of "determinate negation" as a goad or inducement for action: In presuming the determinate end of all action, Hegel leaves little room for the actual individual in which to act. Both presented alternative visions of the individual acting of his or her own accord; both saw in irony a moment in which individuals leap or swerve by themselves. We might say that the difference between Kierkegaard and Marx on the one hand and Hegel on the other was that Kierkegaard and Marx were attempting to find a way of encouraging individuals themselves to apprehend their goals and to act upon them; whereas Hegel could not quite bear the thought of overall goal-lessness and the need for goal-creation (a difference that was brought out in Hegel's heated opposition to Schlegelian irony).

Thomas Mann also belongs on the list of nineteenth century anti-Hegelians. He confirms his membership in this group in a passage in *Reflections of a Nonpolitical Man*, in which he links Hegelianism with all modern politics:

> It is becoming clear: if I am to call my right to patriotism in question, if it needs defense before my conscience, the reason is not so much that I am not really a true German as that my relationship to *politics* is, in a good German fashion, a nonrelationship. For politics is participation in the state, zeal and passion for the state--and people like me have anything but a Hegelian attitude. I do not find that the state is "to be admired as something earthly divine." I see no "self-purpose" in it--I see something technical more than something spiritual, a machine to be supervised and taken care of by the experts. Not only do I disagree that human destiny should be absorbed in state and society, I even find this opinion repulsively inhuman; I think that the most important aspects of the human spirit--religion, philosophy, art, poetry, science--exist beside, above, and beyond the state, and often enough even against it; every application and applicability of these areas of the human intellect as agents of the state--every official, uniformed, and regimented spirit, that is--seems to me to provoke irony.[139]

In the next chapter, we shall examine Mann's dislike for the twentieth century, for politics. Politics, according to Mann, is an *intellectual* affirmation of life; and the presumptuousness of the enterprise, not to mention the hypocrisy and dangerousness of it, is revealed by World War I, for the war showed that the politicians are willing to kill, to go against "life," on the basis of arguments and abstract principles. The "intellect" militates against "life" in the twentieth century, and politics is at the heart of that militancy. Mann's argument is self-consciously borrowed from Nietzsche, who declared that the wars of the twentieth century would be over grand systems, over "ideas." In the above passage, Mann is using Nietzsche against Hegel: Hegelianism is the intellectual force behind all modern politics, for it raises the intellect--principles, arguments, reason-- above "life."

Mann's stated preference for irony over Hegelianism makes him a close, if otherwise unexpected ally of Schlegel, Kierkegaard, and Marx. Mann, we shall see, defined irony as "the self-betrayal of the intellect in favor of life"--a formulation that he claimed was inspired by Nietzsche's project of "questioning the value of truth for life." Hegelianism presumes the coherence of its own enterprise; its followers are sure of their system; the logic of the dialectic is considered impeccable, automatic, inevitable. Hegelianism poses one expectantly toward the future, inspiring confidence for a favorable resolution (a confidence that Mann thought is the *sine qua non* of the act of waging world war). But Mann could not accept a logic that was supposedly based upon organic models, that operated in a realm removed from human involvement. Mann claimed he was ambivalent by nature, a skeptic, and that Hegelianism ultimately cannot accommodate skepticism and ambivalence. But worse, Mann repudiated Hegelianism because it makes "life" dependent upon "reason," it makes life into an "argument." Mann decried Hegel's presumptuousness because, he argued, "life" is not a matter of argument; its worth cannot be demonstrated by logical proof. This is not to say that Mann was an absolutist vis-à-vis life, a romantic. Instead, he realized that his was, equally with Hegelianism, an "intellectual" position, but now it was the intellect militating against the intellect in order to affirm life. Thus we can begin to understand Mann's definition of irony as "the self-betrayal of the intellect in favor of life." The formulation was directed against Hegelianism. Hegelianism essentially shows no self-restraint, no modesty, no ambivalence, whereas irony uses the intellect to restrain the intellect. Yet irony's intellectual self-restraint does not simply end with skepticism, for it is a self-betrayal "in favor of life." For Mann, the ironic stance was essentially a positive, an affirmative stance.

Hence we begin to see similarities in Mann's ironic affirmation of "life" and the ulterior concerns of the other anti-Hegelians of the century: Schlegel's interest in the "dignity of man," Kierkegaard's obsession with the "authentic individual," Marx's regard for the free activity of the "swerving" atom. The opposition of these theorists of irony to Hegel was not simply a continuation of the Romantic rebellion against the Enlightenment, an attempt to give up on reason. Indeed, Schlegel, Kierkegaard, Marx, and Mann all stressed irony's "philosophical" or intellectual character. But the difference was that the logic of irony--for Schlegel, Kierkegaard, Marx, and Mann--issued distinctly from the individual, as a product of conscious choice and free affirmation, rather than being the determinate and necessary result of a general "system." Kierkegaard, for instance, maintained that irony was uniquely an individual stance, and Marx called it a form of "subjective philosophy." For the highly individualistic Mann, too, irony characterized individuals, not systems.

Perhaps now, with a special focus upon the individual, we can reexamine the relationship between art and politics as it pertained to irony in the nineteenth century. Our reexamination to some extent will follow the form of Marx's examination of the relationship between Democritean and Epicurean physics, for we wish to know why the realms of art and politics were so *close* in the minds of the theorists of irony, and yet why at the same time they considered art and politics to be fundamentally separate. The anti-Hegelian turn in our investigation provides an insight into the matter. Those thinkers concerned with "human dignity" tend to look for worldly confirmation of the same, which often brings them to the fields of art and politics; but since such value orientations in some sense reside in the individual (for they need to be appropriated or internalized), it is often difficult to posit a connection from one individual to others. Art has a personal and an interpersonal dimension, but it also has a conspicuous, because visible, bridge between the two: the artwork. One can *see* the essence of art; but politics evinces no such natural foundations, no such obvious bridge between the personal and the impersonal, no such clearly visible borders around its particular easel. If the theorists of irony failed in their attempts to translate their ironic sensibilities from the realm of art to the realm of politics, their failures can be attributed in large part to the inherent difficulty in finding a way to extrapolate from the ironic individual to the ironic collectivity.

What we have learned from the nineteenth-century theorists of irony is that "irony" is indeed unstable and uncertain, that it is reluctant to commit itself, that it does not readily translate into effective action. Thus irony does not *seem* very conducive to politics in the twentieth century and beyond, but this may mean only that politics as we understand it needs to be reexamined and perhaps changed. Irony shifts the burden of proof back upon us: If irony is to work, is to be "effective," then perhaps *we* must make ourselves and our politics more open to irony.[140]

This chapter has presented some of the theoretical failings of irony--failings that attest to possible dangers of an ironic politics. Marx suggested that irony's biggest liability is that it does not translate readily from the individual to the collectivity. Hence irony is most comfortable in the realm of art, where a social basis of communication is naturally provided in the artwork; but in politics, where intersubjective ties are less visible, irony seems to require objective confirmation. The catch-22 of irony in politics is that, in Marx's words, a "material" expression of irony tends to undermine the spirit of irony and yet without external support, irony can hardly inspire "world-historical" movements.

We can perhaps distill some oblique encouragement from Marx regarding the prospects of irony in politics, but in the main Marx's writings do not bode well for such an undertaking. Marx apparently decided to abandon irony, or else to conceal his irony entirely under the guise of the material principle of "repulsion." Yet by the same token we must note that Marx's dissertation would need to be amended for the twentieth century, for the nature of atomic physics has since been drastically changed, and Epicurean physics has been long outdated. We now live in a world in which one wrong "repulsion," one wrong swerve, can set off irreversible catastrophes. Against the background of such absolute determinations, such total triumphs, we may well be facing the possibility that our only option is to redefine our politics, making it and ourselves more conducive to irony, or else we may be running the risk of condemning ourselves to a fate far worse than the "mediocrity" that Marx loathingly imagined.

Notes

1. René Wellek, *A History of Modern Criticism: 1750-1950*, Vol. 2, *The Romantic Age* (New Haven: Yale University Press, 1955), p. 6; Hans Eichner, *Friedrich Schlegel* (New York: Twayne Publishers, 1970), p. 43.

2. Wellek, *A History of Modern Criticism*, Vol 2., p. 25; Eichner, *Friedrich Schlegel*, p. 43.

3. Eichner, *Friedrich Schlegel*, p. 46.

4. *Ibid.*, p. 92.

5. Though Martin Bernal doesn't praise these pioneering efforts; he sees Schlegel's early Sanskrit studies as helping form the concept of an Aryan race. *Black Athena: The Afroasiatic Roots of Classical Civilization*, Vol. 1 (New Brunswick, N.J.: Rutgers University Press, 1987), pp. 230ff.

6. See Steven E. Alford's excellent book, *Irony and the Logic of the Romantic Imagination* (New York and Berne: Peter Lang, 1984).

7. See Raymond Immerwahr, "The Subjectivity or Objectivity of Friedrich Schlegel's Poetic Irony." *Germanic Review* 26 (October, 1951), p. 190; Ingrid Strohschneider-Kohrs, *Die romantische Ironie in Theorie und Gestaltung* (Tübingen: Max Niemeyer Verlag, 1977), p. 7; Eichner, *Friedrich Schlegel*, pp. 120-122; and Alfred E. Lussky, "Friedrich Schlegel's Theory of Romantic Irony," *Tieck's Romantic Irony* (Chapel Hill: University of North Carolina Press, 1932), pp. 2-4.

8. See Wellek, *A History of Modern Criticism*, Vol. 2; Lussky, "Friedrich Schlegel's Theory of Romantic Irony," pp. 45-91; and Charles Taylor, *Hegel* (Cambridge: Cambridge University Press, 1975), pp. 34-50.

9. Leonard P. Wessell, Jr., "The Antinomic Structure of Friedrich Schlegel's 'Romanticism,'" *Studies in Romanticism* 12 (Summer, 1973), p. 649.

10. *Idem, Karl Marx, Romantic Irony, and the Proletariat: The Mythopoetic Origins of Marxism* (Baton Rouge and London: Louisiana State University Press, 1979).

11. Wessell writes: "I agree with H.A. Korff that Novalis' doctrine of 'magical idealism' and Schlegel's theory of romantic irony are two complementary sides of the same ontopoetic coin. Each theory casts light upon the other. Since I am seeking to mediate an overall view of romantic philosophy and poetology, my approach must be composite and schematic. Concrete differences among thinkers must be neglected in order to exposit the general unity." *Karl Marx, Romantic Irony, and the Proletariat*, p. 15.

12. Friedrich Schlegel, *Schlegels Briefe an seinen Bruder August Wilhelm*, ed. Oskar F. Walzel (Berlin: Speyer & Peters, 1890), p. 32; cited in Eichner, *Friedrich Schlegel*, p. 74.

13. Friedrich Schlegel, *Kritische Friedrich-Schlegel-Ausgabe*, ed. Ernst Behler in collaboration with Jean-Jacques Anstett and Hans Eichner (Munich: Ferdinand Schöningh; Zurich: Thomas-Verlag, 1957), Vol. 18, p. 8; cited in Eichner, *Friedrich Schlegel*, p. 76.

14. Eichner, *Friedrich Schlegel*. p. 77.

15. Schlegel, *Kritische Friedrich-Schlegel-Ausgabe*, ed. Hans Eichner (Munich: Ferdinand Schöningh; Zurich: Thomas-Verlag, 1959), Vol. 4, p. 246; cited in Eichner, *Friedrich Schlegel*, p. 107.

16. Schlegel, *Kritische Friedrich-Schlegel-Ausgabe*, ed. Jean-Jacques Anstett (Munich: Ferdinand Schöningh; Zurich: Thomas-Verlag, 1959), Vol. 12, p. 151; cited in Eichner, *Friedrich Schlegel*, p. 107.

17. Eichner, *Friedrich Schlegel*, p. 107.

18. *Ibid.*, p. 79.

19. *Ibid.*, pp. 79, 112.

20. *Ibid.*, p. 130.

21. *Ibid.*, p. 48.

22. *Ibid.*, p. 125.

23. See Eichner, *Friedrich Schlegel*, p. 74; Strohschneider-Kohrs, *Die romantische Ironie in Theorie und Gestaltung*, pp. 14-54.

24. Eichner, *Friedrich Schlegel*, p. 48.

25. *Ibid.*, pp. 121-122.

26. Immerwahr, "The Subjectivity or Objectivity of Friedrich Schlegel's Poetic Irony," p. 190.

27. See for instance, E.M. Butler, *The Tyranny of Greece over Germany* (Boston: Beacon Press, 1935).

28. Friedrich Schlegel, "On Incomprehensibility," *Friedrich Schlegel's Lucinde and the Fragments*, trans. Peter Firchow (Minneapolis: University of Minnesota Press, 1971), p. 263.

29. Schlegel, *Athenaeum Fragments*, #53, *Friedrich Schlegel's* Lucinde *and the Fragments.*, p. 167.

30. *Idem, Lyceum-Fragments*, #108, *Friedrich Schlegel's* Lucinde *and the Fragment*, p. 153.

31. Eichner, *Friedrich Schlegel*, p. 78.

32. *Ibid.*, p. 107.

33. *Ibid.*, p. 108.

34. Schlegel, "On Incomprehensibility," p. 267.

35. *Idem, Ideas*, #106.

36. G.W.F. Hegel, *The Phenomenology of Spirit*, trans. A.V. Miller (Oxford: Oxford University Press, 1977), pp. 50-51.

37. *Ibid.*, p. 51.

38. Lionel Trilling, *Sincerity and Authenticity* (Cambridge: Harvard University Press, 1971), p. 11.

39. See Donal O'Gorman, *Diderot the Satirist* (Toronto: University of Toronto Press, 1971).

40. G.W.F. Hegel, *The Phenomenology of Spirit*, p. 319.

41. *Ibid.*, p. 32.

42. Here I am using the word *hopeful* with an awareness of its vagueness, but I am not overlooking Hegel's discussion of "pure insight" or his distinction between faith and nonfaith.

43. G.W.F. Hegel, *Aesthetics: Lectures on Fine Art*, trans. T.M. Knox, Vol. 1 (Oxford: At the Clarendon Press, 1975), p. 64.

44. *Ibid.*, p. 65.

45. *Ibid.*, p. 66.

46. *Ibid.*

47. I should point out that Hegel attributed some value to irony by way of Karl Solgar's notion of "absolute negative infinity"; see Hegel, *Aesthetics*, p. 68, *The Phenomenology of Spirit*, p. 101.

48. *Idem, The Phenomenology of Spirit*, p. 319.

49. *Idem, Aesthetics*, p. 159.

50. *Ibid.* Friedrich Schlegel, "On Incomprehensibility," *Lucinde and the Fragments*, p. 263.

51. Hegel, *Aesthetics*, p. 160.

52. See Immerwahl, "The Subjectivity or Objectivity of Friedrich Schlegel's Poetic Irony," p. 181; Eichner, *Friedrich Schlegel*, pp. 77-78; and Ernst Behler, "Friedrich Schlegel und Hegel," *Hegel-Studien* 2 (Bonn: H. Bouvier und Co., 1963).

53. Søren Kierkegaard, *The Concept of Irony: With Constant Reference to Socrates*, trans. Lee M. Capel (Bloomington: Indiana University Press, 1965), p. 282.

54. Alford thinks Hegel and Kierkegaard essentially misunderstood the nature of Schlegelian irony. See Alford, *Irony and the Logic of the Romantic Imagination*, p. 21. Furst, however, is one who contends that Kierkegaard ends closer to Schlegel than is generally supposed. Lilian R. Furst, *Fictions of Romantic Irony* (Cambridge: Harvard University Press, 1984), p. 34.

55. Kierkegaard, *The Concept of Irony*, p. 76.

56. *Ibid.*, p. 524.

57. *Ibid.*, p. 340, emphasis added.

58. *Ibid.*

59. *Ibid.*

60. *Ibid.*, p. 341.

61. *Ibid.*

62. Kierkegaard mentions the idea of community in connection with irony, but he does not develop the point at all. Some of what is at stake in the attempt to reconcile irony and community--which requires that Hegel's view of irony be refuted--can be discerned from the following passage: "Womankind--the everlasting irony [in the life] of the community--changes by intrigue the universal end of the government into a private end, transforms its universal activity into a work of some particular individual, and perverts the universal property of the state into a possession and ornament for the Family." Hegel, *The Phenomenology of Spirit*, p. 288.

63. See Hegel, *Aesthetics*, Vol. 1, pp. 64-8; see also Margaret A. Rose, regarding Karl Solgar's influence on Hegel's view of irony. Margaret A. Rose, *Reading the Young Marx and Engels: Poetry, Parody and the Censor* (Totowa, N.J.: Rowman and Littlefield, 1978), pp. 141.

64. G.W.F. Hegel, *The History of Philosophy*, trans. E.S. Haldane (London: Kegan Paul, Trench, Trübner, 1892), p. 307; and *idem, The Philosophy of Right*, trans. T.M. Knox (Oxford: Clarendon Press, 1952), esp. pp. 95, 101.

65. McLellan, by the way, reports that Kierkegaard was in attendance at Schelling's inaugural address in Berlin, a lecture that prompted Marx to append his recently completed thesis. David McLellan, *Karl Marx: His Life and Thought* (New York: Harper and Row, 1973), pp. 40-1.

66. One writer who has made much of Marx's ironic connections with the Schlegels is Wessell, *Karl Marx, Romantic Irony, and the Proletariat*. Wessell's main objective in the book is to indict Marxism by exposing Marx's early associations with Romantic irony; and Wessell's hope is that Marxism will be shown in the process to be a closed, mythic, pseudoreligious and therefore unrealistic political outlook. I believe that the book is mistaken about many things; but I agree with Wessell's premise that Marx and Marxism had certain origins in the theories of "Romantic irony." I think, however, that he has his conclusion reversed, namely that the association of Marxism with irony should suggest a more "open," less "deterministic," reading of Marx's politics.

67. The sixth chapter of the sixth doctoral notebook appears as the immediate foreword to the dissertation in the German version; but in the English the notebooks have been published intact and separate from the dissertation. Karl Marx, *Collected Works*, Vol. 1 (Moscow: Progress Publishers, 1975), pp. 490-500.

68. For example: "The bulk of the *Dissertation*, comparing the natural philosophies of Democritus and Epicurus, is devoid of interest. According to the preface, the object of the work was, as common among Hegel's disciples, to elaborate on a field only very sketchily dealt with by the Master." David

McLellan, "Introduction," *Karl Marx: Early Texts* (New York: Barnes and Noble, 1971), p. xiii; see also Louis Althusser, *For Marx*, trans. Ben Brewster (New York: Penguin Press, 1969), p. 35.

69. Rose, *Reading the Young Marx and Engels.*

70. *Ibid.*, p. 120.

71. *Ibid.*, p. 137.

72. *Ibid.*, p. 84.

73. Though I should note that Rose comments that Marx "never entirely resolved" this "meta-linguistic" problem. *Ibid.*, p. 120.

74. *Ibid.*, p. 119.

75. "In articulating this problem and dissociating himself from it by transferring it back onto the Young Hegelians, Marx speaks directly, without the use of parody or irony, and demonstrates his own release--made within *The German Ideology*--from the fault he condemns. And not only is the above made in direct language, but it is made in relationship to an attempt to analyse the connection between language and the material mode of production." *Ibid.*, p. 120.

76. Marx, *Collected Works*, Vol. 1, p. 491.

77. *Ibid.*, p. 492.

78. *Ibid.*, p. 494, italics added.

79. *Ibid.*, italics added.

80. *Ibid.*, p. 496, italics added.

81. *Ibid.*, p. 497, italics added.

82. *Ibid.*, italics added.

83. *Ibid.*

84. *Ibid.*, p. 498.

85. *Ibid.*, p. 38.

86. *Ibid.*, p. 43.

87. *Ibid.*, pp. 42-3.

88. *Ibid.*, p. 43.

89. *Ibid.*, p. 44.

90. *Ibid.*, pp. 47-8.

91. *Ibid.*, p. 49.

92. *Ibid.*, p. 50.

93. *Ibid.*

94. *Ibid.*, p. 51.

95. *Ibid.*, p. 52.

96. *Ibid.*

97. *Ibid.*, p. 53.

98. *Ibid.*

99. The above is an abbreviated exegesis of the dissertation, but the basic point of the remaining chapters is the same: to demonstrate Epicurus' theoretical perversity in defending the "inner essence" of the atom.

100. Wessell, *Karl Marx, Romantic Irony, and the Proletariat*, p. 102. Note that Norman D. Livergood in his interpretation of Marx's dissertation recognized Marx's break with Hegel, yet Livergood, too, contends that Marx is

trying to out-Hegel Hegel: "In the dissertation Marx is still a philosopher in the Hegelian style. . . . For though Marx is still a Hegelian in the dissertation, he dares to challenge Hegel and attempts to go beyond Hegel." Livergood, *Activity in Marx's Philosophy* (The Hague: Martinus Nijhoff, 1967), pp. viii-ix. S.S. Prawer draws a similar conclusion, namely that early Marx for the most part accepts Hegel's philosophy, and the point is simply to put such ideals into practice. See Prawer,*Karl Marx and World Literature* (Oxford: At the Clarendon Press, 1976), p. 25; and Prawer cites A.C. MacIntyre to support him on this point; see MacIntyre, *Marxism. An Interpretation* (London, 1953), p. 39. McLellan sees Marx as writing under the influence of Bauer's Hegelianism, McLellan, "Introduction," p. xiii. Rose views Marx's project as one of "defending the materialism of Epicurus . . . as 'dynamic,'" Margaret Rose, *Marx's Lost Aesthetic* (Cambridge: Cambridge University Press, 1984), p. 75. Seigel thinks that Marx is supplementing Hegel's view of antiquity by focusing on an ancient Greek physicist who attempts to comprehend the ideal and the material in a single description, but Seigel contends that Marx thinks that Epicurus' inability to go beyond atomism is a shortcoming that finally vindicates later Hegelian thought. Jerrold Seigel, *Marx's Fate: The Shape of a Life* (Princeton: Princeton University Press, 1978). Mins believes Marx is following Hegel in the main, "without coinciding with him." Henry F. Mins, "Marx's Doctoral Dissertation," *Science and Society* 12 (Winter, 1948), pp. 157-69. Berlin writes: "[Marx] had obtained a doctor's degree in the University of Jena, with a characteristically Young Hegelian thesis on the contrast between the views of Democritus and Epicurus, in which he defends theses which he attributed to the latter in terms not much less nebulous than much of what he later himself condemned as typical idealist verbiage." Isaiah Berlin, *Karl Marx: His Life and Environment* (Oxford: Oxford University Press, 1978), p. 59. Mah also considers the dissertation to be a "Young Hegelian tract." Harold Mah, *The End of Philosophy, the Origin of Ideology* (Berkeley: University of California Press, 1987), p. 177. Finally, we might note with interest that the only place where the "early" Althusser sees some Hegelianism in early Marx is in the dissertation; Althusser, *For Marx*, p. 35. For a possible explanation of why Marx might ironize even his teacher Bauer, see Schleifer's related discussion of Kierkegaard's graduate-student need to parody his teachers with only mock approval. Ronald Schleifer, "Irony and the Literary Past," *Kierkegaard and Literature: Irony, Repetition, and Criticism*, ed. Ronald Schleifer and Robert Markley (Norman: University of Oklahoma Press, 1984).

101. Marx, *Collected Works*, Vol. 1, p. 491.

102. *Ibid.*, p. 492.

103. *Ibid.*

104. *Ibid.*, p. 491.

105. *Ibid.*

106. *Ibid.*

107. *Ibid.*, p. 493.

108. *Ibid.*, p. 30.

109. *Ibid.*, p. 492.

110. Marx to Lassalle, December 21, 1857, Karl Marx, *Karl Marx-Friedrich Engels, Werke,* Vol. 29 (Berlin: Dietz Verlag, 1963), p. 547.

111. S.S. Prawer makes the important observation that Marx quotes the lines "Prometheus is the foremost saint and martyr in the philosopher's calendar" in the original Greek; and that "although Prometheus speaks the words Aeschylus put into his mouth, Aeschylus himself could hardly have acknowledged the thought that man's self-consciousness is to be the highest divinity as the thought of *his* Prometheus." Marx drew explicitly a link between Aeschylus and Hegel in his doctoral notes. In short, Marx uses the Prometheus myth in literary, rather than literal, sense--and these lines should interpreted as such. Prawer, *Karl Marx and World Literature,* p. 24. I might add that Marx's religious language here, especially since it is juxtaposed directly against Epicurus' impious "theology," seems possibly to betray a mockingly ironic stance toward Prometheus--e.g., his "confession," is an "aphorism against all heavenly and earthly gods who do not acknowledge human self-consciousness as the highest divinity." In brief, if Marx's tribute to "saint" Prometheus is mocking in part, then it might be that Marx had already adopted the stance toward religious criticism usually associated only with his critique of Feuerbach. Marx, *Collected Works,* Vol. 1, pp. 30-1.

112. Marx, *Collected Works,* Vol. 1, p. 49.

113. "Hence Epicurus feels that here his previous categories break down, that the method of his theory becomes different. And the *profoundest knowledge* achieved by his system, its most thorough consistency, is that he is aware of this and expresses it consciously." *Ibid.,* p. 71.

114. Franz Mehring, *Karl Marx: The Story of His Life* (New York: Covici, Friede, 1935); cited by Mins, "Marx's Doctoral Dissertation."

115. Marx, *Collected Works,* Vol. 1, p. 43.

116. Karl Marx, "The German Ideology," *The Marx-Engels Reader,* ed. Robert Tucker (New York: W.W. Norton, 1972), p. 172.

117. *Ibid.,* p. 193.

118. *Ibid.,* p. 169.

119. *Ibid.,* p. 162.

120. Alvin W. Gouldner, *The Two Marxisms* (New York: Seabury Press, 1980), p. 33.

121. Dominick LaCapra, *Rethinking Intellectual History: Texts, Contexts, Language* (Ithaca and London: Cornell University Press, 1983), pp. 270-1.

122. *Ibid.,* p. 333.

123. *Ibid.,* p. 273.

124. *Ibid.,* p. 280.

125. Karl Marx, *The Eighteenth Brumaire of Louis Bonaparte* (New York: International Publishers, 1963), p. 15.

126. See also Rose's excellent discussion in *"The Eighteenth Brumaire*: History as Parody," *Reading the Young Marx and Engels,* pp. 128-46.

127. Lenin begins *What is to Be Done?* by quoting Marx's "Critique of the Gotha Program": "If you must unite . . . then enter into agreements to satisfy the practical aims of the movement, but do not allow any bargaining over

principles, do not make theoretical 'concessions.' " Vladimir Lenin, *What is to be Done?* (New York: International Publishers, 1969), p. 25; quoted in Gouldner, *The Two Marxisms*, p. 5.

128. Marx, *Collected Works*, Vol. 1, p. 496.

129. *Ibid.*, p. 497.

130. *Ibid.*, Vol. 5, p. 141.

131. Karl Marx, *Capital*, trans. Samuel Moore and Edward Aveling (Moscow: Progress Publishers, 1887), Vol. 1, p. 83; Vol. 3, pp. 330, 598.

132. Marx, May 31, 1858, *Marx-Engels, Werke*, Vol. 29, p. 561. Seigel quotes this letter, but he fails to connect it to Marx's discussion of irony. Seigel, *Marx's Fate*, p. 389. Marx in the letter says that Epicurus, although he bases himself on the natural philosophy of Democritus, "is for ever turning the argument inside out." Marx also seems to say that Epicurus is not completely aware of his own "system," but this contradicts his remark in the dissertation that Epicurus is conscious of his own theoretical contradictions.

133. One can find good evidence of an ironic sensibility in Marx's middle and later works. I am inclined to agree with LaCapra on the point that one of Marx's common literary strategies is to adopt the language of political economists in order to meet them on their own terms--thus it is not at all certain how much "economism" we should ascribe to Marx himself, and the same is true of his "scientism." A similar point is made in Paul Thomas's book *Karl Marx and the Anarchists* (London: Routledge & Kegan Paul, 1980) regarding Marx's complex stance toward Hegel, and his use of Hegel against the anarchists. Thomas writes: "To some extent, Marx's identification of the revolutionary proletariat as the agency of social transformation . . . follows from what Hegel had to say about the dialectics of labour. . . . But the lineaments of Marx's thinking owe more to Hegel than this. Hegel had fastened the idea of community on to the state, and Marx himself in his 'critique' of Hegel's *Philosophy of Right* focused his discussion on Hegel's 'institutional' paragraphs. He was endeavouring to meet Hegel on Hegel's own terms, in order to cast into sharp relief a central question Hegel had posed. If the distinction between state and civil society . . . is as Hegel portrayed it, and if it is not to be overcome by the various institutional mediations Hegel's *Philosophy of Right* outlines, then surely the need to overcome it still remains" (p. 24). Thus we can gain an appreciation for the sense in which Marx's critique projects beyond itself, but not in a programmatic way: "Far from straightforwardly denying it, political emancipation presages human emancipation, blazes its trail, points the way forward--and parodies it in advance. Citizenship in the alien state is a cruel joke upon man, one which mocks the universality, the *Gemeinwesen*, the extension of real, social control he desperately and increasingly needs" (p. 75). Schaar suggests that in missing the "irony" of *Capital*, one might miss Marx's whole point. See John H. Schaar, "The Question of Justice," *Raritan* 3 (Fall, 1983), p. 118.

134. Marx, *Collected Works*, Vol. 1, p. 51.

135. *Ibid.*

136. *Ibid.*

137. *Ibid.*, Vol. 5., p. 492.

138. Certain recent writers, most notably Derrida, Hayden White, and Richard Rorty, have attempted to portray Hegel as an "ironist" generally, but this classification misses the important differences between Solgarian and Schlegelian notions of irony. Moreover, it overlooks Hegel's own discussion of the different kinds of negativities. Despite all of this talk of negations, Hegel quite simply was not a friend of irony.

139. Mann, *Reflections of a Nonpolitical Man*, trans. Walter D. Morris (New York: Frederick Ungar, 1983), p. 107.

140. "It is not the ironist, however, but the man who does not wish to enquire or see, who incites men to war or establishes a totalitarian state. When Anatole France complained that martyrs lacked a sense of irony he might have added, with at least as much point, that a sense of irony did not characterise those who felt a need to martyr them." D.C. Muecke, *The Compass of Irony* (London: Methuen and Company, 1969), p. 246.

5

Political Irony and World War: Thomas Mann's Twentieth-Century Self-Reversal (with Constant Reference to Nietzsche)

Es lockt dich meine Art und Sprach',
Du folgest mir, du gehst mir nach?
Geh nur dir selber treulich nach:--
So Folgst du mir--gemach! gemach!
--Nietzsche, *The Gay Science*

Thomas Mann's book, *Reflections of a Nonpolitical Man*, is an extended descant on the subject of the relationship between art and politics, though it is also a book that defies easy summary. Several commentators, citing the book's World War I context, have in effect slighted the importance of Mann's abstract on art and politics, arguing instead that such pronouncements amount to little more than a thinly veiled justification of German imperialism.[1] For them, the book is above all reactionary, polemical, elitist, and possibly protofascist. Others seem to claim that the larger aesthetic, political, and historical issues are really beside the point, for the underlying narrative is directed at Mann's politically liberal, pro-French brother Heinrich, who had left Germany and who had proposed that all good aesthetes should take a stand against Germany's militarism.[2] Upon such a reading, Thomas Mann's assertion of his aesthetic right to be "nonpolitical" is really his clever way of waging a personal war with his older brother while seeming to be above the fray.[3]

While not wishing to excuse Mann's excesses, I propose that we first examine Mann's discussion of art and politics on its own terms, if only because that discussion already assumes and comprehends both of the above lines of contextual analysis.[4] For Mann's *Reflections of a Nonpolitical Man* is self-consciously a tale of personal transformation; more confessionary and disclaiming than polemical and tendentious; an attempt, even a struggle, to find a bridge between the strictly personal and the generally political. Such a rereading holds implications for the study of Mann's own political biography. His is a fascinating story of self-reversal: the self-described "nonpolitical" aesthete turned political; the antidemocrat turned democrat; the shameless defender of German *Volkskultur* turned fervent anti-Nazi (and anti-McCarthyist); the bourgeois *burgher* turned "world citizen."   Students of Mann commonly identify 1922 as the date of his political about-face--well after the 1918 publication of his *Reflections* and only in response to rising tide of national socialism[5]--but the present reading would suggest that Mann had already embraced democracy, and not only resigned himself to it, before the end of the war and the Kaiser's demise.[6]

Aside, however, from setting the historical record straight, the ultimate purpose of this chapter is to suggest that Mann's story of personal transformation holds broad, maybe stirring, implications for the politics of the twentieth century, in particular with respect to issues of world war. I would like to begin to draw forth some of these implications, finally by comparing Mann's self-reversal with two other twentieth-century models of self-reversal, which I find presented in works by the French theorist Jacques Derrida and the American theorist George Kateb.

The textual evidence for supporting an interpretation of *Reflections* as a rearguard defense of the authoritarian state is abundant and conspicuous. Mann makes explicit his preference for *Obrigkeitsstaat*, the rule of a spiritual aristocracy, as the best safeguard for German aesthetic culture. "I want the monarchy," he frankly admits.[7] Mann himself, in retrospect, made a few statements that would seem to support this reading of *Reflections* as essentially nostalgic and reactionary.[8] But he also refused to retract the book[9] (though given later circumstances he was painfully embarrassed by some of his tributes to German nationalism[10]), and he always resisted the interpretation that his thought had changed drastically in the postwar years. The book took more than two years to write,[11] and it should be pointed out that most of Mann's one-sided tirades are limited to those chapters written in the early years of the war.[12] The chapters written or revised toward the end of the war are more difficult to categorize, especially the last chapter, "Irony and Radicalism."[13] Therein Mann for the first time uses the phrase, "political irony," which critics have generally passed over but which Mann highlights too dramatically to be of little import.[14]

I suggest that Mann's phrase "political irony" indeed is the key to the book, that is, to Mann's final position on the relationship between art and politics and to Mann's personal transformation over the course of writing the book. What did he mean by this phrase? Let us turn to a brief *explication de'text*, for without attending closely to all the twists and turns in Mann's thought, one can too hastily categorize Mann merely as a defeated aristocrat who is clinging to tradition.[15]

*　　　*　　　*

At the outset of *Reflections of a Nonpolitical Man*, Mann declares himself to be "a genuine child of the nineteenth century." The declaration requires that he situate the nineteenth century between the eighteenth and the twentieth. The eighteenth century, he says, sought to adapt the human being to its "utopia." The century was superficial and humane, "enthusiastic for the human being," and it "advocated, with the use of art, *reforms of a social and political nature*."[16] The nineteenth century rebelled against eighteenth-century pretentiousness; the nineteenth century "freed itself from the *domination of ideals*." It turned from reason to beauty, from the intellect to "life."[17] "Romanticism, nationalism, burgherly nature, music, pessimism, humor"--these were its products. But the nineteenth century went in two directions. Some turned "hysterically" to art, as a sentimental return to Renaissance aestheticism. Others, whose aesthetic tendencies were more cerebral in nature, repudiated the eighteenth century by "denying the intellect in favor of life"--an act that required that the intellect turn against itself. Such a stance was the "moral attitude" of what Mann calls *irony*.[18] Mann places himself with the ironists, who, he explains, defined "life" just as the Renaissance aesthetes did, but "with a different, lighter, and more reserved nuance of feeling."[19] Irony seeks "to win for the intellect," but it is very far from placing itself in the service of "ideals." Above all, it is a completely "personal" ethos, not a "social" one.

To observe Mann's distinctions further: The young twentieth century again *believes*--in progress, in the human being, in "mankind," in utopia. Like the eighteenth century, the twentieth century directs its reason and passion to secure "happiness," "love," and "democracy." Once again, "ideals" dominate, and thus one finds "activism, voluntarism, reform, politics, expressionism."[20] Art is again called upon to propagate reforms of a social and political nature; no longer is art inward and personal. "Mankind" is rather the order of the day:

"No more of Goethe's ethos of personal culture: society rather! Politics! Politics!"[21]

Mann calls this twentieth century concern for politics and society "the new passion." Its nature is "optimistic-ameliorative"; it seeks to enlighten, to humanize, to politicize. But the new passion pursues only one kind of politics--the democratic one: "One is not a 'democratic' or, say, a 'conservative' politician. One is a politician or one is not. And if one is, then one is democratic. The political intellectual attitude is the democratic one; belief in politics is belief in democracy, in the *contrat social*."[22]

Mann is forthright in expressing his opposition to the twentieth century: "I do not want politics."[23] He registers his contempt for politics throughout the book, and he finally ends the book "happy that I can do what the nations punishing each other so terribly cannot do for a long time--that I can finish."[24] Looking back, he apologizes for some of the bitter pages in the book, but these repulsions of his "were only a reflection of the great insult that a nation received from a whole articulate world." That world--of politics, of democracy--he says he had to take a position against, that he had to stand with Germany in the war. But he is careful to explain that his patriotism is not "chauvinism."[25] He prefers aristocracy over democracy on "aesthetic" grounds; and he prefers the "nation" over the "state" and "personality" over "individuality" on "metaphysical" grounds. Similarly, his pronouncements against politics and the twentieth century issue from aesthetic, metaphysical preferences. Politics, Mann says, makes one "rough, vulgar, and stupid."[26] But at the same time, Mann insists that the book is really no "polemic against politics": "*Reflections of a Nonpolitical Man*? One will find the word accurate only in a figurative sense. But no matter how much appearances speak against it--I don't side with any party; truly I am not fighting democracy."[27]

The war has brought out complicated sentiments in Mann, and he is especially ambivalent about politics. He confesses that he can "understand completely . . . those who declare 'I cannot love or hate a whole nation; I know only human beings.'" Yet he sides with Germany. He tells us that his nationalism, however, is not itself "political" but issues from an "artistic-intellectual" perspective. He is nationalistic because the war has brought out, and "almost forces," primitive vices and primitive emotions that hold a certain esthetic appeal to the artist in him. Yet in the end he admits that he really is not inwardly opposed to "politics" but that "he had to take a stand." And eventually he seems to make overtures to politics, conceding that "one does not have to play the political activist and demonstrator, that one can be an 'esthete' and still have deep feeling for the political element."[28]

What precisely, then, does Mann mean by "politics?" He asks this question for the first time only after two hundred pages. His answer is characteristically playful, the playfulness of which might not be fully appreciated by professional political scientists:

> What is politics?
> One will answer: "Politics is the science of the state." Or perhaps, as a scholar formulates it with seemingly final exactness: "Politics is a practical behavior, including the rules derived from it, which, whether it be on the part of government, particular groups of people, or even individuals, sets as its goal the maintenance or the reformation of the existing state." But today these are outdated definitions. The true definition of the concept, "politics," is only possible with the help of its opposite concept; it says: "Politics is the opposite of estheticism." Or: "Politics is salvation from estheticism." Or, stated quite strictly: "To be a politician is the only possible way of not being an esthete." We claim and insist that only this offers a living definition of the concept of politics that fits its present conditions, although it does not escape us that we are here defining an unknown with an unknown--that no definition exists as long as we have not defined this second X, the concept of estheticism, as well. We are ready to do this! What is estheticism? What is an esthete?[29]

Mann at first refrains from answering his own question and instead cites examples of "aestheticism." His avoiding the question is intentional, we discover, for he does not wish to "intellectualize" about art and aestheticism. Art, apparently his own writing included, depends upon *ambiguity*, and freedom from commitment; and thus one ought not press too far for an "intellectual" formulation for art. Aestheticism is skepticism, he finally formulates. The rest of the chapter entitled "Politics" is essentially a discursus regarding two fundamental ways of interpreting Nietzsche (more on this later), but the basic point Mann seems to be insinuating is this: Aesthetics and politics are "antithetical" because the former requires freedom *from* commitment and room for *irresponsibility*, whereas "politics" requires a bedrock commitment to and concern for something, namely "the people." Mann, the aesthete, cannot discover in himself this basic, unmitigated, generalized love for humanity. And for him, "Rule of the people" is a phrase that "has its terror."[30]

Up to the very last chapter, the "authoritarian" interpretation of the book could probably still be sustained--Mann's twists, turns, and qualifications notwithstanding--for Mann still adheres to the view that art and politics are fundamentally opposed. Not until the last chapter does Mann truly reveal himself. Let us continue our close reading.

The chapter "Irony and Radicalism" begins abruptly and strangely. An intellectual human being, Mann writes, is confronted with a Kierkegaardian,[31] either/or, decision: One can either be a radical or an ironist. As a radical, one sides with the "intellect." As an ironist, one sides with "life." Mann explains that for the radical, arguments or appeals on the basis of "life" are not intrinsically compelling, and he cites the old adage (invoked approvingly by Kant)--*Fiat justitia, et pereat mundus et vita*--to illustrate this point. The radical is prepared to destroy "life" in the name of principles--truth, justice, or purity--a position Mann refers to as "nihilism." In politics, the radical will defend to the death his principles and ideals, as if "life" were a matter of argument. In brief, radicalism for Mann is the germ cause of the war, a war that puts humanitarianism above human beings, that puts an "argument" above "life."

The ironist, oddly, is not a nihilist, but rather a "conservative." Mann's explanation of this is taxing, but coherent. Conservatism is *ironic* conservatism, he says, only if it is *not* the voice of "life wanting itself" but the voice of the "intellect," not wanting itself, but rather "life." Such a stance is an "affirmation of life by the intellect."[32] This particularly *intellectual* outlook of irony is also *erotic*, Mann adds, and its love and eroticism "is not fanatical, it is ingenious, it is *political*."[33] At this juncture, Mann breaks off the discussion and announces, "It is time to speak of art."

What is art? If one is to speak of function, Mann writes wryly, certainly art is a *meliorative* activity: it is a way of transfiguring and glorifying life. "Originally," he adds, art was "naive"; it was a celebration of life and beauty; it was also a stimulus, a seduction to life. But if art ever once upon a time was purely "naive," now it cannot be so considered. Art now is "problematic," and "critical." Art engages the critical intellect and thus entails a "criticism," not just an expression, of "life." Moreover, this criticism is "far more terrible and shocking than that of pure intellect, as its methods are richer, more emotional, more varied--and more amusing."[34] Art is not simply imitative and playful and glorifying; it is also "moral" in a very complicated sense: "But what psychology can cope with art, this enigmatic being with the deeply cunning eyes that is serious in play and in all seriousness plays a game of form that by deception, brilliant imitation, and earnest illusion, deeply shakes people with ineffable sobbing and ineffable laughter, both at the same time!"[35]

Art's new critical-moral stance enhances its former function, of giving pleasure and enthusiasm to life; but now it should be observed that art's connection to criticism, to the intellect, and even to "nihilism," may sometimes contravene its function of serving life. Art, then, embodies a paradox, a fundamental contradiction, an "irony":

> And still it is precisely this that makes art so lovable and worthy of practice; it is this wonderful contradiction that it is, or at least can be, by its delightful imitation and critical-moral destruction of life, at the same time life's comfort and judgment, praise and glory, that it can have the effect of giving pleasure and awakening *conscience* to the same degree. To put it diplomatically, its mission lies in maintaining equally good relations with life and with pure intellect, in being at the same time conservative and radical; it lies in its central and mediating position between intellect and life. Here is the source of irony.[36]

Throughout the book, Mann has maintained that politics is the opposite of aestheticism: the artist suspends belief; the politician earnestly promotes a cause. Now Mann begins to notice certain "structural similarities" between politics and art. Both art and politics take a "mediating" position between "life" and the "intellect." But it would be a mistake to conclude, he adds, that art's proper function is mediating or meliorative in a *political* sense, that is, with an aim toward the public weal. Preserving the precious *dignity* of art is not the issue here; rather, art must be accorded a nonpolitical status in order to reserve the artist's right to be ambivalent, ironic, even demonic. Mann is quick to add that all art need not be ironic (some modern art is still "naive"), but the point is that we cannot expect art always to be political. Art must be allowed a separate status: "It is basically disloyal to use art's criticism of life for ameliorative propaganda purposes; neither the school nor life in general can be arranged so that the highest moral and esthetic sensitivity, that sensitivity and intellect, can feel at home in them."[37]

To be sure, artistic criticism may frequently produce "political effects" in the real world, may at times express the conscience of the human race, and may improve, ennoble, and moralize. But we must not misunderstand the "ironic leadership" of the artist, pleads Mann, to be "directly" political. The artist is by nature a skeptic, in spite of occasional appearances to the contrary.

So much for art. Now Mann seems to break off again, and he begins to consider, given the "structural similarities" between art and politics, whether there can be such a thing as an "ironic politics." "But 'ironic' politics? The word combination seems all too strange and especially all too frivolous for one ever to find it valid, much less to admit that politics is altogether and always of ironical character."[38]

Yet despite this seeming denial, Mann goes on immediately to cite numerous examples of what he calls "political irony," drawing from Kant, Nietzsche, Ibsen, Adam Müller, and Friedrich von Gentz. Mann sees "political irony" in Kant's charitable self-reversal, for after Kant's "terrible and only too successful epistemological campaign, [he] reintroduced everything again under the name of 'Postulates of *Practical* Reason,' and made possible again what he had just critically crushed."[39] And Mann sees the same ethos of political irony in Nietzsche's philosophical act of "questioning the value of truth for *life*,"[40] which Mann likens to Ibsen's acceptance of "the lie as a condition of life."[41] Mann notes, too, that he, Mann, learned how to achieve an *ironic* stance toward the concept of "life" specifically from Nietzsche.[42]

Irony, he explains, is the "intellect" of conservatism, though conservatism he says can also be simple emotionalism, that is, without wit and melancholy. Conservatism becomes intellectual and ironic, witty and melancholic, only "when international intellectual emphasis joins national emotional emphasis, when a bit of democracy, of literature, complicates its essence."[43] In ironic conservatism, "being and effect contradict one another to a certain extent, and it is possible that it may promote democracy and progress in the way it fights them."[44] Clearly, Mann feels uncomfortable with the label of political "conservative"--there is, he interjects, an "antithesis" between conservatism and his status as writer: "For literature is analysis, intellect, skepticism, psychology; it is democracy, the 'West,' and where it joins the conservative-national disposition, that schism of which I spoke appears, the one between being and effect. Conservative? Naturally I am not."[45]

Only thus, in tortured qualifications and rejoinders, does Mann remain true to his claim of being a nonpolitical man. He walks a fine line when he defends Germany, and it is only a deft intellect such as his that can assert that his patriotism is but a negative political statement, a way of embracing Germany's role in the war without embracing the war itself and the politics behind it. But this position is *not* that of a crypto-authoritarian, nor is it a way simply of rationalizing his wartime opportunism. If one polemicizes in response to Mann, one does so only at the cost of ignoring Mann's plea that his book not be taken as a polemic. Once we respect Mann's ambivalence we can in turn admire his candor in naming his aesthetic preferences as regards politics--but we must not let these more conspicuous assertions obscure the real point of the book and Mann's real intention. *Reflections of a Nonpolitical Man* is essentially and self-consciously a book about politics and democracy, however "nonpolitical" the author's "nature" may be.   Mann understands the irony of his writing such a book--indeed, the act of self-reversal in writing the book is precisely the topic under discussion (and we might go so far as to suggest that the implicit, and ironically concealed, title of the book is "*Political Reflections of a Nonpolitical Man*").   Far from simply "clinging to tradition," Mann is even generous enough to assist the cause he suggests, albeit in passing, that his own "political irony" might even promote the present wave of "democracy." No, Mann's "position" is too complex simply to negate; a polemical response to Mann misses the point or several points, misses the underlying irony of the book.

Hence the otherwise artistically ambivalent Mann finds his ambivalence at odds with his deep scorn. The twentieth century refuses to respect Germany's borders, to let Germany be Germany--"artistic and skeptical"--and that is why Mann defends Germany on principle, namely as a defense of the right to be skeptical. But it must be noted that Mann's underlying opposition to the idea of the war runs even deeper than his professed patriotism and truly reveals his ambivalence, his irony. The war violates "life" and not just as a matter of "argument."[46] Thus the ironist must break with his own policy of refraining from commitment. The ironist Mann must take a stand, in the name of "life," and against those twentieth-century humanitarians and democrats who will fight fanatically to the death, on an unprecedented scale, all in the name of truth, justice, and humanity. The ironist must be unironical (ironically enough) in this one instance: he must oppose the war itself (if by defending Germany).[47]

Mann, then, must be taken pretty much at his word when he contends that his defense of Germany is not a matter of "taking sides,"[48] or that he is not really opposed to democracy. If anything, his nationalism is but a ploy, a way to convey the deeper antiwar sentiments that he harbors but will not fully admit. Considering that his ire, his main charge, is directed toward those democratic hypocrites who will sanction war to promote democracy, perhaps we should not dismiss out of hand Mann's insistence that his outward defense of Germany actually promotes the true spirit of democracy and humanitarianism, appearances to the contrary notwithstanding.

Mann faces a dilemma, which one might say involves a confrontation between art and politics, or between his ironical nature and his stance against the war. He resolves the dilemma by writing a book and thereby using his literary skills to express both his patriotism and his underlying opposition to the war, even though within the book he inveighs against those, such as his brother, who use their art in the direct service of politics. The war has forced Mann to enforce the distinction between the spirit and the letter of his irony--as a concern for "life," as "skepticism turned backward," on the one hand versus its practice in art, as straightforward skepticism, on the other. The book, then, is the story of how an ironist turns against his own irony, how, in other words, a fundamentally nonpolitical man could ever become political, and how an antidemocratic individualist could ever see fit to champion, if only obliquely, the cause of democracy. The answer is, by way of political irony, that "self-betrayal of the intellect in favor of life."

*   *   *

What are we--we political children of the twentieth century--to make of Mann's ironical stance towards politics? I would like to approach this question through examples, by comparing Mann personal transformation with two distinctively twentieth-century models of self-reversal, both of which make claims, I believe, about the implications of Nietzschean aesthetics for politics.

The first example emphasizes the tendency of language to reverse itself. I am referring to Jacques Derrida's strategies of deconstructive interpretation, and I suspect that those readers familiar with Derrida's many works will not find themselves surprised by the above "rereading" of Mann's *Reflections*. The follower of Derrida might well contend that it is not so unusual that Mann would turn against his own discourse, for his inclination toward "politics" was already implicit in his formulation of a "nonpolitical" nature. The Derridean would deconstruct these binary oppositions, between art and politics, literature and commitment, insightfully revealing along the way that Mann, continental romantic idealist that he was, privileged his own consciousness and voluntarism through various linguistic impositions. In fact, Derrida himself often uses the term *irony* as a apparent synonym for "deconstruction"; but the Derridean might add that Mann seems to have been the unwitting victim of his own textual irony.[49]

This is no place for an exhaustive comparison between Mann and Derrida, for I should think that that would require an analysis of their different readings of both Hegel and Nietzsche; but I would like to point out what I see as one major source of divergence. Mann understands himself to be subverting his own terms, his metaphysics, his fictions, his delusions;[50] but he insists that his "self-betrayal" of the intellect is in service of "life." I take Mann's dilemma to be this: How does an ironist--a deconstructionist, as it were--retain *any* important distinctions, how does he or she take any stand at all, how does the individual trace or effect any connection whatsoever between his "constructs" and political "reality"? Mann is attempting to find a way to turn his ironization against itself, to use a bit of nihilism to stave off complete nihilism, to turn his hostilities toward himself (as a self-confessed, self-privileging aesthete) to fight against the war. (And, by the way, Mann later contended that he would have been an anti-Nazi at the time of writing *Reflections* had the issue emerged.[51]) His self-reversal is an act of supreme self-restraint (his "self-discipline"[52]), as opposed to, as it were, an ongoing act of "dissemination."[53] "Life" may be taken playfully, words may be but fictions, but one cannot assume that the whole game will simply go on.[54] As a point of contrast, I am doubtful that Derrida's "strategies" can be of much use, direct or indirect, in staving off holocausts and world wars.[55] Such strategies scarcely reveal (nor coyly conceal) a way whereby textual ambivalence might translate into political resolve.[56] Moreover, Derrida seems not to be at all aware of the possible consequences of the "destructive absolute" when he asserts, for instance, that deconstruction is a "series without finality," or that "thinking is always of presence, never purely of absence."[57] Mann's intrigue with death may at times seem excessive and morbid,[58] but by comparison Derrida's parasitism upon some notion of the abiding discourse of "life" seems presumptuous, to say the least.

The second example of twentieth-century self-reversal shows much more awareness, anguish in fact, by the possibility of ultimate deconstruction. I am referring to a series of articles, "Thinking about Nuclear Extinction," written by George Kateb.[59] Kateb calls for a "change of heart" in the nuclear age, by which he means a personal change of moral philosophy that would cultivate "those thoughts and feelings that would drive people to do all they could to avoid the possibility of extinction."[60] This is not the place to attempt to summarize, with any sense of justice, Kateb's courageous, controlled plea. But as a way of recalling his position, let me say that there is much in Kateb's outlook that resembles the Thomas Mann of *Reflections*: the search for a particularly twentieth-century affirmation of life, a search prompted by "the death of God" and the fear of mankind's potential for massive self-destruction on a scale altogether new; the view that individualism is the best defensive idealism under such nihilistic conditions; an exploration of the idea of a new "attachment to earthly existence as such" through a possible synthesis involving the ideas of Nietzsche, Whitman, aesthetics, and democracy.[61] Kateb's heart, the heart that needs some changing, belongs to American theorists and poets, and to an American political tradition; which is to say that Kateb does not find much solace, or much that is attractive, in the tradition of European philosophy. He finds the best hope for a nuclear "change of heart" in the transcendental, and democratic, poetry of Whitman, Emerson, and Thoreau. He believes, however, that this tradition needs revision by the European antidemocratic individualists Nietzsche and Heidegger. Nietzsche and Heidegger, in brief, suggest to us how life can be affirmed and renewed aesthetically, but through an aestheticism that is neither theological nor humanist. Perhaps thus we can be "attached to existence as such."

Much depends, then, on Nietzsche and Nietzsche's legacy. Let us compare Kateb's rendering of Nietzsche with Mann's. Mann, too, stakes much upon Nietzsche. In fact, we would not be too far afield to assert that *Reflections* in its entirety is a book about Nietzsche: about how to interpret Nietzsche and how to use properly his aesthetics for political purposes.[62] Nietzsche, says Mann, was the first to anticipate the development of democracy in Germany,[63] and Mann discloses that he gained, oddly enough, his first real understanding of democracy from Nietzsche.[64] But Nietzsche was also "the last nonpolitical man"[65]-- hence the title of *Reflections* begins to suggest that the book is a play in some way upon Nietzsche.

More needs to be said about Mann's view of Nietzsche. We eventually realize in reading *Reflections* that a wrangling over Nietzsche is at the center of Mann's debate with his brother Heinrich. Heinrich, evidently, espoused the view, in the name of Nietzsche, that artists should use their aesthetic skills on behalf of politics. In *Reflections* Thomas Mann states that there are "two brotherly possibilities" for appropriating Nietzsche's aesthetics, two ways of interpreting the significance of "life" in the aesthetic act of a "self-denial of intellect in favor of life."[66] The first is a "ruthless Renaissance aestheticism" which "hysterically" glorifies "power, beauty, and life," which archly affects a pose of "life wanting itself." The second is an ironic aestheticism, which modestly admits that its affirmation of life is performed precisely by the intellect.[67] Mann elaborates on the differences between these two stances. The first kind of aesthete takes Nietzsche as the "father of European aestheticism,"[68] and he attempts to apply directly to politics what he believes to be Nietzsche's new aesthetic "truths." Nietzsche's literary style, Mann suggests, his *satire* in particular,[69] seems to invite such a democratic appropriation; just about any latter-day philosophe can believe that he or she is faithfully following Nietzsche in applying, for example, Nietzsche's critique of Christianity to the German *Reich*. But such a caricature of Nietzsche is "grotesque" and "laughable."[70]

Yes, in years in which there was otherwise little to despise, I could despise the esthetic, renaissance-Nietzscheanism that was all around me and that seemed to me to be a boyishly mistaken imitation of Nietzsche. The representatives of this school took Nietzsche at his word, took him literally. It was not Nietzsche whom they had viewed and experienced, but the ideal image of his self-negation, and they cultivated this mechanically. They innocently believed him to be the "immoralist" he called himself; they did not see that this descendent of Protestant ministers had been the most sensitive moralist who ever lived, a morally possessed man, Pascal's brother. But then, what did they see, really? They did not miss a single misunderstanding that his demeanor ever offered them opportunity for. The element of romantic *irony* in his eros--they had no sense for this at all. And his philosophizing inspired them to create quite prosaic celebrations of beauty, novels full of aphrodisiacal, high-school boy's fantasy, catalogues of vices in which absolutely nothing was omitted.[71]

The ironist sees that nonpolitical Nietzsche hated democracy, that he hated Bismarck for having brought Germany to the brink of grand politics;[72] and that Nietzsche's occasional overtures to democracy and to politics were therefore issued *ambivalently*, against his own best instincts, in spite of his own hatred. Democracy must now be accepted, for its march is inevitable and as such it provides the best available defense of "life." "A giant put Germany into the saddle; now she must ride, for she must not fall off."[73] These are the "conservative sentiments" of an ironist, but Mann's point is to insist that the ironic Nietzschean embraces democracy out of "calm necessity" and not because of its inherent "theoretical desirability."[74]

Back to Kateb: I do not mean to belabor the above distinctions in order to imply that Kateb's turn to Europe, to Nietzschean aesthetics, is hysterical and ruthless and doctrinaire. Far from it, for Kateb reveals, in importantly revelatory moments, an acute understanding of the irony of his own project. His discussion, he writes, "is dominated by the irony that a seemingly self-centered sense of life is most truly itself when it loses sight of the self for the sake of becoming newly attached to existence";[75] and he sees another "irony" in his rereading of Nietzsche and Heidegger, for "though Nietzsche and Heidegger are antidemocratic because they say only a few can see philosophically, the fact remains that a good deal of the content of their vision bears a strong resemblance to that of the theorists of democratic individuality."[76] Kateb knows full well, moreover, that Nietzsche's writings cannot be construed to mean that "beauty should be allowed to pose as the reason for wanting existence to go on forever,"[77] and Kateb's subsequent shift to Heidegger and the Heideggerian notion of "wonder"[78] provokes yet another stirring irony: "At its most rigorous,

Heidegger's hint is that the only person who is truly alive is one who is dead while still living."[79] All along, Kateb suggests that the search for a vital "attachment" will require an enhanced ability to "detach" from existence.[80]

Yet at other times in his discussion, Kateb seems to lose touch with his own ironic sensibility, and here Mann can provide some indirect redirection.[81] Kateb poses Nietzsche's question, "To what extent can truth endure incorporation [into life]?" and Kateb answers "without reservation": "It must be incorporated fully if life is to go on."[82] At this and similar junctures, Kateb, in his attempt to discover some virtually new "attachment to existence per se," seems to be using aesthetics to try to find a way, in Mann's terms, that "life" might "want itself." This comes dangerously close to what Mann called a "theoretical" glorification of life, albeit in the name of Nietzsche. We might, in response, repeat Mann's reminder that art must be granted its right to be entirely irresponsible (and not only irreligious).   Art cannot be expected, nor should it be called upon, to save or to justify the world.[83]

What would, in turn, a thoroughly *ironic* affirmation of twentieth-century "life" look like? I can suggest only provisionally that it would probably be a stance that begins by never expecting to find an "attachment to existence per se." The hidden implication of Mann's formula--"the self-betrayal of the intellect in favor of life"--is that "life" may not admit of any intrinsic "reason" for itself: There may literally be no good answer to the Kantian-like question that Kateb quietly begs: "Why *should* we save the world from total destruction?"[84] The beauty of irony is that this particular self-reversal of the intellect does not require an inherent reason--aesthetic, poetic, phenomenological--to affirm the value of all of human existence.[85] Mann's "political irony" may be a way, ironically, of making the world safe for skeptics.[86]

Notes

1. To cite but a few noteworthy examples: Arnold Bauer, *Thomas Mann*, trans. Alexander and Elizabeth Henderson (New York: Frederick Ungar Publishing, 1971); Joseph Brennan, *Thomas Mann's World* (New York: Russell and Russell, 1962); Ignace Feuerlicht, *Thomas Mann* (Boston: Twayne Publishers, 1968); Hans Eichner, "Thomas Mann and Politics," *Thomas Mann: Ein Kolloquium*, ed. Hans H. Schulte and Gerald Chapple (Bonn: Bouvier, 1978), pp. 5-19; Max Rychner, "Thomas Mann und die Politik," *Aufsätze zur Literatur* (Zurich: Manesse Verlag, 1966), pp. 251-304; Manfred Haiduk, "Die Bedeutung der Polemischen Schriften im Schaffen Thomas Manns," *Vollendung und Grösse Thomas Manns*, ed. Georg Wenzel (Halle: Kreuz,

1962), pp. 43-71; Walter E. Anderson, "Thomas Mann: The Dilemma of a 'Nonpolitical Man,'" *The German Enigma* (New York: Vantage Press, 1980), pp. 70-130; Walter E. Berendsohn, *Thomas Mann: Artist and Partisan in Troubled Times*, trans. George C. Buck (University: University of Alabama Press, 1973).

2. See Irving Stock's perceptive article, "Ironic Conservatism: Thomas Mann's Reflections of a Non-Political Man." Stock interprets Mann's *Reflections* as a response to Heinrich Mann's attack on his brother's recent defense of German militarism. Stock, for all of his appreciation of Mann's ironic affirmation, still understands the *Reflections* as an "anomalous" work, from which Mann must distance himself when he later endorses democracy; whereas I see more threads or continuities between these "periods," albeit by way of irony. Stock, "Ironic Conservatism," *Salmagundi*, No. 68-69 (Fall, 1985-Winter, 1986), pp. 166-185. Also see Eichner, "Thomas Mann and Politics," pp. 11-13.

3. I am not convinced by the argument that the later version of *Reflections*, in which Mann deleted thirty-eight and one-half pages, is the reason that the book now seems less "polemical." Certainly Mann softens the blows against his brother, but his ambivalent turn toward democracy carries over from the original. See Max Rychner, "Thomas Mann und die Politik"; and Bernhard Blume, "Aspects of Contradiction: On Recent Criticisms of Thomas Mann," *Thomas Mann: A Collection of Critical Essays*, ed. Henry Hatfield (Englewood Cliffs, N.J.: Prentice-Hall, 1964), p. 156.

4. This chapter will not attempt to position Mann's personal-political development with respect to his literature (the *Betrachtungen*'s connections to *Der Zauberberg*, *Buddenbrooks*, and *Doktor Faustus* often fuel such speculation). Indeed, an implication of the present argument is that the two realms need not show any direct correlation; hence I shall keep the present analysis within such bounds (and the available literature is vast).

5. The turning point is usually identified as Mann's 1922 speech, "Von Deutscher Republik," *Gesammelte Werke*, Vol. 12 (Frankfurt am Main: S. Fischer Verlag, 1955), pp. 491-532; "The German Republic," *Order of the Day*, trans. H.T. Lowe-Porter (Freeport: Books for Libraries Press, 1937), pp. 3-45. See the following related discussions: Hans Rudolf Vaget, "Lukács and Mann," *Thomas Mann in Context*, ed. Kenneth Hughes (Worcester, Mass.: Clark University Press, 1978), p. 56; John F. Madden begins to note a turning point in Mann's thought beginning with *Reflections*, but Madden still thinks the major changes in Mann's views come after this point. See his "Myth as Mask and Model: Agreements and Contrasts between Freud and Mann," *Thomas Mann in Context*, ed. Hughes, pp. 17-36; Berendsohn notices a shift in Mann's attitude toward democracy by the end of *Reflections*, but he still doesn't think Mann is a democrat until 1922; *Thomas Mann: Artist and Partisan in Troubled Times*, pp. 52-59. Walter G. Hesse suspects that Mann's political attitudes show continuities dating back to *Betrachtungen*, but he does not connect this to irony. "Thomas Mann, der unpolitische Deutsche oder Leiden an der Soziologie," *Dichtung, Sprache, Gesellschaft*, ed. Victor Lange and Hans-Gert Roloff (Frankfurt am Main: Athenäum Verlag, 1971), pp. 189-196. Pikulik

reminds us that there may be no definite starting point at which Mann jumped into the political arena. Lothar Pikulik, "Die Politisierung des Ästheten im Ersten Weltkrieg," *Thomas Mann 1875-1975*, ed. Beatrix Bludau et al. (Frankfurt am Main: S. Fischer, 1977).

6. Commentators have made little note of Mann's own statement that his turn toward democracy began with *Reflections*: "My personal allegiance to democracy rests upon a conviction which I was obliged to acquire, since it was basically foreign to my bourgeois-intellectual origins and upbringing. I mean the conviction that the political and the social are parts of the human; that they belong to the totality of human problems and must be assimilated to the whole. Otherwise we leave a dangerous gap in our cultural life. Perhaps it sounds strange that I should so simply equate democracy with politics and define it, without more ado, as the political aspect of the intellect, the readiness of the intellect to be political. But indeed I did that twenty years ago, in a large and laborious work called *The Reflections of an Unpolitical Man*. And therein my definition was not only negative but even belligerently so. I defined democracy as the political functioning of the intellect, and I opposed it with all my power, in the name of culture--and even in the name of freedom. . . . But self-examination, if it is thorough enough, is nearly always the first step towards change. . . . In short, an acknowledgment of democratic feeling rose to my lips. Despite all the inhibitions of my anti-political upbringing, it was not to be suppressed. I did not suppress it--and for that I am grateful to my good genius." "Culture and Politics" (1939), *Order of the Day*, pp. 228-229. In a superb article, J. Lesser notes Mann's motif of "self-contradictions" in the *Betrachtungen*, and Lesser nicely emphasizes the passage on Kant and irony in the book; but at other times in the article, Lesser falls back upon a more conventional reading of Mann's "conversion" to politics. "Of Thomas Mann's Renunciation" (part 1), *Germanic Review* 25, No. 4 (December, 1950), pp. 245-256.

7. Thomas Mann, *Reflections of a Nonpolitical Man*, trans. Walter D. Morris (New York: Frederick Ungar Publishing Co., 1983), p. 188.

8. Commentators frequently quote this later self-assessment of *Reflections*: "The rearward ties of which I spoke, and which had been necessary for me to write the work, now made themselves felt with negative effect: they made me into a reactionary or at least caused me to appear as such for a moment. For the book was basically far more of an experimental and educational novel than a political manifesto; it was, considered psychologically, a long exploration of the conservative and national sphere in polemical form without thought of ultimate and final commitment. Scarcely was it complete in 1918 when I freed myself from it." "Meine Zeit," *Reden und Aufsätze* 2 (Frankfurt am Main: S. Fischer, 1960), p. 578. Stock rightly cites this comment to indicate Mann's later concern about the book: "A more intimate and more misusable diary has never been kept by anyone." From Mann, "In my Defense," *Atlantic Monthly* (October, 1944), p. 12.

9. "My dear friends, I am still here. . . . As for the fall and the [post-*Reflections*] betrayal, that is not quite a fair way to look at it. I retract nothing. I

take back nothing essential." Mann, "The German Republic," p. 22. Mann said in an interview (in 1923) with a Vienna newspaper that he "took back not a single word of all he had said in 1918," and he contended as late as 1950 that his supposed self-reversal in 1922 had been undertaken "without being conscious of any break in [my] existence, without the slightest feeling that [I] had anything at all to recant." Quoted by Anderson, *The German Enigma*, p. 99; see Walter Morris's discussion, "Introduction," *Reflections*, pp. vii-xvi.

10. See Anderson, *The German Enigma*, pp. 101ff.

11. Berendsohn makes the point that by the end of 1915, Mann had already written about 200 pages, and only then read the essay "Zola" that his brother had written. *Thomas Mann: Artist and Partisan in Troubled Times*, p. 53.

12. The last six chapters and the foreword were written after March, 1917, and Mann rewrote the chapter "Politics" after January, 1918. See Hans Bürgin and Hans-Otto Mayer, *Thomas Mann: A Chronicle of his Life*, trans. Eugene Dobson (University: University of Alabama Press, 1969).

13. I am thinking here particularly of the chapters, "Politics," "Some Comments on Humanity," "The Politics of Estheticism," "Irony and Radicalism," and the "Prologue." Kurzke makes the point that these chapters contain the fewest direct quotations, which make up the bulk of the other chapters. Hermann Kurzke, "Die Quellen der 'Betrachtungen eines Unpolitischen,' " *Thomas Mann Studien*, Band 7 (Bern: Francke Verlag: 1986), pp. 291-310.

14. Kurzke offers a systematic analysis of the irony in *Betrachtungen*, but he doesn't mention Mann's combining the term *political irony* as such. Hermann Kurzke, *Epoche-Werk-Wirkung* (Munich: Beck, 1985), pp. 139ff.

15. T.J. Reed offers a plausible, if reductive, reading of Mann's *Reflections*, contending that the book betrays above all Mann's nostalgic adherence to tradition ("the expression of a whole-hearted emotional commitment desperately seeking to rationalize itself"), and little more. This strikes me as an odd approach to understanding a self-proclaimed ironist, and I am very doubtful that Reed's reading does justice to the complexity of Mann's book. T.J. Reed, *Thomas Mann: The Uses of Tradition* (Oxford: At the Clarendon Press, 1974), pp. 179ff.

16. Mann, *Reflections*, p. 11.

17. I am following Morris's translation of "Geist" as "intellect." On the tradition of relating "Geist" and "Leben," see Madden's discussion in "Myth as Mask and Model: Agreements and Contrasts between Freud and Mann," ed. Hughes, pp. 19ff.

18. For a few discussions of Mann's use of irony in his "artistic" writings, see: R.J. Hollingdale, *Thomas Mann: A Critical Study* (London: Rupert Hart-David, 1971), pp. 76-106; Reinhard Baumgardt, *Das Ironische und die Ironie in den Werken Thomas Manns* (Munich: C. Hansen, 1969); Erich Heller, *The Ironic German* (Boston: Little, Brown and Co., 1958); R. Hinton Thomas, *Thomas Mann: The Mediation of Art* (Oxford: At the Clarendon Press, 1956), pp. 171-174; Peter-André Alt, *Ironie und Krise* (Frankfurt am Main: Peter Lang,

1985). Finally, see Mann, "Humor and Irony," *Thomas Mann*, ed. Hatfield, pp. 170-172.

19. Mann, *Reflections*, p. 13.

20. *Ibid.*, p. 14.

21. *Ibid.*

22. *Ibid.*, p. 15.

23. *Ibid.*, p. 189.

24. *Ibid.*, p. 434.

25. *Ibid.*, p. 409.

26. *Ibid.*, p. 187.

27. *Ibid.*, p. 239.

28. *Ibid.*, p. 433.

29. *Ibid.*, p. 160.

30. *Ibid.*, p. 267.

31. Heller contends that Mann "unwittingly" invokes Kierkegaard here, but Mann at this point did at least know of Lukács's *Soul and Form* and that book's fascination with Kierkegaardian "either/ors." I cannot fathom that a chapter on irony, beginning with a reference to "either/or," could so resemble Kierkegaard merely by coincidence. Heller, *The Ironic German*, pp. 229-230.

32. Mann, *Reflections*, p. 419.

33. *Ibid.*, p. 420.

34. *Ibid.*

35. *Ibid.*, pp. 420-1.

36. *Ibid.*, p. 421

37. *Ibid.*, p. 424.

38. *Ibid.*, p. 426.

39. *Ibid.*, p. 429. Cf. Lesser, "Of Thomas Mann's Renunciation," pp. 251-2.

40. Mann, *Reflections*, p. 429.

41. *Ibid.*, p. 12.

42. *Ibid.*, p. 433.

43. *Ibid.*, p. 430.

44. *Ibid.*

45. *Ibid.*, p. 431. See Kurzke's discussion of this passage, "Die Quellen der 'Betrachtungen eines Unpolitischen,' " pp. 305-6.

46. Hence those critics who contend that Mann advances the absurd "argument" that the Allies were fighting Germany to destroy German culture seem to have missed his basic point.

47. Reed ignores entirely the possibility that there exists something more than a hint of irony in Mann's prowar pronouncements: "Heinrich's humanitarianism led to such things as protest against the horrors of war. The tough-minded aesthete with his grasp of many-faceted reality found this trivial. An artist must be capable of relapse in the primitive. He refused to condemn war as such; it is one of the great facts of life, and it would be a degenerate humanity which was not worthy of war." Reed, *Thomas Mann: The Uses of Tradition*, p. 206. Reed accounts for this primitivism by pointing to Mann's liking for Nietzsche, which he says is a "simpler, vitalist Nietzsche," rather than

a "criticial" one. Mann's Nietzsche, according to Reed, "is shorn of his reservations" as well as "subtlety," yielding a nationalism purged of "all irony" (p. 219). As should become clear in this chapter, I disagree. Mann's ironic connections between Nietzsche and democratic politics are evidently lost on Reed.

48. Mann, *Reflections*, p. 186.

49. Erich Heller seems to have anticipated a Derridean-like critique of Mann: "There is, clearly, in Joseph's mind ample room to distinguish between that which *is* and that which is *meant*, between the observance and that which is observed; and once there is room to distinguish, there is also irony--the irony of the conscious need to interpret, to *make* sense rather than to find it as a given attribute of the world. . . . Thus defined, irony seems indeed the natural condition of the human mind at a certain stage of its growth: at the emergence of the multiple vision which was bound ironically to undermine the throne of those unironical royalties of Babel and the two Egypts by revealing that they were embodiments of the sun god only 'from one point of view.' Once 'points of view' have come into the world, the suspicion spreads that all 'meanings' are only so many texts read into life; and who can be sure then that what he reads is the text of the authorized version." Heller, *The Ironic German*, pp. 244-5.

50. "In these pages, I seem to have accepted and adopted as my own the antithesis of political or politicized art, and the art of estheticism. But that was a game; for seriously, I know better what the nature of this antithesis is, I know that it rests on a desired, nobly desired, self-deception that has gradually become all too successful for the one who decrees it, that it is wrong, that it does not exist, that one need not be an esthete when one does not believe in politics, but that one can, as a "serving" social-moralist and herald of resolute love of mankind, remain an arch-esthete." Mann, *Reflections*, p. 401.

51. In a letter to Reinhold Niebuhr on February 19, 1943, Mann wrote: "If I had remained at the level of *Reflections of a Nonpolitical Man*, which was, after all, not an antihumane book, I would still have taken a position with the same rage *and with the same justification* against this horror as I do today--*sit venia verbo*--as a 'democrat.' " Quoted by Morris, "Introduction," *Reflections*, p. xiii.

52. Cf. Lesser, "Of Thomas Mann's Renunciation," p. 252.

53. Jacques Derrida, *Disseminations*, trans. Barbara Johnson (Chicago: University of Chicago Press, 1981; see also Derrida, "From Restricted to General Economy: A Hegelianism Without Reserve," *Writing and Difference*, trans. Alan Bass (Chicago: University of Chicago Press, 1978), pp. 251-277, and *Éperons: Les Styles de Nietzsche (Spurs: Nietzsche's Styles)*, trans. Barbara Harlow (Chicago: University of Chicago Press, 1978).

54. Thomas notes the following remark by Mann (in 1953), which suggests that while Mann realized that he was "playing" his political role, he also took the "game" altogether seriously: "It is fascism and not communism which I, old-fashioned as I know I am, keep regarding as the most repulsive offspring of political history. It was the victories of fascism, and its--at bottom--undesired defeat, which drove me further to the left in social philosophy; it was due to

them that I have been turned at times into a hedge priest of democracy, a role whose comic side I could never ignore, even when I was most passionately longing for Hitler's downfall." Quoted in Thomas, *Thomas Mann*, p. 173.

55. Derrida himself seems to suggest otherwise: "Second, because, paradoxically, I think deconstructions *do have a relation*, but an altogether other relation, to the substance of the problems we are talking about here. To put it in a word, deconstructions have always represented, as I see it, the at least necessary condition for identifying and combatting the totalitarian risk in all the forms already mentioned." But after so many disseminations, I'm not sure Derrida can claim this good intention (or "relation") for his writings. Jacques Derrida, "Like the Sound of the Sea Deep within a Shell: Paul de Man's War," *Critical Inquiry* 14 (Spring, 1988), p. 647. In one essay Derrida explicitly uses the nuclear issue as an occasion to send missives to his readers; while this essay is brilliantly clever, I believe it falls into the category of nuclear criticism that George Kateb calls "distracted." Derrida, "No Apocalypse, No Now (full speed ahead, seven missiles, seven missives)," trans. Catherine Porter and Philip Lewis, *diacritics* 14, No. 2 (Summer, 1984), pp. 20-31.

56. I am aware that several commentators have been attempting to tease a coherent politics out of Derrida's writings, but I think these projects are as yet incomplete. See, for instance, Michael Ryan, *Marxism and Deconstruction: A Critical Articulation* (Baltimore and London: Johns Hopkins University Press, 1982); J. Fisher Solomon, *Discourse and Reference in the Nuclear Age* (Tulsa: University of Oklahoma Press, 1988); and Gayatri Spivak, *In Other Worlds: Essays in Cultural Politics* (New York: Methuen, 1987). Derrida himself is lobbing rhetorical volleys into the court of politics, but these pieces withhold more than they reveal. See Derrida, "The Laws of Reflection: Nelson Mandela, in Admiration," *For Nelson Mandela*, ed. Jacques Derrida and Mustapha Tlili (New York: Henry Holt, 1987), pp. 13-42; "Otobiographies: The Teaching of Nietzsche and the Politics of the Proper Name," trans. Avital Ronell, *The Ear of the Other*, ed. Christie McDonald (New York: Schocken, 1985); "Racism's Last Word," *Critical Inquiry* 12 (1985), pp. 290-299; Derrida, "The Politics of Friendship," *Journal of Philosophy* (1988), pp. 632-644. I think Rorty is right to suggest that Derrida's writings give up on politics, a private project of which Rorty approves; but then I don't find a joint Rorty-Derrida rejection of politics and political theory to be all that compelling (were either ever political to begin with?). Richard Rorty, "From Ironist Theory to Private Allusions: Derrida," *Contingency, Irony, and Solidarity* (Cambridge: Cambridge University Press, 1989), pp. 122-137.

57. I am thinking here primarily of Derrida's essay, "Différance," in *Margins of Philosophy*, trans. Alan Bass (Chicago, University of Chicago Press, 1982), pp. 1-27. But I also worry, for instance, when I read Derrida's deconstruction of "apocalyptic" writing as a philosophical "tone." Jacques Derrida, "Of an Apocalyptic Tone Recently Adopted in Philosophy," trans. John P. Leavey, Jr., *Oxford Literary Review* 6, No. 2 (1984), pp. 3-35.

58. See T.E. Apter, "The Fascination with Disgust," *Thomas Mann: The Devil's Advocate* (London: Macmillan Press, 1978), pp. 58-77.

59. George Kateb, "Nuclear Weapons and Individual Responsibility," *Dissent* (Spring 1986), pp. 161-172; "Thinking About Human Extinction (1): Nietzsche and Heidegger," *Raritan* 6, No. 2 (Fall 1986), pp. 1-28; "Thinking About Human Extinction (2): Emerson and Whitman," *Raritan* 6, No. 3 (Winter 1987), pp. 1-22.

60. *Idem*, "Thinking About Human Extinction (1)," p. 1.

61. Mann's own attempt to add Whitman to the equation, in the synthesis of democracy and Nietzschean aesthetics, probably begins only with "The German Republic." But his thinking in that essay is extraordinarily close to Kateb's, and Mann contends in the talk that his ideas are but an extension of those in *Reflections*. His attitude toward Whitman seems to have changed from an earlier period when he ridiculed Whitman's poetry as "wildwest Rousseauism." In any event, he does not yet invoke Whitman in *Reflections* to explain his new-found inclinations toward fellowship. His later endorsements of Whitman appear straightforward and sincere: "Europe has had much to learn from America as to the nature of democracy. It was your American statesmen and poets such as Lincoln and Whitman who proclaimed to the world democratic thought and feeling, and the democratic way of life, in imperishable words. The world has probably never produced a master of words who has known so well as Whitman how to elevate and translate a social principle such as democracy into intoxicating song, or how to endow it with such powerful emotional content, representing a magnificent fusion of spirituality and sensuousness." Thomas Mann, *The Coming Victory of Democracy*, trans. Agnes E. Meyer (New York: Alfred A. Knopf, 1938), p. 8. I might add that in the same year that Mann paid tribute to Whitman in "The German Republic," he also wrote, with respect to two patricians, that the "problem of irony" was "without exception the profoundest and most fascinating in the world. For we see here that nothing is more foreign to spirit than a desire to convert nature to itself." Thomas Mann, "Goethe and Tolstoy," *Essays by Thomas Mann*, trans. H.T. Lowe-Porter (New York: Vintage Books, 1957), p. 113.

62. Mann later states that this was the theme of the *Reflections*: "Probably my earliest prose writings that saw the light of print betray clearly enough the intellectual and stylistic influence of Nietzsche. In *The Reflections of a Nonpolitical Man* I have described my attitude of mind toward that whole compelling complex and traced it back to the personal factors which delimited and conditioned it. . . . In a word, what I saw above all else in Nietzsche was the victory over self. I took nothing literally; I *believed* him hardly at all; and this precisely it was that made my love for him a passion in two planes—gave it in other words, its depth." Thomas Mann, *A Sketch of My Life*, trans. H.T. Lowe-Porter (Paris: Harrison, 1930), pp. 21-22.

63. *Idem*, *Reflections*, p. 174.

64. *Ibid.*, p. 239.

65. *Ibid.*, p. 176.

66. *Ibid.*, p. 13.

67. *Ibid.*

68. *Ibid.,* p. 398.
69. Cf. Daniel W. Conway, "Solving the Problem of Socrates: Nietzsche's *Zarathustra* as Political Irony," *Political Theory* 16, No. 2 (May, 1988), pp. 257-280.
70. Mann, *Reflections,* p. 252.
71. *Ibid.,* p. 398.
72. *Ibid.,* p. 170.
73. *Ibid.,* p. 176.
74. *Ibid.,* p. 177.
75. Kateb, "Thinking About Human Extinction (1)," p. 4.
76. *Ibid.,* p. 9.
77. *Ibid.,* p. 20. Elsewhere Kateb considers a "nonaesthetic" version of beauty, to be found in Heidegger's notion of *Gelassenheit;* see George Kateb, *Hannah Arendt: Politics, Conscience, Evil* (Totawa, N.J.: Rowman and Allanheld, 1984), pp. 165ff.
78. Randy Newman's lyric "Let's drop the big one, and see what happens," in his song "Political Science," would seem to present a parody of the notion of Heideggerian wonder as a hedge against nuclear annihilation.
79. Kateb, "Thinking About Human Extinction (2)," p. 25.
80. At the celebration of his fiftieth birthday, Mann told a group of friends that he wished that people would say of his work "that it was friendly towards life although it knew of death." And he added: "There are two kinds of friendliness towards life: One that knows nothing of death, and this one is rather silly and robust. The other knows of death, and only this one has full spiritual value." "Tischrede," *Die Forderung des Tages* (Berlin: S. Fischer, 1930), p. 10; quoted in Lesser, "Of Thomas Mann's Renunciation," p. 250.
81. Though I wish to avoid a crude reductionism, I think some account of the striking difference in Heidegger's and Mann's respective views of national socialism is in order. Heidegger's bridge between phenomenology and politics, I want to say, was devoid of irony (Rorty to the contrary notwithstanding). This alone would not make Heidegger or anyone else predisposed toward nazism; but what one can say is that it was necessary for the fascists of Nazi Germany *not* to be open to irony in order for them to do what they did in the concentration camps. As Edwin Good has written (crediting Gilbert Highet with the original insight), "the Nazis fiendishly misunderstood Swift, for their 'final solution to the Jewish problem' followed lines not dissimilar to the *Proposal,* without, however, confining attention to the children." In other words, being a Nazi precludes being (philosophically) ironical; or to put it more positively, an ironic reading of Swift's "A Modest Proposal" would probably make it less likely for one to engage in genocide. Muecke makes a similar point, contending that it was not only because Heinrich Heine was a Jew that the Nazis attacked his works. The Nazis had to represent Heine as a totally irresponsible writer, had to attack his irony, in order to maintain their exclusivistic definition of German nationalism. In no way do I want to suggest that irony--i.e., simply reading a text or writing a text with a sense of irony in mind--automatically prohibits one from being a Nazi. But I do think

irony is philosophically incompatible with nazism; and if, as Kierkegaard claimed, "whoever has essentially irony, has it all day long," is true, then one cannot kill Jews in the morning and be ironical (in the full Kierkegaardian sense) in the afternoon.   Edwin M. Good, *Irony in the Old Testament* (Philadelphia: Westminster Press, 1965), p. 23; D.C. Muecke, *The Compass of Irony* (London: Methuen and Company, 1969), p. 246. Baumgardt connects Mann's antinazism directly with his investment in irony: "Denn der Kampf gegen das dritte Reich war auch ein Kampf für die Möglichkeit der Ironie, die spielend und zögernd offengelassene Wahlfreiheit." *Das Ironische und die Ironie in den Werken Thomas Manns*, p. 95.

82. Kateb, "Thinking About Human Extinction (1)," p. 3.

83. This is not to say that ironic art is inherently nihilistic, either; Mann wrote somewhat later: "[Art] is of all powers the most human and most friendly to humanity, mediating as she does between spirit and life. There can be no greater mistake than to conceive of her irony--the irony of all mediating influences--as a blithe nihilistic avoidance of the struggle and of human duty. She, whose joyous endeavour it is to permeate nature with the human and to take from nature what she needs for the creative heightening of life: she, who is the kindling spirit in matter, the instinctive urge to humanization (for there is such an instinct)—how should she cease to function in an age when the world-- as always dilatory and reluctant in such matters--needs more than ever this spiritual reshaping?" "Mass und Wert," *Order of the Day*, p. 90.

84. See George Kateb's discussion of Arendt's analysis of *Fiat justitia, et pereat mundus*, "Modernity," *Hannah Arendt: Politics, Conscience, Evil*, pp. 149-187.

85. Mann claimed in "The German Republic" that *Reflections* was essentially a declaration of "humanism." "The German Republic," p. 24. And Stock mentions another later retrospective to that effect: "I had never done anything [in *Reflections*] but defend humanity. I shall never do anything else." Mann, "The Years of My Life," *Harpers* (October, 1950), pp. 256-7.

86. This, too, is Rorty's overall project in *Contingency, Irony, and Solidarity*; but for Rorty, while irony permits by default a politics of liberal accommodation, irony suggests no theoretical way to translate itself into the public sphere. Odd, that in his attempt to reconcile things nineteenth century-ish and Nietzschean with things twentieth century-ish and political, Rorty gives scant attention to Thomas Mann's literary mediations and nothing at all to Mann's own project of interpreting Nietzsche ironically for the sake of political democracy.

6

Irony in the Antinuclear Movement

> More than any other time in history, mankind faces a crossroads. One path leads to despair and utter hopelessness. The other, to total extinction. Let us pray we have the wisdom to choose correctly.
> --Woody Allen, *Side Effects*

> I think you guys are going to have to come up with a lot of wonderful *new* lies, or people just aren't going to want to go on living.
> --Kurt Vonnegut, Jr., *Slaughterhouse Five*

June 20, 1983: In protest of the sheer existence of thermonuclear weaponry, groups from around the world, though primarily in Western Europe and the United States, have designated this day "The International Day of Nuclear Disarmament."[1] Numerous acts of nonviolent civil disobedience, in conjunction with several well-publicized peaceful marches and legal demonstrations, have been organized to take place at various strategic locations, mostly military munitions sites or research laboratories where nuclear weapons are designed and produced. One of these laboratories, the Lawrence Livermore National Laboratory, located in Livermore, California, has been targeted for protest by an antinuclear organization in northern California, the Livermore Action Group.[2]

On this day, at a prearranged time, protesters gather at certain street corners on access roads leading to the Livermore laboratory. The initial atmosphere is festive, almost like a carnival.[3] Small bands of persons in the crowd are singing folksongs. Many persons are dressed in brightly colored clothing; some even wear costumes and masks.[4] Nearly every protester is adorned with some extra article: an armband around the sleeve, a button on the shirt, a placard held in hand. Someone has inflated a giant balloon in the shape of a rocket and has deposited it on a nearby lawn. Most of the protesters are here today simply to lend moral "support" to the few who have chosen in advance to risk arrest. People arrive late; the crowd builds. A group of Buddhists continue to beat their small drums as they chant in low monotones.

As if it were all staged, the scene suddenly changes, the atmosphere abruptly turns solemn. A group of six or seven elderly men and women have taken the first step to sit down in the middle of the street, thereby blocking traffic en route to the laboratory. A handicapped woman drives her motorized wheelchair along with the group of elders, thus accompanying them in their open defiance of state traffic laws. Now situated in the center of the street, they stop a large truck from proceeding, and, holding helium-filled balloons, they draw closer to the truck's wheels and front bumper. The onlooking protesters momentarily break the tension with applause and whistles of approval. But, stage right, several squadrons of policemen, dressed in full riot gear, enter the scene, having observed from a distance the elderly make their move. The policemen march single file down both sides of the street, pushing as they go stray spectators and rubbernecks back into the throng, thus preventing the crowd from spilling out into the street. Once the pathway is cleared, another squadron, numbering about twenty-five, marches down the center of the street toward the elderly disobedients. Through a hand-held loudspeaker one of them announces to the elderly that they, the elderly, are acting in violation of the laws of California and will be placed under arrest on behalf of the people of California if they do not move immediately. They do not move. The twenty-five policemen march as a unit closer toward the six elderly persons and the woman in the wheelchair. They pause for their final orders. By twos, the policemen reach down to arrest individual protesters. They apply special armholds to the protesters, twisting their arms so that the protesters will rise to their feet of their own accord (more or less). But one man, his gray hair suggesting an age over sixty, lets his body go limp, thereby passively resisting arrest. The two policemen assigned to him twist both of his arms, forcing him to stand up. They march him down the street, still twisting both arms. He and his fellows are escorted to an awaiting schoolbus, which evidently has been reserved in advance for the purpose of transporting the arrested on this day to a nearby jailing facility. Just before they board the bus, the arrested men and women are handcuffed, their arms bound behind them with a piece of plastic material. The handicapped woman too is arrested and is wheeled down the street. But she is pushed to a special bus, a van designed for the handicapped, which evidently has been reserved in advanced for the purpose of transporting arrested handicapped persons on this day to a nearby jailing facility. One of her attending officers binds her smallish hands with the same plastic-model handcuffs. The crowd has been chanting angrily, the volume steadily building. But now it grows quiet as the woman is placed on a platform that mechanically lifts her up and into the van. As she ascends, she smiles faintly and nods to the crowd below. They yell back, "Thank you, thank you!" and suddenly break into applause and whistles.

A disinterested observer of this spectacle--assuming for the sake of argument that one could remain disinterested standing in witness of this display--might ask these of protesters, and in particular of the handicapped woman: How do they think their actions will actually accomplish anything? Clearly they are guided by the supposedly proven method of Gandhi's *satyagraha*, the idea of nonviolent resistance; but in this case it is difficult to see exactly how songs, buttons, costumes, chants, whistles, and balloons are ever going to dismantle the most powerful weapons mankind has ever invented. For what ripple effect could they possibly hope that might translate into real and widespread political consequences? Put even more directly, why does the handicapped woman, who is obviously so personally powerless, feel that she can militate against a state that is obviously so powerful and against bombs that are so deadly, simply by holding up a balloon while she holds up traffic? Is hers an act of supreme presumptuousness, or misbegotten rebelliousness, or sheer desperation, or plain lunacy, or what?

Critics of the antinuclear movement have in fact already raised these questions and have provided some answers. Typically they argue that the actions of the protesters are either illogical or naïve.[5] The Alameda County district attorney, for instance, has contended in court that the protesters' case depends on their establishing a logical connection between the protests and an actual reduction in the arms race, and such a connection "does not exist."[6] The authors of the Harvard Study Group's book, *Living with Nuclear Weapons*, however, do perceive a vague logic in the protesters' actions but charge that the logic is escapist and naïve. They explain that persons often turn to small doses of humor as a way of avoiding the difficult issues in the nuclear debate. They contend that Stanley Kubrick's movie "Dr. Strangelove" and Tom Lehrer's songs were analogous examples of reversion into black humor; and as such, these and similar antinuclear measures constitute forms of psychological "denial," a way of "treating the subject lightly so as to release the tension" in order to cope with the underlying fear. Black humor, they claim, is "a way to stop worrying" (an interpretation they draw by taking literally Kubrick's subtitle "Or How I Learned to Stop Worrying and Love the Bomb").[7] What the Harvard authors pose as the alternative to such escapism and denial is "a better understanding of the vast problems nuclear weaponry creates." The point of their book is that such an understanding will lead to the conclusion that we must, as their title suggests, learn to live with nuclear weapons, a goal that, they say, is "realistic."[8]

In supposing themselves to have a privileged insight into the inner workings of "reality," the Harvard Study Group assumes a typical stance with respect to the opponents of nuclear weapons. Namely, the critics of the antinuclear movement characteristically take the epistemological highroad, contending that their opponents' "idealistic" sentiments, though perhaps well intended, represent a kind of intellectual naïveté. The hard-line version of such criticism argues that the antinuclear movement in the Western world plays unwittingly into the hands of the Soviets; the more modest version of this charge is that the movement's participants simply cannot grasp the paradox that in order to preserve the peace in a world with belligerent enemies, a nation must prepare for "worst-case scenarios." To such critics, then, the issue dividing them from the antinuclear activists is not one of "ends" (for neither side wants nuclear war, is the common refrain) but simply one of "means," of realistic strategy and military effectiveness.[9] Thus the Harvard Study Group argues that the problem of nuclear weapons is strictly technical: "The choice the United States faces is not, and has never been, 'Better Red than Dead.' Most Americans reject both alternatives. It is better to be 'Armed than Harmed,' and if the nation pursues intellectual policies it need never choose between surrender or death. Where people who have studied these issues disagree is over what kind of arms policy the United States should follow."[10]

In sum, the main criticism of the antinuclear movement is that it is on the whole anti-intellectual, or is at least without reputable theoretical backing. The movement has not comprehended the intractability of the international weapons game and thus has tended to flee into the utopian world of balloons and humor. As the Harvard group and other critics claim, the movement entertains the "myth" of a world without such weapons.[11] It lacks the intellectual wherewithal to confront the world as it is and to proceed from there. Moreover, occasionally the criticism extends beyond the charge of simple naïveté and turns into the charge of closed-mindedness and even seditiousness. A mass demonstration, it is said, subverts rational political discourse and encourages mob rule. The chants, slogans, songs, buttons, balloons, and bumper stickers trivialize national debate and may even leave the protesters susceptible to covert Soviet manipulation (a charge leveled by the *Reader's Digest* magazine and once echoed by then-president Ronald Reagan).

Such criticism of the antinuclear movement is deeply mistaken, I think. The final purpose of this entire book, and especially of this chapter, is to give a theoretical voice to the antinuclear movement, to reveal its intellectual underpinnings and its contribution to national political discourse.[12] To put it more specifically, I intend to articulate the political theory behind the handicapped woman's action on June 20, 1983. To this end I will not be forwarding an argument as to the relative merits of missiles on either side of the Ukraine, nor will I be reciting the up-to-the-minute numbers regarding the respective mega-tonnage and throw-weight capacities in the arsenals of the super-powers. I am excluding such purely factual material not because I think it is irrelevant to the nuclear debate--of course it is not--but rather because my argument takes a completely different form, adopts a very different approach. Much of the literature on the nuclear issue, I have found, focuses exclusively upon technical matters. I want to say that this common approach--the careful weighing of the history of the arms race and the subsequent attempt to draw a conclusion from the interpretation of numbers--belongs, as it were, to the realm of the "literal." As purely technical accounts, these arguments are not directly *political*; indeed, the expressed purpose of deterrence and "redundancy scenarios" is precisely to eliminate *political* considera-tions from nuclear calculations and to substitute predictably adminis-trative and procedural factors in their place.[13] As exclusively "literal" arguments they are, I suggest, woefully shortsighted and limited in addressing the larger issues of the nuclear dilemma, a perspective something like--in counting missiles, they miss the forest.

As an alternative method, I want to recover (for it surely seems to have been dropped by the wayside) the significance of the *political* in nuclear matters, and I intend to do this by focusing upon the *ironic* consciousness, the sense of irony, displayed by the antinuclear movement in particular, and by the strategy of nonviolent resistance in general. To the question I posed earlier--how can the handicapped woman, who is so obviously weak in her physical person, militate against the state and its bombs, which are so obviously powerful?--I will now disclose the preliminary and indirect answer: *Literally*, she cannot. She cannot fight fire with fire, meet force with force, match might with might. Instead, her actions make an appeal, on the basis of irony, to a larger democratic populace beyond her own person and beyond the antinuclear movement itself. In sharp opposition to the critics of the antinuclear movement (who seem to have missed the irony altogether), I want to propose that this ironic appeal is *coherent*, that it has a logic, a positive direction, especially within the context and against the background of the threat of nuclear annihilation. The logic can be followed by others--hers is not an appeal to magic, whim, or fantasy--and implicit in that logic is a program for an expansive politics in the nuclear age. This view of an ironic politics in the nuclear age, I will argue, includes at least indirect implications for national policy as well as for international policy and international relations.

Nonviolent Criticism

Let us therefore examine the logic of the antinuclear movement. Since the movement's protests and demonstrations are deliberately nonviolent, we should first examine the theory of nonviolent resistance to see whether it contains a plausible strategy for an effective politics. Much has been written on the topic of nonviolent resistance, though most of the commentary is devoted to the question of whether nonviolent acts of civil disobedience are morally or legally justified. Inevitably, the question of justification turns on an acceptance of some variation upon a social contract theory of politics. Instead of heading down this path, I would like to examine the question of strategy separate from the question of justification, and I would like to avoid the presumption that a social contract theory necessarily characterizes contemporary political relations.

As an alternative, I propose that we ask the question: How can the strategy of nonviolent resistance work in a "Nietzschean/Weberian" world? By "Nietzschean" I mean a world in which "God is dead"; that is, a world in which professed belief in transcendent universals no longer binds people naturally together; a world, in other words, that is likely to be ethically fragmented. By "Weberian" I mean the attempt to act in such a world "in spite of all!"; that is, the attempt to take public or "worldly" action--action that affects others--despite one's sense of the absence of a transcendental basis for political community, despite deep-seated ethical differences among people. The original question could be rephrased, "How can a political movement expect to avoid annihilating others in an age of nihilism?" or "How can a political movement expect to avoid violating others in an age of violence?"

If we look to the writings of the most famous champions of nonviolence--Thoreau, Gandhi, and King--we shall come away dissatisfied or mystified about the strategy of nonviolence (given our complicating conditions), for each of these writers explains the strategy of nonviolence by appealing to some literal notion of universalism. Thoreau did not concern himself with the interpersonal consequences of his personal act of "civil disobedience"; his justification of his crime was based upon a view of the primacy of the rights of the individual over the authority of the state. His act expressed the view that personal conscience should be inviolate, that the inner life of the individual ought to be universally regarded as sacred. He did not consider, however, that consciences could clash over particular issues, or that, as Hegel warned, a Reign of Virtue could turn quickly into a Reign of Terror.[14]

Gandhi spent considerably more time than Thoreau in elaborating the intersubjective dynamics of nonviolent action that issues from personal conscience; but his notion of *satyagraha* must remain a mystery to the unbelieving skeptic.[15] *Satya* means "truth" or "love," and *agraha* is "force"; thus *satyagraha* is "truth-force" or "soul-force" or the "power of love." How exactly this truth and soulfulness and love win over one's adversaries is, however, open to question. Sometimes Gandhi wrote that *satyagraha* is an appeal to the opponent's intellect and sense of principle;[16] sometimes he wrote that *satyagraha* attempts to shame the opponent;[17] frequently he wrote that the technique is an appeal to the opponent's "heart," elicited by an open display of self-imposed suffering.[18] Nonetheless, Gandhi's explanations hardly seem applicable outside the context of British rule, in which some common moral ground between ruler and resister could have been presumed to exist; and thus his notion of *satyagraha* seems extremely vulnerable to the criticism that if the "strategy of nonviolent resistance had met with a different enemy--Stalin's Russia, Hitler's Germany, even prewar Japan, instead of England--the outcome would not have been decolonization, but massacre and submission."[19]

Martin Luther King, Jr., was explicit in his view that a Nietzschean outlook had to be repudiated before one could consider the strategy of nonviolent resistance "a potent instrument for social and collective transformation."[20] In describing his intellectual pilgrimage leading to an acceptance of nonviolence, King wrote that his "faith in love was temporarily shaken by the philosophy of Nietzsche."[21] Nietzsche had attacked the "whole of the Hebraic-Christian morality," which made King despair about "the power of love in solving social problems." But after reading Gandhi, King became convinced that Nietzsche had been utterly mistaken, for Gandhi taught how "to lift the love ethic of Jesus above mere interaction between individuals to a powerful and effective social force on a large scale."[22] Eventually, King endorsed a Greek version of love, as *agape*. *Agape* is a willingness to "restore community,"[23] a "recognition of the fact that all life is interrelated. All humanity is involved in a single process, and all men are brothers." *Agape* is the "only cement that can hold this broken community together."[24] The question could be posed to King whether one and one's adversaries must be believing Christians, or else believers in *agape*, in order for nonviolence to work. His answer was forthright. One need not believe in a personal God, but the parties involved must believe "in the existence of some creative force that works for universal wholeness. Whether we call it an unconscious process, an impersonal Brahman, or a Personal Being of matchless power and infinite love, there is a creative force in this universe that works to bring the disconnected aspects of reality into a harmonious whole."[25] From this statement it could easily be inferred that King would not have considered nonviolence a plausible or viable strategy given a "Nietzschean/Weberian" world.

Several writers, while inspired by Thoreau, Gandhi, and King, have attempted to give more secular, less mystical explanations of how nonviolence effects political change.[26] Yet their answers, too, involve some version of universalism that implicitly ignores or simply denies the Nietzschean challenge to universalist ethics. Richard B. Gregg, for instance, argues in his book, *The Psychology and Strategy of Gandhi's Nonviolent Resistance*, that Gandhi's *satyagraha* is "universally valid" and that it can be understood in "secular" (i.e., "psychological and philosophical") terms.[27] Gregg proposes the idea that nonviolence involves a process of moral jujitsu, whereby one in effect holds up a moral mirror to one's opponent. Yet this argument rests finally upon Gregg's belief that Western ethics and Eastern religion hold certain ideals in common that can be understood and accepted by either side in a political conflict.

George T. Lakey responds that Gregg's book presents a first approximation of "just how nonviolent action works, when it does," but he complains that Gregg's thesis suffers from outdated psychological concepts. Lakey identifies instead three "sociological mechanisms"-- coercion, conversion, and persuasion--that he claims describe the various forms of nonviolent action; and then he reveals what he thinks to be the dominant psychological process underwriting two of these sociological mechanisms. He argues that no prior morality or "feeling of kinship" need characterize the opponents for a strategy of nonviolent resistance to work. Rather, nonviolence brings the suffering of the victims out into the open and thereby makes an appeal to the combatants' "common ability to suffer," which underscores their "common humanity."[28] This leads, claims Lakey, to a Freudian identification of the oppressor with the sufferer. (Lakey argues that the Nazis would have identified more in human terms with the Jews had

the Jews taken an open, collective stand against Hitler's regime.[29])
Perceiving the sufferer as a fellow human being is the first step toward
the inner conversion of the oppressor.

Gene Sharp has been the most prolific contemporary writer on the
subject of nonviolent action. In his impressively researched three-
volume work, *The Politics of Nonviolent Action*, Sharp shifts emphasis
away from Gregg's concern with common morality and away from
Lakey's concern with inner conversion, and instead focuses upon what
Sharp calls the *politics* of nonviolent action. He argues that the success
of nonviolent strategies does not require shared standards and
principles, a high degree of community, or even a high degree of
psychological closeness between resister and oppressor.[30] Sharp contends that most forms of nonviolent action involve a process of *political*
(as opposed to moral) jujitsu, whereby one turns the oppressor's *power*
back against him to disable him. This technique works, however,
because political power ultimately derives, according to Sharp, from
society. Sharp devotes the first volume of his trilogy to an explication
of the theory of this view of political power. His argument amounts to
what Arendt called a "vertical" contract theory,[31] namely that a group
of people collectively enter into a covenant with a supreme secular
authority and thereby confer power and legitimacy upon that
authority. For nonviolent activists, the importance of this insight into
the social bases of political power is that consent (and hence power)
may be withdrawn from authorities just as it was once conferred.

The problem with Sharp's analysis is that he makes no mention
and offers no analysis of what Arendt termed the "horizontal" contract,
namely "that aboriginal contract which brought about not government
but society,"[32] an alliance among all individual members; and it would
seem that incumbent upon Sharp is the need to discuss the "horizontal"
basis of society since he relies upon it so heavily, if implicitly, in his
theory of nonviolence. Sharp focuses so completely upon the
relationship between oppressor and resister that he ignores the
internal dynamics of society, wherein the roots of all power supposedly
lie. This omission becomes most evident in Sharp's discussions of Max
Weber; and it points to the main problem in his account of the political
dynamics of nonviolence. To establish the social and nonviolent bases
of power, Sharp feels he must wrest from Weber the latter's alleged
identification of power with *violence.*[33] Essentially Sharp argues that
Gandhi and King demonstrated that nonviolent action *could* prove
effective and responsible, which obversely implies something about
the societal basis of power. In short, Sharp's critique of Weber's
violent view of politics turns on a benign view of society.

But Sharp misreads Weber's Nietzscheanism and thus misunderstands why Weber viewed modern politics as inherently violent. In his essay "Politics as a Vocation," Weber forced a distinction between ultimate ends and responsible means *not* because he was convinced that only violent means could be effective in the modern world. Rather, his views of violence were *derived from* his almost uncritically complete acceptance of Nietzsche's depiction of the modern world (or, "society") as ethically fragmented, as riddled by moral paradoxes and torn by a "war of beliefs."[34] Deep cultural and religious differences were seen as characterizing persons and as fundamentally dividing them (and throughout his life Weber had held to the conviction that ideals go to the heart of human beings). Politics, however, is the art of living together, despite these ingrained differences. Now, perhaps Weber overestimated the independent force of ideals, perhaps he respected them too much; but given this worldview, his conclusion follows that the politician necessarily will step on some toes if he attempts to bridge these differences. "Violence" in Weber's scheme of things means physical force only on the assumption that one's ideals govern one's entire person. Weber seems to have felt that modern politics necessarily would "violate" persons in their innermost being and *therefore* would require physically forceful sanctions. "Whoever wants to engage in politics at all . . . must know that he is responsible for what may become of himself under the impact of these [ethical] paradoxes."[35]

Weber saw no neat way to mediate "ideal" differences between persons and within society, and perhaps we can take issue with him on this score. But it will not do for theorists of nonviolence simply to assert the validity of an abiding horizontal social contract against the objections of a Nietzschean nonbeliever. In one's zeal to sever the modern concept of violence from the modern concept of power one must not attempt merely to recover a lost innocence: The phrase "nonviolent power" is *not* a redundancy, as Arendt claimed it was.[36] If a strategy of nonviolent action is to be regarded as practical for modern politics, then we must develop a theory of politics that recognizes and accommodates the possibility of the inherent "ethical irrationality"[37] of the modern world.

Arendt herself provides a starting point for developing a theory of politics such that nonviolence might seem plausible within an ethically dubious world. In a section in *The Human Condition* in which she distinguishes between power and strength (as they relate to political efficacy), Arendt makes the following comment:

Popular revolt against materially strong rulers . . . may engender an
almost irresistible power even if it forgoes the use of violence in the
face of materially vastly superior forces. To call this "passive
resistance" is certainly an ironic idea; it is one of the most active and
efficient ways of action ever devised, because it cannot be countered
by fighting, where there may be defeat or victory, but only by mass
slaughter in which even the victor is defeated, cheated of his prize,
since nobody can rule over dead men.[38]

Why is calling such popular revolt "passive" resistance an "ironic
idea"? Arendt's choice of the word *ironic* may have been casual or
intuitive, but she uses the word in this passage in a very complicated
way. Irony in this context, she writes, is an "idea" (and surely more is
at stake in the above passage than simply the correct labeling of the
phenomenon of popular revolt). What, then, is the idea about?

First what it is not about: The idea is not, as the social contract
theorists of nonviolence suggest, simply about the withdrawal of
consent and thus of actual power from authorities, power that is
ultimately rooted in the firm foundations of society. Nonviolent action
is not simply moral or political jujitsu. No, the way Arendt has
presented the idea of nonviolence is to suggest that the rulers and the
resisters enter into a kind of active and noncombative relationship *with
each other* (and not simply through the wielding of moral canons or the
power of numbers as "weapons"[39] against one another); certainly we can
see parallels between this active, mutually engaging, noncombative
relationship and what Arendt understood as a uniquely *political*
relationship. What, then, is the basis, are the details, are the
dynamics of this particular relationship?

The nonviolent resisters Arendt describes have literally put their
lives on the line to make a point; the point is apparently more
important to them than life itself. Now surely this action must be
viewed as a strategy of sorts, containing a partial bluff; certainly the
resisters must hope that they are not taken too literally, that their
bluff not be automatically called. They cannot intend that their ruler
simply kill them and that the matter end abruptly there. There is an
indirect appeal, then, being made to the ruler, a deal being proposed:
make certain concessions, or else lose the entire basis of your authority
(for without us followers, you will be no authority at all). Arendt calls
this an "efficient" way of acting and bargaining, but I am not so sure of
that. It seems to me that the ruler is left with a *difficult* calculation to
make: Kill the resisters, and adhere abstractly to one's principles of
ruling; or let them live, grant them some concessions, and retain only
partial (even if actual) command. To my mind, it *could* go either way.

On what basis will the ruler make his decision? Everything will depend on whether the ruler chooses to respect the lives and concerns of the resisters more than he values the principles of his rule (as considered abstractly and separately from the actual exercise of his authority). In the above passage, Arendt obliquely suggests (assuming that the material to the right of her semicolon is an explication of the material to the left) that an "ironic idea" is implicitly revealed when the ruler chooses the former option over the latter one (i.e., when commentators call this particular result the product of "passive" resistance).

Calling popular revolt "passive resistance" is ironic because the process actually involves a kind of active, if subliminal, dialogue or interaction between human actors in which matters of the highest importance are carefully presented, the stakes of the issue made clear, and decisions deliberately made. The resisters *could* have chosen not to resist in the first place or they could have chosen to fight to the death; the ruler *could* have chosen to kill them from the outset. That both parties agreed to settle matters in a nonviolent manner, chose to recognize each other as the basis for negotiations, runs contrary to a certain set of expectations, represents a possible irony. That choice--made by both parties--holds many implications for politics (an insight of which Arendt was at least implicitly aware as evidenced in her occasional claim that many resistance movements in history have embodied an essential moment of free political activity). Taking Arendt's view of the "ironic idea" potentially involved in nonviolent resistance as our cue, let us return to our antinuclear scenario with the handicapped woman in order to see whether we can identify an element of irony at work within the protests and demonstrations of the antinuclear movement.

Reading Balloons and Bumper Stickers

We will approach the antinuclear scenario in Livermore as a text to be read, but we must bear in mind the difficulties discussed in Chapter 3 regarding the understanding of irony primarily as a textual phenomenon. Because we have defined irony as a process of reading and writing and interactive communication rather than as a syntactical structure or a set textual matrix, and because we have embraced a notion of irony as an inherently unstable concept, we must make certain allowances at the outset for the likelihood of an eventually *unstable* interpretation. We will not reach a firm final conclusion about whether irony "exists" or not. Rather, reading irony is an ongoing process of interpretation: posing questions, making guesses, reflecting further, inclining perhaps toward an answer. Because irony is indeed complex, requiring from a reader more involvement than simply the application of a formula or the recognition of a textual mechanism, we must to some extent repeat the "experiential" approach to reading irony that we described and employed in earlier chapters.

As we have learned, the process of interpreting irony--or we should say rather, that of only suspecting irony--begins typically (though not always) with the recognition of a particular kind of textual discrepancy, a subtle incongruity that at first seems accidental or occasional but that, upon reflection, shows signs of deliberateness. Taking our cue from these telltale signs, we begin to question the validity of the literal text.

The antinuclear protests of the early 1980s have contained several general incongruities that may strike the observer. Perhaps most notable is the observation that the movement seems composed mainly of "mainstream" personalities from society: professionals (physicians, architects, educators, et al.), the clergy and religious groups, all ages including the very young and the very old, and many women.[40] To be sure, the movement includes its share of young, white, bearded males, but conspicuously the demonstrations attract a greater cross section of the population than simply the rebellious youth and marginal radicals associated with the college protests of the two previous decades. No outward characteristic or common creed (except antinuclearism) seems to hold the motley assortment of various persons and groups together, and thus the observer cannot easily impute a self-interested motive to the movement as a whole (as one could perhaps to the student protests of the sixties, for instance on the grounds of youthful self-indulgence, unresolved Oedipalism, or fear of body bags).

Second, the general gaiety and festive atmosphere characterizing most antinuclear demonstrations (as opposed to the morose or angry atmospheres surrounding other protest movements) seem out of place considering the gravity of the subject under protest, viz., nuclear weapons. Perhaps even more poignant is that the theatrical props-- the bands, songs, buttons, and balloons--which under normal circum- stances would be associated with playful and peacetime pursuits, seem especially anomalous in this confrontational setting, in which the police carry shields, guns, and billy clubs.

The handicapped woman's presence sharpens these contrasts almost to a point of melodramatic absurdity. Certainly the sight of policemen carting out a helpless handicapped woman, as if she were physically a real threat to society, makes us wince a bit, perhaps more out of a sense of confusion or embarrassment or of the bizarre rather than from a straight identification either with her or with her attending officers. Her act of holding the balloon underscores the absurdity of the situation.

But here is the point at which reading irony becomes tricky, for, I suggest, a complete interpretation cannot be made on the textual level alone,[41] cannot be made merely on the basis of the balloon. The woman calls attention to herself by holding the balloon, dramatizing her passivity, and thus calls attention to the disparity between her level of strength and that of the police. Yet she is, so to speak, only floating a balloon; she is extending an invitation to *us* to examine the situation further (for the complete story does not unfold immediately before our eyes). "Why is she doing this?" seems the appropriate question to ask. Now at this point we have the option of taking leave of the text completely: We can quickly conclude that she is crazed, or that she is nicely nonviolent but naïvely childlike, or that she is "grandstanding" for personal attention, and so on. But none of these answers is completely satisfying intellectually, because her act seems *so* contrived, *so* melodramatic, *so* overt and thus so *deliberate*, that surely she must have some further reason for it. If we accept what seems to be her silent invitation to us to probe further, then we will be led to examine the logic of her apparent illogic. If we think about the situation, there is ample reason to suspect that the woman *herself* must know that holding balloons alone will not dismantle any bombs.

As described in Chapter 3, at some key point in the process of reading irony, one will need to shift interpretive strategies. If the reader pushes himself or herself sufficiently, he or she will be virtually forced to go beyond the text itself, to abstract from the text, and will seek instead some general account of the author's motivations. The reader will be prompted to inquire into what might be called the *function* as opposed to the *structure* of the language of balloons in the context of a protest demonstration. By directing us to focus upon a balloon, the handicapped woman has offered us a tangible, if in some sense indirect, way of thinking about the whole nuclear dilemma.

Some General Nuclear Notations

Reflections upon nuclear matters may lead in a number of directions, but one book in particular helps very much, I think, to understand the actions and the logic of the handicapped woman as being part of a strong undercurrent of thought within the twentieth century. Paul Fussell, in *The Great War and Modern Memory*, posits that the consciousness, or in his words "the mode of memory" of the twentieth century is predominantly *ironic*, and the reason has to do with the experience of world war in this century. Every war engenders irony, writes Fussell, for every war "constitutes an irony of situation because its means are so melodramatically disproportionate to its presumed ends."[42] But World War I in particular was "more ironic than any other"--so much so, contends Fussell, that the irony of that war continues to affect the way we think about wars and warfare in general.

Irony for Fussell is a study in contrasts, a recognition of situational reversals and odd juxtapositions that attest to some discrepancy between expectations or ideals and reality.[43] Irony is a form of consciousness that attaches in particular to the experience of warfare--and especially world warfare--because warfare, according to Fussell, provides images that shock and numb the psyche; and virtually the only way to confront and to assimilate such images, and yet to put up a personal defense against them, is to approach their horrors by indirection. Irony provides such a strategy of indirection, a way of juxtaposing the terrifying stream of events in warfare with more comprehensible and accessible notions, thereby "dramaticiz[ing] the fantastic and normaliz[ing] the unspeakable."[44] While warfare seems incomprehensible and devastating on the one hand, the strategy of ironic juxtaposition allows the survivors to remember their experiences with a special vividness: "The very enormity of the proceedings, their absurd remove from the usages of the normal world, will guarantee that a structure of irony sufficient for ready narrative recall will attach to them."[45]

Fussell examines the literature and poetry of the post-World War I period and concludes that the experience of trench warfare engendered several varieties of ironic association unique to that form of warfare and that war: e.g., juxtapositions between warfare and pastoral themes, sexual themes, or theater and stage metaphors. But Fussell makes a larger claim in the book, namely that the ironic war consciousness has entrenched itself in our memories, that it continues to occupy and to invade our psyches. He suggests, for instance, that much of the dichotomous thinking in this century; the use of military euphemisms and jargon in our language; and the haunting idea of endless warfare can be traced back to World War I. Fussell finds evidence for this thesis in the novels of Thomas Pynchon and Norman Mailer, authors too young to have experienced first hand the Great War but whose works he says are clearly part of the thematic legacy of that war. Mailer, for example, seems to conceive of human consciousness as a form of lifelong warfare; and his recurring motif of walking the parapet--a World War I image--suggests that the ironic war consciousness has become a permanent feature of human existence: "a sense of anxiety without end, life without purpose, perpetual self-testing, doubts about one's identity and values" and "a fascinated love-loathing of the threatening, alien terrain on the other side."[46]

Fussell's thesis suggests several ways to understand the handicapped woman's actions as a use of irony as a *rhetorical* technique. First, several other authors have argued that nuclear war is difficult to think about simply because it is abstract.[47] As Jonathan Schell has pointed out, the problem is not one of moral indifference to evil; it is not as if the population has been "Eichmannized," because, says Schell, the expressions of evil are different in the cases of Nazi Germany and the present nuclear situation. Eichmann participated unflinchingly, banally, in an act occurring in his presence. Whereas one could argue that the nuclear buildup is going on right under *our* noses, it is also true that nuclear war has *not* yet occurred.[48] The antinuclear movement, then, must face the tactical problem of how to activate persons, how to goad them to commit themselves to the prevention of something that has not really impinged upon their daily lives.

In view of this problem, we can understand the woman's balloon as providing a tangible point of reference, a graphic reminder that *this* balloon would burst should there be a nuclear war. The element of rhetorical irony involved in the woman's act of holding the balloon consists in the extent to which she is indeed simply *floating* a balloon in order for her spectators to think about bombs. Hers is a strategy of indirection: Because the balloon is *so* unlike the bomb, it can be used as an allusion to the bomb and all its abstract horrors.[49]

But in earlier chapters I have argued that the rhetoric of irony is not *simply* a mechanism for inversion; it is not simply a straight declination from the literal text. Regarding our protest scenario, this qualification means that there is indeed some validity to the balloon on its own terms, and that a double perspective is thus suggested. Balloons connote an ideal, perhaps imaginary world, a world of play and color and innocence. In an antinuclear demonstration, certainly balloons symbolize on some level the possibility of a world without bombs. This symbolism, however, is not merely an appeal to fantasy, to utopia, to a child's world; it is not simply and literally the use of balloon-power (or the former "flower-power") against bomb-power. Rather, the woman's holding the balloon appears to be the use of a child's toy as an intellectual foil to the horrible world of bombs; and the power of the symbol has to do with the salient fact that the balloon is very real indeed and not just "utopian." Thus the balloon gives us a tangible point of reference allowing us to imagine not only abstract horrors but also abstract alternatives--yet the paradoxical point should be emphasized that a balloon presents tangibly an abstract alternative to the present nuclear world only to a person who sees a certain irony in all of that.

Second, the woman's actions appeal to or provoke a sense of irony not only because they emerge within the Fussellian context of twentieth-century warfare but also because they take place precisely within a liberal-democratic polity. Holding up a balloon while holding up traffic is an openly defiant act; and the apparent deliberateness of the act conveys the indirect statement that normal channels for democratic dialogue and reform have been somehow closed off or have become grossly inadequate. The irony here emerges from a sense of disparity between theory and practice. If undertaken in a spirit of irony, however, such actions indirectly validate the theory and thus can represent an ultimate endorsement of democratic principles, not their subversion (and the indirect proof of this proposition is that in undemocratic states, the act of holding up a balloon while holding up traffic would most probably be manifestly unironic). The woman's actions represent a kind of subliminal appeal, which represents an indirect affirmation of the value of democratic dialogue itself. Indeed, since balloons themselves cannot dismantle bombs, such actions make sense only insofar as they constitute appeals to a larger population outside the antinuclear movement itself. But such actions must be explained not merely on the basis of good intentions but also upon the credibility of the claim that channels for democratic reform have in fact been foreclosed.

Some of the same arguments that have been used to justify civil disobedience can help to explain the rationale behind the use of ironic techniques of protest within a democratic polity. Bertrand Russell argued that there is one very large class of cases in which laws do not merit absolute respect and obedience. The usual argument for respecting laws, he reasoned, is that laws provide procedural impartiality between disputants. But this argument becomes problematic when one of the disputants is the state itself. Since the state makes the laws, it can also tilt laws in its own favor, which may not be what is for "the public good" (which Russell distinguished from "the state," that strictly formal institution, which may not at all times embody the public weal even in democratic states; moreover, the institutional gap between the legislative and judiciary branches attests to the need, Russell and others have noted, for the occasional testing of the constitutionality of laws through deliberate civil disobedience). The Nuremberg war trials in fact established, contended Russell, that *failure* to practice civil disobedience in certain instances may deserve punishment. This conditional argument holds even for democracies, for democracies are not immune to abuses and to corruption by those in authority. Russell argued that the possibility of abuses in democracies was especially great in matters pertaining to nuclear weapons. He seemed disturbed by what is now known as the phenomenon of "nuke-speak":

> There are a number of questions in dispute. I will mention a few of them. What is the likelihood of a nuclear war by accident? What is to be feared from fall-out? What proportion of the population is likely to survive an all-out nuclear war? On every one of these questions independent students find that official apologists and policymakers give answers which, to an unbiased inquirer, appear grossly and mur-derously misleading. To make known to the general population what independent inquirers believe to be the true answers to those questions is a very difficult matter. Where the truth is difficult to ascertain there is a natural inclination to believe what official authorities assert. This is especially the case when what they assert enables people to dismiss uneasiness as needlessly alarmist. The major organs of publicity feel themselves part of the Establishment and are very reluctant to take a course which the Establishment will frown on. Long and frustrating experience has proved, to those among us who have endeavoured to make unpleasant facts known, that orthodox methods, alone, are insufficent.[50]

The need for unorthodox and unofficial methods of publicity in nuclear affairs--even in democratic polities--justified for Russell the recourse to nonviolent acts of civil disobedience. (And he argued further that the urgency of the nuclear problem also presented grounds for particularly *extralegal* methods of reform.[51]) We can apply Russell's argument to the case of ironic methods in particular. If the bomb by its very nature tends to foreclose democratic debate--for the bomb is inherently undemocratic, inherently under the strict control of a handful of experts, inherently threatening so as to make debate closed and one-sided--then we can understand the use of ironic techniques as a way of opening a subliminal dialogue on the issues. Indeed, it is not necessarily a favorable reflection upon the Western democracies that the nuclear issue in particular has inspired such a profusion of artistic or figurative methods of communication and protest--artworks, plays, films, bumper stickers, buttons--on the subject. The handicapped woman's actions in particular, by their paradoxical appearance, are designed to provide a intellectual jolt that breaks through nukespeak, that shatters the clichés of nuclear discourse. If we recognize specifically an element of irony in her actions, then we shall understand that her point is not to substitute literally the language of balloons for a more forthright discussion of the issues, not merely to substitute slogans for extended dialogue, not finally to subvert traditional democratic channels however corrupt; but rather her balloon-speak issues an invitation, an appeal, for *further* reflection and an expanded discussion on nuclear matters.[52]

But if that is all there is to irony, if it is merely an indirect means of discourse that happens to flourish in the antinuclear movement, then the thesis regarding the presence of irony in the antinuclear movement would not be very interesting or important. If irony is merely a form of verbal camouflage, then we could write numerous parallel theses on the presence of political satire, allegory, black humor, or tragicomedy in the antinuclear movement. Throughout this book, however, I have insisted that irony is much more than a simple rhetorical figure, that it entails an entire outlook, a certain *philosophical* posture. To be sure, the handicapped woman holds up a balloon to get our attention, but I think there are even deeper reasons why she does what she does-- reasons that even she may not be able to articulate fully. If we inquire further into the logic of her actions, I believe that we will discover that precisely an element of irony informs these deeper reasons of hers; and that her ironic reasoning implies a general theory concerning the nature of moral and political interaction in the nuclear world.

Kant and Universal Suicide

Let us first consider a few theoretical problems created by the invention and subsequent proliferation of the hydrogen bomb. In his *Groundwork of the Metaphysic of Morals*, Immanuel Kant set out to give a general description of morality (i.e., "pure ethics"). His argument--that morality is to be based upon a "good will," which is defined as duty to and reverence for law irrespective of consequences and personal inclinations--is well known. Let us, then, consider the act of initiating a nuclear war with respect to Kant's supreme principle of morality.

First, according to Kant's argument, the consequences of nuclear warfare, however horrible and repulsive, do not directly affect the consideration of whether pushing the nuclear button meets the requirements of a "good will." Although Kant clearly recognizes that formal ethics includes certain "empirical" considerations, he is equally clear that the goodness of a will is not dependent upon actual consequences. He argues that ethics must proceed instead from "pure" or "*a priori*" logic. We cannot therefore judge the act of instigating nuclear war according to its aftermath, and instead we are to make an evaluation based strictly upon the notion of duty involved in that act.

Thus we are led to Kant's "categorical imperative," the first formulation of which reads: "I ought never to act except in such a way that I can also will the maxim of my action to be a universal law." As several Kantian commentators have pointed out, this first formulation is but a negative expression of the concept of duty; that is, it does not imply that one is positively obliged to act upon any and all maxims that can be universalized just because they can be universalized. Furthermore, by "can will," Kant means "able to conceive without logical contradiction"; it not a question of personal capacity or practical feasibility.

Despite these clarifications, the act of commencing nuclear war presents strange complications to Kant's dictum, mainly because the possible totality of the eventual destruction completely obliterates the distinction between pure logic and actual consequences. First, the technological possibility of destroying the entire world in one fell swoop makes the act of universalizable self-destruction at least conceivable--though the crucial Kantian question is whether that act can be willed in a logically consistent manner. Kant did entertain certain examples of "material maxims," or actual circumstances that may have some bearing upon one's moral judgements. The first of these illustrations was the case of suicide, which we should reconsider for its obvious parallels with the act of nuclear self-annihilation.

Kant posed the issue of suicide as, "From self-love I make it my principle to shorten my life if its continuance threatens more evil than it promises pleasure." He concluded that this application of self-love was not logically universalizable and thus failed the limiting test of morality. His argument rested upon his loading the terms "suicide" and "self-love." First he equated suicide with self-love, and then he defined the purpose of self-love as "stimulating the furtherance of life." From this series of definitions the conclusion followed that it would be logically impossible, i.e., logically self-contradictory, for everyone to commit suicide out of "self-love"[53] because the generalized destruction of human life could not be reconciled with the purpose of stimulating the furtherance of life. Universalized suicide "could not subsist as a system of nature."[54]

Kant's argument thus comes down to this: Individual acts of suicide are not moral because they contravene the principle of the "furtherance of life" and undermine the idea of the "system of nature." Kant's argument is a more formal version of the familiar adage that suicide is really an indirect affirmation of the importance of life. But in Kant's version, the crux of the issue is not the individual's appreciation of this importance of life or his actual happiness, whether dead or alive. Rather, according to the first formulation of the categorical imperative, the *concept* of suicide is logically self-contradictory because it is dependent upon or derivative of the *concept* of life. The issue is really that an individual act of suicide militates *logically* against the category of "life"--for the *actual* adverse systemic consequences of one act of suicide are quite small--and it is precisely because individual suicide is foremost a logical rather than empirical militancy against life that Kant felt that the point needed amplification by an exercise of the imagination, namely the idea of universalization.

Nuclear war, however, raises the "empirical" stakes of the issue. The question of pushing the nuclear button is one not simply of logical militancy against "life" or "nature" as an *a priori* category or pure concept. Rather, the question of instigating nuclear war can be posed as a question of life itself, of whether one *ought* "to stimulate the furtherance of life" and to support "the system of nature" at all. To phrase the question in perverse Kantian terms, nuclear annihilation is a question of whether one ought to retain even one's *a priori* categories.

Kant himself recognized the problems involved in appealing to a general "system of nature" as the *a priori* bedrock on the basis of which one would identify logical inconsistencies for purposes of ethical elucidation. This apparently was the reason that Kant switched from a negative formulation of morality (albeit based upon positively inviolate *a priori* categories) to a positive formulation of obligation. This shift is evident in his restatement of the categorical imperative as, "Act so as to use humanity, both in your person and in the person of every other, always at the same time as an end, never simply as a means." But we should note that the act of blowing up all of humanity can be undertaken with a view that the perpetrator is using humanity as an end-in-itself; indeed, the act would carry such finality that it is difficult to see any way in which the act could be considered as a means toward some further worldly end. Kant's reformulating the categorical imperative in this way does not settle the question of the ethical propriety of nuclear war, for in the case of instigating nuclear war the overriding question involved is the very *value* of humanity and human life itself.

The problem with Kant's ethical system that emerges when it is applied to the case of nuclear warfare is that Kantianism renders morality into a matter of objective categories, whereas nuclear war renders even Kantian categories supremely contingent upon human choice. Kant attempts to describe the conditions of morality, to tell us what it means to act morality; but the overwhelming *question* of the nuclear issue is out of the range of Kant's system, for the act of pushing the button is a question of the morality of the entire system itself, not "merely" the conditions of morality *given* the system. Kantianism thus cannot be appealed to as a way of thinking morally about nuclear matters; which means that if, for whatever reasons, we wish to avert annihilation, we will need to look to some other basis for morality and interpersonal commitment.

Weber and Science

Max Weber presented an explicit answer to Kant's attempt to reconcile ethics and epistemology. In his address "Science as a Vocation," Weber writes that Kant took his point of departure from the proposition, "'Scientific truth exists and it is valid,'" and then asked, "Under which presuppositions of thought is truth possible and meaningful?"[55] Weber argues in response that such a view of science is no longer credible, and in the address he warns prospective young scientists not to enter into the field of science with the expectation that science leads to or is founded upon some ultimate or apodictic truth. Instead, Weber contends that dedication to science--the scientific *ethos*--must be based upon the understanding that the very *meaning* of science is precisely that it does not ask whether there *should* be science. Science does not answer the question, "What shall we do and how shall we live?"[56]--even with respect to the question of whether to engage in scientific activity. Science does not, Weber insists, ask for the answers to the questions whether "the existence of the world which these sciences describe is worth while, [whether] it has any 'meaning,' or [whether] it makes sense to live in such a world."[57]

In elaboration of this strange scientific ethos, Weber explains that scientific work is chained to the course of progress.[58] The very *meaning* of such activity, he says, is to be found in the expectation that all scientific work will become antiquated in the future. The scientist does not work for "gratifications" along the way. In other words, the scientific ethos is a kind of devotion to progress for the sake of progress--without any presumption that it is eventually leading somewhere. This view of scientific activity fits into Weber's larger picture of the process of rationalization, which in modern times has relegated ultimate values or "ends" to the sphere of human activity in general: "The fate of our times is characterized by rationalization and intellectualization and, above all, by the 'disenchantment of the world.' Precisely the ultimate and most sublime values have retreated from public life either into the trancendental realm of mystic life or into the brotherliness of direct and personal human relations."[59] The activity of science, which historically provided the means toward ends, now has become a life of pure means without real ends--a life of unending means that becomes valued for its own sake (or one that perpetually defers the question of value), almost but not quite as an "end-in-itself." According to Weber, the inherent value of such an enterprise is that it can be performed fulfillingly without the need for an ultimate answer to the question, "Why does one engage in doing something that in reality never comes, and never can come, to an end?"[60]

Weber, in advocating such a vision of science, seems to have found a functional substitute for common or universal values in the "common fate"[61] of the scientific process. His is a world in which "the ultimately possible attitudes toward life are irreconcilable, and hence their struggle can never be brought to a final conclusion."[62] Within such a world, the process of science will seem liberating or inherently valuable because it relieves one of having to try to reconcile such differences. Yet the coherence and meaning of Weber's enterprise do depend upon the ongoingness of a scientific community. And thus the prospect of nuclear annihilation throws a monkey wrench into Weber's world, for such a threat means that even the scientist, who supposedly has forsworn questions of universal ethics, is in fact engaging "in doing something that in reality . . . can come to an end." Given the possibility of nuclear destruction, Weber's scientific activity loses its very meaning--for now the scientist *cannot* reasonably expect that his work will be surpassed. What's worse, Weber from his scientific perspective--one that by Weber's definition refrains from ethical commentary--cannot give any positive reason to *save* the world, or to save even the scientific community, from nuclear devastation. Weberian science disabuses one of Kantian pretensions, but it cannot provide the basis for a positive ethos in the nuclear world.

To the extent that Weber's view of scientific activity describes and informs modern scientific practice, modern science reveals a serious methodological error when it attempts to apply its insights to the larger questions of the nuclear issue, e.g., the questions of the very value of human existence, the qualify of life of those living under the nuclear threat, the question of how far to risk destruction as a tactic of deterrence. Weberian science substitutes an ongoing *process* for a positive epistemology; it presumes that a scientific construct--a theory or a model--is valid until proven otherwise, valid until disconfirmed by future data. (Usually this view of scientific activity and scientific truth is attributed not to Weber but to Karl Popper, as the idea of a process of "ongoing falsification.") But the problem with a strictly procedural version of science is that it mortgages its coherence to the future; that is, its methodological consistency rests upon the presumption of the continued presence of an ongoing scientific community--a presumption that cannot be relied upon in the face of nuclear destruction.[63] The hard reality in the nuclear age is that a scientist who wishes to abide by the scientific method (as described by Weber) cannot accept the risk that is posed by the nuclear threat, namely of the total, empirical disconfirmation of his models, especially if he and his fellows are relying upon those models to avert nuclear warfare (e.g., in the case of nuclear "deterrence theory").

Kant tried to make morality (i.e., universal morality) a virtual consequence of logic and epistemology. Weber, revealing vestiges of Kantianism, encouraged dedication to an ongoing process--sort of a protracted version of Kantian universalism (albeit applicable only to the scientific community). Both Kantian ethics and Weberian science subordinate questions of the ultimate value of the world and of human existence to the systems of epistemology and methodology, respectively. But in the nuclear age, even these systems are subject to the threat of destruction and thus themselves become the subject of moral inquiry. As such, neither Kant's ethics nor Weber's ethos provides a firm framework for moral or political reasoning in the nuclear world.

Nuclear Morality and Politics

That Kantian ethics or modern science provides few insights into the great moral complexities of the day is but an indication of the far-reaching effect that the invention of the nuclear bomb has had upon the human world. As George Ball has written, the technology of the bomb introduced into world affairs a radically new level of contingency based purely upon human choice: "In opening the box of the atom's secrets, man did not unleash evil, he merely acquired the capacity to unleash it. This left him with the oppressive burden of free choice--the power to decide whether or not to blow up the world."[64] Indeed, the power to decide whether to destroy the entire world raises for the first time in history questions of the ultimate value of all of existence in *practical* terms. Why life at all? is now a *question* to consider, a pressing and a legitimate question, and not simply a topic for philosophical contemplation in leisurely circles.

Our individual moral reflexes may jump intuitively to the conclusion that the burden of proof is upon those who would dare choose to destroy the world, but the matter is not so easily resolved. Perhaps the biggest danger of nuclear weapons, and perhaps the source of their seductive appeal as well, is that they beg for absolute and world wide reasons to go on living, to save the world at large. Particularistic and pluralistic and proceduralistic responses will not suffice, for the answer or answers would seem to bear the new categorical imperative to encompass substantially the *entire* human world, to extend across rivals' borders and to traverse seemingly irreconcilable value systems. But because of the immense difficulty of this task, the bomb seems instead to invite a thoroughgoing skepticism: If pressed, we human beings may be forced to conclude that the world admits of *no* inherent reason why it is better to be than not to be. Not reason, not instinct, not the values of self or of intimacy, not the institutions of religion or philosophy or anthropology, not the force of tradition or ethnicity or of national heritage--none of these can be wholly relied upon to decide the ultimate questions of the value of existence posed by the nuclear bomb. That it is no longer a foregone conclusion that mothers across the globe want to wean their offspring in order to raise them to inhabit the present nuclear world may be the most profound evidence of the *moral* devastation that the bomb is wreaking upon the world.[65]

The bomb potentially devastates not only the moral world of the individual, over and above the damage that it could do to his or her physical person, but it threatens the foundations of the political world, of politics, as well. Just as the bomb taunts the individual with the threat of a moral abyss, of the possibility that there is no ultimate or existential answer to the question of why one should go on living, so too does the bomb threaten what meaning that membership and participation in a collectivity may hold. Without the presumption or promise that the polity may endure, it becomes hard to see how the political ideas of justice or community could hold any importance and command any respect. Hannah Arendt well understood that the bomb so threatens the sheer *possibility* of politics in the modern world, a point she underscored by noting that the adage *Fiat justitia, et pereat mundus* (Let justice be done even if the world perishes)[66] is now used only as a rhetorical statement. Only Kant, she wryly observed, would sacrifice the world for the sake of justice. But Arendt herself endorsed a modified version of the adage, as *Fiat veritas, et pereat mundus* (Let there be truth or truthfulness, or let the world perish). For Arendt, the world, especially the political world, was not worth saving if truthfulness were to be sacrificed. Much of Arendt's theory can be understood as a response to the bomb, a response that is intended to recover the truthfulness of the political world as an answer to the nihilistic questions posed by the bomb.[67]

We also find a continuation of Arendt's nuclear project in Jonathan Schell's book *The Fate of the Earth*. Explicitly following Arendt's conception of the "common world" of politics, Schell attempts to enumerate the principles for such commonality in the nuclear age. He names three. The first would be "respect for human beings, born and unborn, based on our common love of life and our common jeopardy in the face of our own destructive powers and inclinations."[68] The second would be respect for the ecology of the earth, and the third would be respect for "God or nature, or whatever one chooses to call the universal dust that made, or became, us."[69] Schell likens these principles and affirmations to marital love, parental love, and religious faith. The respect for the life of all human beings, he says, "would grow out of each generation's gratitude to past generations for having permitted it to exist."[70] But Schell stops short of laying down a political agenda for eliciting this respect, which he evidently believes all individuals and all peoples are capable of cultivating.

Arendt's and Schell's projects are indeed admirable, perhaps even heroic given the odds. But finally both issue their appeals to believers--in truth or truthfulness and worldliness, or in love and commonality and the intrinsic value of the "gift of life."[71] Arendt's theoretical efforts testifying to the truthfulness of the political world were considerable, as well as reassuring. But her endorsement of the adage *Fiat veritas, et pereat mundus* is shocking when we realize that Arendt was willing to let the world perish if the world did not admit of inherent truthfulness. For Arendt, the world was acceptable, worthy of one's commitment, only if *true*; and in this regard, Arendt was herself a believer (and that she accepted the above adage in the conditional suggests that she was not entirely convinced by the pure logic of her own efforts). An obvious problem, then, with the claims of nuclear theorists, such as Arendt and Schell, who issue their appeals exclusively to believers is that they must accept an extremely heavy burden of proof, showing ontologically, epistemologically, factually, and practically that life in this world is indeed good and true and worth saving. And if the theorist fails to meet those requirements, his or her whole system tends to fall apart, the edifice starts to crumble.

The problem of Arendt's and Schell's similar approaches to the nuclear issue is that neither can accommodate skepticism. Philosophically and theoretically this exclusion means that one must have truth in hand in order to justify existence, a "reason" in order to work to save the world. Politically and practically it means that one's truth system must extend to all peoples, that it be not only absolute but also universalistic. Such heavy burdens may have the effect of defeating, rather than inspiring, action designed to avert annihilation. But perhaps even more disturbing is that neither Arendt nor Schell throws a rope to the thoroughgoing skeptic, to him or her who entertains seriously, or at least with a profound degree of ambivalence, the idea that the world of politics is based upon a lie, that the value and meaning of human affairs do not intrinsically warrant resistance to the threat of annihilation, and that the world's people may after all have little in common. To the skeptic, *Fiat justitia, et pereat mundus* makes some sense (but not for Kant's reasons).

Is there no answer to the nuclear skeptic, the nihilist, the nonbeliever? Must we simply ignore his or her contempt for our sanguine sentiments of meaningful survival? Worse, are we prepared to outlaw skepticism altogether, lest the skeptic might be the one to push the button? In the nuclear age, the theoretical question of how to accommodate skeptics may eventually be more important to our survival than the immediately tactical question of how to convert believers from believing in the bomb.

The Politics of Antinuclear Irony

The ironist is one who can engage the skeptic in meaningful dialogue over nuclear issues, who can hold his attention and possibly coax what little respect the skeptic might hold in reserve. For the ironist is himself mostly a skeptic; he understands detachment and ambivalence; and he is not shocked by the skeptic's blasphemies and his flirtations with death. Thus the ironist can appeal to the skeptic on his own terms and in ways that do not provoke his ire or reproval. The ironist accepts the skeptic's premises--that individual existence may hold no meaning in the face of death, that notions of political community are false, and that there may be after all no good reason to save the world from nuclear annihilation. But the ironist makes an appeal to the skeptic's wayward and irreverent tendencies. He invites the skeptic to choose to affirm the world in spite of all, to accept life on the basis of nothing except the quirk of choice, a choice to act *as if* it all matters. He invites the skeptic to turn his skepticism against itself, to draw forth commitment on a whim, to make an affirmation out of a posture of pretense.

Irony is the spirit of free return. It is exemplified by Plato's philosopher who returns to the cave; by Thomas Mann's intellectual self-betrayals; perhaps also by Weber's injunction to proceed "in spite of all!" Life in this world may be illusory and devoid of inherent meaning, community may be at bottom a big lie; but one can pretend otherwise, nevertheless, without having to sacrifice entirely one's tentativeness or to let down completely one's guard against credulity. Yet irony is much more than mere pretense, for irony is a technique of pretense that can have a peculiar, and substantive, effect. If the skeptic accepts the ironist's invitations and overtures, subsequently their mutual pretense toward one another creates the conditions for a very real dialogue with one another.[72] Similarly, Plato realized that an initial commitment toward the "lie" of community could create--ironically--the conditions for a very real community.

It would be an exaggeration to claim that the entire antinuclear movement self-consciously holds and acts upon precisely these rarefied sentiments. But there are strong indications that something very much like a logic of irony informs the movement at the deepest level, even if that logic is inchoate and poorly understood. Perhaps this evidence of irony can be glimpsed only negatively, ferreted out by a process of elimination: In the nuclear age, holding a balloon while holding up traffic is an act of absurdism, escapism, or sheer nihilism *unless* that act is backed by the chastening attitude of irony--and in our example, the handicapped woman's obvious deliberateness suggests that her actions are ironic in a most profoundly unsettling way. The balloon is a symbol of life--but what a pathetic, fragile symbol! Upon reflection, we realize that the woman is *truly* floating the balloon, that her act is not so innocent and naïvely childlike as it first appears, that it reveals more skepticism than sanguinity about our nuclear future.

Holding up a balloon while holding up traffic presents a modest proposal to think about the meaning of life itself. The point should be underscored in order to understand the ironical ways of the antinuclear protesters: They invite us to question, to doubt, to reflect, to be skeptical. Often their slogans, more witty and wry in tone than angry and adversarial, employ the ironic technique of rhetorical echoing, a mimicking and parodying of the platitudes by which many persons supposedly live their nuclear lives. The echoing device attempts to shatter the clichés of everyday language and thinking, by encouraging the reader or listener to reflect upon language from a distanced perspective, from afar, through the rebounds of echoes. For instance, the antinuclear bumper sticker, "One Nuclear Bomb Will Ruin Your Entire Day," echoes and plays upon another prevalent bumber sticker theme, "Have a Nice Day!" The antinuclear version imitates the facile tone of the "nice day" bumper sticker; but it also parodies and thus subverts (i.e., invites the observer to subvert) the ostensibly affable tone of this genre of bumper stickers by juxtaposing the threat of catastrophe with the concern for dailiness and niceness. Similarly, a popular antinuclear T-shirt shows a cartoon of a tearfully hysterical woman who is exclaiming, "Nuclear War? There goes my career!" Both of these examples of antinuclear rhetoric *could* be read as (merely) moderately satirical, directed against those persons who send their greetings via banalities and bumper stickers or against those persons so oblivious to the arms race that the news of the possibility of nuclear war comes as a total surprise. But I suggest that these slogans reveal an even deeper skepticism toward life, a more startling and stinging parody, a suggestion of ultimate nihilism: When push comes to shove, what does it really matter if our days and our careers are destroyed?

So, too, can the woman's balloon easily burst--and this visual pun reveals an important part, though not all, of the logic behind her antinuclear rhetoric. If we push still onward in our speculations about her motives, her deliberately self-deprecating posture may disclose not so much an attitude of outright defiance, or supreme chutzpah, or superficial mawkishness as ironic *pretense*. On the most elementary level she exhibits a pretense toward the balloon as a technique of opposition against the weapons lab, the state, and the police--the balloon cannot *literally* counteract these institutions. But the balloon also suggests a broader pretense toward life--*as if* it matters. The woman's pretense betrays on the one hand an underlying skepticism; the whimsy in her act is finally an appeal to the skeptical rather than to the credulous, and it is also designed to provoke a skepticism, a questioning attitude, in the otherwise unreflective observer. But then we must understand her actions, her deliberate affirmation of life (also symbolized in the balloon), *against* the background of her countervailing skepticism. Her pretense, while implicitly condoning disengagement from life, at the same time invites the skeptic to play along. She has revealed her conscious decision to affirm life in the nuclear age. She also has given the skeptic sufficient leeway in which to make his own decision, for her appeal is based solely on the force of her own person, her own deliberateness, her own choice. Her appeal is *not* based, by contrast, upon "natural categories," such as the intrinsic "gift of life" or the universal "brotherhood of mankind." The whole affair involves risk and some arbitrariness, depending finally upon whether the skeptic chooses to seek her out. If he happens to pick up the cue, accepting her personal appeal and following her lead, then they will have formed a unique tie with each other. That two skeptics should form an alliance, mutually pledged to the affirmation of life, on the basis of a juxtaposition of bombs with balloons is essentially an episode in irony.

The trick to irony is that this form of pretense can indeed have an effect, for it can procure a commitment from a skeptic. The possible *political* implications of an antinuclear protester's ironic action lie in the fact that although an ironist's appeal to a skeptic is *personal*, because the author of irony sustains his inscrutability, that suggests that the commitment procured can perhaps be generalized beyond strictly personal and textual forms of interaction. At this juncture in our discussion, then, we can finally provide an answer to the question: Can the strategy of nonviolence work in a Nietzschean/Weberian world? As mentioned above, explanations of the strategy of nonviolence as issuing an appeal on the basis of religion, morality, or even political power presume and are thus contingent upon the prior existence of a common social tie or some notion of naturally abiding community. Hence the classic explanations become mystifications given a profoundly skeptical view of society (not to mention cross-cultural and international contact). I want to propose that the strategy of nonviolence (or at least certain kinds of nonviolent action) *can* be viewed as logical from within a skeptic's scheme of things, but that it operates fundamentally according to a logic of *irony*. Understanding the element of irony inherent in the strategy of nonviolence is the final key to understanding the political theory of the antinuclear movement.

I have labored repeatedly against viewing irony as a merely deflationary, corrosive technique. This major misconception of irony goes way back to the criticism of Socrates in his role as gadfly. The standard interpretation of Socrates is that he was a *dissembler*, that he was feigning ignorance. On the contrary, I think that if we in some sense take seriously his assertions that he knew nothing, we will begin to suspect that his irony consisted in a feigning of *knowledge* rather than ignorance.[73] His dialectic was not an exercise in "aporetics" but was a kind of bluffing: Pretending that he had coherent answers, he alluded to the possibility of absolute knowledge; and thereby he could engage the sophistic sophists and hold their attention. The result of that pretense was a real dialogue, an intense, searching, interactive experience with other featherless bipeds. Even if based initially upon a falsehood of sorts, the dialogue could assume a validity and vitality on its own terms.

Socrates' irony has parallels in Gandhi's nonviolent resistance. For all of Gandhi's writings on the power of love and soul-force and the intrinsic value of life, his *practice* of nonviolence embodied and revealed a much different proposition. For just as the handicapped woman conveys indirectly her acknowledgment that a balloon can easily burst, so too did Gandhian *satyagraha* evince the proposition that human life, if in theory sacred, is in practice *dispensable*. That one would be willing to sacrifice one's own life represents a partially deflationary attitude toward that life; it is an attitude of *not* taking oneself, one's life, completely seriously. The *satyagraha* floated a balloon, as it were, with their own bodies. Yet the deliberateness in their approach, revealed by their extreme restraint in forgoing violence, indicated a decision to affirm life, in spite of all. In other words, *satyagraha* overall makes an appeal to the *skeptic* and not just to the believer; it is an invitation to respect the resisters' lives, based upon nothing but a choice--made amidst countervailing sentiments--to accept provisionally the proposition that life, and the lives of the resisters in particular, is valuable. (As a psychological ploy, it is probably cleverly accommodating to try to convince someone to recognize your life on the reverse logic that you yourself do not consider your life to be very important.) Yet even if its successes were obtained under partially false pretenses, Gandhi's approach did strike some common ground between ruler and resister, did obtain some basis for an ongoing dialogue. When both parties had agreed provisionally to the possible falsehood that the lives of the resisters were important, they then had found some terms for ongoing negotiations. Then and only then could politics commence.

The practice of nonviolent resistance, and the form employed by the antinuclear movement in particular, contains within itself a working strategy for establishing dialogue and negotiations--but this strategy leading to negotiations first requires a triumph of conceptual definition, a commitment to certain common terms as a basis for communication, and this commitment presupposes an acknowledgment and acceptance of basic differences between the parties involved. *The element of irony in nonviolent resistance and in the antinuclear movement is contained within the idea that this initial triumph of conceptual definition is based essentially upon a lie,* that it issues from mutual adherence to a falsehood of sorts. Gandhian resisters present a proposition in favor of the dignity of individual life by offering individual death as a foil. The antinuclear movement attempts to bring people together in solidarity against the bomb by alluding to possibility of collective death. Neither the Gandhians nor the antinuclear resisters are entirely serious about the literalness of their respective claims concerning the value of life or the meaning of community--and that is partly the reason for their effectiveness, when in fact their methods meet with success. In the way in which they self-consciously invoke *death* as an organizing principle for *life*, both the Gandhians and the antinuclear protesters employ a notion of a political community that is based on irony.[74]

This claim about the underlying irony involved in the strategy of nonviolent resistance must be distinguished from most other explanations and theories of nonviolence. For instance, the civil rights protesters of the 1960s were making claims about the *literal* universality and brotherhood of mankind. *By contrast, the antinuclear protesters--at least some of them--seem to be attempting to define a community by default or indirection, in their implicit claim that all of us humans have something "in common" by virtue of our shared orientation toward the nuclear possibility of collective death.*[75] The proposition that collective death holds implications for life and for political action is not in and of itself ironic (for after all, the world religions generally have organized themselves according to very unironic views of the meaning of individual death, and surely many antinuclear protesters see nothing ironic about articulating a community on the basis of future annihilation). But I have seized upon the handicapped woman's balloon statement to argue that, in its most public demonstrations, the antinuclear movement exhibits and induces a deeply ironic understanding of what its members mean by a political community based on the threat of nuclear devastation.

As I argued in Chapter 2 with respect to Plato's *Republic*, an ironic view of political community is *not* tantamount to a *deflationary* view of political community. I read Plato's *Republic* as proposing that though the world of politics may be based upon an enormous fiction, the ironist is one who can affirm and act in such a world, nonetheless. Such a stance reflects a double perspective upon political affairs, a worldliness that accommodates ambivalence. Likewise, it follows from an ironic reading of the strategy of nonviolent resistance that the commitment to ongoing dialogue embraced by the parties involved does not require inner "conversions," a joint acceptance of ultimate principles, or preexisting social ties. Rather, successful nonviolent ventures reflect tenuous and tentative affirmations of "life"--and therewith others' lives--from the perspective of death. Such choices and commitments are made amidst doubts; such pretenses are sustained amidst countervailing beliefs. Thus the question of ironic politics should not be posed so sharply as an issue of belief versus skepticism; for an ironic view of political community does not finally preclude belief and exclude believers.

Because the sense of irony *can* be provoked in the hitherto nonironic observer, because irony can sometimes induce the troglodyte to moderate his absolutism, and because it appeals to skeptics, irony holds the potential for forwarding an expansive political program. This hidden potential has to do with the fact that because ironic communities are based upon pretenses, if not lies, the choice to affirm such communities then becomes a free one.

An Immodest Proposal

We might say in sweeping fashion that the decisive political issue for our nuclear age is the question of *boundaries*. On the one hand, the bomb has made the world smaller; all peoples and nations are implicated in the threat of nuclear warfare. And because the nuclear threat holds truly global ramifications, the conclusion suggests itself that some kind of internationally coordinated attempt to avert nuclear annihilation--if nuclear annihilation is to be *deliberately* averted--is called for. On the other hand, the world is populated by a plethora of peoples, nations, factions, ideologies, races, and cultures, all of which divide the world and inherently put up resistance to most attempts for deliberate coordination. In short, the question of liberal politics is now writ large on a global scale, viz., how are we human beings to achieve some kind of theoretical unity amidst (actual) diversity? How are we to find or to erect some transnational or international authority that will effectively mediate disputes and adjudicate differences so that sovereign nations need not resort to war as the final way of settling differences? Occasionally the notion of a world government with far-reaching coercive authority is submitted, but usually this idea is quickly dismissed as far fetched, impractical, and undesirable. With that option out of the running, the liberal model, based mostly upon consent rather than coercion, remains as the leading alternative to consider. But then we face the question of the *nature* of that consensual unity which would bind human beings on a global scale, for worldwide "integration" could not be simply procedural and formal--as in liberal nation-states--but would need some substantive clout, some positive imperative directing that authority to rid us of or to reduce the nuclear threat.

Hannah Arendt argued that human beings could achieve some sense of rootedness in the modern world--and rootlessness for her was the real problem underlying the threat of nuclear warfare--only by *adhering* to their differences and then entering into an international federation on the basis of their respective interests.[76] The crux of Arendt's case was that the sense of "worldliness" admits of positive criteria--based on people's backgrounds--for the sake of which human beings will necessarily save the world from nuclear destruction.

I am skeptical about Arendt's claim. To my mind, one would be hard pressed to state a literal case, to find positive criteria, justifying why all the world's peoples should and would strive to coexist. I am very skeptical that worldliness or rootedness provides a theoretical framework on the basis of which persons actually would peaceably engage with each other and would mediate their outstanding disputes the world over. The problem with natural foundational schemes, such as Arendt's, is that they require some literal notion of universalism, even if presented in the popular form of "equilibrium theory" (with a self-adjusting, overlapping, intersecting pattern of self-interests). My skepticism with respect to international foundational schemes issues from what I think is a respect for differences among peoples and nations; to my way of thinking, a scheme of "self-interests" can be used to rationalize stalemates, stand offs, and even escalations as much as it might suggest "congruence" and natural equilibrium. At any rate, the overall problem with such foundational schemes is that they require of the theorist that he or she accept a world wide burden of proof, and I'm not sure even Arendt was up to that awesome task.

Instead, I propose irony as a more auspicious alternative, as a way of thinking and interacting that holds the potential for an expansive political agenda. The key to political irony is that it is based, not upon positive or true criteria, but the acceptance of a possible falsehood, a noble lie, e.g., that all men and women are brothers and sisters, that all peoples are interrelated solely by virtue of their common humanity. The advantages of using a falsehood as the basis for community are potentially enormous, for it relieves the theorist, as well as the practitioner, of having to find some substantive and verifiable One over the Many, some cosmopolitan standard that actually encompasses the entire globe. Political definition and negotiation--in short, coexistence--can be based entirely upon the quirk of choice, upon a posture of pretense. In practical terms this means: It does not matter whether one is Russian or American, Jew or Arab, white or black, for one to choose to engage ironically with one's supposed adversary. Ironic interaction gives one ample room in cross-cultural confrontations not to take oneself, or one's other, completely seriously; for the ironic consciousness is not based upon "natural" or "organic" categories, is not beholden to "primary" interests and "natural" identifications. Irony allows one to act in a spirit that runs contrary to these expectations, in a way however that does not require a *total* repudiation of those primary allegiances and traditional identifications to which one has been pledged. In short, irony is a kind of pretense--toward oneself, toward texts, toward life--but a pretense that can also be extended toward others, such that irony can encourage productive and peaceful interaction with other, and very "different" human beings. The spirit of irony suggests a spirit of politics appropriate for the nuclear world, a way of achieving theoretical unity amidst great, worldwide diversity --based on little more than choice, a decision to return to the political world.

Evidence of irony's political potential can already be found in microcosm within the antinuclear movement. By most counts, the composition of the movement is incredibly diverse, traversing the entire spectrum of social and economic categories. The protesters have little "in common" with each other--if by commonality one understands the "positive" criteria of class, ethnicity, race, religion, age, gender, or sexual orientation.[77] Part of the reason the antinuclear movement has attracted such a diverse membership is, I suspect, that one does not have to be cut from a certain cloth to participate. The threat of literal destruction (based upon mostly speculative criteria) certainly helps to helps to swell the ranks. But the bomb's literalness does not alone account for extraordinary composition of the movement. I suggest that an ironic consciousness of the meaning of life as viewed with respect to the bomb--a certain blend of skeptical detachment and deliberate implication--informs the movement and helps explain its wide appeal. But the important point for our purposes is that this appeal has the potential of extending well beyond the already committed. The logic behind the apparent illogic of holding up balloons while holding up traffic rests upon the strategy of issuing an invitation to nonprotesters to enter into dialogue. This appeal makes sense primarily within a democracy, for in democracies if a movement turns enough heads and wins enough votes, it can effect real change. It is very unlikely that the handicapped woman believes that her actions alone are sufficient; and neither is it likely that they are meant simply as "symbolic" gestures. She is making an appeal, on the basis of irony, to the democratic populace at large; and she hopes eventually to effect change through established democratic channels. She knows that she cannot fight fire with fire, match might with might. But her ironic sensibility *can* provoke reflection in observers; perhaps she *can* win over a number of people; and perhaps her actions *can* in fact set off a chain reaction resulting in a change of national nuclear policy.[78]

But the quick rebuttal to the above argument is that domestic strategies alone are insufficient and naïve in the nuclear age. The people of a nation can be in well-intended solidarity with one another, in favor of "life" and against the bomb, but such sentiments are of little consequence and might even be dangerous in the actual context of international affairs. It is often argued that in this monumental life-or-death competition for ever more effective weaponry, the safety and defense of a nation must not be left to chance--and trusting one's adversaries is chancy. Thus a nation must not act unilaterally in the weapons game, hoping wistfully that that act will be received as a gesture of goodwill. Rather, nations must negotiate and interact only the basis of well-defined and calculable "interests." Bargaining, bartering, and batting about interests is an exercise in pure power ploys; it does not require any deeply involved human contact and needs only the minimum of shared concerns. States do not in fact subscribe to and abide by any cosmopolitan standards, nor do they play by a common set of rules. Knowing this and accepting it as a fact of life, democratic statespersons must conduct "foreign policy" such that reciprocities, proportionalities, and fair trade-offs are their highest practical aims.

Yet the antinuclear protesters' logic does make some sense within an international context. First it should be noted that both Gandhi and Martin Luther King, Jr., insisted that nonviolent methods could and must be applied on an international level,[79] and Gene Sharp has documented several cases where nonviolence has worked in international disputes.[80] In addition, the argument that I have forwarded-- that the underlying irony of the antinuclear movement appeals to the skeptic--has several implications for international affairs. Just as the protesters' unilateral actions create subliminally the conditions for a dialogue with and within an entrenched state power, so in theory can democratic nations (as international "actors") create the ironic conditions for *effective* nuclear negotiations with totalitarian (and other) state powers. Ironic engagement is based not upon blind trust but rather upon partial pretense and tentative commitment. The point of finding some common conceptual ground--even if based initially upon a lie--is that negotiations (and by "negotiations" here I mean not simply a front with the adversary, the point of which is to gain an advantage through world sentiment; not simply "negotiations" as warfare and competition by other means) presuppose some political tie, some mutual recognition, some prior political definition; and heretofore the superpower governments have maintained that the business of bargaining interests could be conducted in the midst and in spite of a climate of "bad faith." Irony does not ignore underlying hostilities and "bad faith" but instead attempts to use that very skepticism to secure commitments. To put the potential of irony obversely: Looking for *reasons* why totalitarian leaders would willingly and without a fight forfeit some power may be a futile activity; yet irony offers a choice to such leaders based upon the very unreasonableness of this proposition. The contingency, rather than the necessity, of this choice may give democratic statespersons a foot in the door, some basis for discussions. The alternative--negotiations on the basis of crude interests--reduces dialogue to a sheer power play and, I contend, completely eliminates *politics* from the picture.

The advocates of irony, however, need not accept the full burden of proof for their arguments. If they can show *some* rationale to the ironic attempt to rid the world of nuclear weapons, then their case cripples the nuclear proponents' claim that weapons must be deployed, not because of their intrinsic worth as objects of strange love or because any one really welcomes nuclear warfare, but because the threatening posture of the enemy simply warrants deployment. This shifting of the burden of proof means that the argument between the advocates of nuclear weapons deployment and their opponents no longer can be reduced to a question of nuclear weapons as a mere "means" to peace (as the advocates often claim), for by playing the irony card the antinuclear protesters have at least put in their own bid for finding a nonviolent, nonnuclear "means" of negotiating with a hostile enemy.

Yet irony carries with it no guarantees, and the practitioners of antinuclear irony themselves would hardly hedge any bets that their efforts will in fact have a significant long-term effect. Irony involves considerable risks, and there is no guarantee that an ironic transmission will "take" or that it will even be understood. But the potential of irony must be assessed in relative terms. Again, present reality affords abundant material with which to draw a few contrasts. With large literary license, we can draw a rough dichotomy between ironic politics and modern politics, which latter we will summarily call--taking our cue from Thomas Mann's analysis of twentieth-century politics-- "Hegelian." Ironic politics is inspired by lies, whereas Hegelian politics is organized according to "positive" or "literal" or "organic" criteria--in short, the categories of Truth and Reason and Nature. According to this rough scheme of things, both the Soviet Union and the Western democracies pursue some version of Hegelianism. Hegelianism recommends action and pursues policies only upon the presumption that a thread of logical continuity can be extrapolated from the criteria of the present to the consequences of the future. It poses its proponents expectantly toward the future, promising them positive developments and eventual resolutions. The indirect result is that Hegelianism teaches patience and self-confidence as much as it explicitly propounds progressiveness; and such patience and self-assurance are the sentiments that sustain the arms race (even if they are also responsible for forestalling total destruction for the time being), for they are the sentiments that allow the superpowers to wait for the right moment-- the golden opportunity, the critical juncture, the turning point, the pregnant pause--before taking decisive steps to roll back the weapons.[81]

Ironic politics--and again I draw upon insights of Marx, Kierkegaard, and Mann--are characterized by self-initiated deviations, by action that is based upon a "negative way," which Kierkegaard explained as "not the way whereby one who imagines himself to have a result comes to possess it, but the way whereby the result forsakes him."[82] As Mann contended, irony is action and commitment that follows--paradoxically--from tentativeness, ambivalence, and skepticism. As Marx suggested, irony is to Hegelianism as Epicureanism was to Democriteanism: The ironist is interested in contingencies and abstract possibilities, whereas the determinist is concerned only with necessities and absolute possibilities.[83]

Let us now ask the burning question: What kind of political consciousness will prevent annihilation? The question requires not an "argument from apocalypse backwards"[84] but rather a speculative projection toward the partly real, partly imaginary state of nonannihilation. George Ball, in several writings, has implied that the answer cannot be Hegelian, for the telos of the bomb must never be realized.[85] The above question can be rephrased as: How is it that persons will act decisively on the basis of a negative goal, will participate painstakingly in order that a particular state of affairs *not* come about? The difficulty of this task is immense. It would require that the truth of the adage, If weapons work, they will be used, be denied. It would require that the momentum of a major technological wave be reversed, that a powerful historical process not be allowed to run its full course. Stopping such potentialities, deviating from such paths downward, would entail that persons, many persons, cultivate an ability to delight in the negative, to entertain a sense of accomplishment and triumph in the defeat of what seems to be the predominant march of history. Such a theoretical outlook would contrast with Hegelianism in the sense that nuclear survival would require an orientation toward the future wherein a person would act purposively but *not* for the sake of an ultimate resolution. Such an outlook would require, moreover, a keen ability to live with ambivalence and ambiguity--even while one is acting deliberately and decisively. In short, the answer to the above question calls for a posture of radical *forbearance*, a way of acting positively for a negative--and such requirements *ipso facto* eliminate Hegelianism from the running.[86]

Gandhi praised forbearance as one of the virtues of nonviolence.[87] By forbearance he meant not so much the common Christian sentiment of "turning the other cheek," but rather the active pursuit of a nonentity, a nonstate of affairs; and it was because nonviolence required such activity, such resolve and purposiveness that Gandhi repeatedly insisted that the term "passive resistance" was a misnomer for his *satyagraha*.[88]

Hegelianism needs reasons to act decisively; it needs the promise and logical lure of eventual resolution in order to meet with an other, to hold talks, to negotiate settlements. Hegelianism now needs *reasons* to save the world, if saving the world will entail positive acts of forbearance. By contrast, the beauty and benefit of irony is that it is a mode of consciousness that does not need hard and irrefutable evidence proving that life is important, that the enemy is trustworthy, or that all peoples should live, in order to countenance and to counsel action. Of the two alternatives presented somewhat drastically here--Hegelianism and irony--only irony is capable of considering seriously the sentiment that the bomb affords an odd opportunity to unite, in theory and in practice, the peoples of the world.

What, then, are the possible practical consequences of a politics of irony? The question is a bit perverse, a kind of request for the utilitarian implications of what I have been suggesting is a profoundly nonutilitarian stance. But then again, *of course* I believe that there are worldly benefits to a politics of irony and tangible returns to the act of returning, just as I suspect that the handicapped woman, though nobody's fool, entertains the idea that her actions might turn out *not* to have been in vain. The ironic stance is appropriate for the nuclear age, but *not* because irony will directly map out concrete solutions with respect to the immediate questions of nuclear arms policy and so on. Instead, the benefits of irony are analogous to what Max Weber-- demonically rather than ironically--claimed was the very *meaning* of the vocation of modern science, namely that the scientist need not ask whether there *should* be science. Similarly, the value of irony in the nuclear age is that the ironist need not ask for *reasons* to work to save the world and to affirm the value of all of human existence. This, I believe, was the meaning behind Thomas Mann's definition of irony as "the self-betrayal of the intellect in favor of life." Such a life- affirming stance is *unconditional* and *undiscriminating*--which is why it entailed for Mann a condemnation of warfare per se--but it should be noted that Mann's affirmation of life was not based upon straight reason, not based upon, as it were, some foundational scheme. The morality of irony *is* a morality of the intellect; but now it is the intellect that works *against* the intellect in order to produce an unqualified affirmation of life. The particular benefit of irony in the nuclear age is that it frames the monumental life-or-death decisions-- which are an inescapable part of modern politics--in such a way that an *argument* or a reason or some natural foundation scheme is *not* required proving incontrovertibly why the various peoples of the world should be allowed to be rather than not to be.

In this chapter, and in several ways in this book as a whole, I have attempted to uncover, explicate, and elaborate the element of irony at work within the antinuclear movement in particular and within the strategy of nonviolent protest in general. The approach has been highly interpretive, and I have tried to retrace the logic of the antinuclear movement on its own terms. But many of the preceding pages in the book attest to the coherence of the movement's ironic ways from a wider point of view, for I have suggested herein that the irony of the antinuclear movement has long and illustrative precedents in the history of political theory. That history goes back at least to Socrates, and there are direct parallels between Socrates' ironical ways and those of the antinuclear protesters. But now we should be explicit in acknowledging this legacy: The antinuclear protesters are *the* modern- day gadflies in this nuclear age. Before we brush them off, let us understand them better than the Athenian court understood Socrates. Socrates' irony was an exercise in self-parody, an implicit admission of limitations, an indirect acknowledgment of ignorance--but Socrates somehow made his ignorance into a mode of dialogue, his questioning into a means of interaction, his examinations into an entire way of life with others. Socrates, however, left open the question for us--as he did for Plato--of whether an entire politics can be based upon ignorance and even lies. The insight of the ironist is that out of ignorance, there can indeed be affirmation; from examination and questioning, there can be dialogue and interaction; from lies and pretense, there can be an odd sort of community. The political question posed ironically to us by the antinuclear protesters is whether, with the threat of total oblivion on the horizon, we will continue talking with each other, as individuals and as nations.[89]

Notes

1. This day should not be confused with the mass demonstrations in New York and San Francisco (and elsewhere) that took place in June a year earlier. In 1982, approximately 1,300 people were arrested in Livermore blockades; in 1983 the number dropped to around 1,100.

2. The Livermore Action Group is an umbrella organization for approximately 200 affinity groups from northern California. The names of some of these affinity groups are worth mentioning: Arms for Embracing, Bay Area Martial Artists for Nuclear Disarmament, Bombs Away, Burning Bridges Collective, Chuckling Doves, Communist Dupes, Cosmic Compost, Critical Mass, Cut the Rhetoric, Dr. Spock's Youth Brigade, East Bay Deadheads for Peace, Elders for Survival, Fission Impossible, Gone Fission, Men Against Phallic Weaponry, No Nukes and Hold the Anchovies, Women on the Edge of Time. For a list of antinuclear organizations in northern California, see "The Disarmament Directory: A Guide to the Movement Against Nuclear Weapons and War in Central and Northern California," published by the Resource Center for Nonviolence, Santa Cruz, California.

3. This festive atmosphere does not characterize all protest demonstrations in northern California. It has been my observation that, for instance, protest marches against U.S. policy in Central America are, by contrast, much more grim. For example, far fewer participants come dressed in funny costumes; the chants are much more angry than witty; and the attention is focused much more sharply upon an identifiable opponent than it is at antinuclear demonstrations.

4. I saw persons dressed in Ronald Reagan masks, skeleton outfits, and missile costumes. One cluster of protesters dressed up as trees, and at some point they sneaked onto the roadway, giving the appearance that trees had suddenly sprouted out of the concrete. Anyway, in the subsequent scene, the policemen were arresting the trees.

5. A few examples of the criticism of the antinuclear movement can be found in the collection of essays: Ernest W. Lefever and E. Stephen Hunt, ed.

The Apocalyptic Premise (Washington, D.C.: Ethics and Public Policy Center, 1982). Among the contributors, Charles Krauthammer directs his criticism toward the freeze movement in particular, arguing that the movement simply cannot understand the paradoxes of deterrence (see "In Defense of Deterrence, " esp. p. 74). William Griffith also bases his attack on the freeze movement on the charge of naïveté ("Ban Whose Bomb?" pp. 107-110). Rael Jean Isaac and Erich Isaac lay out the case that the movement is a target for Soviet manipulation ("The Counterfeit Peacemakers," pp. 139-164).

6. *Oakland Tribune* (October 19, 1984).

7. Albert Carnesale et al., *Living With Nuclear Weapons* (New York: Bantam Books, 1983), p. 13; and see Alfie Kohn, "Laughing at the Unlaughable," *In These Times* (July 13-26, 1983), pp. 12-13.

8. Albert Carnesale et al., *Living With Nuclear Weapons,* p. 13.

9. Not to be pedantic, but whoever in the Harvard Nuclear Study Group wrote the following passage was not in control of his prose: "Weapons are tools. And like other tools, they should serve a purpose or they should not be built. They should be means to an end and not ends in themselves." *Ibid.,* p. 133.

10. *Ibid.,* p. 7.

11. *Ibid.,* p. 254.

12. For an excellent history and analysis of the successes and failings of the 1980s freeze campaign, see David S. Meyer, *A Winter of Discontent: The Nuclear Freeze and American Politics* (New York: Praeger, 1990).

13. For example, the Harvard Nuclear Study Group writes: "Such debates [over Soviet policy] obscure the central issue, which is the effect, not the motive, of Soviet actions. We can never "know" exactly what motivates the Soviet leadership. What the West *can* know is that certain Soviet actions are not in its interests and the central issue is, then, how best to encourage Soviet restraint in such dangerous areas." *Ibid.,* p. 36.

14. See H.B. Acton, "Political Justification," *Civil Disobedience: Theory and Practice,* ed. Hugo Adam Bedau (Indianapolis and New York: Pegasus, 1969), p. 227.

15. Joan Bondurant's account of *satyagraha* emphasizes that although Gandhi was a seeker after truth, he had yet to find it; and his practice of *ahimsa* issues from an awareness of one's own epistemological shortcomings. Bondurant, *Conquest of Violence* (Princeton: Princeton University Press, 1958), pp. 16ff.

16. See Gene Sharp, *Power and Struggle,* Part 1, *The Politics of Nonviolent Action* (Boston: Porter Sargent Publishers, 1973), p. 32.

17. See *idem, The Dynamics of Nonviolence,* Part 3, *The Politics of Nonviolent Action,* p. 707.

18. See M.K. Gandhi, *The Law of Love,* ed. Anand T. Hingorani (Bombay: Bharatiya Vidya Bhavan, 1962), p. 57; *Non-Violence in Peace and War,* Vol. 1 (Ahmedabad: Navajivan Publishing House, 1942), p. 2.

19. Hannah Arendt, "On Violence," *Crises of the Republic* (New York: Harcourt Brace Jovanovich, 1969), p. 152.

20. Martin Luther King, Jr., "Pilgrimage to Nonviolence," *Stride Toward Freedom: The Montgomery Story* (New York: Harper & Brothers, 1958), p. 97.

21. *Ibid.*, pp. 95-6.

22. *Ibid.*, p. 97.

23. *Ibid.*, p. 105.

24. *Ibid.*, p. 106.

25. *Ibid.*, p. 107.

26. See also Bondurant, *Conquest of Violence*; Leo Kuper, *Passive Resistance in South Africa* (London: Jonathan Cape, 1956); Eric H. Erikson, *Gandhi's Truth: On the Origins of Militant Nonviolence* (New York: W.W. Norton and Company, 1969); Paul A. Hare and Herbert H. Blumberg, *Nonviolent Direct Action* (Washington D.C.: Corpus Books, 1968); Leroy H. Pelton, *The Psychology of Nonviolence* (New York: Pergamon Press, 1974); Judith Stiehm, *Nonviolent Power* (Lexington, Mass.: D.C. Heath and Company, 1972); April Carter, *Direct Action and Liberal Democracy* (New York: Harper and Row, 1973); John Lofland and Michael Fink, *Symbolic Sit-Ins: Protest Occupations at the California Capitol* (Washington, D.C.: University Press of America, 1982); T.K.N. Unnithan and Yogendra Singh, *Traditions of Non-Violence* (New Delhi: Arnold-Heinemann, 1973); and M.K. Gandhi, *The Science of Satyagraha*, ed. Anand T. Hingorani (Bombay: Bharatiya Vidya Bhavan, 1962).

27. Richard B. Gregg, *The Psychology and Strategy of Gandhi's Nonviolent Resistance* (New York and London: Garland Publishing, 1972); *The Power of Nonviolence* (Nyack, N.Y.: Fellowship Publications, 1959).

28. George T. Lakey, "The Sociological Mechanisms of Non-Violent Action," *Peace Research Reviews* 2 (December, 1968), p. 19.

29. *Ibid.*, p. 20.

30. Sharp, *Power and Struggle*, p. 71.

31. Arendt, "Civil Disobedience," *Crises of the Republic*, p. 86.

32. *Ibid.*

33. See Gene Sharp, "Ethics and Responsibility in Politics: A Critique of the Present Adequacy of Max Weber's Classification of Ethical Systems," *Inquiry* (Oslo) 7, No. 3 (Autumn, 1964), pp. 304-317.

34. Max Weber, "Politics as a Vocation," *From Max Weber: Essays in Sociology*, ed. H.H. Gerth and C. Wright Mills (New York: Oxford University Press, 1946), p. 126.

35. *Ibid.*, p. 125.

36. Arendt, "On Violence," *Crises of the Republic*, p. 155.

37. Weber, "Politics as a Vocation," p. 122.

38. Hannah Arendt, *The Human Condition* (Chicago: University of Chicago Press, 1958), p. 201.

39. Gene Sharp repeatedly refers to nonviolent means of opposition as "weapons." See *The Methods of Nonviolent Action*, Part 2, *The Politics of Nonviolent Action*, p. 113.

40. Though I do not intend to develop the point here, I want to insist that my thesis about the Orphic-ironic tradition is not exclusively a "male-

privileging" narrative. The antinuclear movement attracted great numbers of women, and most of its leaders and principals were women: Women's Action for Nuclear Disarmament (WAND), Greenham Common Camp, Helen Caldicott, Randall Forsberg, Petra Kelly, Mary Kaldor, Pam Solo, Christa Wölf, Katya Komisaruk, and my anonymous handicapped protester.

41. See David Simpson, *Irony and Authority* (London: The Macmillan Press, 1979), pp. 97-98.

42. Paul Fussell, *The Great War and Modern Memory* (London: Oxford University Press, 1975), p. 7.

43. Fussell on the whole uses the term *irony* in a narrow way, namely as a recognition of the defeat of ideals, but he is not explicit about this in *The Great War and Modern Memory*. For a clearer articulation of Fussell's view of irony, see his "The New Irony and the Augustans," *Encounter* 34 (June, 1970), pp. 68-74.

44. *Idem, The Great War and Modern Memory*, p. 74.

45. *Ibid.*, p. 326.

46. *Ibid.*, p. 320.

47. See Robert Jay Lifton, *Indefensible Weapons: The Political and Moral Case Against Nuclear Arms* (New York: Basic Books, 1982).

48. Jonathan Schell, *The Fate of the Earth* (New York: Alfred A. Knopf, 1982), pp. 142-3.

49. See Chapter 3, on Schlegelian irony as a strategy of artistic representation.

50. Bertrand Russell, "Civil Disobedience and the Threat of Nuclear Weapons," *Civil Disobedience: Theory and Practice*, ed. H.A. Bedau (Indianapolis and New York: Pegasus Books, 1969), p. 157.

51. Robert Bolt gives a good argument for civil disobedience as a form of nuclear reform (though he finally thinks conventional channels will suffice): "It is the whole of humanity that is threatened with disaster, not this or that section of it. And we are threatened, not because of wicked or wickedly incompetent statesmen on this or that side of the Iron Curtain, but because we are all helplessly caught up in attitudes of national interest, national hate, above all national fear, which simply are not adequate to our actual situation. . . . The national statesmen cannot break the circle because their mandate is to act in the national interest. Only the private individual can act in the name of humanity; the lead must come from below. And the lead must come in a form so definite and vigorous that statesmen can see that a new force has been placed at their disposal, and a new mandate given them. That is the justification on non-violent civil disobedience." In Clara Urquhart, ed., *A Matter of Life* (London: Jonathan Cape, 1963), pp. 44-5.

52. After their protests, the Livermore Action Group spokespersons often complain about insufficient or distorted coverage from the local media. I think it is significant that in one blockade, protesters held signs along the road in Livermore that read simply "Talk to us."

53. A lively debate between Jonathan Harrison and J. Kemp over Kant's view of suicide appears in Robert Paul Wolff, ed., *Kant: A Collection of Critical*

Essays (Notre Dame: University of Notre Dame Press, 1968). Harrison argues, "It is obvious to the meanest intelligence, however, that there is no contradiction whatsoever in the idea of everyone's committing suicide if they would be happier dead, and, what is more, Kant makes no attempt whatsoever to show that there is such a contradiction." But Kemp responds, rightly I think, that the issue is not whether persons would be "happier dead"; it is rather a question of whether there is a logical contradiction between suicide as an act of self-love and self-love as the furtherance of life.

54. Immanuel Kant, *Groundwork of the Metaphysic of Morals*, trans. H.J. Paton (New York: Harper Torchbooks, 1948), p. 89.

55. Weber, "Science as a Vocation," p. 154.

56. *Ibid.*, p. 147.

57. *Ibid.*, p. 144.

58. *Ibid.*, p. 137.

59. *Ibid.*, p. 155.

60. *Ibid.*, p. 138.

61. *Ibid.*

62. *Ibid.*, p. 152.

63. Cf. Harry Redner, *In the Beginning Was the Deed: Reflections on the Passage of Faust* (Berkeley: University of California Press, 1982).

64. George W. Ball, "White House Roulette," *New York Review of Books* (November 8, 1984), p. 5.

65. I have read a few news articles and heard personal testimonials to this effect. I mention these mothers' fears because I think they contravene Arendt's hope that the process of "natality" will continue in a given fashion to renew the world. (*The Human Condition*, p. 27). That women might balk at having or raising children, or that nuclear war would instill, not severe suffering, but fear so great as to cause one to shy away from life also subverts reassuring propositions such as this: "Now to speak of our having an insatiable thirst for phenomenology, so defined, seems to be a way of referring to the familiar fact that we are attached to life in an unconditional manner. That is, our urge to go on living is normally not based on expectations of success or pleasure, though we can be driven to desire death by severe suffering." Charles Taylor, "Design for Living," *New York Review of Books* (November 22, 1984), p. 53. A belief in the our "insatiable thirst for phenomenology" is a good way of paraphrasing the main argument, the main sentiment in Freeman Dyson's *Weapons and Hope* (New York: Harper and Row, 1984).

66. Arendt, "Civil Disobedience," *Crises of the Republic*, p. 62; "Truth and Politics," *Between Past and Future* (New York: Viking Press, 1954), p. 228.

67. See George Kateb, "Modernity," *Hannah Arendt: Politics, Conscience, Evil* (Totowa, N.J.: Rowman and Allanheld, 1984), pp. 149-187.

68. Schell, *The Fate of the Earth*, p. 177.

69. *Ibid.*, p. 178.

70. *Ibid.*, p. 177.

71. *Ibid.*

72. The final lines of Woody Allen's *Annie Hall* come to my mind here: "I guess it's like that old joke: 'Doctor, my brother thinks he's a chicken.' The doctor says, 'Oh yeah, why haven't you done something about it?' And the fellow replies, 'I would, but I need the eggs.'--That's the way I feel about relationships: they're crazy and irrational, but we keep on having them because we need the eggs."

73. See Gregory Vlastos, "Socrates' Disavowal of Knowledge," *Philosophical Quarterly* 35 (January, 1985), pp. 1-31.

74. Hobbesians (i.e., nonironists) and Socratics (i.e., ironists) both invoke death as an organizing principle for political life, but whereas Hobbes presumes that one should be fearful about death, Socrates is supremely ambivalent about what death may or may not bring.

75. This is very close, I think, to what Gunther Anders meant by "negative universality."

76. See Kateb, "Modernity," *Hannah Arendt: Politics, Conscience, Evil*, pp. 153, 166. Kateb quotes the following passages from Arendt's writings to make this point: "Just as man and woman can be the same, namely human, only by being absolutely different from each other, so the national of every country can enter this world history of humanity only by remaining and clinging stubbornly to what he is. A world citizen, living under the tyranny of a world empire, and speaking and thinking in a kind of glorified Esperanto, would be no less a monster than a hermaphrodite." Hannah Arendt, "Karl Jaspers: Citizen of the World?" *Men in Dark Times* (New York: Harcourt, Brace & World, 1968), p. 89; and, "I have always regarded my Jewishness as one of the indisputable factual data of my life, and I have never had the wish to change or disclaim facts of this kind. There is such a thing as a basic gratitude for everything that is as it is; for what has been given and was not, could not be *made*, for things that are *physei* and not *nomo*." Hannah Arendt, *The Jew as Pariah*, ed. Ron H. Feldman (New York: Grove, 1978), p. 246.

77. Though it should be noted that the Livermore Action Group is a "coalition" of "affinity groups," which means that at least part of the strategy of antinuclear mobilization involves the appeal to "common ties" on local levels.

78. One is also reminded of the student referendum at Brown University in which students voted to have the student medical center stock cyanide pills, to be distributed in the event of nuclear war.

79. Martin Luther King, Jr., "Non-Violence and Social Change," *Conscience for Change*, Massey Lectures (Canada: CBC Publications, 1967), p. 36; Gandhi, "The Greatest Force," *Non-violence in War and Peace*, pp. 110-113.

80. See Sharp, *The Methods of Nonviolent Action*, Part 2, *The Politics of Nonviolent Action*, pp. 340-346.

81. Listen to the sweet patience of the Harvard Nuclear Study Group: "Perhaps it makes no difference whether the twentieth nuclear weapon state joins the ranks in 2000 or 2020. It is more reasonable, however, to expect that the rate is important. If the rate can be slowed, there are better chances of managing the destabilizing effects and the prospects of nuclear use. For every extra year in which an additional country does *not* have nuclear weapons, there

is at least some reduction in the likelihood of nuclear war." Carnedale et al., *Living With Nuclear Weapons*, p. 223.

82. Søren Kierkegaard, *The Concept of Irony: With Constant Reference to Socrates*, trans. Lee M. Capel (Bloomington: Indiana University Press, 1965), p. 340.

83. Karl Marx, "On the Difference Between the Democritean and Epicurean Philosophy of Nature," *Collected Works* 1 (Moscow: Progress Publishers, 1975), pp. 43-44.

84. Leon Wieseltier, *Nuclear War, Nuclear Peace* (New York: Holt, Rinehart and Winston, 1983), p. 19.

85. See George W. Ball, "Sovietizing U.S. Policy," *New York Review of Books* (February 2, 1984).

86. To be sure, Hegel's dialectic is based upon an acute appreciation of the negative; but it is a negative that is moving toward a positive. That Hegel himself could not tolerate "absolute negativities" is discussed at length in Kierkegaard, *The Concept of Irony*.

87. Gandhi, *The Law of Love*, pp. 80-81.

88. *Idem, The Science of Satyagraha*, p. 27.

89. My ending echoes some of the ideas expressed at the end of D.C. Muecke's *The Compass of Irony* (London: Methuen and Company, 1969): "Those who close their eyes to the ambivalences of the human condition--the proponents and adherents of systems, the sentimental idealists, the hardheaded realists, the panacea-mongering technologists--will naturally find an enemy in the ironist and accuse him of flippancy, nihilism, or sitting on the fence. Though some ironists may be guilty of these charges, irony is properly to be regarded as more an intellectual than a moral activity. That is the say, the morality of irony, like the morality of science, philosophy, and art, is a morality of intelligence. The ironist's virtue is mental alertness and agility. His business is to make life unbearable to troglodytes, to keep open house for ideas, and to go on asking questions" (p. 247).

7

Irony in Politics and Theory

> It seemed to her such nonsense--inventing differences, when people,
> heaven knows, were different enough without that.
> > --Virginia Woolf, *To the Lighthouse*

The end of a project is the best time for definition. Here is a pretty
good definition of politics: Politics is the art of living together, despite
differences. And here is a fair approximation of irony: Irony, in all of
its forms and varieties, generally indicates a reversal of expectations.
Much could be said to elaborate these encapsulations further. My aim
in this final chapter is to draw them together, and thereby elucidate
them jointly. I hope to underscore, in schematic fashion, the sense in
which the concept of politics, at least in its most theoretically coherent
formulations, contains implicitly an element of irony.

Definitions of politics abound, and it is very difficult to get any
group of political theorists to agree upon a single definition of the
beast. We therefore are delving into a hotly disputed subject matter, so
let us proceed in the spirit of self-imposed simplification, aware that
our categories are rough hewn, our designs ahistorical and no doubt
culture bound, our distinctions more than just a bit crude and compromis-
ing. Having issued those disclaimers, let me make the sweeping
suggestion that political theorists who define politics belong to either
of two basic camps: those who emphasize the importance of considerations of political "justice," and those who emphasize "power" relations
among political actors. (For now, I am also disregarding those theorists

who teach us, rightly I think, to avoid dichotomization.) Slogging along, I believe we can put the "justice-power" dichotomy in other oppositional terms without too much loss: "consensus" versus "coercion," "community" versus "conflict," or "normative unities" versus "empirical differences."

The first part of the above definition of politics--*politics as an art of living together*--roughly corresponds to the concern with justice, consensus, community, and shared norms. The latter part of the definition--*despite differences*--refers to the concern with power, coercion, conflict, and empirical differences.

The definition attempts to recognize "both" features of politics--justice and power--but it is also clearly weighted in favor of justice and community. I am one of those theorists who is fascinated with the notion of political community--which to my mind represents an extraordinary human achievement--but I very much recognize and appreciate the "differences" that persons often ascribe to themselves. Yet I believe that those theorists who focus primarily upon "differences" and "conflict" and "power" overlook the extent to which conflictual relations necessarily presuppose some initial or overriding attempt to live together; and further, I believe that that attempt presupposes an even "deeper" agreement about, or call it tacit justification of, living together. My belief, to write frankly, issues from a profound skepticism regarding human relations: When pressed, I see no *natural* reason why human beings should live together, let alone live and endure as individuals (and functionalist or pragmatist appeals make absolutely no purchase upon my Rousseau-like, Sartre-like frame of mind). Hence I suggest that political association, in all its contingency, requires or depends upon--even if that requirement "exists" or can be perceived to exist only episodically or else by default--a strong element of choice and agreement and compliance.

To be sure, power theorists study what is often the most interesting aspect of politics: power. Conflict provides the drama of politics, the pathos, the edge; difference provides the spice of life, the stakes of the game. And the skeptic in me thinks that power theorists are quite right to remind communitarian theorists that the latter have ignored profound, probably inexorable differences among human beings. But I also think that power theorists ignore the contingency of politics, and hence the hidden fact that conflict presupposes some kind of underlying consensus. Warfare is not *political* per se. If political "conflict" escalates into all-out warfare, then that relation is no longer, by definition, "political." No longer are the principal actors attempting to live *together*. They have exceeded and violated the normal bounds of political interaction.

Politics attempts, then, to adjudicate differences so that persons can live together after a fashion that at the least avoids warfare; hence politics is concerned to some extent with *order*. Order means stability and continuity, a degree of permanence, an enduring if not shared reality. But politics cannot be reduced to a workaday concern with order and prosaic procedures, as some theorists would have it. The reason politics cannot be so reduced is that the concern for order and stability grows out of, and thus bears a necessary relation to, an underlying awareness of *contingency, change,* and *impermanence.* Moreover, order is no end in itself; order requires justification.

So, too, might we say that political togetherness presupposes or betrays the idea of natural *separation.* Politics may aim for shared reality, community, stability, order, permanence, continuity, and so forth; but these aims, indeed politics itself, necessarily operates *in the face of* human impermanence, separation, mortality, change, rootlessness, meaninglessness. Politics poignantly if implicitly recognizes a dark side to human existence and for the most part attempts to withstand it. Politics, as Aeschylus knew perhaps best of all the Greeks, grows out of *tragedy,* that sense of profound loss and limitation which so often (perhaps inevitably) descends upon human existence and human relations.

Politics grows out of tragedy, is a response to tragedy, is an attempt to overcome tragedy. Political community must be viewed as a precarious triumph over the radical separateness of human existence; political order must be understood as a rare achievement given the chaos and flux of life. Community and order, to be sure, are principal aims of politics; but it must be quickly added that if politics emerges out of an awareness of tragedy, as a response to tragedy, then politics is an endeavor that can never fulfill itself, can never finally attain its highest goals. For politics can never *fully* defy the tragedy of human existence; political community can never completely repair human separateness; and what semblance of order politics imposes can thus be only temporary. Politics, then, is an activity that is always at odds with itself, always ambivalent about itself, never satisfied, ever incomplete.

To digress for a moment: My complaint with most theoretical formulations of politics is that they ignore the underlying ambivalence of politics, mainly because they ignore the extent to which politics emerges out of, and hence presupposes, an awareness of tragedy. Most formulations of politics are "literalist," for they revolve around the presumption that politics can literally achieve its ends. Radical communitarians seem to presume that a happy human community is actually possible, if only we get our attitudes, words, or practices right.

Anticommunitarian liberals advise us to lower our expectations about political possibilities, to accept second-best states, to "de-center" our political designs. But such advice seems to be based upon the presumption that our "interests" and our freedoms lie elsewhere, that is, somewhere outside of the political realm, wherein human happiness again can in fact be attained (if in diminished form). Once again, such formulations lack a strong sense of tragedy. What, after all, are one's "interests" in the face of death?

To return to the main discussion: A politics that acknowledges and accommodates a tragic perspective cannot be entirely rationalist, for tragedy contravenes, even defies, the communitarian tendencies of politics, and reason cannot correct that discrepancy. By default, a politics that recognizes tragedy will need to be based upon a fiction of some sort, a partial pretense, a lie, a construct, a self-imposed myth. Somehow that politics will have to retain its goals and yet also accept tragic subversion of those goals. That double perspective corresponds closely, I think, to what can be properly called an *ironic* outlook, that peculiar outlook first expressed by the ancient Greeks, later revived by nineteenth-century theorists, and most recently displayed, as I've argued, by antinuclear activists. A politics that actively accommodates tragedy, we might now say, is an ironic politics, or a politics that is aware of its own implicit irony.

Why is politics implicitly "ironic?" Politics involves an affirmation of the idea of human community, but that affirmation grows out of, or is attendant upon, a profound awareness of human difference, as well of human tragedy. Such an affirmation requires, I suggest, the kind of reversal of expectations typically associated with the concept of irony. To choose to affirm human community in the face of human mortality, to seek order against the background of chaos, to hold out for worldly justice even though death ultimately defeats or mocks all such efforts, to be dedicated when one is also deeply doubtful--all of this suggests a philosophical stance that involves a double perspective on things, though a stance in which one's affirmative side finally (if barely) triumphs over, that is, partially reverses, one's cynical expectations. Given a deep appreciation of tragedy, one would expect cynicism, skepticism, fatalism, even nihilism, to reign. That instead one affirms human association at all--human differences notwithstanding--entails what I think is best called an ironical attitude.

But let us approach the question from a different angle. Why does irony *affirm*--rather than merely toy with or subvert--the idea of political community? Why, in other words, does the concept of irony find a resolution, a stopping point, in the *political* realm (whereas to some rhetoricians and artists, irony is deliciously unending)? The answer is actually simple: To the ironist, whose outlook on things is already detached, life is *fundamentally* tragic, finally devoid of inherent meaning; human activity is framed by the inescapable facts of mortality and separation. These facts of nature simply cannot be reversed any farther, no matter how playful, how talented the ironist. At some point irony can go no farther; finally irony must affirm human existence. The last twist of irony, as Thomas Mann contended, is to turn its own skepticism "backwards" upon itself, in order to affirm existence. "Political irony," as Mann called it, becomes "eroticism" in the sense that it entails an unconditional affirmation of human life.

Political irony explores the recesses of tragedy, and only by indirection does it "transcend" or reverse a tragic outlook. This reversal of expectations is the reason irony informed the ancient *katabasis*. The ancients explored a symbolic realm of death and destruction in order to gain moral insight into the activity of *this* world, but at the same time they realized that this netherworldly investigation was indeed a roundabout approach to ethics.

Again compare the irony of the ancient *katabasis* with the literalism of certain modern approaches to ethics and political justification, such as John Rawls's work. In his famous book, *A Theory of Justice*, Rawls tried to make Kant's transcendental principles more worldly and accessible, but note that Rawls's own categories remained decidedly "above ground." He earnestly believed that a literalist approach to political justification was possible, and political theorists everywhere admired him for his efforts. More recently Rawls has been looking for principles of political justification that are not "comprehensive and general," but that still bring persons together under the same moral framework. Never, as I have suggested, has Rawls considered the idea of political definition by indirection (though I am tempted to say that the original position is indeed roundabout), nor does it seem that Rawls has considered *death* as an organizing category for life. He has not gone underground in his investigations, his work does not descend into an underworld of death and destruction, his theory has neither confronted nor accommodated a tragic outlook, and it certainly is not ironic, at least not deliberately so.

Yet I should mention furthermore that Rawls's critics--those who have descried his "analytic" approach, his "Cartesian" approach to justification--also remain for the most part tethered to a "literalist" approach to politics. I am thinking here of certain Nietzscheans, several Marxists, many modern feminist theorists--all of whom contend, to speak collectively, that political justification must go beyond the "ideational" level of Rawls's words and pretty principles. The notion of human community is much deeper, they suggest, human beings are more complicated than Rawls might suppose; and to *change* political societies, entire selves must be transfigured, entire patterns of production must be overcome, entire routines of gender differentiation must be altered. As sympathetic as I am to the good intentions of these anti-Cartesians,[1] I must respond by noting that their critique of analytic political philosophy seems based upon a presumption that a deeper human community can be literally founded; and however strong my sympathies, I am not optimistic about their chances for founding such communities (though try they must).

I am not optimistic about modern communitarian theorizing when I attempt to think through the nuclear dilemma by way of such theory. True, I grant that "the bomb" is only the tip of an iceberg of sociocultural, historical, economic, and gender-related problems (and nonproblems); only an index of a totality of underlying world tensions, loyalties, forces, feelings and configurations. To address the bomb is to address the whole world, and therefore a theorist should not by lulled into the temptation of embracing quick fixes. But I am not sure that we can afford the luxury of contemplating the overthrow, for instance, of the whole of patriarchy, of trying to transfigure human selves and societies in their entireties, before we attend to the weapons themselves. I think that we need a theory of politics that addresses the issue of nuclear weapons in a way that, while respecting the difficulties and complexities and enormities of the whole mad affair, and while bearing in mind that the effort eventually may well be in vain, allows and encourages us to act, in a spirit "in spite of all!"

Nuclear weapons are here now, and their abrupt and earth shattering consequences would seem to demand some sense of urgency (something short of apocalyptic hysteria) even on the part of theorists who theorize for the sake of pure theory. Time is not necessarily on our side, and if we wait too long, holding out for a better bargain or a more subtle theory, there may not be any owls of Minerva left to take flight at dusk, nor any phoenixes to rise from the ashes.

In contrast to many modern communitarian theorists, I have been drawn to a theory of political irony as a way of beginning to confront what options are available in the nuclear age; as a way of rediscovering human agency and the human ability to act; as a way of returning to politics. From a theoretical perspective, irony seems appropriate for addressing nuclear matters and the likely disparity between intentions and consequences, subjects and objects, theories and practices; for irony *begins* with the premise that theory is preciously limited, but unlike literalist theorists, ironic theorists make a method, construct a creative conceit, out of that very awareness of their own limitations and the preciousness of their enterprise. Similarly, irony holds the general potential for inviting choice and encouraging political action in a way in which persons could be freed from prior inhibitions, previous engagements, and past commitments--so that they might be able to embrace, ironically, some nuclear-free notion of political community. The spirit of irony is not merely that of reversal; it is rather one of free affirmation against the background of skepticism. Myself, I am often utterly amazed that politics should even *be*; and irony I think is a good way of expressing and cultivating that sense of contingency which is contained within the very concept, and is crucial for the practice, of politics itself. None of this should be construed to mean that irony is a panacea for our nuclear troubles; nor should irony be seen as precluding more "literal" or prosaic approaches to politics. Rather, irony should be viewed as a starting point or a recovery, as a slight "deviation" in Marx's sense.

The infernal traveler of antiquity descended imaginatively into an underworld of death and destruction in order to create, uncover, and renew his moral and political ties with other human beings. So renewed, the traveler would return to the above ground, where his epic understanding would help him to found a new, often an expansive political community. The real question of the nuclear age is not whether we can find particular ways of staving off the next holocaust, but rather whether we can find any moral reason at all, applicable at large, to work to find ways of staving off the next holocaust: Why should we care? Antinuclear actors have provided us with appropriately modern visions of apocalypse, and now our political theorists, realizing the moral irony of these actors' ways, would do well to listen to their poetic exhortations.

Notes

1. Though to those modern theorists who are so eager to reconcile the mind with the body, I might point out that the ancient Egyptians, too, held such a presumption--which was the very idea behind preserving the body after death, in mummified form.

Bibliography

Adam, James, ed. *The Republic of Plato*. 2 Volumes. Cambridge: Cambridge University Press, 1902.

Agress, Lynne. *The Feminine Irony: Women on Women in Early-Nineteenth-Century English Literature*. Cranbury, N.J.: Associated University Press, 1978.

Alford, Steven A. *Irony and the Logic of the Romantic Imagination*. New York and Berne: Peter Lang, 1984.

Allemann, Beda. *Ironie und Dichtung*. Stuttgart: Neske Pfullingen, 1956.

Allen, Woody. *Side Effects*. New York: Random House, 1975.

Almansi, Guido. *L'Ironie de l'ironie*. Urbino: Centro Internazionale di Semiotica e di Linguistica, 1979.

Alt, Peter-André. *Ironie und Krise*. Frankfurt am Main: Peter Lang, 1985.

Althusser, Louis. *For Marx*. Translated by Ben Brewster. New York: Penguin Press, 1969.

_____. *Politics and History: Montesquieu, Rousseau, Hegel and Marx*. Translated by Ben Brewster. London: NLB, 1970.

Anders, Gunther. "Reflections on the H Bomb." Translated by Norbert Guterman. *Dissent* 1 (Spring, 1956): 146-155.

Anderson, Walter E. *The German Enigma*. New York: Vantage Press, 1980.

Annas, Julia. *An Introduction to Plato's Republic*. Oxford: Clarendon Press, 1981.

Apter, T.E. "The Fascination with Disgust," *Thomas Mann: The Devil's Advocate* (London: Macmillan Press, 1978), pp. 58-77

Arendt, Hannah. *Between Past and Future*. New York: Viking Press, 1954.

_____. *Crises of the Republic*. New York: Harcourt Brace Jovanovich, Inc., 1969.

_____. "Karl Jaspers: Citizen of the World?" *Men in Dark Times*. New York: Harcourt, Brace & World, 1968.

_____. *On Revolution*. New York: Viking Press, 1963.

_____. *The Human Condition*. Chicago: University of Chicago Press, 1958.

_____. *The Jew as Pariah*. Edited by Ron H. Feldman. New York: Grove, 1978.

_____. *The Origins of Totalitarianism*. New York and London: Harcourt Brace Jovanovich, 1951.

Babbitt, Irving. *Rousseau and Romanticism*. Cleveland and New York: World Publishing Company, 1955.

347

Bakhtin, Mikhail. *Rabelais and His World*. Translated by Helene Iswolsky. Cambridge, Mass: MIT Press, 1968.

Baldwin, Charles Sears. *Ancient Rhetoric and Poetic*. Gloucester, Mass.: Peter Smith, 1959.

Ball, George W. "Sovietizing U.S. Policy." *New York Review of Books* (February 2, 1984): 34-35.

_____. "White House Roulette." *New York Review of Books* (November 8, 1984): 5-11.

Bambrough, Renford. *Plato, Popper and Politics*. Cambridge: W. Heffer and Sons, 1967.

Bauer, Arnold. *Thomas Mann*. Translated by Alexander and Elizabeth Henderson. New York: Frederick Ungar Publishing, 1971.

Baumgardt, Reinhard. *Das Ironische und die Ironie in den Werken Thomas Manns*. Munich: C. Hanser, 1964.

Becker, William A. "Concepts of Irony with Special Reference to Applications in the Visual Arts." Dissertation, Columbia University, 1970.

Bedau, Hugo Adam. *Civil Disobedience: Theory and Practice*. Indianapolis and New York: Pegasus Books, 1969.

Behler, Ernst. "Der Urspung des Begriffs der Tragischen Ironie." *Arcadia* 5 (1970): 113-142.

_____. *Friedrich Schlegel*. Reinbek bei Hamburg: Rowohlt, 1967.

_____. "Friedrich Schlegel und Hegel." *Hegel-Studien* 2. Bonn: H. Bouvier und Company, 1963: 203-250.

_____. *Klassische Ironie, Romantische Ironie, Tragische Ironie*. Darmstadt: Wissenschaftliche Buchgesellschaft, 1972.

_____. "Nietzsches Auffassung der Ironie." *Nietzsche-Studien* 4 (1975): 1-35.

Bell, Daniel. *The End of Ideology: On the Exhaustion of Political Ideas in the Fifties*. New York: Free Press, 1960.

Benjamin, Walter. "Der Begriff der Kunstkritik in der deutschen Romantik." *Gesammelte Schriften*. Edited by Rolf Tiedemann and Hermann Schweppenhäuser. Frankfurt: Suhrkamp, 1955. Vol. 2: 420-528.

Berendsohn, Walter E. *Thomas Mann: Artist and Partisan in Troubled Times*. Translated by George C. Buck. University: University of Alabama Press, 1973.

Berlin, Isaiah. "Does Political Theory Still Exist?" *Philosophy, Politics and Society*. Second Series. Edited by Peter Laslett and W.G. Runciman. Oxford: Basil Blackwell, 1969: 1-34.

_____. *Karl Marx: His Life and Environment*. Oxford: Oxford University Press, 1978.

Berman, Marshall. "All That Is Solid Melts into Air: Marx, Modernism, Modernization." *Dissent* 25 (Winter, 1978): 54-73.

Bernal, Martin. *Black Athena: The Afroasiatic Roots of Classical Civilization*. New Brunswick, N.J.: Rutgers University Press, 1987.

Blackwell, Marilyn Johns. *C.J.L. Almqvist and Romantic Irony: The Aesthetics of Self-Consciousness*. Stockholm: Almqvist & Wiksell International, 1983.

Blanchot, Maurice. *The Gaze of Orpheus.* Translated by Lydia Davis. Edited by P. Adams Sitney. Barrytown, N.Y.: Station Hill Press, 1981.

_____. *The Space of Literature.* Translated by Ann Smock. Lincoln: University of Nebraska Press, 1982.

Bloom, Allan. *The Closing of the American Mind.* New York: Simon and Schuster, 1987.

_____. "Interpretive Essay." *The Republic of Plato.* New York: Basic Books, 1968: 307-436.

_____. "Response to Hall." *Political Theory* 5 (August, 1977): 315-330.

Bloom, Harold, ed., et al. *Deconstruction and Criticism.* New York: Seabury Press, 1979.

Blumberg, Herbert H. *Nonviolent Direct Action.* Washington, D.C.: Corpus Books, 1968.

Bondurant, Joan V. *Conquest of Violence: The Gandhian Philosophy of Conflict.* Princeton: Princeton University Press, 1958.

Booth, Wayne C. "A New Strategy for Establishing a Truly Democratic Criticism." *Daedalus* 112 (Winter, 1983): 193-214.

_____. *The Rhetoric of Fiction.* Chicago: University of Chicago Press, 1961.

_____. *A Rhetoric of Irony.* Chicago: University of Chicago Press, 1974.

Bosanquet, Bernard. *A History of Aesthetics.* London: George Allen and Unwin Ltd., 1892.

Bourne, Randolph. *History of a Literary Radical.* New York: B.W. Heubsch, 1920.

_____. "The Life of Irony." *Youth and Life.* Cambridge, Mass.: Riverside Press, 1913.

Bowra, C.M. "Orpheus and Eurydice," *Classical Quarterly* 2 (1952): 113-124.

Brennan, Joseph. *Thomas Mann's World.* New York: Russell and Russell, 1962.

Brooks, Cleanth. "Irony as a Principle of Structure." *Literary Opinion in America.* Edited by Morton Dauwen Zabel. New York: Harper and Brothers, 1951.

_____. "Irony and 'Ironic' Poetry." *College English* 9 (February, 1948): 231-237.

_____. *The Well Wrought Urn: Studies in the Structure of Poetry.* London: Dennis Dobson, 1949.

Brown, Katharine Holland. "The Birth of Irony." *Lippincott's Monthly Magazine* 81 (January-June, 1908): 750-757.

Brown, Norman O. *Life Against Death: The Psychoanalytical Meaning of History.* Middletown, Conn.: Wesleyan University Press, 1959.

Brown, Wendy. *Manhood and Politics: A Feminist Reading in Political Theory.* Totowa, N.J.: Rowman & Littlefield, 1988.

Bruss, Elizabeth W. *Beautiful Theories: The Spectacle of Discourse in Contemporary Criticism.* Baltimore and London: Johns Hopkins University Press, 1982.

Büchner, Wilhelm. "Über den Begriff der Eironeia." *Hermes* 76 (1941): 339-358.

Bürgin, Hans, and Hans-Otto Mayer. *Thomas Mann: A Chronicle of his Life.* Translated by Eugene Dobson. University: University of Alabama Press, 1969.

Burke, Kenneth. *A Grammar of Motives.* New York: George Braziller, 1955.

_____. *The Philosophy of Literary Form.* Berkeley: University of California Press, 1973.

Burkert, Walter. "Oriental and Greek Mythology: The Meeting of Parallels." *Interpretations of Greek Mythology.* Edited by Jan Bremmer. London and Sydney: Croom Helm, 1987: 10-40.

Burnyeat, M.F. "Sphinx Without a Secret." *New York Review of Books* (November 30, 1985).

Butler, E.M. *The Tyranny of Greece over Germany.* Boston: Beacon Press, 1958.

Butterfield, Fox. "Anatomy of the Nuclear Protest." *New York Times Magazine* (July 11, 1982): 14ff.

Carnesale, Albert, Paul Doty, Stanley Hoffmann, Samuel P. Huntington, Joesph S. Nye, Jr., and Scott Sagan. *Living with Nuclear Weapons.* Harvard Nuclear Study Group. New York: Bantam Books, 1983.

Carter, April. *Direct Action and Liberal Democracy.* New York: Harper and Row, 1973.

Cassirer, Ernst. "Plato's Republic." *The Myth of the State.* New Haven: Yale University Press, 1946: 61-77.

Catlin, George. "Political Theory: What 'Is It?" *Political Science Quarterly* 72 (March, 1957): 1-29.

Cavarnos, Constantine. *Plato's View of Man.* Belmont, Mass.: Institute for Byzantine and Modern Greek Studies, 1979.

Cavell, Stanley. *The Claim of Reason: Wittgenstein, Skepticism, Morality, and Tragedy.* Oxford: Clarendon Press, 1979.

_____. *Must We Mean What We Say?* Cambridge: Cambridge University Press, 1976.

Chapman, John Jay. *Lucien, Plato, and Greek Morals.* Boston and New York: Houghton Mifflin Co., 1931.

Chevalier, Haakon M. *The Ironic Temper: Anatole France and his Time.* New York: Oxford University Press, 1932.

Clark, Raymond J. *Catabasis: Virgil and the Wisdom Tradition.* Amsterdam: Gruner, 1979.

Clough, Wilson O. "Irony: A French Approach." *Sewanee Review* 47 (April-June, 1939): 175-183.

Cobban, Alfred. "The Decline of Political Theory." *Political Science Quarterly* 68 (September, 1953): 321-337.

Collingwood, R.G. *The Principles of Art.* Oxford: Clarendon Press, 1960.

Collins, Anthony A. *A Discourse Concerning Ridicule and Irony in Writing.* London: J. Brotherton, Printer, 1729.

Conway, Daniel W. "Solving the Problem of Socrates: Nietzsche's *Zarathustra* as Political Irony." *Political Theory* 16, No. 2 (May, 1988): 257-280.

Cornford, F.M. "Plato's Commonwealth." *The Unwritten Philosophy and Other Essays.* Cambridge: Cambridge University Press, 1950.

Crane, R.S. "The Critical Monism of Cleanth Brooks." *Critics and Criticism: Ancient and Modern*. Edited by R.S. Crane. Chicago: University of Chicago Press, 1952.

Croce, Benedetto. *Guide to Aesthetics*. Translated by Patrick Romonell. New York: Bobbs Merrill, 1965.

Cross, R.C., and A.D. Woozley. *Plato's Republic: A Philosophical Commentary*. New York: St. Martin's Press, 1966.

Crossman, R.H.S. *Plato To-Day*. New York: Oxford University Press, 1959.

Culler, Jonathan. *Structural Poetics: Structuralism, Linguistics, and the Study of Literature*. London: Routledge and Kegan Paul, 1975.

Cumming, Robert D. *Human Nature and History: A Study of the Development of Liberal Political Thought*. 2 Vols. Chicago: University of Chicago Press, 1969.

Cushman, Robert E. *Therapeia*. Westport, Conn.: Greenwood Press, 1958.

Dahl, Robert A. *Controlling Nuclear Weapons: Democracy Versus Guardianship*. Syracuse: Syracuse University Press, 1985.

_____. "Political Theory: Truth or Consequences." *World Politics* 11 (October, 1958): 89-102.

Dannhauser, Werner J. *Nietzsche's View of Socrates*. Ithaca and London: Cornell University Press, 1974.

Darnton, Robert. "Readers Respond to Rousseau: The Fabrication of Romantic Sensitivity." *The Great Cat Massacre and Other Episodes in French Cultural History*. New York: Basic Books, 1984: 215-236.

Davies, John L., and David J. Vaughan, trans. *The Republic of Plato*. London: Macmillan and Company, 1950.

de Crespigny, Anthony, and Kenneth Minogue, ed. *Contemporary Political Philosophers*. New York: Dodd, Mead and Co., 1975.

Dekker, Annie F. *Ironie in de Odyssee*. Leiden: E.J. Brill, 1965.

de Man, Paul. *Allegories of Reading: Figural Language in Rousseau, Nietzsche, Rilke, and Proust*. New Haven: Yale University Press, 1979.

_____. "The Rhetoric of Temporality." *Interpretation: Theory and Practice*. Edited by Charles S. Singleton. Baltimore: Johns Hopkins University Press, 1969: 173-209.

DeMott, Benjamin. "The New Irony: Sickniks and Others." *The American Scholar* 31 (Winter, 1961-62): 108-119.

de Rougemont, Denis. *Love in the Western World*. Translated by Montgomery Belgion. Princeton: Princeton University Press, 1983.

Derrida, Jacques. *Disseminations*. Translated by Barbara Johnson. Chicago: University of Chicago Press, 1981.

_____. *Éperons: Les Styles de Nietzsche (Spurs: Nietzsche's Styles)*. Translated by Barbara Harlow. Dual language edition. Chicago: University of Chicago Press, 1979.

_____. "The Laws of Reflection: Nelson Mandela, in Admiration." *For Nelson Mandela*. Edited by Jacques Derrida and Mustapha Tlili. New York: Henry Holt, 1987: 13-42.

_____. "Like the Sound of the Sea Deep Within a Shell: Paul de Man's War." *Critical Inquiry* 14 (Spring, 1988): 591-652.

————. *Margins of Philosophy*. Translated by Alan Bass. Chicago: University of Chicago Press, 1982.

————. "No Apocalypse, No Now (full speed ahead, seven missiles, seven missives)." Translated by Catherine Porter and Philip Lewis. *diacritics* 14, No. 2 (Summer, 1984): 20-31.

————. "Of an Apocalyptic Tone Recently Adopted in Philosophy." Translated by John P. Leavey, Jr. *Oxford Literary Review* 6, No. 2 (1984): 3-35.

————. *Of Grammatology*. Translated by Gayatri Spivak. Baltimore: Johns Hopkins University Press, 1979.

————. "Otobiographies: The Teaching of Nietzsche and the Politics of the Proper Name." Translated by Avital Ronell. *The Ear of the Other*. Edited by Christie McDonald. New York: Schocken, 1985.

————. "Plato's Pharmacy." *Disseminations*. Translated by Barbara Johnson. Chicago: University of Chicago Press, 1981: 61-172.

————. "The Politics of Friendship." *Journal of Philosophy* (1988): 632-644.

————. "Racism's Last Word," *Critical Inquiry* 12 (1985): 290-299.

————. *Writing and Difference*. Translated by Alan Bass. Chicago: University of Chicago Press, 1978.

Diderot, Denis. *Rameau's Nephew*. Translated by Jacques Barzun and Ralph H. Bowen. New York: Bobbs-Merrill Company, 1964.

Dieterich, A. *Nekyia: Beiträge zur Erklärung der neuentdeckten Petrusapokalypse*. 2d ed. Annotated by R. Wünsch. Leipzig and Berlin: Teubner, 1913.

Diès, M.A. "Le Nombre Nuptial De Platon." *Mémoires à l'Académie Des Inscriptions et Belles-Lettres* 14. Paris: Imprimerie Nationale, 1940.

Dikkers, S.J.E. *Ironie als Vorm van Communicatie*. The Hague: Kruseman, n.d.

Dodds, E.R. *The Greeks and the Irrational*. Berkeley: University of California Press, 1963.

Douglass, Frederick. "What to the Slave Is the Fourth of July?" *The Frederick Douglass Papers*. Edited by John W. Blassingame. Series One: *Speeches, Debates, and Interviews*. Volume 2: 1847-54. New Haven: Yale University Press, 1982: 359-387.

Draenos, Stan. "The Totalitarian Theme in Horkheimer and Arendt." *Salgamundi* (Spring, 1982): 155-169.

Dronke, Peter. "The Return of Eurydice." *Classica et Mediaevalia* 23 (1962): 198-215.

Dyson, A.E. *The Crazy Fabric: Essays in Irony*. London: Macmillan and Co., 1959.

Dyson, Freeman. *Weapons and Hope*. New York: Harper and Row, 1984.

Easton, David. *The Political System*. New York: Alfred A. Knopf, 1953.

Eichner, Hans. *Friedrich Schlegel*. New York: Twayne Publishers, 1970.

————. "Thomas Mann and Politics." *Thomas Mann: Ein Kolloquium*. Edited by Hans H. Schulte and Gerald Chapple. Bonn: Bouvier, 1978: 5-19.

Elshtain, Jean Bethke, ed. *The Family in Political Thought*. Amherst: University of Massachusetts Press, 1982.

Empson, William. *Seven Types of Ambiguity.* New York: New Directions, 1947.
_____. "The Voice of the Underdog." *New York Review of Books* 12 (June, 1975): 37-38.
Enright, D.J. *The Alluring Problem: An Essay on Irony.* Oxford and New York: Oxford University Press, 1986.
Erikson, Erik H. *Gandhi's Truth: On the Origins of Militant Nonviolence.* New York: W.W. Norton and Company, 1969.
Ernst, Fritz. *Die Romantische Ironie.* Zurich: Schulthess, 1915.
Feinberg, Leonard. *Introduction to Satire.* Ames, Iowa: Iowa State University Press, 1967.
Feuerlicht, Ignace. *Thomas Mann.* Boston: Twayne Publishers, 1968.
Finley, M.I. *The World of Odysseus.* London: Chatto and Windus, 1956.
Firchow, Peter. "Introduction." *Friedrich Schlegel's* Lucinde *and the Fragments.* Minneapolis: University of Minnesota Press, 1971.
Fischer, Michael. "Redefining Philosophy as Literature: Richard Rorty's 'Defense' of Literary Culture." *Soundings* 65 (Fall, 1984): 312-324.
Fish, Stanley E. *Self-Consuming Artifacts: The Experience of Seventeenth-Century Literature.* Berkeley: University of California Press, 1972.
_____. "Short People Got No Reason to Live: Reading Irony." *Daedalus* 112 (Winter, 1983): 175-191.
Fite, Warner. *The Platonic Legend.* New York and London: Charles Scribner's Sons, 1934.
Fletcher, Angus. *Allegory: The Theory of a Symbolic Mode.* Ithaca: Cornell University Press, 1964.
Fletcher, F.T.H. *Montesquieu and English Politics (1750-1800).* Philadelphia: Porcupine Press, 1980.
Foley, Helen P. *Ritual Irony: Poetry and Sacrifice in Euripedes.* Ithaca and London: Cornell University Press, 1985.
Foster, M.B. *The Political Philosophies of Plato and Hegel.* Oxford: Clarendon Press, 1965.
Foucault, Michel. *The Foucault Reader.* Edited by Paul Rabinow. New York: Pantheon Books, 1984.
Freccero, John. *Dante: The Poetics of Conversion.* Cambridge: Harvard University Press, 1986.
Freud, Sigmund. "Humor." *Collected Papers* 5. Edited by James Strachey. New York: Basic Books, 1959.
_____. *Jokes and their Relation to the Unconscious.* Translated by James Strachey. New York: W.W. Norton, 1960.
Friedländer, Paul. *Plato: An Introduction.* Translated by Hans Meyerhoff. Bollingen Series 14. Princeton: Princeton University Press, 1958.
Friedman, John Block. *Orpheus in the Middle Ages.* Cambridge: Harvard University Press, 1970.
Frye, Northrop. *Anatomy of Criticism.* Princeton: Princeton University Press, 1957.
Furst, Lilian R. *Fictions of Romantic Irony.* Cambridge: Harvard University Press, 1984.

Fussell, Paul. *The Great War and Modern Memory.* London: Oxford University Press, 1975.

_____. "The New Irony and the Augustans." *Encounter* 34 (June, 1970): 68-74.

Gadamer, Hans-Georg. *Dialogue and Dialectic: Eight Hermeneutical Studies on Plato.* Translated by P. Christopher Smith. New Haven: Yale University Press, 1980.

Gandhi, M.K. *The Law of Love.* Pocket Gandhi Series, no. 3. Edited by Anand T. Hingorani. Bombay: Bharatiya Vidya Bhavan, 1962.

_____. *Non-Violence in Peace and War.* Ahmedabad: Navajivan Publishing House, 1942.

_____. *Satyagraha.* Ahmedabad: Navajivan Publishing House, 1951.

_____. *The Science of Satyagraha.* Pocket Gandhi Series, no. 4. Edited by Anand T. Hingorani. Bombay: Bharatiya Vidya Bhavan, 1962.

Geertz, Clifford. *The Interpretation of Cultures.* New York: Basic Books, 1973.

Germino, Dante. *Beyond Ideology.* New York: Harper and Row Publishers, 1967.

_____. "The Revival of Political Theory." *Journal of Politics* 25 (August, 1963): 437-460.

Girard, René. "Generative Violence and the Extinction of the Social Order." Translated by Thomas Wieser. *Salgamundi*, No. 63-4 (Spring/Summer, 1984): 204-237.

Glicksberg, Charles I. *The Ironic Vision in Modern Literature.* The Hague: Martinus Nijhoff, 1969.

Goethe, Johann Wolfgang. "Plato, als Mitgenosse einer christlichen Offenbarung (1796)." *Schriften zur Literatur* 1. Edited by Edith Nahler (Berlin: Akademic-Verlag, 1970): 180-184.

_____. *Schriften zur Farbenlehre.* Stuttgart: J.G. Cotta'sche Buchhandlung Nachfolger, 1810.

Gompert, David C., J.H. Barton, M. Mandelbaum, and R.L. Garwin. *Nuclear Weapons and World Politics.* 1980s Project/Council on Foreign Relations. New York: McGraw-Hill Books, 1977.

Good, Edwin M. *Irony in the Old Testament.* Philadelphia: Westminster Press, 1965.

Gouldner, Alvin W. *Enter Plato: Classical Greece and the Origins of Social Theory.* New York: Basic Books, 1965.

_____. *The Two Marxisms.* New York: Seabury Press, 1980.

Graf, Fritz. "Orpheus: A Poet among Men. " *Interpretations of Greek Mythology.* Edited by Jan Bremmer. London and Sydney: Croom Helm, 1987: 80-106.

Grant, Mary A. "The Ancient Rhetorical Theories of the Laughable; the Greek Rhetoricians and Cicero." University of Wisconsin Studies in Language and Literature 21. Madison, 1924.

Graves, Robert. *The Greek Myths.* Baltimore: Penguin Books, 1948.

Greenblatt, Stephen J. *Renaissance Self-Fashioning: From More to Shakespeare.* Chicago: University of Chicago Press, 1980.

_____. *Sir Walter Raleigh: The Renaissance Man and His Roles.* New Haven and London: Yale University Press, 1973.

Greene, William Chase. *Plato's View of Poetry.* Cambridge: Harvard Studies in Classical Philosophy, 1918.

Gregg, Richard B. *The Power of Nonviolence.* Nyack, N.Y.: Fellowship Publications, 1959.

_____. *The Psychology and Strategy of Gandhi's Nonviolent Resistance.* New York and London: Garland Publishing, 1972.

Grey, D.R. "Art in the Republic." *Philosophy* 28 (October, 1952): 291-310.

Grice, Paul. "Presupposition and Conversational Implication." *Radical Pragmatics.* Edited by Peter Cole. New York: Academic Press, 1981: 183-198.

Gross, Barry, ed. *The Great Thinkers on Plato.* New York: G.P. Putnam's Sons, 1968.

Ground Zero. *Nuclear War: What's in it for You?* New York: Pocket Books, 1982.

Grube, G.M.A., trans. *Plato's Republic.* Indianapolis: Hackett, 1974.

Gurewitch, Morton L. *European Romantic Irony.* Ann Arbor, Mich.: University Microfilms International Microfilms, 1980.

Guthrie, W.K.C. *Orpheus and Greek Religion.* New York: W.W. Norton & Co., 1966.

Habermas, Jürgen. *Toward a Rational Society: Student Protest, Science, and Politics.* Translated by Jeremy J. Shapiro. London: Heinemann Educational Books, 1971.

Haiduk, Manfred. "Die Bedeutung der Polemischen Schriften im Schaffen Thomas Manns." *Vollendung und Grösse Thomas Manns.* Edited by Georg Wenzel. Halle: Kreuz, 1962: 43-71.

Hall, Dale. "The *Republic* and the 'Limits of Politics.' " *Political Theory* 5 (August, 1977): 293-313.

Hall, David L. *Eros and Irony: A Prelude to Philosophical Anarchism.* Albany: State University of New York Press, 1982.

Hamlin, Cyrus. "Platonic Dialogue and Romantic Irony: Prolegomenon to a Theory of Literary Narrative." *Canadian Review of Comparative Literature* 3 (1976): 5-26.

_____. "The Temporality of Selfhood: Metaphor and Romantic Poetry." *New Literary History* 6 (1974): 169-193.

Handwerk, Gary J. *Irony and Ethics in Narrative: From Schlegel to Lacan.* New Haven and London: Yale University Press, 1985.

Hare, Paul A., and Herbert H. Blumberg. *Nonviolent Direct Action.* Washington, D.C.: Corpus Books, 1968.

Hass, Hans-Egon. "Die Ironie als literarische Phänomen." Dissertation, Bonn, 1950.

Hatfield, Henry, ed. *Thomas Mann: A Collection of Critical Essays.* Englewood Cliffs, N.J.: Prentice-Hall, 1964.

Havelock, Eric A. *Preface to Plato.* Cambridge, Mass.: Belknap Press, 1963.

Hegel, G.W.F. *Aesthetics: Lectures on Fine Art.* 2 Vols. Translated by T.M. Knox. Oxford: Clarendon Press, 1975.

_____. Lectures on the History of Philosophy. 3 Vols. Translated by E.S. Haldane and Frances H. Simson. London: Routledge and Kegan Paul, 1974.

_____. Lectures on the Philosophy of Religion. 3 Vols. Translated by E.B. Speirs. London: Kegan Paul, Trench, Trübner and Co., 1895.

_____. The Phenomenology of Spirit. Translated by A.V. Miller. Oxford: Oxford University Press, 1979.

_____. The Philosophy of History. Translated by J. Sibree. New York: Dover Publications, 1956.

_____. The Philosophy of Mind. Translated by William Wallace. Oxford: Clarendon Press, 1971.

_____. The Philosophy of Right. Translated by T.M. Knox. Oxford: Clarendon Press, 1952.

Heine, Heinrich. The Works of Heinrich Heine. Translated by Charles Godfrey Leland. Volume 5: Germany. New York: E.P. Dutton, 1906.

Heller, Erich. The Disinherited Mind: Essays in Modern German Literature and Thought. Cambridge: Bowes & Bowes, 1952.

_____. The Ironic German: A Study of Thomas Mann. Boston: Little, Brown and Company, 1958.

Henrich, Dieter. "Formen der Negation in Hegels Logik." Hegel-Jahrbuch 1974. Cologne: Pahl-Rugenstein, 1975: 245-256.

Hesse, Walter G. "Thomas Mann, der unpolitische Deutsche oder Leiden an der Soziologie." Dichtung, Sprache, Gesellschaft. Edited by Victor Lange and Hans-Gert Roloff. Frankfurt: Athenäum Verlag, 1971: 189-196.

Highet, Gilbert. The Anatomy of Satire. Princeton: Princeton University Press, 1962.

Hill, Melvyn A., ed. Hannah Arendt: The Recovery of the Public World. New York: St. Martin's Press, 1979.

Himmelfarb, Martha. Tours of Hell: An Apocalyptic Form in Jewish and Christian Literature. Philadelphia: University of Pennsylvania Press, 1983.

Holland, Norman. Dynamics of Literary Response. New York: Oxford University Press, 1968.

Hollingdale, R.J. Thomas Mann: A Critical Study. London: Rupert Hart-David, 1971.

Homer. The Odyssey of Homer. Translated by Richmond Lattimore. New York: Harper and Row, 1965.

Hopper, Stanley R. "Irony--The Pathos of the Middle." Cross Currents 12 (Winter, 1962): 31-40.

Howey, Richard L. "Some Reflections on Irony in Nietzsche." Nietzsche-Studien 4 (1975): 36-51.

Hughes, Kenneth, ed. Thomas Mann in Context. Worcester, Mass.: Clark University Press, 1978.

Hutchens, Eleanor N. "The Identification of Irony." ELH 27. Baltimore: Johns Hopkins University Press, 1960: 352-363.

_____. Irony in Tom Jones. University: University of Alabama Press, 1965.

Immerwahr, Raymond. "The Subjectivity or Objectivity of Friedrich Schlegel's Poetic Irony." Germanic Review 26 (October, 1951): 173-191.

Irwin, Eleanor. "The Songs of Orpheus and the New Song of Christ." *Orpheus: The Metamorphoses of a Myth.* Edited by John Warden. Toronto: University of Toronto Press, 1982: 51-62

Jaeger, Werner. *Paideia: The Ideals of Greek Culture.* Vol. 1 and 2. Translated by Gilbert Highet. New York: Oxford University Press, 1939 and 1943.

Jankélévitch, Vladimir. *L'Ironie.* Paris: Librairie Félix Alcon, 1936.

Japp, Uwe. *Theorie der Ironie.* Frankfurt: Vittorio Klostermann, 1983.

Jaspers, Karl. *The Future of Mankind.* Translated by E.B. Ashton. Chicago: University of Chicago Press, 1961.

Jebb, R.C., trans. *The Characters of Theophrastus.* Edited by J.E. Sandys. London: Macmillan and Company, 1909.

Johnston, Ian C. *The Ironies of War: An Introduction to Homer's Iliad.* Lanham, Maryland: University Press of America, 1988.

Jowett, B. "Analysis." *The Republic of Plato.* New York: Hearst's International Library Co., n.d.

_____, trans. "On the Structure of Plato's Republic and Its Relation to Other Dialogues." *Plato's Republic: The Greek Text.* Vol 2. Edited by B. Jowett and Lewis Campbell. Oxford: Clarendon Press, 1894.

_____. *The Republic of Plato: Two Volumes in One.* New York: Hearst's International Library, n.d.

Jowett, B., and Lewis Campbell, eds. *Plato's Republic: The Greek Text.* 3 Vols. Oxford: Clarendon Press, 1864.

Kant, Immanuel. *Groundwork of the Metaphysic of Morals.* Translated by H.J. Paton. New York: Harper Torchbooks, 1948.

Kariel, Henry S. "Affirming a Politics of Inconsequence." *Polity* 17 (Fall, 1984): 145-160.

_____. *In Search of Authority: Twentieth-Century Political Thought.* Glencoe, Ill.: Free Press, 1964.

Kartsonis, Anna D. *Anastasis: The Making of an Image.* Princeton: Princeton University Press, 1986.

Kateb, George. "Hannah Arendt: Alienation and America." *Raritan* 3, No.1 (Summer, 1983): 4-34.

_____. *Hannah Arendt: Politics, Conscience, Evil.* Totowa, N.J.: Rowman & Allanheld, 1984.

_____. "Nuclear Weapons and Individual Responsibility." *Dissent* (Spring, 1986): 161-172.

_____. *Political Theory: Its Nature and Uses.* New York: St. Martin's Press, 1968.

_____. "Thinking About Human Extinction (1): Nietzsche and Heidegger." *Raritan* 6, No. 2 (Fall, 1986): 1-28.

_____. "Thinking About Human Extinction (2): Emerson and Whitman," *Raritan* 6, No. 3 (Winter, 1987):1-22.

_____. *Utopia and Its Enemies.* New York: Schocken Books, 1972.

Kaufmann, Walter. *Nietzsche: Philosopher, Psychologist, Antichrist.* Princeton: Princeton University Press, 1968.

Kelly, George Armstrong. *Idealism, Politics and History: Sources of Hegelian Thought.* Cambridge: Cambridge University Press, 1969.

_____. "Mortal Politics in Eighteenth-Century France." *Historical Reflections* 13, No. 1 (Spring, 1986).

Keohane, Nannerl O. *Philosophy and the State in France: The Renaissance to the Enlightenment*. Princeton: Princeton University Press, 1980.

Kérenyi, Karl. *Pythagoras und Orpheus*. Zurich: Rhein-Verlag, 1950.

Kérenyi, Karl, and C.G. Jung. *Essays on a Science of Mythology*. Translated by R.F.C. Hull. New York: Pantheon Books, 1949.

Kierkegaard, Søren. *The Concept of Irony: With Constant Reference to Socrates*. Translated by Lee M. Capel. Bloomington: Indiana University Press, 1965.

_____. *Concluding Unscientific Postscript*. Translated by David F. Swenson and Walter Lowrie. Princeton: Princeton University Press, 1941.

_____. *Either/Or*. Vol. 1. Translated by David and Lillian Swenson. Princeton: Princeton University Press, 1944.

_____. [Climacus, Johannes, pseud.]. *Philosophical Fragments*. Translated by David F. Swenson. Princeton: Princeton University Press, 1962.

King, Martin Luther, Jr. "Non-Violence and Social Change." *Conscience for Change*. Massey Lectures. Canada: CBC Publications, 1967.

_____. *Stride Toward Freedom: The Montgomery Story*. New York: Harper & Brothers, 1958.

_____. *Where Do We Go From Here: Chaos or Community*. New York: Harper & Row Publishers, 1967.

Kinsley, William. "Encompassing Irony" (rev. Muecke, *The Compass of Irony*). *Satire News* 9 (Fall, 1971): 97-99.

Kissinger, Henry A. "Nuclear Weapons and the Peace Movement." *Washington Quarterly* 5 (Summer, 1983): 31-39.

Klein, Jacob. *A Commentary on Plato's Meno*. Chapel Hill: University of North Carolina Press, 1965.

Knox, Norman. "Irony." *Dictionary of the History of Ideas*. Vol. 11. Edited by Philip D. Wiener. New York: Charles Scribner's Sons, 1973: 626-634.

_____. "On the Classification of Ironies." *Modern Philology* (August, 1972): 53-62.

_____. *The Word Irony and Its Context, 1500-1755*. Durham, N.C.: Duke University Press, 1961.

Kohn, Alfie. "Laughing at the Unlaughable." *In These Times* (July 13-26, 1983): 12-13.

Kraut, Richard. *Socrates and the State*. Princeton: Princeton University Press, 1984.

Kuper, Leo. *Passive Resistance in South Africa*. London: Jonathan Cape, 1956.

Kurzke, Hermann. "Die Quellen der 'Betrachtungen eines Unpolitischen.' " *ThomasMann Studien*. Band 7. Bern: Francke Verlag, 1986: 291-310.

_____. *Epoche-Werk-Wirkung*. Munich: Beck, 1985.

LaCapra, Dominick. *Rethinking Intellectual History: Texts, Contexts, Language*. Ithaca and London: Cornell University Press, 1983.

Lakey, George. *Non Violent Action: How it Works*. Lebanon, Pa.: Pendle Hill Pamphlet, 1963.

_____. "The Sociological Mechanisms of Non-Violent Action." *Peace Research Reviews* 11 (December, 1968).

Lang, Candace D. *Irony/Humor: Critical Paradigms*. Baltimore and London: Johns Hopkins University Press, 1988.

Larson, Raymond, trans. *The Republic*. Arlington Heights, Ill.: AHM Publishing Corporation, 1979.

Laslett, Peter, ed. *Philosophy, Politics and Society*. Oxford: Basil Blackwell, 1956.

Laslett, Peter, and W.G. Runciman, eds. *Philosophy, Politics and Society*. Second Series. Oxford: Basil Blackwell, 1969.

Lee, Desmond. "Introduction." *Plato: The Republic*. Edited and Translated by Desmond Lee. New York: Penguin Books, 1974.

Lee, M. Owen. "Orpheus and Eurydice: Some Modern Versions." *Classical Quarterly* 11 (1952): 113-126.

Lefever, Ernest W., and E.Stephen Hunt, eds. *The Apocalyptic Premise*. Washington, D.C.: Ethics and Public Policy Center, 1982.

Lenin, Vladimir. *What Is to Be Done?* New York: International Publishers, 1969.

Lens, Sidney. *The Day Before Doomsday: An Anatomy of the Nuclear Arms Race*. Garden City, N.Y.: Doubleday & Company, 1977.

Lesser, J. "Of Thomas Mann's Renunciation." *Germanic Review* 25, No. 4 (December, 1950): 245-256.

Levinson, Ronald. *In Defense of Plato*. Cambridge: Harvard University Press, 1953.

Lifton, Robert Jay. *Indefensible Weapons: The Political and Moral Case Against Nuclear Arms*. New York: Basic Books, 1982.

Lindsay, A.D., trans. *The Republic of Plato*. New York: E.P. Dutton, 1957.

Linforth, Ivan M. *The Arts of Orpheus*. Berkeley: University of California Press, 1941.

Livergood, Norman O. *Activity in Marx's Philosophy*. The Hague: Martinus Nijhoff, 1967.

Lodge, Rupert C. *Plato's Theory of Art*. London: Routledge and Kegan Paul Ltd., 1953.

Lofland, John, and Michael Fink. *Symbolic Sit-Ins: Protest Occupations at the California Capitol*. Washington, D.C.: University Press of America, 1982.

Lovejoy, Arthur O. *The Great Chain of Being*. Cambridge: Harvard University Press, 1936.

Lowell, Robert. "Orpheus, Eurydice and Hermes." *Imitations*. New York: Farrar, Straus and Giroux, 1978.

Lukács, Georg. *Soul and Form*. Translated by Anna Bostock. Cambridge, Mass.: MIT Press, 1974.

_____. *The Theory of the Novel*. Translated by Anna Bostock. Cambridge, Mass.: MIT Press, 1973.

Lussky, Alfred E. *Tieck's Romantic Irony*. Chapel Hill: University of North Carolina Press, 1932.

Macchioro, Vittorio D. *From Orpheus to Paul: A History of Orphism*. New York, Henry Holt and Company, 1930.

MacDonald, Ronald R. *The Burial-Places of Memory: Epic Underworlds in Vergil, Dante, and Milton.* Amherst: University of Massachusetts Press, 1987.

MacIntyre, A.C. *Marxism. An Interpretation.* London, 1953.

McKee, John B. *Literary Irony and the Literary Audience: Studies in the Victimization of the Reader in Augustan Fiction.* Amsterdam: Rodopi N.V., 1974.

McLellan, David. *Karl Marx: Early Texts.* New York: Barnes and Noble, 1971.

_____. *Karl Marx: His Life and Thought.* New York: Harper and Row, 1973.

Macpherson, C.B. *Democratic Theory: Essays in Retrieval.* Oxford: Clarendon Press, 1973.

Madden, John F. "Myth as Mask and Model: Agreements and Contrasts between Freud and Mann." *Thomas Mann in Context.* Edited by Kenneth Hughes. Worcester, Mass.: Clark University Press, 1978: 17-36.

Mah, Harold. *The End of Philosophy, the Origin of Ideology.* Berkeley: University of California Press, 1987.

Mann, Thomas. *The Coming Victory of Democracy.* Translated by Agnes E. Meyer. New York: Alfred A. Knopf, 1938.

_____. "The German Republic." *Order of the Day.* Translated by H.T. Lowe-Porter. Freeport, N.Y.: Books for Libraries Press, 1937.

_____. "Goethe and Tolstoy." *Essays of Three Decades.* Translated by H.T. Lowe-Porter. New York: Vintage Books, 1957.

_____. "Humor and Irony." *Thomas Mann: A Collection of Critical Essays.* Edited by Henry Hatfield. Englewood Cliffs, N.J.: Prentice-Hall, 1964: 170-172.

_____. "In My Defense." *Atlantic Monthly* (October, 1944).

_____. "Mass und Wert." *Achtung Europa! Aufsatze zur Zeit.* Stockholm: Bermann-Fischer, 1938.

_____. "Meine Zeit." *Reden und Aufsätze 2.* Frankfurt am Main: S. Fischer, 1960.

_____. *Order of the Day.* Translated by H.T. Lowe-Porter. Freeport, N.Y.: Books for Libraries Press, 1937.

_____. *Reflections of a Nonpolitical Man.* Translated by Walter D. Morris. New York: Frederick Ungar Publishing Co., 1983.

_____. *A Sketch of My Life.* Translated by H.T. Lowe-Porter. Paris: Harrison, 1930.

_____. "The Years of My Life." *Harpers* (October, 1950): 256-7.

_____. "Tischrede." *Die Forderung des Tages.* Berlin: S. Fischer, 1930.

_____. "Von Deutscher Republik." *Gesammelte Werke* 12. Frankfurt am Main: S. Fischer, 1955: 491-532.

Marcuse, H. *Eros and Civilization: A Philosophical Inquiry into Freud.* Boston: Beacon Press, 1955.

Marx, Karl. *Capital.* Translated by Samuel Moore and Edward Aveling. Edited by Friedrich Engels. Moscow: Progress Publishers, 1887.

_____. *Collected Works.* Moscow: Progress Publishers, 1975.

_____. *The Eighteenth Brumaire of Louis Bonaparte.* New York: International Publishers, 1963.

_____. *Karl Marx-Friedrich Engels, Werke.* Berlin: Dietz Verlag, 1963.

_____. "On the Difference Between the Democritean and Epicurean Philosophy of Nature." *Collected Works.* Vol. 1. Moscow: Progress Publishers, 1975: 25-131.

_____. *The Marx-Engels Reader.* Edited by Robert Tucker. New York: W.W. Norton, 1972.

Mathieu, Bertrand. *Orpheus in Brooklyn: Orphism, Rimbaud, and Henry Miller.* The Hague-Paris: Mouton, 1976.

Mazlish, Bruce. *James and John Stuart Mill: Father and Son in the Nineteenth Century.* New York: Basic Books, 1975.

Mehring, Franz. *Karl Marx: The Story of His Life.* New York: Covici, Friede, 1935.

Mellor, Anne K. *English Romantic Irony.* Cambridge: Harvard University Press, 1980.

_____. "On Romantic Irony, Symbolism and Allegory." *Criticism* 21 (Summer, 1979): 217-229.

Merlan, Philip. "Form and Content in Plato's Philosophy." *Journal of the History of Ideas* 8 (October, 1947): 406-430.

Meuli, K. *Odyssee und Argonautika.* Basel, 1921.

Meyer, David S. *A Winter of Discontent: The Nuclear Freeze and American Politics.* New York: Praeger, 1990.

Miller, Arthur. "Introduction to the Collected Plays," *Arthur Miller's Collected Plays* (New York: Viking Press, 1957).

Mins, Henry F. "Marx's Doctoral Dissertation." *Science and Society* 12 (Winter, 1948): 157-69.

Moglen, Helene. *The Philosophical Irony of Laurence Sterne.* Gainesville: University Presses of Florida, 1975.

Moloney, Brian. "Psychoanalysis and Irony in 'La Coscienza di Zeno.' " *Modern Language Review* 67 (April, 1972): 309-318.

Muecke, D.C. *The Compass of Irony.* London: Methuen and Company, 1969.

_____. *Irony.* London: Methuen and Company, 1970.

_____. *Irony and the Ironic.* The Critical Idiom Series No. 13. London: Methuen and Company, 1982.

Mueller, Gustav E. "Solgar's Aesthetics--A Key to Hegel (Irony and Dialectic)." *Corona: Studies in Celebration of the Eightieth Birthday of Samuel Singer.* Edited by Arno Schirokauer and Wolfgang Paulsen. Durham, N.C.: Duke University Press, 1941.

Murdoch, Iris. *The Fire and the Sun: Why Plato Banished the Artists.* Oxford: Oxford University Press, 1977.

Nagler, Michael N. *America without Violence.* Covelo, Calif.: Island Press, 1982.

Nehamas, Alexander. "Predication and Forms of Opposites in the *Phaedo.*" *Review of Metaphysics* 26 (March, 1973): 461-491.

Nelson, John S. "Political Theory as Political Rhetoric." *What Should Political Theory Be Now?* Edited by John S. Nelson. Albany: State University of New York Press, 1983.

Nettleship, R.L. *The Theory of Education in Plato's Republic.* London: Oxford University Press, 1935.

Niebuhr, Reinhold. *The Irony of American History.* New York: Charles Scribner's Sons, 1952.

Nietzsche, Friedrich. *The Birth of Tragedy.* Translated by Walter Kaufmann. New York: Vintage Books, 1967.

_____. *The Gay Science.* Translated by Walter Kaufmann. New York: Vintage Books, 1974.

_____. *On the Geneology of Morals/Ecce Homo.* Translated by Walter Kaufmann. New York: Vintage Books, 1969.

Novak, Maximillian E., and Herbert J. Davis. *Irony in Defoe and Swift.* Los Angeles: William Andrews Clark Memorial Library, 1966.

Nussbaum, Martha. "Allan Bloom's 'American Mind.' " *New York Review of Books* (November 5, 1987).

O'Brien, Conor Cruise. *Writers and Politics.* New York: Pantheon Books, 1955.

Oakeshott, Michael. *Rationalism in Politics.* New York: Basic Books, 1962.

O'Gorman, Donal. *Diderot the Satirist.* Toronto: University of Toronto Press, 1971.

Okin, Susan Moller. "Philosopher Queens and Private Wives: Plato on Women and the Family." *The Family in Political Thought.* Edited by Jean Bethke Elshtain. Amherst: University of Massachusetts Press, 1982.

_____. *Women in Western Political Thought.* Princeton: Princeton University Press, 1971.

Ortega y Gasset, José. *The Dehumanization of Art and Notes on the Novel.* Translated by Helene Weyl. Princeton: Princeton University Press, 1948.

Page, Denys. *Folktales in Homer's Odyssey.* Cambridge: Harvard University Press, 1973.

Parfit, Derek. *Reasons and Persons.* Oxford: Clarendon Press, 1984.

Pater, Walter. *Plato and Platonism.* London: Macmillan, 1895.

Paulson, Ronald. *The Fictions of Satire.* Baltimore: Johns Hopkins University Press, 1967.

Pelton, Leroy H. *The Psychology of Nonviolence.* New York: Pergamon Press, Inc., 1974.

Perkins, Robert L. "Hegel and Kierkegaard: Two Critics of Romantic Irony." *Review of National Literature* 1 (Fall, 1970): 232-254.

Pikulik, Lothar. "Die Politisierung des Ästheten im Ersten Weltkrieg." *Thomas Mann 1875-1975.* Edited by Beatrix Bludau, et al. Frankfurt am Main: S. Fischer, 1977.

Pitkin, Hanna Fenichel. *Wittgenstein and Justice.* Berkeley: University of California Press, 1972.

Plass, Paul. "Philosophic Anonymity and Irony in the Platonic Dialogues." *American Journal of Philology* 35 (1964): 254-278.

Popper, Karl R. *The Logic of Scientific Discovery.* New York: Basic Books, 1959.

_____. *The Open Society and Its Enemies.* Princeton: Princeton University Press, 1950.

Prang, Helmut. *Die Romantische Ironie.* Darmstadt: Wissenschaftliche Buchgesellschaft, 1972.

Prawer, S.S. *Karl Marx and World Literature.* Oxford: Clarendon Press, 1976.

Price, John Valdimir. *The Ironic Hume.* Austin: University of Texas Press, 1965.

Radcliffe-Brown, A.R. "On Joking Relationships." *Structure and Function in Primitive Society.* New York: Free Press, 1952: 90-104.

Randall, John Herman, Jr. *Plato: Dramatist of the Life of Reason.* New York: Columbia University Press, 1970.

Rankin, H.D. "A Modest Proposal about the *Republic.*" *Apeiron* 2 (1968): 20-22.

Raven, J.E. *Plato's Thought in the Making.* Cambridge: Cambridge University Press, 1965.

Rawls, John. *A Theory of Justice.* Cambridge: Harvard University Press, 1971.

Redner, Harry. *In the Beginning Was the Deed: Reflections on the Passage of Faust.* Berkeley: University of California Press, 1982.

Reed, T.J. *Thomas Mann: The Uses of Tradition.* Oxford: Clarendon Press, 1974.

Reik, Theodor. "Saint Irony." *The Secret Self: Psychoanalytical Experiences in Life and Literature.* New York: Farrar, Straus, and Young, 1952: 161-183.

Reinitz, Richard. *Irony and Consciousness: American Historiography and Reinhold Niebuhr's Vision.* Lewisburg, Pa.: Bucknell University Press, 1980.

Reiss, Edmund. "Medieval Irony." *Journal of the History of Ideas* 42 (April-June, 1981): 209-226.

Ribbeck, Otto. "Über den Begriff des *Eiron.*" *Rheinisches Museum* 31 (1876): 381-400.

Richards, I.A. *Principles of Literary Criticism.* New York: Harcourt, Brace and Company, 1952.

_____, ed. and trans. *Plato's Republic.* Cambridge: Cambridge University Press, 1966.

Richter, Melvin. *The Political Theory of Montesquieu.* Cambridge: Cambridge University Press, 1977.

Robbins, Emmet. "Famous Orpheus." *Orpheus: The Metamorphoses of a Myth.* Edited by John Warden. Toronto: University of Toronto Press, 1982.

Robinson, Richard. *Plato's Earlier Dialectic.* Oxford: Clarendon Press, 1953.

Root, John G. "Stylistic Irony in Thomas Mann." *Germanic Review* 35 (April, 1960): 93-103.

Rorty, Richard. *Consequences of Pragmatism.* Minneapolis: University of Minnesota Press, 1982.

_____. *Contingency, Irony, and Solidarity.* Cambridge: Cambridge University Press, 1989.

Rose, Margaret A. *Reading the Young Marx and Engels: Poetry, Parody and the Censor.* Totowa, N.J.: Rowman and Littlefield, 1978.

Rose, Margaret. *Marx's Lost Aesthetic.* Cambridge: Cambridge University Press, 1984.

Rosen, Stanley. "The Role of Eros in Plato's *Republic*." *Review of Metaphysics* 18 (March, 1965): 452-475.

Rossman, Vladimir R. *Perspectives of Irony in Medieval French Literature.* The Hague: Mouton, 1975.

Rousseau, Jean-Jacques. *Essay on the Origin of Language.* Translated by John H. Moran and Alexander Gode. Chicago: University of Chicago Press, 1986.

Rudnick, Paul, and Kurt Andersen. "The Irony Epidemic." *Spy Magazine* (March, 1989): 93-101.

Russell, Bertrand. "Civil Disobedience and the Threat of Nuclear Weapons." *Civil Disobedience: Theory and Practice.* Edited by H.A. Bedau. Indianapolis and New York: Pegasus Books, 1969.

_____. *Common Sense and Nuclear Warfare.* New York: Simon and Schuster, 1959.

_____. *Has Man a Future?* London: George Allen and Unwin, 1961.

Ryan, Michael. *Marxism and Deconstruction: A Critical Articulation.* Baltimore and London: Johns Hopkins University Press, 1982.

Rychner, Max. "Thomas Mann und die Politik." *Aufsätze zur Literatur.* Zurich: Manesse Verlag, 1966: 251-304.

Ryle, Gilbert. *The Concept of Mind.* London: Hutchinson and Co., 1949.

Sabine, George H. "What is a Political Theory?" *Journal of Politics* 1 (February, 1939): 1-16.

Salomon, Roger B. *Desperate Storytelling: Post-Romantic Elaborations of the Mock-Heroic Mode.* Athens and London: University of Georgia Press, 1987.

Sandel, Michael J., ed. *Liberalism and Its Critics.* Oxford: Basil Blackwell, 1984.

Sarton, May. "The Shield of Irony." *Nation* (April 14, 1956): 314-316.

Saxonhouse, Arlene W. "Comedy in Callipolis: Animal Imagery in the *Republic*." *American Political Science Review* (September, 1978): 888-901.

Schaar, John H. "The Question of Justice." *Raritan* 3 (Fall, 1983).

Schaeffer, John D. "Ironic Discourse and the Creation of Secularity." *Soundings* 66 (Fall, 1983): 319-330.

Schein, Seth L. *The Mortal Hero: An Introduction to Homer's Iliad.* Berkeley: University of California Press, 1984.

Schell, Jonathan. *The Fate of the Earth.* New York: Alfred A. Knopf, 1982.

Schlegel, A.W. *Lectures on Dramatic Art and Literature .* Translated by John Black. New York: AMS Press, 1965.

Schlegel, Friedrich. *The Aesthetic and Miscellaneous Works.* Translated by E.J. Millington. London: George Bell and Sons, 1889.

_____. *Dialogue on Poetry and Literary Aphorisms.* Translated by Ernst Behler and Roman Struc. University Park: Pennsylvania State University Press, 1968.

_____. "Fragmente zur Geschichte und Politik: 1820-1828." *Kritische Friedrich-Schlegel-Ausgabe.* Edited by Ursula Behler. Vol. 22. Munich: Ferdinand Schöningh; Zurich: Thomas-Verlag, 1979.

_____. *Gespräch über die Poesie.* Cologne: Der Kölner Presse, 1924.

_____. *Lectures on the History of Literature, Ancient and Modern.* Philadelphia: Moss and Brother, 1848.

_____. *Literary Notebooks, 1797-1801.* Edited by Hans Eichner. London: Athlone Press, 1957.

_____. *Friedrich Schlegel's* Lucinde *and the Fragments.* Translated by Peter Firchow. Minneapolis: of Minnesota Press, 1971.

_____. *The Philosophy of History.* Translated by J.B. Robertson. London: Henry G. Bohn, 1846.

_____. *Schlegels Briefe an seinen Bruder August Wilhelm.* Edited by Oskar F. Walzel. Berlin: Speyer & Peters, 1890.

_____. "Studien zur Geschichte und Politik." *Kritische Friedrich-Schlegel-Ausgabe.* Vol. 17. Munich: Ferdinand Schöningh; Zurich: Thomas-Verlag, 1979.

Schleiermacher, F.E.D. *Introduction to the Dialogues of Plato.* Translated by William Dobson. New York: Arno Press, 1973.

Schleifer, Ronald. "Irony and the Literary Past. " *Kierkegaard and Literature: Irony, Repetition, and Criticism.* Edited by Ronald Schleifer and Robert Markley. Norman: University of Oklahoma Press, 1984.

Schutz, Charles E. *Political Humor: From Aristophanes to Sam Ervin.* London: Associated University Press, 1977.

Searle, J.R. *Speech Acts.* Cambridge: Cambridge University Press, 1970.

_____, ed. *The Philosophy of Language.* Oxford Readings in Philosophy. London: Oxford University Press, 1971.

_____. "The Word Turned Upside Down." *New York Review of Books* XXX (October 27, 1983): 74-79.

Sedgewick, G.G. *Of Irony: Especially in Drama.* Toronto: University of Toronto Press, 1948.

Segal, Charles. *Orpheus: The Myth of the Poet.* Baltimore: Johns Hopkins University Press, 1989.

Seigel, Jerrold. *Marx's Fate: The Shape of a Life.* Princeton: Princeton University Press, 1978.

Sesonske, Alexander, ed. *Plato's Republic: Interpretation and Criticism.* Belmont, Calif.: Wadsworth Publishing Co., 1966.

Shapiro, Marianne. "The Status of Irony." *Stanford Literature Review* 2, No. 1 (Spring, 1985): 5-26.

Sharp, Gene. "Ethics and Responsibility in Politics: A Critique of the Present Adequacy of Max Weber's Classification of Ethical Systems." *Inquiry* (Oslo) 7, No. 3 (Autumn, 1964): 304-317.

_____. *The Politics of Nonviolent Action.* 3 Vols. Boston: Porter Sargent Publishers, 1973.

Sharpe, Robert Boies. *Irony in the Drama: An Essay on Impersonation, Shock, and Catharsis.* Chapel Hill: University of North Carolina Press, 1959.

Shklar, Judith N. *After Utopia: The Decline of Political Faith.* Princeton: Princeton University Press, 1957.

_____, ed. *Political Theory and Ideology.* Toronto: MacMillan Company, 1966.

Shorey, Paul, trans. *The Republic.* Bollingen Series 71. Edited by Edith Hamilton and Huntington Cairns: *Plato: The Collected Dialogues.* Princeton: Princeton University Press, 1961.

Sidgwick, Arthur. "On Some Forms of Irony in Literature." *Cornhill Magazine,* 3rd ser. 22 (April, 1907): 497-508.

Sikes, E.E. *The Greek View of Poetry.* London: Methuen, 1931.

Simpson, David. *Irony and Authority in Romantic Poetry.* London: Macmillan Press, 1979.

Sinclair, Thomas. "Plato's Philosophic Dog." *Classical Review* 62 (September, 1948): 61-62.

Smyth, John Vignauz. *A Question of Eros: Irony in Sterne, Kierkegaard, and Barthes.* Tallahassee: Florida State University Press, 1984.

Solomon, J. Fisher. *Discourse and Reference in the Nuclear Age.* Tulsa: University of Oklahoma Press, 1988.

Spector, Leonard S. *Nuclear Proliferation Today.* New York: Vintage Books, 1984.

Spence, Larry D. "Political Theory as a Vacation." *Polity* 12 (Summer, 1980): 697-710.

Sperber, Dan, and Deirdre Wilson. "Irony and the Use-Mention Distinction." *Radical Pragmatics.* Edited by Peter Cole. New York: Academic Press, 1981: 295-318.

Spivak, Gayatri. *In Other Worlds: Essays in Cultural Politics.* New York: Methuen, 1987.

Spragens, Thomas A., Jr. *The Dilemma of Contemporary Political Theory: Toward a Postbehavioral Science of Politics.* New York: Dunellen, 1973.

_____. *The Irony of Liberal Reason.* Chicago: University of Chicago Press, 1981.

_____. *Understanding Political Theory.* New York: St. Martin's Press, 1976.

States, Bert O. *Irony and Drama: A Poetics.* Ithaca and London: Cornell University Press, 1971.

Stiehm, Judith. *Nonviolent Power: Active and Passive Resistance in America.* Lexington, Mass.: D.C. Heath and Company, 1972.

Stock, Irving. "Ironic Conservatism: Thomas Mann's Reflections of a Non-Political Man." *Salmagundi.* No. 68-69 (Fall, 1985/Winter, 1986): 166-185

Strauss, Leo. *The City and Man.* Chicago: University of Chicago Press, 1964.

_____. *Liberalism Ancient and Modern.* New York: Basic Books, 1968.

_____. *On Tyranny.* Ithaca, N.Y.: Cornell University Press, 1968.

_____. *Persecution and the Art of Writing.* Glencoe, Ill.: Free Press, 1952.

_____. "Political Philosophy and the Crisis of Our Time." *The Post-Behavioral Era.* Edited by G.J. Graham, Jr., and G.W. Carey. New York: David McKay Co., 1972: 17-242.

_____. *Socrates and Aristophanes.* Chicago and London: University of Chicago Press, 1966.

_____. "What Is Political Philosophy?" *Journal of Politics* 19 (August, 1957): 343-368.

_____. *What Is Political Philosophy? And Other Studies.* Glencoe, Ill.: Free Press, 1959.

Strauss, Walter A. *Descent and Return: The Orphic Theme in Modern Literature.* Cambridge: Harvard University Press, 1971.

Strohschneider-Kohrs, Ingrid. *Die romantische Ironie in Theorie und Gestaltung.* Tübingen: Max Niemeyer Verlag, 1977.

Suleiman, Susan. "Interpreting Ironies." *diacritics* (Summer, 1976): 15-21.

Swift, Jonathan. *The Drapier's Letters to the People of Ireland.* Edited by Herbert Davis. Oxford: Clarendon Press, 1935.

_____. "A Modest Proposal (1729)." *The Prose Works of Jonathan Swift, D.D.* Vol. 7. Edited by Temple Scott. London: George Bell and Sons, 1905.

Tarrant, Dorothy. "Plato as Dramatist." *Journal of Hellenic Studies* 55 (1955): 82-89.

Tate, J. "Plato and 'Imitation.' " *Classical Quarterly* 26. (1932): 161-169.

Taylor, A.E. *Plato: The Man and His Work.* London: Methuen and Company, 1926.

Taylor, Charles. "Design for Living." *New York Review of Books* (November 22, 1984).

_____. *Hegel.* Cambridge: Cambridge University Press, 1975.

Thirlwall, Connop. "On the Irony of Sophocles." *The Philological Museum.* Vol. 2. Cambridge: J. Smith, Printer, 1833: 483-537.

Thomas, D. Paul. *Karl Marx and the Anarchists.* London: Routledge and Kegan Paul, 1980.

Thomas, R. Hinton. *Thomas Mann: The Mediation of Art.* Oxford: Clarendon Press, 1956.

Thompson, Alan Reynolds. *The Dry Mock.* Berkeley: University of California Press, 1948.

Thompson, E.P. *Beyond the Cold War.* New York: Pantheon Books, 1982.

Thompson, E.P., and Dan Smith. *Protest and Survive.* New York: Penguin Books, 1980.

Thomson, J.A.K. *Irony: An Historical Introduction.* London: George Allen and Unwin, 1926.

Thoreau, Henry David. "Civil Disobedience." *The Portable Thoreau.* Edited by Carl Bode. New York: Viking Press, 1947: 109-137.

Thorson, Thomas Landon, ed. *Plato: Totalitarian or Democrat?* Englewood Cliffs, N.J.: Prentice-Hall, 1963.

Traugott, John. "A Voyage to Nowhere with Thomas More and Jonathan Swift: Utopia and The Voyage to the Houyhnhnms." *Swift: A Collection of Critical Essays.* Edited by Ernest Tuveson. Englewood Cliffs, N.J.: Prentice-Hall, 1964: 143-169.

_____. "The Yahoo in the Doll's House: *Gulliver's Travels* the Children's Classic." *The Yearbook of English Studies* 14. London: Modern Humanities Research Association, 1984: 127-150.

Trilling, Lionel. *Sincerity and Authenticity.* Cambridge: Harvard University Press, 1971.

Unnithan, T.K.N., and Yogendra Singh. *Traditions of Non-Violence.* New Delhi: Arnold-Heinemann, 1973.

Urquhart, Clara., ed. *A Matter of Life.* London: Jonathan Cape, 1963.

Vellacott, Philip. *Ironic Drama: A Study of Euripedes' Method and Meaning.* Cambridge: Cambridge University Press, 1975.

Verdenis, Willem Jacob. *Mimesis: Plato's Doctrine of Artistic Imitation and its Relation to Us.* Leiden: E.J. Brill, 1949.

Vicari, Patricia. "Sparagmos: Orpheus among the Christians." *Orpheus: The Metamorphoses of a Myth.* Edited by John Warden. Toronto: University of Toronto Press, 1982.

Vico, Giambattista. *The New Science.* Translated by Thomas G. Bergin and Max H. Fisch. Ithaca, N.Y.: Cornell University Press, 1948.

Vlastos, Gregory. "The Historical Socrates and Athenian Democracy." *Political Theory* 11 (November, 1983): 495-516.

_____. *Plato's Universe.* Seattle: University of Washington Press, 1975.

_____. "Socrates' Disavowal of Knowledge." *Philosophical Quarterly* 35 (January, 1985): 1-31.

_____. "The Theory of Social Justice in the *Polis* in Plato's *Republic.*" *Interpretations of Plato.* Edited by Helen F. North. Leiden: E.J. Brill, 1977.

_____, ed. *Plato II.* Garden City, N.Y.: Anchor Books, 1971.

Voegelin, Eric. *The New Science of Politics.* Chicago: University of Chicago Press, 1952.

_____. *Plato and Aristotle.* Vol. 3 of *Order and History.* Baton Rouge: Louisiana State University Press, 1966.

Walcutt, Charles Child. "Irony: Vision or Retreat?" *Pacific Spectator* 10 (Autumn, 1956): 354-366.

Walker, D.P. *The Decline of Hell: Seventeenth-Century Discussions of Eternal Torment.* Chicago: University of Chicago Press, 1964.

Walser, Martin. *Selbstbewußtsein und Ironie.* Frankfurt: Suhrkamp, 1981.

Walzel, Oskar. *German Romanticism.* Translated by Alma Lussky. New York: G.P. Putnam's Sons, 1932.

Walzer, Michael. *Just and Unjust Wars: A Moral Argument with Historical Illustrations.* New York: Basic Books, 1977.

Warden, John, ed. *Orpheus: The Metamorphoses of a Myth.* Toronto: University of Toronto Press, 1982.

Weber, Max. *From Max Weber: Essays in Sociology.* Edited by H.H. Gerth and C. Wright Mills. New York: Oxford University Press, 1946.

Webster, T.B.L. *The Art of Greece: The Age of Hellenia.* New York: Greyston Press, 1953.

Wellek, René. *A History of Modern Criticism: 1750-1950.* Volume 2: *The Romantic Age.* New Haven: Yale University Press, 1955.

Wessell, Leonard P., Jr. "The Antinomic Structure of Friedrich Schlegel's Romanticism." *Studies in Romanticism* 12 (Summer, 1973): 648-669.

_____. *Karl Marx, Romantic Irony and the Proletariat: The Mythopoetic Origins of Marxism.* Baton Rouge and London: Louisiana State University Press, 1979.

West, M.L. *The Orphic Poems.* Oxford: Clarendon Press, 1983.

White, Hayden. *Metahistory: The Historical Imagination in Nineteenth-Century Europe.* Baltimore: Johns Hopkins University Press, 1973.

Wieseltier, Leon. *Nuclear War, Nuclear Peace.* New York: Holt, Rinehart and Winston, 1983.

Wilamowitz-Moellendorff, Ulrich von. *Platon.* Berlin: Weidmann, 1920.

Wilde, Alan. *Horizons of Assent: Modernism, Postmodernism, and the Ironic Imagination.* Baltimore and London: Johns Hopkins University Press, 1981.

Wimsatt, W.K., Jr. *The Verbal Icon.* Lexington: University of Kentucky Press, 1954.

Wolff, Robert Paul, ed. *Kant: A Collection of Critical Essays.* Notre Dame: University of Notre Dame Press, 1968.

Wolin, Sheldon S. "Political Theory as a Vocation." *American Political Science Review* 63 (December, 1969): 1062-1082.

_____. "Political Theory: 2. Trends and Goals." *International Encyclopedia of the Social Sciences* 12 (New York: Macmillan, 1968): 318-329.

_____. *Politics and Vision: Continuity and Innovation in Western Political Thought.* Boston: Little, Brown and Company, 1960.

Wood, Gordon S. "The Fundamentalists and the Constitution." *New York Review of Books* (February 18, 1988).

Woolf, Virginia. *To the Lighthouse.* San Diego: Harcourt Brace Jovanovich, 1927.

Worcester, David. *The Art of Satire.* Cambridge: Harvard University Press, 1940.

Wright, Andrew H. "Irony and Fiction." *Journal of Aesthetics and Art Criticism* 12 (September, 1953): 111-118.

Zuckerman, Solly. *Nuclear Illusion and Reality.* New York: Vintage Books, 1982.

Zumwalt, Eugene. "Divine and Diabolic Irony: The Growth of a Tudor Dramatic Sense." Dissertation, University of California, Berkeley, 1956.

Index